ARTHUR CONAN DOYLE

*Sherlock Holmes:*
*The Major Stories*
*with Contemporary*
*Critical Essays*

ARTHUR CONAN DOYLE

# Sherlock Holmes: The Major Stories with Contemporary Critical Essays

EDITED BY
**John A. Hodgson**

**Bedford Books** *of* **St. Martin's Press**
BOSTON • NEW YORK

PR
4621
.H64
1994

**For Bedford Books**
*Publisher:* Charles H. Christensen
*Associate Publisher/General Manager:* Joan E. Feinberg
*Managing Editor:* Elizabeth M. Schaaf
*Developmental Editor:* Stephen A. Scipione
*Production Editor:* Jonathan R. Burns
*Copyeditor:* Helen Webber
*Text Design:* Sandra Rigney, The Book Department
*Cover Design:* Donna Lee Dennison
*Cover Art:* Photograph of Scotland Yard. Greater London Photograph Library, London, England.

*For information, write:* St. Martin's Press, Inc.
175 Fifth Avenue, New York, NY 10010

*Editorial Offices:* Bedford Books *of* St. Martin's Press
29 Winchester Street, Boston, MA 02116

ISBN: 0–312–08945–7 (paperback)
ISBN: 0–312–10304–2 (hardcover)

Published and distributed outside North America by:

MACMILLAN PRESS LTD.
Houndmills, Basingstoke, Hampshire RG21 2XS and London
Companies and representatives throughout the world.

ISBN: 0–333–53137–X

## Acknowledgments

Catherine Belsey, "Deconstructing the Text: Sherlock Holmes." From *Critical Practice.* Copyright © 1980 Methuen & Co.

Peter Brooks, "Reading for the Plot." From *Reading for the Plot* by Peter Brooks. Copyright © 1984 by Peter Brooks. Reprinted by permission of Alfred A. Knopf, Inc.

Gian Paolo Caprettini, "Sherlock Holmes: Ethics, Logic, the Mask." From *The Sign of Three: Dupin, Holmes, Peirce.* Translated by Roberto Cagliero. Edited by Umberto Eco and Thomas A. Sebeok. Copyright Indiana University Press, 1983.

*Acknowledgments and copyrights are continued at the back of the book on page 447, which constitutes an extension of the copyright page.*

# About This Book

Arthur Conan Doyle's Sherlock Holmes stories today stand at an important intersection of general and scholarly interest. Always popular with multitudes of readers, they are now attracting significant attention from a wide array of literary critics as well. During the past dozen years this critical attention to the stories has developed into a rich and sustained dialogue. Critics of Victorian literature and culture, analysts of genre and of narrative, literary theoreticians representing a variety of emphases — all these and more are contributing to the discussion.

*Sherlock Holmes: The Major Stories with Contemporary Critical Essays* presents Doyle's most important and influential Sherlock Holmes stories in the context of the contemporary critical and theoretical interest they have excited. The Introduction discusses the relation of Sherlock Holmes to Doyle's own life, reviews the history of the stories' publication and reception, and provides a brief overview of the contemporary critical essays. Part One includes the opening chapters of *A Study in Scarlet* and fourteen major stories; each selection is followed by a brief critical commentary. Part Two presents nine important contemporary critical essays, with a brief introduction to each. These essays are grouped in two clusters, reflecting two general emphases that have especially characterized recent Holmes criticism. The first group includes essays emphasizing detection, plot, and narrative; the second, essays emphasizing society, gender, culture, and ideology.

For the convenience of the reader the introductory material, story commentaries, and critical essays have all been thoroughly cross-referenced, by page number, with the Sherlock Holmes stories included in this volume.

This book also contains a variety of auxiliary materials intended to enhance its usefulness. These include a chronology of Doyle's life, a note on Doyle's personal list of the best Holmes stories, and footnotes glossing obscure allusions and references in the stories and essays. There are also two comprehensive guides to a wide range of other Sherlock Holmes materials: first, an annotated bibliography of texts, bibliographies, biographies, and recent critical studies; and second, an exhaustive listing of the film and video treatments of all the Holmes stories included in this collection. Finally, a thorough index to the entire volume is provided as a service and encouragement to browsers and scholars alike.

## ABOUT THE TEXT OF THE STORIES

There is no standard, authoritative text of the Sherlock Holmes stories. The standard English collection is the two-volume set published by Murray in 1928–29, during Doyle's lifetime; the standard American collection, that published by Doubleday in 1930, the year of Doyle's death. Both editions contain errors and inconsistencies, and both almost without exception simply reproduce the similarly flawed earlier editions of the individual novels and story collections. The editors of the American edition apparently made an effort to correct obvious errors in the English version, but they also introduced some new typographical errors and occasionally changed correct English words or phrases they found obscure or mistakenly regarded as incorrect.

The text of the Sherlock Holmes stories in the present volume is based on the first English publications of these works in book form (listed below), which I have compared against later editions, both English and American. I have corrected obvious errors of spelling and usage and have consistently regularized such matters as the use of quotation marks, the form of possessives, the spellings of proper names, the formatting of internal documents, the style of specifying time of day ("6:30" rather than the English "6.30"), and so forth. Otherwise I have edited quite conservatively, retaining Doyle's occasionally idiosyncratic punctuation and even his inconsistent use of alternative acceptable spellings (for example, both "despatch" and "dispatch").

Many of the Holmes stories originally appeared under the title "The

Adventure of . . .": thus, for example, "The Adventure of the Blue Car-buncle," "The Adventure of the Speckled Band." Doyle condensed these titles to their shorter, familiar versions, or allowed his editors to do so, in the 1928 collected edition of his stories, and I have followed that practice here.

*A Study in Scarlet.* In *Beeton's Christmas Annual.* London: Ward, Lock, 1887.
*The Adventures of Sherlock Holmes.* London: George Newnes, 1892.
*The Memoirs of Sherlock Holmes.* London: George Newnes, 1894.
*The Return of Sherlock Holmes.* London: George Newnes, 1905.

## ACKNOWLEDGMENTS

Many of my own ideas about the Sherlock Holmes stories were prompted by my teaching, and I am grateful to my students at Harvard College and Harvard Extension School for their participation in those seminal classes, which incidentally taught me the desirability of a book such as this. I am grateful also to Charles Rzepka for the timely impetus he gave when he invited me to participate in a special session on Sherlock Holmes at the Modern Language Association's annual convention.

I have been very fortunate in my publisher. At Bedford Books, Steve Scipione has been a model editor — a sensitive and careful reader, an efficient manager and negotiator of the larger editorial process, and above all a person with the intelligent reader's interests always in mind and at heart. I am very happy, and very grateful, to have been able to work with him. Charles Christensen's and Joan Feinberg's early enthusiasm for and continued interest in the book were always encouraging. Jonathan Burns did a masterly job of seeing the book through production. Helen Webber's fine copyediting discovered several errors in the original Sherlock Holmes texts.

# Contents

# PART TWO
# Contemporary Critical Essays

## Appendices

## Index

ARTHUR CONAN DOYLE

*Sherlock Holmes:*
*The Major Stories*
*with Contemporary*
*Critical Essays*

# Arthur Conan Doyle and Sherlock Holmes: Biographical and Critical Contexts

Sherlock Holmes, the world's first "unofficial consulting detective" (*The Sign of Four*), entered the pages of English literature slightly more than one hundred years ago and soon thereafter entered the English-speaking world's common knowledge as well. From an obscure beginning in a cheap shilling paperback in 1887, he quickly became one of the world's most famous literary characters, and he remains so today. "Sherlock" and "Holmesian," and even "Watsonian," are now part of the language, while the popular image of the brilliant, incisive sleuth and his loyal, conventional friend and chronicler has become an archetype and cliché of our culture.

A popular image, of course, is not always entirely trustworthy. The common iconography of Sherlock Holmes, for example — the tall, lean figure and the sharp, handsome face; the deerstalker cap, curved pipe, and cape — derives much more from Sidney Paget's original illustrations of the stories (though Doyle tacitly accepted these and adapted to them) and William Gillette's turn-of-the-century dramatic impersonations than from Doyle's narratives. The common reader trusting to such images thereby plays the role of an interpretative Watson, in whom Holmes finds a similar carelessness: "You see, but you do not observe" ("A Scandal in Bohemia," p. 34).

In the stories collected here, readers can see and observe for themselves what Sherlock Holmes is about. The critical essays that follow the stories demonstrate how a variety of contemporary literary critics have done the same.

## SHERLOCK HOLMES AND
## SIR ARTHUR CONAN DOYLE

In about 1907, Sir Arthur Conan Doyle received a request for detective advice from a countrywoman. Her favorite cousin, she wrote, had a week ago disappeared. He had traveled to London and stopped at a large hotel there. That evening he attended a music-hall performance, returned to his hotel at about ten o'clock, and had not been seen since, though a man in the next room stated that he had heard him moving during the night. The police were baffled. What had happened to her cousin?

As he occasionally would, Doyle decided to take the case. He solved it in perhaps an hour, without leaving his home. By return mail he wrote, "Your cousin is in Scotland. Look for him in Glasgow or Edinburgh, and I will guarantee you will find him" (Higham 203). And so it proved: the man was found in Scotland and had indeed gone initially from London to Edinburgh.

Doyle had solved the mystery so quickly by simply "endeavouring to see the matter through the eyes of Mr. Holmes." By telephone he quickly learned that the man had withdrawn his bank balance of £40 before going to London. The woman feared that her cousin "had been murdered for the sake of the money," but to Doyle the fact suggested something quite different: "the man had meant to disappear. Why else should he draw all his money?" And when that night had he left the hotel? He had been seen entering his room there after ten; but Doyle mistrusted the testimony of the hotel guest in the next room who had heard the missing man during the night: there are so many sounds, after all, in a large hotel. It was much more likely that the man had left earlier, as Doyle could reasonably infer from his own familiarity with the routine of London hotels:

> He had got out of the hotel during the night. But there is a night porter in all hotels, and it is impossible to get out without his knowledge when the door is once shut. The door is shut after the theatre-goers return — say at twelve o'clock. Therefore the man left the hotel before twelve o'clock. He had come from the music-hall at ten . . . and had departed with his bag. No one had seen him do so. The inference is that he had done it at the moment when the hall was full of the returning guests, which is from

eleven to eleven-thirty. After that hour, even if the door
open, there are few people coming and going so that he
bag would certainly have been seen.

Doyle next asked

why a man who desires to hide himself should go out at such an
hour. If he intended to conceal himself in London he need never
have gone to the hotel at all. Clearly then he was going to catch a
train which would carry him away. But a man who is deposited by
a train in any provincial station during the night is likely to be noticed. . . . Therefore, his destination would be some large town
which he would reach as a terminus where all his fellow passengers
would disembark and where he would lose himself in the crowd.
When one turns up the time table and sees that the great Scotch
expresses bound for Edinburgh and Glasgow start about midnight, the goal is reached.

As this anecdote illustrates and as many others amply confirm, there
was much of Sherlock Holmes in Arthur Conan Doyle. Like his famous
protagonist, Doyle had a sensitivity to significant detail, a ready imagination, a wide range of social and intellectual experience, and a flair for
the dramatic. Most important, he also had a genuinely shrewd and analytic turn of mind.

Doyle's analytic ability did not come to him by chance; he was educated and professionally trained in it, first through eight years of Jesuit
schooling (chiefly at Stonyhurst, the most prominent Jesuit school in
England) and then through five years of medical study at Edinburgh
University. After graduating from Edinburgh he practiced medicine for
ten years before abandoning a physician's career for a writer's. His medical training, particularly, seems to lie behind his conception of Sherlock
Holmes as "a scientific detective who solved cases on his own merits and
not through the folly of the criminal," an investigator both masterful in
his grasp of analytic principles and keenly aware of the importance of
details. Expert medical diagnosis (detection) required both the
scientist's training in inductive reasoning and the clinician's educated
eye for the often subtle symptoms (clues) of disease. As one of Conan
Doyle's Edinburgh teachers wrote, "The precise and intelligent recognition and appreciation of minor differences is the real essential factor in
all successful medical diagnosis. Carried into ordinary life, . . . you have
Sherlock Holmes as he astonishes his somewhat dense friend Watson;
carried out in a specialized training, you have Sherlock Holmes the
skilled detective."

The author of these words was, as Conan Doyle frequently acknowledged, the model for Sherlock Holmes himself. Dr. Joseph Bell, who lectured on clinical surgery at the Edinburgh Infirmary, was famous among the Edinburgh students for his wonderful ability to discover almost instantly not only the medical complaints but also the occupations and backgrounds of his clinic's outpatients, people who were entire strangers to him. Conan Doyle became Bell's outpatient clerk, the student who first took each patient's medical history before ushering each in turn into the presence of the surgeon and his students; thus, as he later wrote, "I had ample chance of studying his methods and of noticing that he often learned more of the patient by a few quick glances than I had done by my questions." Many anecdotes of Bell's abilities survive. "In one of his best cases," Conan Doyle recalled,

> he said to a civilian patient: "Well, my man, you've served in the army."
> "Aye, sir."
> "Not long discharged?"
> "No, sir."
> "A Highland regiment?"
> "Aye, sir."
> "A non-com. officer?"
> "Aye, sir."
> "Stationed at Barbados?"
> "Aye, sir."
> "You see, gentlemen," he would explain, "the man was a respectful man but did not remove his hat. They do not in the army, but he would have learned civilian ways had he been long discharged. He has an air of authority and he is obviously Scottish. As to Barbados, his complaint is elephantiasis, which is West Indian and not British."

Several years later Doyle recalled the impact of these incidents when, early in his writing career, he was casting about for ideas for a new book, perhaps something in the detective line:

> Gaboriau had rather attracted me by the neat dovetailing of his plots, and Poe's masterful detective, M. Dupin, had from boyhood been one of my heroes. But could I bring an addition of my own? I thought of my old teacher Joe Bell, of his eagle face, of his curious ways, of his eerie trick of spotting details. If he were a detective he would surely reduce this fascinating but unorganized business to something nearer to an exact science. I would try if I could get this effect. It was surely possible in real life, so why

should I not make it plausible in fiction? It is all very well to say that a man is clever, but the reader wants to see examples of it — such examples as Bell gave us every day in the wards.

And thus did Sherlock Holmes come into being in *A Study in Scarlet* (1887).

The analytic ability fostered by Conan Doyle's medical training was always a notable part of his character. It was on display most famously in his public investigative crusades on behalf first of George Edalji and later of Oscar Slater, two victims of British xenophobia who, in egregious miscarriages of justice, had been convicted of and imprisoned for crimes they had clearly not committed. It also showed in his foresight, before World War I, of the threat that a submarine blockade could pose to England. It appeared again during the war in his recognition of the need for life preservers for troops and sailors at sea (Doyle himself first proposed the inflatable swimming collar that was the precursor of the life jacket) and in his devising of a secret cipher for communicating with British prisoners of war. Like Sherlock Holmes, Arthur Conan Doyle was a rationalist role model for the late Victorian and Edwardian era.

But unlike Holmes, Doyle did not confine himself to rationalism. This was most forcefully brought home to his contemporaries in 1918, only a year after the fourth collection of Sherlock Holmes stories (*His Last Bow*) appeared, when Doyle published *The New Revelation* and revealed himself as a committed exponent and prophet of spiritualism (the belief that the spirits of the dead survive the body's death and can communicate — whether through mediums in séances, through automatic writing, through telepathy, or in many other possible ways — with the living), a cause and credo to which he wholeheartedly devoted the remainder of his life. Sherlock Holmes was both skeptical of and uninterested in the supernatural: "Of course, if . . . we are dealing with forces outside the ordinary laws of Nature, there is an end of our investigation. But we are bound to exhaust all other hypotheses before falling back upon this one" (*The Hound of the Baskervilles*). But Doyle had been intrigued by the supernatural for years, ever since the very beginnings of Sherlock Holmes. He published his first article on psychic phenomena in 1887, the year *A Study in Scarlet* appeared, and joined the British Society for Psychical Research in 1893, while the stories that would be collected as *The Memoirs of Sherlock Holmes* were appearing in the *Strand* magazine. This final commitment entangled Doyle in his later years in some most un-Holmeslike embarrassments, most notably his happy conviction that two young English girls had photographically documented the existence of fairies. Despite strong evidence of a hoax, Doyle wrote a book, *The Coming of the Fairies* (1922), declaring for the photographs' — and the fairies' — genuineness.

These writings and tendencies affected Doyle's reputation among his contemporaries but had no significant impact on the Sherlock Holmes stories: Holmes carefully held himself apart from such investigations. They testify, however, to a deeper, more fundamental strain of romanticism in Doyle's character, which in other ways affected the Holmes stories very much indeed. This strain seems to have been fostered especially by his mother, Mary Foley Doyle — "the Ma'am," as Conan Doyle titled and addressed her throughout his adult life — to whom he was always very close. (His father, a retiring, impractical civil servant and artist manqué who was institutionalized for alcoholism, epilepsy, and depression by the time Arthur was twenty, did not figure largely in his upbringing.) Mary Doyle, a spirited, forceful, intelligent woman with great ambitions for her eldest son, was devoted to the ideas and ideals of chivalry and, moreover, fiercely proud of her and her son's lineage; she had worked out her family tree back more than five hundred years, to the Plantagenets. She raised Arthur on a strong diet of national pride, genealogy, heraldry, and tales of chivalric valor and virtue (which were often also tales of family history), and imbued him with an utter respect for the "ancient standards" of knightly honor and courtesy.

Doyle's chivalric sense of honor, England's honor as well as his own, dominated the historical novels that were his proudest accomplishments, especially *The White Company* (1891) and *Sir Nigel* (1906), tales of fourteenth-century English knighthood. It also figured largely in many of the causes to which he lent his name and devoted his energies and talents. The Edalji and Slater cases each seemed to Doyle "a blot upon the record of English justice" that "should be wiped out." The heraldic allusion to "a blot on the escutcheon" is significant and characteristic. *The War in South Africa: Its Causes and Conduct,* his widely disseminated 1902 paperbound book defending Britain's conduct of the Boer War (in which Doyle had served heroically as a volunteer doctor) against severe European criticism — "defamation," Doyle thought it — was in essence a sustained, documented defense of English honor; appropriately enough, it brought him his own knighthood.

Both Holmes and Watson share with their creator an unwavering devotion to a chivalric code, a sure sense of the values and duties of a gentleman. "Honour is a medieval conception," a German diplomatist says dismissively in "His Last Bow"; but Holmes and Watson soon patriotically demonstrate that it remains a vital English conception still. As Watson once avows of his "word of honour," "I never broke it in my life" ("Charles Augustus Milverton," p. 278). This code of honor guides them to champion the right, defend the wronged, protect the weak. Many of the stories, in fact, do not involve actual crimes at all, as Holmes himself readily acknowledges ("The Blue Carbuncle," p. 134); but all involve honor and justice.

A man's chivalric code of honor, of course, is not least of all a code of his conduct with respect to women; and for both Doyle and Holmes these relationships provided challenges. Doyle himself was — and not inconsistently by his own lights — both a strong advocate of divorce law reform and an opponent of women's suffrage. On a personal level, he found himself particularly affected by the requirements of his code when in 1897, some eleven years after his marriage and some three after his wife had fallen ill with tuberculosis, he met and fell overwhelmingly in love with another woman, Jean Leckie, who both loved him equally in return and shared his strong and particular sense of honor. For the next ten years they maintained a secret but scrupulously platonic and proper relationship — with the full awareness and approval of "the Ma'am" throughout — not marrying until a proper year-plus after the death of his wife. Such, Doyle believed, was the only course that honor permitted him.

Sherlock Holmes's attitude toward women was similarly chivalric and genteel, though, as a confirmed bachelor, his most significant difficulties with them were professional rather than personal. "I have been beaten four times — three times by men, and once by a woman," he declares in "The Five Orange Pips"; but the defeats by men remain apocryphal, whereas Irene Adler's outmaneuvering of him in "A Scandal in Bohemia" is central to the Holmes legend. Holmes is again professionally humbled owing to his misjudgment of a woman in "The Yellow Face"; and even when, as is usually the case, he interprets women as accurately as he does his fellow men, he learns to interpret with particular caution:

> "You must have observed, Watson, how she manœuvered to have the light at her back. She did not wish us to read her expression. . . . And yet the motives of women are so inscrutable. You remember the woman at Margate whom I suspected for the same reason. No powder on her nose — that proved to be the correct solution. How can you build on such a quicksand? Their most trivial action may mean volumes, or their most extraordinary conduct may depend upon a hairpin or a curling tongs." ("The Second Stain," p. 297)

For both the analytic Doyle and the superanalytic Holmes, rational inquiry or interpretation can be baffled when it is blinded by a confidence in its own assumptions; and for both, the misleading assumption is apt to be a moral one. Some of the critical essays collected in this volume will consider certain such instances from the Sherlock Holmes stories. A striking instance from Doyle's own life appears in his account of his days with the army in South Africa during the Boer War, in 1900. Taking advantage of a lull in his medical duties after a hellish four weeks fighting an epidemic of typhoid, Doyle and a friend joined the advancing army for several days to see the war firsthand. As they then journeyed back across the broad plains toward their hospital, they encountered a native who told them of an injured Englishman lying far out on the veldt, and they rode off to find him. It was an Australian soldier, "shot, overlooked, and abandoned," who had been killed in the previous day's fighting but not yet discovered by the medical and burial parties.

> We examine him for injuries. Obviously he had bled to death.
> There is a horrible wound in his stomach. His arm is shot
> through. Beside him lies his water-bottle — a little water still in it,
> so he was not tortured by thirst. And there is a singular point. On
> the water-bottle is balanced a red chess pawn. Has he died playing
> with it? It looks like it. Where are the the other chessmen? We
> find them in a haversack out of his reach. A singular trooper this,
> who carried chessmen on a campaign. Or is it loot from a farm-
> house? I shrewdly suspect it.

They took the body back two miles to a point where they could turn it over to an approaching convoy for burial. "So he met his end," Doyle concludes — "somebody's boy. Fair fight, open air, and a great cause — I know no better death."

It was utterly characteristic of Doyle both to acknowledge the all-too-human flaws of the individual (the soldier had probably done some looting) and yet insist on the nobility and glory of the larger English cause ("I know no better death"). Yet his uncertainty about the "singular point" of the chess pawn so pointedly singled out by this "singular trooper" is stunning, even haunting. As he had already had Sherlock Holmes proclaim (in "The Boscombe Valley Mystery," p. 91), "Singularity is almost invariably a clue"; and this particular clue is hardly subtle. It is in fact quite difficult not to conclude that this abandoned, wounded soldier, come from one continent in the service of an emperor on another to die fighting the empire's enemy on a third, at the last felt himself but a mere sacrificial pawn in someone else's game, and wanted to say so. But this, even though couched in the courtly figures of chess, was precisely the kind of code-rejecting message that Doyle would not be able to read.

## THE SHERLOCK HOLMES STORIES

The first Sherlock Holmes story, *A Study in Scarlet,* was a short novel published as "cheap fiction" (the publisher's own phrase to Doyle) in *Beeton's Christmas Annual* in 1887 for very little recompense and to very little attention. But one of its readers, an editor of the American *Lippincott's Monthly Magazine,* came to London to contract with both Conan Doyle and Oscar Wilde for new books. Doyle produced a second Holmes novel, *The Sign of Four* (1890); Wilde produced *The Picture of Dorian Gray.* As this conjunction might promise, *The Sign of Four,* with its new stress on Holmes's moodiness, world-weariness, and use of cocaine, its wild tale of a stolen Indian treasure, its love interest (here Watson meets and wins his future wife), its exotic dangers (most notably a dwarfish, misshapen aborigine armed with poisoned darts), is the "Wildest," most sensational and fin-de-siècle of the Holmes stories.

The next year Doyle, who had closed his medical practice at Southsea, set up a new and signally unsuccessful medical practice as an oculist in London. He never had a single patient; but he spent the time in his consulting-room writing stories for a new, popular monthly magazine, the *Strand,* and soon decided to abandon medicine and write full-time. A monthly organ, Doyle speculated, offered interesting publishing possibilities. "A single character running through a series," he thought, "if it only engaged the attention of the reader, would bind that reader to that particular magazine." But a serialized novel had an obvious liability: the reader who missed a single installment might well then lose interest in subsequent ones. "Clearly the ideal compromise was a character which carried through, and yet instalments which were each complete in themselves, so that the purchaser was always sure that he could relish the whole contents of the magazine." And his existing character Sherlock Holmes, he believed, "would easily lend himself to a succession of short stories."

So Doyle submitted to the *Strand* two new Holmes stories he had written in his consulting-room, "A Scandal in Bohemia" and "The Red-headed League." The editor of the *Strand* immediately accepted both and asked for four more. The series that would become *The Adventures of Sherlock Holmes* (1892) was under way.

The stories were hugely popular. Quickly the *Strand* wanted more. Doyle hesitated, wanting instead to begin work on another historical novel (*The White Company* was currently appearing in serialization), but finally agreed to write six more Holmes stories. As he neared the end of this new commitment, he revealed to "the Ma'am," "I think of slaying Holmes in the last and winding him up for good and all. He takes my mind from better things." His mother, a Holmes enthusiast, wrote sharply in reply, "You won't! You can't! You *mustn't!*" (Carr 66); he shelved the thought.

The *Strand* already wanted another Holmes series and readily agreed to pay an unusually high sum for twelve more stories. These, appearing in 1892 and 1893, would (with one exception) be collected in *The Memoirs of Sherlock Holmes* (1894). In the last of these stories, "The Final Problem," Doyle resolutely put an end to his hero: Holmes and his archenemy, Professor Moriarty, plunge to their deaths in a final struggle at Switzerland's fearful Reichenbach Falls.

Doyle was relieved to be free of his troublesomely popular hero: Holmes, he felt, was "taking up an undue share of my imagination." Now he could devote himself again to higher literary pursuits. But readers were stunned, grief-stricken, outraged. More than twenty thousand cancelled their subscriptions to the *Strand,* and thousands more wrote to protest; people wore mourning in the streets of London. One letter of remonstrance to Doyle from a lady opened bluntly, "You Brute." But he remained firm in his insistence that Holmes was dead.

For eight years Holmes remained not only dead, but gone. In 1901, however, Doyle decided to bring him back — in an earlier, pre-Reichenbach adventure — as the protagonist of a mystery he had already begun to plot, *The Hound of the Baskervilles.* Published serially in the *Strand* in 1901–02 and then in the latter year in book form, *The Hound* was a great success. Upon the appearance of its first installment, the *Strand*'s circulation increased by a remarkable thirty thousand copies. And finally, in 1903, prompted in part by a lucrative offer from an American publisher for more Sherlock Holmes stories — provided, however, that Holmes's supposed death should be explained away — he agreed to resurrect his hero. The first new story, "The Empty House," appeared later that year, to a wildly enthusiastic reception. Doyle collected it and the next twelve stories as *The Return of Sherlock Holmes* in 1905.

After his *Return,* Holmes continued to appear in new adventures for another two decades and more, though with decreasing frequency. Doyle wrote a fourth and final Holmes novel, *The Valley of Fear* (1915), and also continued to publish Sherlock Holmes stories occasionally in the *Strand* until 1927. These later stories, bringing the total to fifty-six in all, were collected in *His Last Bow* in 1917 and *The Case-Book of Sherlock Holmes* in 1927; with a few exceptions, they reveal a significant decline in quality from those written earlier.

Doyle himself was never willing to acknowledge this — not, at least, in so many words. Though he had always claimed to regard his Sherlock Holmes stories as "a lower stratum of literary achievement," "lighter sketches" unworthy of serious comparison with his "higher work," he had come to think of them nonetheless as masterpieces of their short-story kind; and "It takes more exquisite skill to carve the cameo than the statue" (*Through the Magic Door* 116). There was thus a curiously ambivalent pathos, part humility, part pride, in his reaction to the sense that, in his words, "there was a falling off in the stories" in later years. Though he was ready enough to tell on himself the story of the Cornish boatman who said to him, "I think, sir, when Holmes fell over that cliff, he may not have killed himself, but all the same he was never quite the same man afterwards," he was also very quick to disagree. "[T]he last story is as good as the first," Doyle insisted. "I was determined . . . never again to write anything which was not as good as I could possibly make it, and therefore I would not write a Holmes story without a worthy plot and without a problem which interested my own mind." Any perception of a falling off was more properly attributable, he suggested, to readerly overfamiliarity, a liability he shared with far more illustrious authors: "When the same string is still harped upon, however cunningly one may vary the melody, there is still the danger of monotony. The mind of the reader is less fresh and responsive, which may unjustly prejudice him against the writer."

But Doyle could scarcely complain of an unresponsive or unjustly prejudiced audience for his detective; his readers, he knew, had been remarkable for their "constancy," their "patience and loyalty." And even while positing their jadedness he could not seriously credit it. As he wrote to them in the *Strand* in 1927 (and reprinted in his Preface to *The Case-Book of Sherlock Holmes* later the same year), "I fear that Mr. Sherlock Holmes may become like one of those popular tenors who, having outlived their time, are still tempted to make repeated farewell bows to their indulgent audiences." Since Holmes had already made his explicitly proclaimed "Last Bow" in the story and collection of that name in 1917, the relevance of this 1927 acknowledgment is quite pointed, and quite poignant.

Holmes himself, upon his return in "The Empty House," had

happily arrogated Enobarbus's famous praise of Cleopatra to himself: "'I trust that age doth not wither nor custom stale my infinite variety,' said he, and I recognized in his voice the joy and pride which the artist takes in his own creation" (p. 239). It was an attitude — the trust, perhaps, no less than the joy and pride — that his author shared.

## HOLMES AND THE CRITICS

For much of this century, critical analysis of the Sherlock Holmes stories was almost exclusively the preserve of a cult of devotees — "Sherlockians," practitioners of the so-called Higher Criticism — who produced voluminously what one scholar has called "the most tedious pseudo-scholarship in the history of letters, most of it premised on the facetious assumption that Holmes was a historical character whose biography needs filling in" (Clausen 105). Now, in the last decade or so, that situation is changing: increasingly Doyle is being studied seriously both as a literary artist and as a representative of his culture, and a genuine critical discussion of the Holmes works is now in progress.

Two general emphases, broadly distinguishable though by no means mutually exclusive, have characterized this recent Holmes criticism. First, many critics have been particularly interested in the stories as detective fiction: they have pursued inquiries into the detective story's stress on and exposure of plot, into the detective's and the reader's modes of interpretation and how these relate to each other, into the structure, logic, and nature of detection itself. Critics asking some very different questions, meanwhile, have examined the same stories more for their cultural and historical implications and resonances, attending especially to their subtexts of sexual, class, and political relationships.

The articles collected in this volume, all of them recent (five first appeared in the 1980s, the remaining four in the early 1990s), show the richness and variousness of both these contemporary critical dialogues. They are grouped here according to the broad topical distinctions just indicated: the first cluster includes essays emphasizing detection, plot, and narrative, and the second, essays emphasizing society, gender, culture, and ideology. Each group opens with a broadly contextualizing essay (Priestman on Doyle's development of the "series" mode; Knight on the relation of the early Sherlock Holmes stories to the cultural and especially the sexual issues of their era). Next in each group comes an essay in critical theory (Brooks's narratological meditation on the detective story and the nature of narrative plot; Belsey's deconstructive approach to the repressed sexual ideology of the stories). Each section then offers two sustained critical studies of particular Sherlock Holmes stories (Caprettini on "A Scandal in Bohemia" and Hodgson on "The Speckled Band"; Hennessy and Mohan on "The Speckled Band" and Jaffe on "The Man with the Twisted Lip"). At the end of the first section and connecting it to the second, Alastair Fowler's essay on "The Dancing Men" begins by considering a particularly pure opportunity for Holmes's ratiocination, the solving of a cipher, but ends by discovering in both cipher and solution a "symbolic romance," an "eloquent means of expressing social ideas" (p. 366).

Not surprisingly, the essays within each cluster have much to say to each other, and the different arguments they pose and debate about the stories as detective fiction (the first group) and about the stories as artifacts of late Victorian culture (the second group) are collectively as well as individually instructive. Even more fascinating, perhaps, are the dialogues implicit or potential between essays from the two groups. The two essays on "The Speckled Band," for example, approach the story in dramatically different ways but show some curious, unexpected affinities in their perceptions of the mystifyings and overwritings of authorial (Hodgson) or of patriarchal (Hennessy and Mohan) control. Again, Peter Brooks's presentation of detection as an interpretative repetition and plot as the reworking of story in and by discourse (he looks particularly at "The Musgrave Ritual") stands in provocative juxtaposition to Catherine Belsey's suggestion (with particular reference to "Charles Augustus Milverton," "The Dancing Men," and "The Second Stain") that the stories bespeak the limitations of detection and that their plots are often not merely reworkings but also contradictory hauntings of their stories. Fowler, too, debates Belsey, both on the "realist" status of Doyle's fiction and on Doyle's possible repression in his stories of the woman's voice. Similarly, the implications of opposed maskings or disguises is a central concern of both Caprettini's semiotic attention to Holmes's method in "A Scandal in Bohemia" and Jaffe's new historicist reading of the ambivalences of capitalism in "The Man with the Twisted Lip." Such intersections abound in the essays; they suggest that even after years of familiarity we, like Watson, have still only begun to appreciate the complexities of Sherlock Holmes.

## WORKS CITED

Bell, Joseph. "Mr. Sherlock Holmes," Preface to *A Study in Scarlet*. London: Ward, Locke and Bowden, 1893.

Carr, John Dickson. *The Life of Sir Arthur Conan Doyle*. New York: Harper, 1949.

Clausen, Christopher. "Sherlock Holmes, Order, and the Late-Victorian Mind." *Georgia Review* 38 (1984): 104–23.

Doyle, Arthur Conan. *Memories and Adventures*. London: Hodder and Stoughton, 1924.

———. "A Sherlock Holmes Competition: Mr. Sherlock Holmes to His Readers." *Strand*, March, 1927.

———. *Through the Magic Door*. New York: McClure, 1908.

Higham, Charles. *The Adventures of Conan Doyle: The Life of the Creator of Sherlock Holmes*. New York: Norton, 1976.

# PART ONE

# The Major
# Sherlock Holmes
# Stories

# From *A Study in Scarlet*

## PART 1: BEING A REPRINT FROM THE REMINISCENCES OF JOHN H. WATSON, M.D., LATE OF THE ARMY MEDICAL DEPARTMENT

### Chapter 1. Mr. Sherlock Holmes

In the year 1878 I took my degree of Doctor of Medicine of the University of London, and proceeded to Netley to go through the course prescribed for surgeons in the Army. Having completed my studies there, I was duly attached to the Fifth Northumberland Fusiliers as assistant surgeon. The regiment was stationed in India at the time, and before I could join it, the second Afghan war had broken out. On landing at Bombay, I learned that my corps had advanced through the passes, and was already deep in the enemy's country. I followed, however, with many other officers who were in the same situation as myself, and succeeded in reaching Candahar in safety, where I found my regiment, and at once entered upon my new duties.

The campaign brought honours and promotion to many, but for me it had nothing but misfortune and disaster. I was removed from my brigade and attached to the Berkshires, with whom I served at the fatal battle of Maiwand. There I was struck on the shoulder by a Jezail bullet, which shattered the bone and grazed the subclavian artery. I should have fallen into the hands of the murderous Ghazis had it not been for the devotion and courage shown by Murray, my orderly, who threw me across a pack-horse, and succeeded in bringing me safely to the British lines.

Worn with pain, and weak from the prolonged hardships which I had undergone, I was removed, with a great train of wounded sufferers, to the base hospital at Peshawar. Here I rallied, and had already improved so far as to be able to walk about the wards, and even to bask a little upon the veranda, when I was struck down by enteric fever, that curse of our Indian possessions. For months my life was despaired of, and when at last I came to myself and became convalescent, I was so weak and emaciated that a medical board determined that not a day should be lost in sending me back to England. I was despatched, accordingly, in the troopship *Orontes,* and landed a month later on

First published in *Beeton's Christmas Annual,* November 1887.

Portsmouth jetty, with my health irretrievably ruined, but with permission from a paternal government to spend the next nine months in attempting to improve it.

I had neither kith nor kin in England, and was therefore as free as air — or as free as an income of eleven shillings and sixpence a day will permit a man to be. Under such circumstances I naturally gravitated to London, that great cesspool into which all the loungers and idlers of the Empire are irresistibly drained. There I stayed for some time at a private hotel in the Strand, leading a comfortless, meaningless existence, and spending such money as I had, considerably more freely than I ought. So alarming did the state of my finances become, that I soon realized that I must either leave the metropolis and rusticate somewhere in the country, or that I must make a complete alteration in my style of living. Choosing the latter alternative, I began by making up my mind to leave the hotel, and take up my quarters in some less pretentious and less expensive domicile.

On the very day that I had come to this conclusion, I was standing at the Criterion Bar, when someone tapped me on the shoulder, and turning round I recognized young Stamford, who had been a dresser under me at Bart's.[1] The sight of a friendly face in the great wilderness of London is a pleasant thing indeed to a lonely man. In old days Stamford had never been a particular crony of mine, but now I hailed him with enthusiasm, and he, in his turn, appeared to be delighted to see me. In the exuberance of my joy, I asked him to lunch with me at the Holborn, and we started off together in a hansom.

"Whatever have you been doing with yourself, Watson?" he asked in undisguised wonder, as we rattled through the crowded London streets. "You are as thin as a lath and as brown as a nut."

I gave him a short sketch of my adventures, and had hardly concluded it by the time that we reached our destination.

"Poor devil!" he said, commiseratingly, after he had listened to my misfortunes. "What are you up to now?"

"Looking for lodgings," I answered. "Trying to solve the problem as to whether it is possible to get comfortable rooms at a reasonable price."

"That's a strange thing," remarked my companion; "you are the second man to-day that has used that expression to me."

"And who was the first?" I asked.

"A fellow who is working at the chemical laboratory up at the hos-

---

[1] *Bart's:* St. Bartholomew's Hospital, in London.

pital. He was bemoaning himself this morning because he could not get someone to go halves with him in some nice rooms which he had found, and which were too much for his purse."

"By Jove!" I cried; "if he really wants someone to share the rooms and the expense, I am the very man for him. I should prefer having a partner to being alone."

Young Stamford looked rather strangely at me over his wineglass. "You don't know Sherlock Holmes yet," he said; "perhaps you would not care for him as a constant companion."

"Why, what is there against him?"

"Oh, I didn't say there was anything against him. He is a little queer in his ideas — an enthusiast in some branches of science. As far as I know he is a decent fellow enough."

"A medical student, I suppose?" said I.

"No — I have no idea what he intends to go in for. I believe he is well up in anatomy, and he is a first-class chemist; but, as far as I know, he has never taken out any systematic medical classes. His studies are very desultory and eccentric, but he has amassed a lot of out-of-the-way knowledge which would astonish his professors."

"Did you never ask him what he was going in for?" I asked.

"No; he is not a man that it is easy to draw out, though he can be communicative enough when the fancy seizes him."

"I should like to meet him," I said. "If I am to lodge with anyone, I should prefer a man of studious and quiet habits. I am not strong enough yet to stand much noise or excitement. I had enough of both in Afghanistan to last me for the remainder of my natural existence. How could I meet this friend of yours?"

"He is sure to be at the laboratory," returned my companion. "He either avoids the place for weeks, or else he works there from morning till night. If you like, we will drive round together after luncheon."

"Certainly," I answered, and the conversation drifted away into other channels.

As we made our way to the hospital after leaving the Holborn, Stamford gave me a few more particulars about the gentleman whom I proposed to take as a fellow-lodger.

"You mustn't blame me if you don't get on with him," he said; "I know nothing more of him than I have learned from meeting him occasionally in the laboratory. You proposed this arrangement, so you must not hold me responsible."

"If we don't get on it will be easy to part company," I answered. "It seems to me, Stamford," I added, looking hard at my companion, "that

ome reason for washing your hands of the matter. Is this
nper so formidable, or what is it? Don't be mealymouthed
about it.

"It is not easy to express the inexpressible," he answered with a
laugh. "Holmes is a little too scientific for my tastes — it approaches to
cold-bloodedness. I could imagine his giving a friend a little pinch of
the latest vegetable alkaloid, not out of malevolence, you understand,
but simply out of a spirit of inquiry in order to have an accurate idea of
the effects. To do him justice, I think that he would take it himself with
the same readiness. He appears to have a passion for definite and exact
knowledge."

"Very right too."

"Yes, but it may be pushed to excess. When it comes to beating the
subjects in the dissecting-rooms with a stick, it is certainly taking rather
a bizarre shape."

"Beating the subjects!"

"Yes, to verify how far bruises may be produced after death. I saw
him at it with my own eyes."

"And yet you say he is not a medical student?"

"No. Heaven knows what the objects of his studies are. But here we
are, and you must form your own impressions about him." As he spoke,
we turned down a narrow lane and passed through a small side-door,
which opened into a wing of the great hospital. It was familiar ground
to me, and I needed no guiding as we ascended the bleak stone staircase
and made our way down the long corridor with its vista of whitewashed
wall and dun-coloured doors. Near the farther end a low arched passage
branched away from it and led to the chemical laboratory.

This was a lofty chamber, lined and littered with countless bottles.
Broad, low tables were scattered about, which bristled with retorts, test-
tubes, and little Bunsen lamps, with their blue flickering flames. There
was only one student in the room, who was bending over a distant table
absorbed in his work. At the sound of our steps he glanced round and
sprang to his feet with a cry of pleasure. "I've found it! I've found it,"
he shouted to my companion, running towards us with a test-tube in his
hand. "I have found a re-agent which is precipitated by hæmoglobin,
and by nothing else." Had he discovered a gold mine, greater delight
could not have shone upon his features.

"Dr. Watson, Mr. Sherlock Holmes," said Stamford, introducing us.

"How are you?" he said cordially, gripping my hand with a strength
for which I should hardly have given him credit. "You have been in
Afghanistan, I perceive."

"How on earth did you know that?" I asked in astonishment.

"Never mind," said he, chuckling to himself. "The question now is about hæmoglobin. No doubt you see the significance of this discovery of mine?"

"It is interesting, chemically, no doubt," I answered, "but practically ——"

"Why, man, it is the most practical medico-legal discovery for years. Don't you see that it gives us an infallible test for blood stains? Come over here now!" He seized me by the coat-sleeve in his eagerness, and drew me over to the table at which he had been working. "Let us have some fresh blood," he said, digging a long bodkin into his finger, and drawing off the resulting drop of blood in a chemical pipette. "Now, I add this small quantity of blood to a litre of water. You perceive that the resulting mixture has the appearance of pure water. The proportion of blood cannot be more than one in a million. I have no doubt, however, that we shall be able to obtain the characteristic reaction." As he spoke, he threw into the vessel a few white crystals, and then added some drops of a transparent fluid. In an instant the contents assumed a dull mahogany colour, and a brownish dust was precipitated to the bottom of the glass jar.

"Ha! ha!" he cried, clapping his hands, and looking as delighted as a child with a new toy. "What do you think of that?"

"It seems to be a very delicate test," I remarked.

"Beautiful! beautiful! The old guaiacum test was very clumsy and uncertain. So is the microscopic examination for blood corpuscles. The latter is valueless if the stains are a few hours old. Now, this appears to act as well whether the blood is old or new. Had this test been invented, there are hundreds of men now walking the earth who would long ago have paid the penalty of their crimes."

"Indeed!" I murmured.

"Criminal cases are continually hinging upon that one point. A man is suspected of a crime months perhaps after it has been committed. His linen or clothes are examined and brownish stains discovered upon them. Are they blood stains, or mud stains, or rust stains, or fruit stains, or what are they? That is a question which has puzzled many an expert, and why? Because there was no reliable test. Now we have the Sherlock Holmes test, and there will no longer be any difficulty."

His eyes fairly glittered as he spoke, and he put his hand over his heart and bowed as if to some applauding crowd conjured up by his imagination.

"You are to be congratulated," I remarked, considerably surprised at his enthusiasm.

"There was the case of Von Bischoff at Frankfort last year. He would certainly have been hung had this test been in existence. Then there was Mason of Bradford, and the notorious Muller, and Lefevre of Montpellier, and Samson of New Orleans. I could name a score of cases in which it would have been decisive."

"You seem to be a walking calendar of crime," said Stamford with a laugh. "You might start a paper on those lines. Call it the 'Police News of the Past.'"

"Very interesting reading it might be made, too," remarked Sherlock Holmes, sticking a small piece of plaster over the prick on his finger. "I have to be careful," he continued, turning to me with a smile, "for I dabble with poisons a good deal." He held out his hand as he spoke, and I noticed that it was all mottled over with similar pieces of plaster, and discoloured with strong acids.

"We came here on business," said Stamford, sitting down on a high three-legged stool, and pushing another one in my direction with his foot. "My friend here wants to take diggings; and as you were complaining that you could get no one to go halves with you, I thought that I had better bring you together."

Sherlock Holmes seemed delighted at the idea of sharing his rooms with me. "I have my eye on a suite in Baker Street," he said, "which would suit us down to the ground. You don't mind the smell of strong tobacco, I hope?"

"I always smoke 'ship's' myself," I answered.

"That's good enough. I generally have chemicals about, and occasionally do experiments. Would that annoy you?"

"By no means."

"Let me see — what are my other shortcomings? I get in the dumps at times, and don't open my mouth for days on end. You must not think I am sulky when I do that. Just let me alone, and I'll soon be right. What have you to confess now? It's just as well for two fellows to know the worst of one another before they begin to live together."

I laughed at this cross-examination. "I keep a bull pup," I said, "and I object to rows because my nerves are shaken, and I get up at all sorts of ungodly hours, and I am extremely lazy. I have another set of vices when I'm well, but those are the principal ones at present."

"Do you include violin playing in your category of rows?" he asked, anxiously.

"It depends on the player," I answered. "A well-played violin is a treat for the gods — a badly played one ——"

"Oh, that's all right," he cried, with a merry laugh. "I think we may

consider the thing as settled — that is, if the rooms are a[  ]
you."

"When shall we see them?"

"Call for me here at noon to-morrow, and we'll go together and settle everything," he answered.

"All right — noon exactly," said I, shaking his hand.

We left him working among his chemicals, and we walked together towards my hotel.

"By the way," I asked suddenly, stopping and turning upon Stamford, "how the deuce did he know that I had come from Afghanistan?"

My companion smiled an enigmatical smile. "That's just his little peculiarity," he said. "A good many people have wanted to know how he finds things out."

"Oh! a mystery is it?" I cried, rubbing my hands. "This is very piquant. I am much obliged to you for bringing us together. 'The proper study of mankind is man,' you know."

"You must study him, then," Stamford said, as he bade me good-bye. "You'll find him a knotty problem, though. I'll wager he learns more about you than you about him. Good-bye."

"Good-bye," I answered, and strolled on to my hotel, considerably interested in my new acquaintance.

## Chapter 2.   The Science of Deduction

We met next day as he had arranged, and inspected the rooms at No. 221B, Baker Street, of which he had spoken at our meeting. They consisted of a couple of comfortable bedrooms and a single large airy sitting-room, cheerfully furnished, and illuminated by two broad windows. So desirable in every way were the apartments, and so moderate did the terms seem when divided between us, that the bargain was concluded upon the spot, and we at once entered into possession. That very evening I moved my things round from the hotel, and on the following morning Sherlock Holmes followed me with several boxes and portmanteaus. For a day or two we were busily employed in unpacking and laying out our property to the best advantage. That done, we gradually began to settle down and to accommodate ourselves to our new surroundings.

Holmes was certainly not a difficult man to live with. He was quiet in his ways, and his habits were regular. It was rare for him to be up after ten at night, and he had invariably breakfasted and gone out before I rose in the morning. Sometimes he spent his day at the chemical laboratory, sometimes in the dissecting-rooms, and occasionally in long walks, which appeared to take him into the lowest portions of the city. Nothing could exceed his energy when the working fit was upon him; but now and again a reaction would seize him, and for days on end he would lie upon the sofa in the sitting-room, hardly uttering a word or moving a muscle from morning to night. On these occasions I have noticed such a dreamy, vacant expression in his eyes, that I might have suspected him of being addicted to the use of some narcotic, had not the temperance and cleanliness of his whole life forbidden such a notion.

As the weeks went by, my interest in him and my curiosity as to his aims in life gradually deepened and increased. His very person and appearance were such as to strike the attention of the most casual observer. In height he was rather over six feet, and so excessively lean that he seemed to be considerably taller. His eyes were sharp and piercing, save during those intervals of torpor to which I have alluded; and his thin, hawk-like nose gave his whole expression an air of alertness and decision. His chin, too, had the prominence and squareness which mark the man of determination. His hands were invariably blotted with ink and stained with chemicals, yet he was possessed of extraordinary delicacy of touch, as I frequently had occasion to observe when I watched him manipulating his fragile philosophical instruments.

The reader may set me down as a hopeless busybody, when I confess how much this man stimulated my curiosity, and how often I endeavoured to break through the reticence which he showed on all that concerned himself. Before pronouncing judgment, however, be it remembered how objectless was my life, and how little there was to engage my attention. My health forbade me from venturing out unless the weather was exceptionally genial, and I had no friends who would call upon me and break the monotony of my daily existence. Under these circumstances, I eagerly hailed the little mystery which hung around my companion, and spent much of my time in endeavouring to unravel it.

He was not studying medicine. He had himself, in reply to a question, confirmed Stamford's opinion upon that point. Neither did he appear to have pursued any course of reading which might fit him for a degree in science or any other recognized portal which would give him an entrance into the learned world. Yet his zeal for certain studies was remarkable, and within eccentric limits his knowledge was so extraordinarily ample and minute that his observations have fairly astounded me. Surely no man would work so hard or attain such precise information unless he had some definite end in view. Desultory readers are seldom remarkable for the exactness of their learning. No man burdens his mind with small matters unless he has some very good reason for doing so.

His ignorance was as remarkable as his knowledge. Of contemporary literature, philosophy and politics he appeared to know next to nothing. Upon my quoting Thomas Carlyle, he inquired in the naïvest way who he might be and what he had done. My surprise reached a climax, however, when I found incidentally that he was ignorant of the Copernican Theory and of the composition of the Solar System. That any civilized human being in this nineteenth century should not be aware that the earth travelled round the sun appeared to me to be such an extraordinary fact that I could hardly realize it.

"You appear to be astonished," he said, smiling at my expression of surprise. "Now that I do know it I shall do my best to forget it."

"To forget it!"

"You see," he explained, "I consider that a man's brain originally is like a little empty attic, and you have to stock it with such furniture as you choose. A fool takes in all the lumber of every sort that he comes across, so that the knowledge which might be useful to him gets crowded out, or at best is jumbled up with a lot of other things, so that  he has a difficulty in laying his hands upon it. Now the skilful workman is very careful indeed as to what he takes into his brain-attic. He will have nothing but the tools which may help him in doing his work, but of these he has a large assortment, and all in the most perfect order. It is a mistake to think that that little room has elastic walls and can distend to any extent. Depend upon it there comes a time when for every addition of knowledge you forget something that you knew before. It is of the highest importance, therefore, not to have useless facts elbowing out the useful ones."

"But the Solar System!" I protested.

"What the deuce is it to me?" he interrupted impatiently: "you say that we go round the sun. If we went round the moon it would not make a pennyworth of difference to me or to my work."

I was on the point of asking him what that work might be, but something in his manner showed me that the question would be an unwelcome one. I pondered over our short conversation, however, and endeavoured to draw my deductions from it. He said that he would acquire no knowledge which did not bear upon his object. Therefore all the knowledge which he possessed was such as would be useful to him. I enumerated in my own mind all the various points upon which he had shown me that he was exceptionally well informed. I even took a pencil and jotted them down. I could not help smiling at the document when I had completed it. It ran in this way:

*Sherlock Holmes — his limits*

1. Knowledge of Literature. — Nil.
2.       "          "   Philosophy. — Nil.
3.       "          "   Astronomy. — Nil.
4.       "          "   Politics. — Feeble.
5.       "          "   Botany. — Variable.
    Well up in belladonna, opium, and poisons generally.
    Knows nothing of practical gardening.
6. Knowledge of Geology. — Practical, but limited.
    Tells at a glance different soils from each other. After walks
    has shown me splashes upon his trousers, and told me by
    their colour and consistence in what part of London he had
    received them.
7. Knowledge of Chemistry. — Profound.
8.       "          "   Anatomy. — Accurate, but unsystematic.
9.       "          "   Sensational Literature. — Immense.
    He appears to know every detail of every horror perpetrated
    in the century.
10. Plays the violin well.
11. Is an expert singlestick[2] player, boxer, and swordsman.
12. Has a good practical knowledge of British law.

When I had got so far in my list I threw it into the fire in despair. "If I can only find what the fellow is driving at by reconciling all these accomplishments, and discovering a calling which needs them all," I said to myself, "I may as well give up the attempt at once."

I see that I have alluded above to his powers upon the violin. These were very remarkable, but as eccentric as all his other accomplishments. That he could play pieces, and difficult pieces, I knew well, because at my request he has played me some of Mendelssohn's *Lieder,* and other favourites. When left to himself, however, he would seldom produce any music or attempt any recognized air. Leaning back in his armchair of an evening, he would close his eyes and scrape carelessly at the fiddle which was thrown across his knee. Sometimes the chords were sonorous and melancholy. Occasionally they were fantastic and cheerful. Clearly they reflected the thoughts which possessed him, but whether the music aided those thoughts, or whether the playing was simply the result of a whim or fancy, was more than I could determine. I might have rebelled

---

[2]*singlestick:* A stick with a hand guard, used with one hand as in fencing.

against these exasperating solos had it not been that he usually terminated them by playing in quick succession a whole series of my favourite airs as a slight compensation for the trial upon my patience.

During the first week or so we had no callers, and I had begun to think that my companion was as friendless a man as I was myself. Presently, however, I found that he had many acquaintances, and those in the most different classes of society. There was one little sallow, rat-faced, dark-eyed fellow, who was introduced to me as Mr. Lestrade, and who came three or four times in a single week. One morning a young girl called, fashionably dressed, and stayed for half an hour or more. The same afternoon brought a grey-headed, seedy visitor, looking like a Jew peddler, who appeared to me to be much excited, and who was closely followed by a slipshod elderly woman. On another occasion an old white-haired gentleman had an interview with my companion; and on another, a railway porter in his velveteen uniform. When any of these nondescript individuals put in an appearance, Sherlock Holmes used to beg for the use of the sitting-room, and I would retire to my bedroom. He always apologized to me for putting me to this inconvenience. "I have to use this room as a place of business," he said, "and these people are my clients." Again I had an opportunity of asking him a point-blank question, and again my delicacy prevented me from forcing another man to confide in me. I imagined at the time that he had some strong reason for not alluding to it, but he soon dispelled the idea by coming round to the subject of his own accord.

It was upon the 4th of March, as I have good reason to remember, that I rose somewhat earlier than usual, and found that Sherlock Holmes had not yet finished his breakfast. The landlady had become so accustomed to my late habits that my place had not been laid nor my coffee prepared. With the unreasonable petulance of mankind I rang the bell and gave a curt intimation that I was ready. Then I picked up a magazine from the table and attempted to while away the time with it, while my companion munched silently at his toast. One of the articles had a pencil mark at the heading, and I naturally began to run my eye through it.

Its somewhat ambitious title was "The Book of Life," and it attempted to show how much an observant man might learn by an accurate and systematic examination of all that came in his way. It struck me as being a remarkable mixture of shrewdness and of absurdity. The reasoning was close and intense, but the deductions appeared to me to be far fetched and exaggerated. The writer claimed by a momentary expression, a twitch of a muscle or a glance of an eye, to fathom a man's inmost thoughts. Deceit, according to him, was an impossibility in the case of one trained to observation and analysis. His conclusions were as infallible as so many propositions of Euclid. So startling would his results appear to the uninitiated that until they learned the processes by which he had arrived at them they might well consider him as a necromancer.

"From a drop of water," said the writer, "a logician could infer the possibility of an Atlantic or a Niagara without having seen or heard of one or the other. So all life is a great chain, the nature of which is known whenever we are shown a single link of it. Like all other arts, the Science of Deduction and Analysis is one which can only be acquired by long and patient study, nor is life long enough to allow any mortal to attain the highest possible perfection in it. Before turning to those moral and mental aspects of the matter which present the greatest difficulties, let the inquirer begin by mastering more elementary problems. Let him, on meeting a fellow-mortal, learn at a glance to distinguish the history of the man, and the trade or profession to which he belongs. Puerile as such an exercise may seem, it sharpens the faculties of observation, and teaches one where to look and what to look for. By a man's finger-nails, by his coat-sleeve, by his boots, by his trouser-knees, by the callosities of his forefinger and thumb, by his expression, by his shirt-cuffs — by each of these things a man's calling is plainly revealed. That all united should fail to enlighten the competent inquirer in any case is almost inconceivable."

"What ineffable twaddle!" I cried, slapping the magazine down on the table; "I never read such rubbish in my life."

"What is it?" asked Sherlock Holmes.

"Why, this article," I said, pointing at it with my eggspoon as I sat down to my breakfast. "I see that you have read it since you have marked it. I don't deny that it is smartly written. It irritates me, though. It is evidently the theory of some armchair lounger who evolves all these neat little paradoxes in the seclusion of his own study. It is not practical. I should like to see him clapped down in a third-class carriage on the Underground, and asked to give the trades of all his fellow-travellers. I would lay a thousand to one against him."

"You would lose your money," Holmes remarked calmly. "As for the article, I wrote it myself."

"You!"

"Yes; I have a turn both for observation and for deduction. The theories which I have expressed there, and which appear to you to be so chimerical, are really extremely practical — so practical that I depend upon them for my bread and cheese."

"And how?" I asked involuntarily.

"Well, I have a trade of my own. I suppose I am the only one in the world. I'm a consulting detective, if you can understand what that is. Here in London we have lots of government detectives and lots of private ones. When these fellows are at fault, they come to me, and I manage to put them on the right scent. They lay all the evidence before me, and I am generally able, by the help of my knowledge of the history of crime, to set them straight. There is a strong family resemblance about misdeeds, and if you have all the details of a thousand at your finger ends, it is odd if you can't unravel the thousand and first. Lestrade is a well-known detective. He got himself into a fog recently over a forgery case, and that was what brought him here."

"And these other people?"

"They are mostly sent on by private inquiry agencies. They are all people who are in trouble about something and want a little enlightening. I listen to their story, they listen to my comments, and then I pocket my fee."

"But do you mean to say," I said, "that without leaving your room you can unravel some knot which other men can make nothing of, although they have seen every detail for themselves?"

"Quite so. I have a kind of intuition that way. Now and again a case turns up which is a little more complex. Then I have to bustle about and see things with my own eyes. You see I have a lot of special knowledge which I apply to the problem, and which facilitates matters wonderfully. Those rules of deduction laid down in that article which aroused your scorn are invaluable to me in practical work. Observation with me is second nature. You appeared to be surprised when I told you, on our first meeting, that you had come from Afghanistan."

"You were told, no doubt."

"Nothing of the sort. I *knew* you came from Afghanistan. From long habit the train of thoughts ran so swiftly through my mind that I arrived at the conclusion without being conscious of intermediate steps. There were such steps, however. The train of reasoning ran, 'Here is a gentleman of a medical type, but with the air of a military man. Clearly an army doctor, then. He has just come from the tropics, for his face is dark, and that is not the natural tint of his skin, for his wrists are fair. He has undergone hardship and sickness, as his haggard face says clearly. His left arm has been injured. He holds it in a stiff and unnatural manner. Where in the tropics could an English army doctor have seen much hardship and got his arm wounded? Clearly in Afghanistan.' The whole train of thought did not occupy a second. I then remarked that you came from Afghanistan, and you were astonished."

"It is simple enough as you explain it," I said, smiling. "You remind me of Edgar Allan Poe's Dupin.[3] I had no idea that such individuals did exist outside of stories."

Sherlock Holmes rose and lit his pipe. "No doubt you think that you are complimenting me in comparing me to Dupin," he observed. "Now, in my opinion, Dupin was a very inferior fellow. That trick of his of breaking in on his friends' thoughts with an apropos remark after a quarter of an hour's silence is really very showy and superficial. He had some analytical genius, no doubt; but he was by no means such a phenomenon as Poe appeared to imagine."

"Have you read Gaboriau's works?"[4] I asked. "Does Lecoq come up to your idea of a detective?"

Sherlock Holmes sniffed sardonically. "Lecoq was a miserable bungler," he said, in an angry voice; "he had only one thing to recommend him, and that was his energy. That book made me positively ill. The question was how to identify an unknown prisoner. I could have done it in twenty-four hours. Lecoq took six months or so. It might be made a textbook for detectives to teach them what to avoid."

I felt rather indignant at having two characters whom I had admired treated in this cavalier style. I walked over to the window and stood looking out into the busy street. "This fellow may be very clever," I said to myself, "but he is certainly very conceited."

"There are no crimes and no criminals in these days," he said, querulously. "What is the use of having brains in our profession? I know well that I have it in me to make my name famous. No man lives or has ever lived who has brought the same amount of study and of natural talent to the detection of crime which I have done. And what is the result? There is no crime to detect, or, at most, some bungling villainy with a motive so transparent that even a Scotland Yard official can see through it."

I was still annoyed at his bumptious style of conversation. I thought it best to change the topic.

"I wonder what that fellow is looking for?" I asked, pointing to a stalwart, plainly dressed individual who was walking slowly down the other side of the street, looking anxiously at the numbers. He had a large blue envelope in his hand, and was evidently the bearer of a message.

"You mean the retired sergeant of Marines," said Sherlock Holmes.

---

[3] *Poe's Dupin:* C. Auguste Dupin, the protagonist of Edgar Allan Poe's seminal stories of detection, "The Murders in the Rue Morgue" (1841), "The Mystery of Marie Roget" (1842), and "The Purloined Letter" (1845).

[4] *Gaboriau:* Emile Gaboriau, who in the late 1860s popularized the detective novel in France; Monsieur Lecoq was his detective protagonist.

"Brag and bounce!" thought I to myself. "He knows that I cannot verify his guess."

The thought had hardly passed through my mind when the man whom we were watching caught sight of the number on our door, and ran rapidly across the roadway. We heard a loud knock, a deep voice below, and heavy steps ascending the stair.

"For Mr. Sherlock Holmes," he said, stepping into the room and handing my friend the letter.

Here was an opportunity of taking the conceit out of him. He little thought of this when he made that random shot. "May I ask, my lad," I said, in the blandest voice, "what your trade may be?"

"Commissionaire,[5] sir," he said, gruffly. "Uniform away for repairs."

"And you were?" I asked, with a slightly malicious glance at my companion.

"A sergeant, sir, Royal Marine Light Infantry, sir. No answer? Right, sir."

He clicked his heels together, raised his hand in salute, and was gone.

## AFTERWORD

Doyle brings his two major characters together skillfully through the agency of their common acquaintance Stamford. "Whatever have you been doing with yourself, Watson?" is Stamford's first query. This is precisely the sort of information that Holmes, in contrast, will gain at a glance, as his own first words to Watson soon demonstrate: "How are you? . . . You have been in Afghanistan, I perceive." The puzzle of Holmes's remarkable perceptiveness greatly interests Watson, for, as he declares (quoting a famous line from Pope's *Essay on Man*), "'The proper study of mankind is man,' you know." But the man Watson now begins to study, he will soon learn, himself makes a particular and very novel business of studying mankind.

Watson's early analysis of Holmes's limits will soon, in subsequent stories, prove to be inadequate or mistaken, particularly on the score of Holmes's apparent ignorances. But Doyle liked the idea of a well-ordered "brain-attic" workshop with a reference library in the background. Holmes recurs to the notion in "The Five Orange Pips," and throughout the stories frequently consults his index, his case-book, and his various encyclopedias and other reference materials for background

---

[5] *Commissionaire:* A member of the Corps of Commissionaires, an association of pensioned soldiers, grandly uniformed, who worked as messengers, porters, and odd-job men.

information (see, for example, "A Scandal in Bohemia," "The Speckled Band," and "The Empty House").

Doyle later insisted that in his "cavalier" dismissal of Poe's Auguste Dupin as "a very inferior fellow," Holmes was speaking in character for himself only, and not for his author. For his own part, Doyle celebrated Poe as "the supreme original short story writer of all time" and Dupin as Holmes's great original: "After all, mental acuteness is the one quality which can be ascribed to the ideal detective, and when that has once been admirably done, succeeding writers must necessarily be content for all time to follow in the same main track" (*Through the Magic Door* 117–18).

"The Science of Deduction," the title of Chapter 2 of *A Study in Scarlet*, is also the title of Chapter 1 of the next Sherlock Holmes novel, *The Sign of Four*, where Holmes further elaborates on "the curious analytical reasoning from effects to causes" that is his strength.

# A Scandal in Bohemia

## I

To Sherlock Holmes she is always *the* woman. I have seldom heard him mention her under any other name. In his eyes she eclipses and predominates the whole of her sex. It was not that he felt any emotion akin to love for Irene Adler. All emotions, and that one particularly, were abhorrent to his cold, precise, but admirably balanced mind. He was, I take it, the most perfect reasoning and observing machine that the world has seen: but, as a lover, he would have placed himself in a false position. He never spoke of the softer passions, save with a gibe and a sneer. They were admirable things for the observer — excellent for drawing the veil from men's motives and actions. But for the trained reasoner to admit such intrusions into his own delicate and finely adjusted temperament was to introduce a distracting factor which might throw a doubt upon all his mental results. Grit in a sensitive instrument, or a crack in one of his own high-power lenses, would not be more disturbing than a strong emotion in a nature such as his. And yet there was but one woman to him, and that woman was the late Irene Adler, of dubious and questionable memory.

From *The Adventures of Sherlock Holmes* (1892). First published in the *Strand*, July 1891.

I had seen little of Holmes lately. My marriage had drifted us away from each other. My own complete happiness, and the home-centred interests which rise up around the man who first finds himself master of his own establishment, were sufficient to absorb all my attention; while Holmes, who loathed every form of society with his whole Bohemian soul, remained in our lodgings in Baker Street, buried among his old books, and alternating from week to week between cocaine and ambition, the drowsiness of the drug, and the fierce energy of his own keen nature. He was still, as ever, deeply attracted by the study of crime, and occupied his immense faculties and extraordinary powers of observation in following out those clues, and clearing up those mysteries, which had been abandoned as hopeless by the official police. From time to time I heard some vague account of his doings: of his summons to Odessa in the case of the Trepoff murder, of his clearing up of the singular tragedy of the Atkinson brothers at Trincomalee, and finally of the mission which he had accomplished so delicately and successfully for the reigning family of Holland. Beyond these signs of his activity, however, which I merely shared with all the readers of the daily press, I knew little of my former friend and companion.

One night — it was on the 20th of March, 1888 — I was returning from a journey to a patient (for I had now returned to civil practice), when my way led me through Baker Street. As I passed the well-remembered door, which must always be associated in my mind with my wooing, and with the dark incidents of the Study in Scarlet, I was seized with a keen desire to see Holmes again, and to know how he was employing his extraordinary powers. His rooms were brilliantly lit, and, even as I looked up, I saw his tall spare figure pass twice in a dark silhouette against the blind. He was pacing the room swiftly, eagerly, with his head sunk upon his chest, and his hands clasped behind him. To me, who knew his every mood and habit, his attitude and manner told their own story. He was at work again. He had risen out of his drug-created dreams, and was hot upon the scent of some new problem. I rang the bell, and was shown up to the chamber which had formerly been in part my own.

His manner was not effusive. It seldom was; but he was glad, I think, to see me. With hardly a word spoken, but with a kindly eye, he waved me to an arm-chair, threw across his case of cigars, and indicated a spirit case and a gasogene in the corner. Then he stood before the fire, and looked me over in his singular introspective fashion.

"Wedlock suits you," he remarked. "I think, Watson, that you have put on seven and a half pounds since I saw you."

"Seven," I answered.

"Indeed, I should have thought a little more. Just a trifle more, I fancy, Watson. And in practice again, I observe. You did not tell me that you intended to go into harness."

"Then, how do you know?"

"I see it, I deduce it. How do I know that you have been getting yourself very wet lately, and that you have a most clumsy and careless servant girl?"

"My dear Holmes," said I, "this is too much. You would certainly have been burned had you lived a few centuries ago. It is true that I had a country walk on Thursday and came home in a dreadful mess; but, as I have changed my clothes, I can't imagine how you deduce it. As to Mary Jane, she is incorrigible, and my wife has given her notice; but there again I fail to see how you work it out."

He chuckled to himself and rubbed his long nervous hands together.

"It is simplicity itself," said he; "my eyes tell me that on the inside of your left shoe, just where the firelight strikes it, the leather is scored by six almost parallel cuts. Obviously they have been caused by some one who has very carelessly scraped round the edges of the sole in order to remove crusted mud from it. Hence, you see, my double deduction that you had been out in vile weather, and that you had a particularly malignant boot-slitting specimen of the London slavey. As to your practice, if a gentleman walks into my rooms smelling of iodoform, with a black mark of nitrate of silver upon his right forefinger, and a bulge on the side of his top hat to show where he has secreted his stethoscope, I must be dull indeed if I do not pronounce him to be an active member of the medical profession."

I could not help laughing at the ease with which he explained his process of deduction. "When I hear you give your reasons," I remarked, "the thing always appears to me to be so ridiculously simple that I could easily do it myself, though at each successive instance of your reasoning I am baffled, until you explain your process. And yet I believe that my eyes are as good as yours."

"Quite so," he answered, lighting a cigarette, and throwing himself down into an arm-chair. "You see, but you do not observe. The distinction is clear. For example, you have frequently seen the steps which lead up from the hall to this room."

"Frequently."

"How often?"

"Well, some hundreds of times."

"Then how many are there?"

"How many! I don't know."

"Quite so! You have not observed. And yet you have seen. That is just my point. Now, I know that there are seventeen steps, because I have both seen and observed. By the way, since you are interested in these little problems, and since you are good enough to chronicle one or two of my trifling experiences, you may be interested in this." He threw over a sheet of thick pink-tinted note-paper which had been lying open upon the table. "It came by the last post," said he. "Read it aloud."

The note was undated, and without either signature or address.

There will call upon you to-night, at a quarter to eight o'clock [it said], a gentleman who desires to consult you upon a matter of the very deepest moment. Your recent services to one of the Royal Houses of Europe have shown that you are one who may safely be trusted with matters which are of an importance which can hardly be exaggerated. This account of you we have from all quarters received. Be in your chamber then at that hour, and do not take it amiss if your visitor wear a mask.

"This is indeed a mystery," I remarked. "What do you imagine that it means?"

"I have no data yet. It is a capital mistake to theorise before one has data. Insensibly one begins to twist facts to suit theories, instead of theories to suit facts. But the note itself. What do you deduce from it?"

I carefully examined the writing, and the paper upon which it was written.

"The man who wrote it was presumably well-to-do," I remarked, endeavouring to imitate my companion's processes. "Such paper could not be bought under half a crown a packet. It is peculiarly strong and stiff."

"Peculiar — that is the very word," said Holmes. "It is not an English paper at all. Hold it up to the light."

I did so, and saw a large *E* with a small *g*, a *P*, and a large *G* with a small *t* woven into the texture of the paper.

"What do you make of that?" asked Holmes.

"The name of the maker, no doubt; or his monogram, rather."

"Not at all. The *G* with the small *t* stands for 'Gesellschaft,' which is the German for 'Company.' It is a customary contraction like our 'Co.' *P*, of course, stands for 'Papier.' Now for the *Eg*. Let us glance at our Continental Gazetteer." He took down a heavy brown volume from his shelves. "Eglow, Eglonitz — here we are, Egria. It is in a German-speaking country — in Bohemia, not far from Carlsbad. 'Remarkable as being the scene of the death of Wallenstein, and for its numerous glass factories and paper mills.' Ha, ha, my boy, what do you make of that?" His eyes sparkled, and he sent up a great blue triumphant cloud from his cigarette.

"The paper was made in Bohemia," I said.

"Precisely. And the man who wrote the note is a German. Do you note the peculiar construction of the sentence — 'This account of you we have from all quarters received.' A Frenchman or Russian could not have written that. It is the German who is so uncourteous to his verbs. It only remains, therefore, to discover what is wanted by this German who writes upon Bohemian paper, and prefers wearing a mask to showing his face. And here he comes, if I am not mistaken, to resolve all our doubts."

As he spoke there was a sharp sound of horses' hoofs and grating wheels against the kerb, followed by a sharp pull at the bell. Holmes whistled.

"A pair by the sound," said he. "Yes," he continued, glancing out of the window. "A nice little brougham and a pair of beauties. A hundred and fifty guineas apiece. There's money in this case, Watson, if there is nothing else."

"I think that I had better go, Holmes."

"Not a bit, Doctor. Stay where you are. I am lost without my Boswell.[1] And this promises to be interesting. It would be a pity to miss it."

"But your client——"

"Never mind him. I may want your help, and so may he. Here he comes. Sit down in that arm-chair, Doctor, and give us your best attention."

A slow and heavy step, which had been heard upon the stairs and in the passage, paused immediately outside the door. Then there was a loud and authoritative tap.

"Come in!" said Holmes.

A man entered who could hardly have been less than six feet six inches in height, with the chest and limbs of a Hercules. His dress was rich with a richness which would, in England, be looked upon as akin to bad taste. Heavy bands of astrakhan were slashed across the sleeves and fronts of his double-breasted coat, while the deep blue cloak which was thrown over his shoulders was lined with flame-coloured silk, and se-

---

[1] **Boswell:** His famous biography of Samuel Johnson (1791) made James Boswell's name a synonym for a devoted biographer.

cured at the neck with a brooch which consisted of a single flaming
beryl. Boots which extended half-way up his calves, and which were
trimmed at the tops with rich brown fur, completed the impression of
barbaric opulence which was suggested by his whole appearance. He
carried a broad-brimmed hat in his hand, while he wore across the
upper part of his face, extending down past the cheek-bones, a black
vizard mask, which he had apparently adjusted that very moment, for
his hand was still raised to it as he entered. From the lower part of the
face he appeared to be a man of strong character, with a thick, hanging
lip, and a long straight chin, suggestive of resolution pushed to the
length of obstinacy.

"You had my note?" he asked, with a deep, harsh voice and a
strongly marked German accent. "I told you that I would call." He
looked from one to the other of us, as if uncertain which to address.

"Pray take a seat," said Holmes. "This is my friend and colleague,
Dr. Watson, who is occasionally good enough to help me in my cases.
Whom have I the honour to address?"

"You may address me as the Count von Kramm, a Bohemian nobleman. I understand that this gentleman, your friend, is a man of honour and
discretion, whom I may trust with a matter of the most extreme importance. If not, I should much prefer to communicate with you alone."

I rose to go, but Holmes caught me by the wrist and pushed me
back into my chair. "It is both, or none," said he. "You may say before
this gentleman anything which you may say to me."

The Count shrugged his broad shoulders. "Then I must begin,"
said he, "by binding you both to absolute secrecy for two years; at the
end of that time the matter will be of no importance. At present it is not
too much to say that it is of such weight that it may have an influence
upon European history."

"I promise," said Holmes.

"And I."

"You will excuse this mask," continued our strange visitor. "The
august person who employs me wishes his agent to be unknown to you,
and I may confess at once that the title by which I have just called myself
is not exactly my own."

"I was aware of it," said Holmes dryly.

"The circumstances are of great delicacy, and every precaution has
to be taken to quench what might grow to be an immense scandal and
seriously compromise one of the reigning families of Europe. To speak
plainly, the matter implicates the great House of Ormstein, hereditary
kings of Bohemia."

"I was also aware of that," murmured Holmes, settling himself down in his arm-chair, and closing his eyes.

Our visitor glanced with some apparent surprise at the languid, lounging figure of the man who had been no doubt depicted to him as the most incisive reasoner, and most energetic agent in Europe. Holmes slowly reopened his eyes, and looked impatiently at his gigantic client.

"If your Majesty would condescend to state your case," he remarked, "I should be better able to advise you."

The man sprang from his chair, and paced up and down the room in uncontrollable agitation. Then, with a gesture of desperation, he tore the mask from his face and hurled it upon the ground. "You are right," he cried, "I am the King. Why should I attempt to conceal it?"

"Why, indeed?" murmured Holmes. "Your Majesty had not spoken before I was aware that I was addressing Wilhelm Gottsreich Sigismond von Ormstein, Grand Duke of Cassel-Falstein, and hereditary King of Bohemia."

"But you can understand," said our strange visitor, sitting down once more and passing his hand over his high, white forehead, "you can understand that I am not accustomed to doing such business in my own person. Yet the matter was so delicate that I could not confide it to an agent without putting myself in his power. I have come *incognito* from Prague for the purpose of consulting you."

"Then, pray consult," said Holmes, shutting his eyes once more.

"The facts are briefly these: Some five years ago, during a lengthy visit to Warsaw, I made the acquaintance of the well-known adventuress Irene Adler. The name is no doubt familiar to you."

"Kindly look her up in my index, Doctor," murmured Holmes, without opening his eyes. For many years he had adopted a system of docketing all paragraphs concerning men and things, so that it was difficult to name a subject or a person on which he could not at once furnish information. In this case I found her biography sandwiched in between that of a Hebrew Rabbi and that of a staff-commander who had written a monograph upon the deep-sea fishes.

"Let me see," said Holmes. "Hum! Born in New Jersey in the year 1858. Contralto — hum! La Scala, hum! Prima donna Imperial Opera of Warsaw — Yes! Retired from operatic stage — ha! Living in London — quite so! Your Majesty, as I understand, became entangled with this young person, wrote her some compromising letters, and is now desirous of getting those letters back."

"Precisely so. But how——"

"Was there a secret marriage?"

"None."

"No legal papers or certificates?"

"None."

"Then I fail to follow Your Majesty. If this young person should produce her letters for blackmailing or other purposes, how is she to prove their authenticity?"

"There is the writing."

"Pooh, pooh! Forgery."

"My private note-paper."

"Stolen."

"My own seal."

"Imitated."

"My photograph."

"Bought."

"We were both in the photograph."

"Oh, dear! That is very bad! Your Majesty has indeed committed an indiscretion."

"I was mad — insane."

"You have compromised yourself seriously."

"I was only Crown Prince then. I was young. I am but thirty now."

"It must be recovered."

"We have tried and failed."

"Your Majesty must pay. It must be bought."

"She will not sell."

"Stolen, then."

"Five attempts have been made. Twice burglars in my pay ransacked her house. Once we diverted her luggage when she travelled. Twice she has been waylaid. There has been no result."

"No sign of it?"

"Absolutely none."

Holmes laughed. "It is quite a pretty little problem," said he.

"But a very serious one to me," returned the King, reproachfully.

"Very, indeed. And what does she propose to do with the photograph?"

"To ruin me."

"But how?"

"I am about to be married."

"So I have heard."

"To Clotilde Lothman von Saxe-Meningen, second daughter of the King of Scandinavia. You may know the strict principles of her family.

She is herself the very soul of delicacy. A shadow of a doubt as to my conduct would bring the matter to an end."

"And Irene Adler?"

"Threatens to send them the photograph. And she will do it. I know that she will do it. You do not know her, but she has a soul of steel. She has the face of the most beautiful of women, and the mind of the most resolute of men. Rather than I should marry another woman, there are no lengths to which she would not go — none."

"You are sure that she has not sent it yet?"

"I am sure."

"And why?"

"Because she has said that she would send it on the day when the betrothal was publicly proclaimed. That will be next Monday."

"Oh, then, we have three days yet," said Holmes, with a yawn. "That is very fortunate, as I have one or two matters of importance to look into just at present. Your Majesty will, of course, stay in London for the present?"

"Certainly. You will find me at the Langham, under the name of the Count von Kramm."

"Then I shall drop you a line to let you know how we progress."

"Pray do so. I shall be all anxiety."

"Then, as to money?"

"You have *carte blanche.*"

"Absolutely?"

"I tell you that I would give one of the provinces of my kingdom to have that photograph."

"And for present expenses?"

The King took a heavy chamois leather bag from under his cloak, and laid it on the table.

"There are three hundred pounds in gold, and seven hundred in notes," he said.

Holmes scribbled a receipt upon a sheet of his note-book, and handed it to him.

"And mademoiselle's address?" he asked.

"Is Briony Lodge, Serpentine Avenue, St. John's Wood."

Holmes took a note of it. "One other question," said he. "Was the photograph a cabinet?"[2]

"It was."

---

[2] *cabinet:* A photograph of appropriate size for placing in a cabinet — 3⅞ by 5½ inches.

"Then, good night, Your Majesty, and I trust that we shall soon have some good news for you. And good night, Watson," he added, as the wheels of the Royal brougham rolled down the street. "If you will be good enough to call to-morrow afternoon, at three o'clock, I should like to chat this little matter over with you."

## II

At three o'clock precisely I was at Baker Street, but Holmes had not yet returned. The landlady informed me that he had left the house shortly after eight o'clock in the morning. I sat down beside the fire, however, with the intention of awaiting him, however long he might be. I was already deeply interested in his inquiry, for, though it was surrounded by none of the grim and strange features which were associated with the two crimes which I have elsewhere recorded, still, the nature of the case and the exalted station of his client gave it a character of its own. Indeed, apart from the nature of the investigation which my friend had on hand, there was something in his masterly grasp of a situation, and his keen, incisive reasoning, which made it a pleasure to me to study his system of work, and to follow the quick, subtle methods by which he disentangled the most inextricable mysteries. So accustomed was I to his invariable success that the very possibility of his failing had ceased to enter into my head.

It was close upon four before the door opened, and a drunken-looking groom, ill-kempt and side-whiskered with an inflamed face and disreputable clothes, walked into the room. Accustomed as I was to my friend's amazing powers in the use of disguises, I had to look three times before I was certain that it was indeed he. With a nod he vanished into the bedroom, whence he emerged in five minutes tweed-suited and respectable, as of old. Putting his hands into his pockets, he stretched out his legs in front of the fire, and laughed heartily for some minutes.

"Well, really!" he cried, and then he choked; and laughed again until he was obliged to lie back, limp and helpless, in the chair.

"What is it?"

"It's quite too funny. I am sure you could never guess how I employed my morning, or what I ended by doing."

"I can't imagine. I suppose that you have been watching the habits, and perhaps the house, of Miss Irene Adler."

"Quite so, but the sequel was rather unusual. I will tell you, however. I left the house a little after eight o'clock this morning, in the character of a groom out of work. There is a wonderful sympathy and freemasonry among horsey men. Be one of them, and you will know all that there is to know. I soon found Briony Lodge. It is a bijou villa, with a garden at the back, but built out in front right up to the road, two stories. Chubb lock to the door. Large sitting-room on the right side, well furnished, with long windows almost to the floor, and those preposterous English window fasteners which a child could open. Behind there was nothing remarkable, save that the passage window could be reached from the top of the coach-house. I walked round it and examined it closely from every point of view, but without noting anything else of interest.

"I then lounged down the street, and found, as I expected, that there was a mews in a lane which runs down by one wall of the garden. I lent the ostlers a hand in rubbing down their horses, and I received in exchange twopence, a glass of half-and-half, two fills of shag tobacco and as much information as I could desire about Miss Adler, to say nothing of half a dozen other people in the neighbourhood in whom I was not in the least interested, but whose biographies I was compelled to listen to."

"And what of Irene Adler?" I asked.

"Oh, she has turned all the men's heads down in that part. She is the daintiest thing under a bonnet on this planet. So say the Serpentine Mews, to a man. She lives quietly, sings at concerts, drives out at five every day, and returns at seven sharp for dinner. Seldom goes out at other times, except when she sings. Has only one male visitor, but a good deal of him. He is dark, handsome, and dashing; never calls less than once a day, and often twice. He is a Mr. Godfrey Norton, of the Inner Temple. See the advantages of a cabman as a confidant. They had driven him home a dozen times from Serpentine Mews, and knew all about him. When I had listened to all that they had to tell, I began to walk up and down near Briony Lodge once more, and to think over my plan of campaign.

"This Godfrey Norton was evidently an important factor in the matter. He was a lawyer. That sounded ominous. What was the relation between them, and what the object of his repeated visits? Was she his client, his friend, or his mistress? If the former, she had probably transferred the photograph to his keeping. If the latter, it was less likely. On the issue of this question depended whether I should continue my work at Briony Lodge, or turn my attention to the gentleman's chambers in the Temple. It was a delicate point, and it widened the field of my inquiry. I fear that I bore you with these details, but I have to let you see my little difficulties, if you are to understand the situation."

"I am following you closely," I answered.

"I was still balancing the matter in my mind when a hansom cab drove up to Briony Lodge, and a gentleman sprang out. He was a remarkably handsome man, dark, aquiline, and moustached — evidently the man of whom I had heard. He appeared to be in a great hurry, shouted to the cabman to wait, and brushed past the maid who opened the door with the air of a man who was thoroughly at home.

"He was in the house about half an hour, and I could catch glimpses of him, in the windows of the sitting-room, pacing up and down, talking excitedly and waving his arms. Of her I could see nothing. Presently he emerged, looking even more flurried than before. As he stepped up to the cab, he pulled a gold watch from his pocket and looked at it earnestly. 'Drive like the devil,' he shouted, 'first to Gross and Hankey's in Regent Street, and then to the church of St. Monica in the Edgware Road. Half a guinea if you do it in twenty minutes!'

"Away they went, and I was just wondering whether I should not do well to follow them, when up the lane came a neat little landau, the coachman with his coat only half buttoned, and his tie under his ear, while all the tags of his harness were sticking out of the buckles. It hadn't pulled up before she shot out of the hall door and into it. I only caught a glimpse of her at the moment, but she was a lovely woman, with a face that a man might die for.

"'The Church of St. Monica, John,' she cried, 'and half a sovereign if you reach it in twenty minutes.'

"This was quite too good to lose, Watson. I was just balancing whether I should run for it, or whether I should perch behind her landau, when a cab came through the street. The driver looked twice at such a shabby fare; but I jumped in before he could object. 'The Church of St. Monica,' said I, 'and half a sovereign if you reach it in twenty minutes.' It was twenty-five minutes to twelve, and of course it was clear enough what was in the wind.[3]

"My cabby drove fast. I don't think I ever drove faster, but the others were there before us. The cab and the landau with their steaming horses were in front of the door when I arrived. I paid the man and hurried into the church. There was not a soul there save the two whom I had followed, and a surpliced clergyman, who seemed to be expostulating with them. They were all three standing in a knot in front of the altar. I lounged up the side aisle like any other idler who has dropped

[3] *what was in the wind:* Until 1886, marriages could legally be performed in England only from eight to twelve in the morning.

into a church. Suddenly, to my surprise, the three at the altar faced round to me, and Godfrey Norton came running as hard as he could towards me.

"'Thank God!' he cried. 'You'll do. Come! Come!'

"'What then?' I asked.

"'Come, man, come, only three minutes, or it won't be legal.'

"I was half dragged up to the altar, and before I knew where I was, I found myself mumbling responses which were whispered in my ear, and vouching for things of which I knew nothing, and generally assisting in the secure tying up of Irene Adler, spinster, to Godfrey Norton, bachelor. It was all done in an instant, and there was the gentleman thanking me on the one side and the lady on the other, while the clergyman beamed on me in front. It was the most preposterous position in which I ever found myself in my life, and it was the thought of it that started me laughing just now. It seems that there had been some informality about their licence, that the clergyman absolutely refused to marry them without a witness of some sort, and that my lucky appearance saved the bridegroom from having to sally out into the streets in search of a best man. The bride gave me a sovereign, and I mean to wear it on my watch-chain in memory of the occasion."

"This is a very unexpected turn of affairs," said I; "and what then?"

"Well, I found my plans very seriously menaced. It looked as if the pair might take an immediate departure, and so necessitate very prompt and energetic measures on my part. At the church door, however, they separated, he driving back to the Temple, and she to her own house. 'I shall drive out in the Park at five as usual,' she said as she left him. I heard no more. They drove away in different directions, and I went off to make my own arrangements."

"Which are?"

"Some cold beef and a glass of beer," he answered, ringing the bell. "I have been too busy to think of food, and I am likely to be busier still this evening. By the way, Doctor, I shall want your co-operation."

"I shall be delighted."

"You don't mind breaking the law?"

"Not in the least."

"Nor running a chance of arrest?"

"Not in a good cause."

"Oh, the cause is excellent!"

"Then I am your man."

"I was sure that I might rely on you."

"But what is it you wish?"

"When Mrs. Turner has brought in the tray I will make it clear to you. Now," he said, as he turned hungrily on the simple fare that our landlady had provided, "I must discuss it while I eat, for I have not much time. It is nearly five now. In two hours we must be on the scene of action. Miss Irene, or Madame, rather, returns from her drive at seven. We must be at Briony Lodge to meet her."

"And what then?"

"You must leave that to me. I have already arranged what is to occur. There is only one point on which I must insist. You must not interfere, come what may. You understand?"

"I am to be neutral?"

"To do nothing whatever. There will probably be some small unpleasantness. Do not join in it. It will end in my being conveyed into the house. Four or five minutes afterwards the sitting-room window will open. You are to station yourself close to that open window."

"Yes."

"You are to watch me, for I will be visible to you."

"Yes."

"And when I raise my hand — so — you will throw into the room what I give you to throw, and will, at the same time, raise the cry of fire. You quite follow me?"

"Entirely."

"It is nothing very formidable," he said, taking a long cigar-shaped roll from his pocket. "It is an ordinary plumber's smoke rocket, fitted with a cap at either end to make it self-lighting. Your task is confined to that. When you raise your cry of fire, it will be taken up by quite a number of people. You may then walk to the end of the street, and I will rejoin you in ten minutes. I hope that I have made myself clear?"

"I am to remain neutral, to get near the window, to watch you, and, at the signal, to throw in this object, then to raise the cry of fire, and to await you at the corner of the street."

"Precisely."

"Then you may entirely rely on me."

"That is excellent. I think perhaps it is almost time that I prepared for the new rôle I have to play."

He disappeared into his bedroom, and returned in a few minutes in the character of an amiable and simple-minded Nonconformist clergyman. His broad black hat, his baggy trousers, his white tie, his sympathetic smile, and general look of peering and benevolent curiosity, were such as Mr. John Hare[4] alone could have equalled. It was not merely that Holmes changed his costume. His expression, his manner, his very soul seemed to vary with every fresh part that he assumed. The stage lost a fine actor, even as science lost an acute reasoner, when he became a specialist in crime.

It was a quarter past six when we left Baker Street, and it still wanted ten minutes to the hour when we found ourselves in Serpentine Avenue. It was already dusk, and the lamps were just being lighted as we paced up and down in front of Briony Lodge, waiting for the coming of its occupant. The house was just such as I had pictured it from Sherlock Holmes's succinct description, but the locality appeared to be less private than I expected. On the contrary, for a small street in a quiet neighbourhood, it was remarkably animated. There was a group of shabbily-dressed men smoking and laughing in a corner, a scissors-grinder with his wheel, two guardsmen who were flirting with a nurse-girl, and several well-dressed young men who were lounging up and down with cigars in their mouths.

"You see," remarked Holmes, as we paced to and fro in front of the house, "this marriage rather simplifies matters. The photograph becomes a double-edged weapon now. The chances are that she would be as averse to its being seen by Mr. Godfrey Norton, as our client is to its coming to the eyes of his Princess. Now the question is — Where are we to find the photograph?"

"Where, indeed?"

"It is most unlikely that she carries it about with her. It is cabinet size. Too large for easy concealment about a woman's dress. She knows that the King is capable of having her waylaid and searched. Two attempts of the sort have already been made. We may take it then that she does not carry it about with her."

"Where, then?"

"Her banker or her lawyer. There is that double possibility. But I am inclined to think neither. Women are naturally secretive, and they like to do their own secreting. Why should she hand it over to anyone else? She could trust her own guardianship, but she could not tell what indirect or political influence might be brought to bear upon a business man. Besides, remember that she had resolved to use it within a few days. It must be where she can lay her hands upon it. It must be in her own house."

"But it has twice been burgled."

[4] *John Hare:* A prominent English actor of the day.

"Pshaw! They did not know how to look."

"But how will you look?"

"I will not look."

"What then?"

"I will get her to show me."

"But she will refuse."

"She will not be able to. But I hear the rumble of wheels. It is her carriage. Now carry out my orders to the letter."

As he spoke, the gleam of the sidelights of a carriage came round the curve of the avenue. It was a smart little landau which rattled up to the door of Briony Lodge. As it pulled up, one of the loafing men at the corner dashed forward to open the door in the hope of earning a copper, but was elbowed away by another loafer who had rushed up with the same intention. A fierce quarrel broke out, which was increased by the two guardsmen, who took sides with one of the loungers, and by the scissors-grinder, who was equally hot upon the other side. A blow was struck, and in an instant the lady, who had stepped from her carriage, was the centre of a little knot of flushed and struggling men who struck savagely at each other with their fists and sticks. Holmes dashed into the crowd to protect the lady; but just as he reached her, he gave a cry and dropped to the ground, with the blood running freely down his face. At his fall the guardsmen took to their heels in one direction and the loungers in the other, while a number of better dressed people who had watched the scuffle without taking part in it, crowded in to help the lady and to attend to the injured man. Irene Adler, as I will still call her, had hurried up the steps; but she stood at the top with her superb figure outlined against the lights of the hall, looking back into the street.

"Is the poor gentleman much hurt?" she asked.

"He is dead," cried several voices.

"No, no, there's life in him," shouted another. "But he'll be gone before you can get him to hospital."

"He's a brave fellow," said a woman. "They would have had the lady's purse and watch if it hadn't been for him. They were a gang, and a rough one, too. Ah, he's breathing now."

"He can't lie in the street. May we bring him in, marm?"

"Surely. Bring him into the sitting-room. There is a comfortable sofa. This way, please!"

Slowly and solemnly he was borne into Briony Lodge, and laid out in the principal room, while I still observed the proceedings from my post by the window. The lamps had been lit, but the blinds had not been drawn, so that I could see Holmes as he lay upon the couch. I do not know whether he was seized with compunction at that moment for the part he was playing, but I know that I never felt more heartily ashamed of myself in my life than when I saw the beautiful creature against whom I was conspiring, or the grace and kindliness with which she waited upon the injured man. And yet it would be the blackest treachery to Holmes to draw back now from the part which he had entrusted to me. I hardened my heart and took the smoke rocket from under my ulster. After all, I thought, we are not injuring her. We are but preventing her from injuring another.

Holmes had sat up upon the couch, and I saw him motion like a man who is in want of air. A maid rushed across and threw open the window. At the same instant I saw him raise his hand, and at the signal I tossed my rocket into the room with a cry of "Fire." The word was no sooner out of my mouth than the whole crowd of spectators, well dressed and ill — gentlemen, ostlers, and servant maids — joined in a general shriek of "Fire." Thick clouds of smoke curled through the room, and out at the open window. I caught a glimpse of rushing figures, and a moment later the voice of Holmes from within, assuring them that it was a false alarm. Slipping through the shouting crowd I made my way to the corner of the street, and in ten minutes was rejoiced to find my friend's arm in mine, and to get away from the scene of the uproar. He walked swiftly and in silence for some few minutes, until we had turned down one of the quiet streets which lead towards the Edgware Road.

"You did it very nicely, Doctor," he remarked. "Nothing could have been better. It is all right."

"You have the photograph!"

"I know where it is."

"And how did you find out?"

"She showed me, as I told you that she would."

"I am still in the dark."

"I do not wish to make a mystery," said he, laughing. "The matter was perfectly simple. You, of course, saw that every one in the street was an accomplice. They were all engaged for the evening."

"I guessed as much."

"Then, when the row broke out, I had a little moist red paint in the palm of my hand. I rushed forward, fell down, clapped my hand to my face, and became a piteous spectacle. It is an old trick."

"That also I could fathom."

"Then they carried me in. She was bound to have me in. What else could she do? And into her sitting-room which was the very room which I suspected. It lay between that and her bedroom, and I was determined to see which. They laid me on a couch, I motioned for air, they were compelled to open the window and you had your chance."

"How did that help you?"

"It was all-important. When a woman thinks that her house is on fire, her instinct is at once to rush to the thing which she values most. It is a perfectly overpowering impulse, and I have more than once taken advantage of it. In the case of the Darlington Substitution Scandal it was of use to me, and also in the Arnsworth Castle business. A married woman grabs at her baby — an unmarried one reaches for her jewel box. Now it was clear to me that our lady of to-day had nothing in the house more precious to her than what we are in quest of. She would rush to secure it. The alarm of fire was admirably done. The smoke and shouting was enough to shake nerves of steel. She responded beautifully. The photograph is in a recess behind a sliding panel just above the right bell-pull. She was there in an instant, and I caught a glimpse of it as she half drew it out. When I cried out that it was a false alarm, she replaced it, glanced at the rocket, rushed from the room, and I have not seen her since. I rose, and, making my excuses, escaped from the house, I hesitated whether to attempt to secure the photograph at once; but the coachman had come in, and as he was watching me narrowly, it seemed safer to wait. A little over-precipitance may ruin all."

"And now?" I asked.

"Our quest is practically finished. I shall call with the King to-morrow, and with you, if you care to come with us. We will be shown into the sitting-room to wait for the lady, but it is probable that when she comes she may find neither us nor the photograph. It might be a satisfaction to His Majesty to regain it with his own hands."

"And when will you call?"

"At eight in the morning. She will not be up, so that we shall have a clear field. Besides, we must be prompt, for this marriage may mean a complete change in her life and habits. I must wire to the King without delay."

We had reached Baker Street, and had stopped at the door. He was searching his pockets for the key, when some one passing said:

"Good night, Mister Sherlock Holmes."

There were several people on the pavement at the time, but the greeting appeared to come from a slim youth in an ulster who had hurried by.

"I've heard that voice before," said Holmes, staring down the dimly lit street. "Now, I wonder who the deuce that could have been."

## III

I slept at Baker Street that night, and we were engaged upon our toast and coffee when the King of Bohemia rushed into the room.

"You have really got it!" he cried, grasping Sherlock Holmes by either shoulder, and looking eagerly into his face.

"Not yet."

"But you have hopes?"

"I have hopes."

"Then, come. I am all impatience to be gone."

"We must have a cab."

"No, my brougham is waiting."

"Then that will simplify matters."

We descended, and started off once more for Briony Lodge.

"Irene Adler is married," remarked Holmes.

"Married! When?"

"Yesterday."

"But to whom?"

"To an English lawyer named Norton."

"But she could not love him?"

"I am in hopes that she does."

"And why in hopes?"

"Because it would spare Your Majesty all fear of future annoyance. If the lady loves her husband, she does not love Your Majesty. If she does not love Your Majesty there is no reason why she should interfere with Your Majesty's plan."

"It is true. And yet——! Well! I wish she had been of my own station! What a queen she would have made!" He relapsed into a moody silence which was not broken until we drew up in Serpentine Avenue.

The door of Briony Lodge was open, and an elderly woman stood upon the steps. She watched us with a sardonic eye as we stepped from the brougham.

"Mr. Sherlock Holmes, I believe?" said she.

"I am Mr. Holmes," answered my companion, looking at her with a questioning and rather startled gaze.

"Indeed! My mistress told me that you were likely to call. She left this morning with her husband, by the 5:15 train from Charing Cross, for the Continent."

"What!" Sherlock Holmes staggered back, white with chagrin and surprise. "Do you mean that she has left England?"

"Never to return."

"And the papers?" asked the King hoarsely. "All is lost."

"We shall see." He pushed past the servant, and rushed into the drawing-room, followed by the King and myself. The furniture was scattered about in every direction, with dismantled shelves, and open drawers, as if the lady had hurriedly ransacked them before her flight. Holmes rushed at the bell-pull, tore back a small sliding shutter, and, plunging in his hand, pulled out a photograph and a letter. The photograph was of Irene Adler herself in evening dress, the letter was superscribed to "Sherlock Holmes, Esq. To be left till called for." My friend tore it open and we all three read it together. It was dated at midnight of the preceding night, and ran in this way:

MY DEAR MR. SHERLOCK HOLMES,
You really did it very well. You took me in completely. Until after the alarm of fire, I had not a suspicion. But then, when I found how I had betrayed myself, I began to think. I had been warned against you months ago. I had been told that if the King employed an agent, it would certainly be you. And your address had been given me. Yet, with all this, you made me reveal what you wanted to know. Even after I became suspicious, I found it hard to think evil of such a dear, kind old clergyman. But, you know, I have been trained as an actress myself. Male costume is nothing new to me. I often take advantage of the freedom which it gives. I sent John, the coachman, to watch you, ran upstairs, got into my walking clothes, as I call them, and came down just as you departed.

Well, I followed you to your door, and so made sure that I was really an object of interest to the celebrated Mr. Sherlock Holmes. Then I, rather imprudently, wished you good night, and started for the Temple to see my husband.

We both thought the best resource was flight when pursued by so formidable an antagonist; so you will find the nest empty when you call to-morrow. As to the photograph, your client may rest in peace. I love and am loved by a better man than he. The King may do what he will without hindrance from one whom he has cruelly wronged. I keep it only to safeguard myself, and to preserve a weapon which will always secure me from any steps which he might take in the future. I leave a photograph which he might care to possess; and I remain, dear Mr. Sherlock Holmes,

Very truly yours,
IRENE NORTON, *née* ADLER.

"What a woman — oh, what a woman!" cried the King of Bohemia, when we had all three read this epistle. "Did I not tell you how quick and resolute she was? Would she not have made an admirable queen? Is it not a pity she was not on my level?"

"From what I have seen of the lady, she seems, indeed, to be on a very different level to Your Majesty," said Holmes, coldly. "I am sorry that I have not been able to bring Your Majesty's business to a more successful conclusion."

"On the contrary, my dear sir," cried the King. "Nothing could be more successful. I know that her word is inviolate. The photograph is now as safe as if it were in the fire."

"I am glad to hear Your Majesty say so."

"I am immensely indebted to you. Pray tell me in what way I can reward you. This ring——" He slipped an emerald snake ring from his finger and held it out upon the palm of his hand.

"Your Majesty has something which I should value even more highly," said Holmes.

"You have but to name it."

"This photograph!"

The King stared at him in amazement.

"Irene's photograph!" he cried. "Certainly, if you wish it."

"I thank Your Majesty. Then there is no more to be done in the matter. I have the honour to wish you a very good morning." He bowed, and, turning away without observing the hand which the King had stretched out to him, he set off in my company for his chambers.

And that was how a great scandal threatened to affect the kingdom of Bohemia, and how the best plans of Mr. Sherlock Holmes were beaten by a woman's wit. He used to make merry over the cleverness of women, but I have not heard him do it of late. And when he speaks of Irene Adler, or when he refers to her photograph, it is always under the honourable title of *the* woman.

## AFTERWORD

As several critics have noted, the King of Bohemia in this story both in behavior and in appearance would have reminded Doyle's contemporaries of the most un-Victorian Prince of Wales, the future Edward VII. The shadow of the Prince appears again in "The Beryl Coronet" as the distinguished man whose name "is a household word all over the earth —

one of the highest, noblest, most exalted names in England," who in order to pay a private debt seeks to pawn "a national possession," "one of the most precious public possessions of the empire" — implicitly, some of the crown jewels. Edward VII, however, apparently never took offense, or perhaps never even perceived any. The notoriously unliterary king read almost no literature, but he did read and enjoy Doyle's stories.

Since "A Scandal in Bohemia" turns ultimately on a contest of disguisings, its beginning with the king's own attempted but inadequate disguise and its progress through Holmes's first disguise as a groom are particularly worth noting.

Irene Adler is the first of Holmes's opponents to know her antagonist by reputation and proceed accordingly. Her defenses against Holmes are in fact oddly reflective of Holmes's own moves, as her farewell letter to him reminds us: she uses her coachman as an agent much as Holmes uses Watson, disguises herself the better to spy on Holmes much as he had earlier spied on her, "takes him in" much as he had taken her in (when she took him into her house), and makes him reveal what she wants to know. Holmes's reaction to her greeting — "Now, I wonder who the *deuce* that could have been" (emphasis added) — even contains its own hint of her resourceful duplicity. The dramatic touch of her wishing him goodnight by name is one that Doyle would later vary elegantly in a similar situation, when a disguised man shadowing Holmes's client notices Holmes shadowing him in turn and dashes off in a cab, leaving his name with the cabman in case Holmes should track him thus far: "'His name,' said the cabman, 'was Mr. Sherlock Holmes'" (*The Hound of the Baskervilles*).

## The Red-headed League

I had called upon my friend, Mr. Sherlock Holmes, one day in the autumn of last year, and found him in deep conversation with a very stout, florid-faced, elderly gentleman, with fiery red hair. With an apology for my intrusion, I was about to withdraw, when Holmes pulled me abruptly into the room, and closed the door behind me.

"You could not possibly have come at a better time, my dear Watson," he said cordially.

From *The Adventures of Sherlock Holmes* (1892). First published in the *Strand*, August 1891.

"I was afraid that you were engaged."

"So I am. Very much so."

"Then I can wait in the next room."

"Not at all. This gentleman, Mr. Wilson, has been my partner and helper in many of my most successful cases, and I have no doubt that he will be of the utmost use to me in yours also."

The stout gentleman half rose from his chair, and gave a bob of greeting, with a quick little questioning glance from his small, fat-encircled eyes.

"Try the settee," said Holmes, relapsing into his arm-chair, and putting his finger-tips together, as was his custom when in judicial moods. "I know, my dear Watson, that you share my love of all that is bizarre and outside the conventions and humdrum routine of everyday life. You have shown your relish for it by the enthusiasm which has prompted you to chronicle, and, if you will excuse my saying so, somewhat to embellish so many of my own little adventures."

"Your cases have indeed been of the greatest interest to me," I observed.

"You will remember that I remarked the other day, just before we went into the very simple problem presented by Miss Mary Sutherland, that for strange effects and extraordinary combinations we must go to life itself, which is always far more daring than any effort of the imagination."

"A proposition which I took the liberty of doubting."

"You did, Doctor, but none the less you must come round to my view, for otherwise I shall keep piling fact upon fact on you, until your reason breaks down under them and acknowledges me to be right. Now, Mr. Jabez Wilson here has been good enough to call upon me this morning, and to begin a narrative which promises to be one of the most singular which I have listened to for some time. You have heard me remark that the strangest and most unique things are very often connected not with the larger but with the smaller crimes, and occasionally, indeed, where there is room for doubt whether any positive crime has been committed. As far as I have heard, it is impossible for me to say whether the present case is an instance of crime or not, but the course of events is certainly among the most singular that I have ever listened to. Perhaps, Mr. Wilson, you would have the great kindness to recommence your narrative. I ask you not merely because my friend Dr. Watson has not heard the opening part, but also because the peculiar nature of the story makes me anxious to have every possible detail from your lips. As a rule, when I have heard some slight indication of the course of events I am able to guide myself by the thousands of other similar cases which occur to my memory. In the present instance I am forced to admit that the facts are, to the best of my belief, unique."

The portly client puffed out his chest with an appearance of some little pride, and pulled a dirty and wrinkled newspaper from the inside pocket of his greatcoat. As he glanced down the advertisement column, with his head thrust forward, and the paper flattened out upon his knee, I took a good look at the man, and endeavoured after the fashion of my companion to read the indications which might be presented by his dress or appearance.

I did not gain very much, however, by my inspection. Our visitor bore every mark of being an average commonplace British tradesman, obese, pompous, and slow. He wore rather baggy grey shepherd's check trousers, a not over-clean black frock-coat, unbuttoned in the front, and a drab waistcoat with a heavy brassy Albert chain, and a square pierced bit of metal dangling down as an ornament. A frayed top-hat, and a faded brown overcoat with a wrinkled velvet collar lay upon a chair beside him. Altogether, look as I would, there was nothing remarkable about the man save his blazing red head, and the expression of extreme chagrin and discontent upon his features.

Sherlock Holmes's quick eye took in my occupation and he shook his head with a smile as he noticed my questioning glances. "Beyond the obvious facts that he has at some time done manual labour, that he takes snuff, that he is a Freemason, that he has been in China, and that he has done a considerable amount of writing lately, I can deduce nothing else."

Mr. Jabez Wilson started up in his chair, with his forefinger upon the paper, but his eyes upon my companion.

"How, in the name of good fortune, did you know all that, Mr. Holmes?" he asked. "How did you know, for example, that I did manual labour? It's as true as gospel, and I began as a ship's carpenter."

"Your hands, my dear sir. Your right hand is quite a size larger than your left. You have worked with it, and the muscles are more developed."

"Well, the snuff, then, and the Freemasonry?"

"I won't insult your intelligence by telling you how I read that, especially as, rather against the strict rules of your order, you use an arc and compass breastpin."

"Ah, of course, I forgot that. But the writing?"

"What else can be indicated by that right cuff so very shiny for five inches, and the left one with the smooth patch near the elbow where you rest it upon the desk."

"Well, but China?"

"The fish which you have tattooed immediately above your right wrist could only have been done in China. I have made a small study of tattoo marks, and have even contributed to the literature of the subject. That trick of staining the fishes' scales of a delicate pink is quite peculiar to China. When, in addition, I see a Chinese coin hanging from your watch-chain, the matter becomes even more simple."

Mr. Jabez Wilson laughed heavily. "Well, I never!" said he. "I thought at first you had done something clever, but I see there was nothing in it after all."

"I begin to think, Watson," said Holmes, "that I make a mistake in explaining. '*Omne ignotum pro magnifico,*'[1] you know, and my poor little reputation, such as it is, will suffer shipwreck if I am so candid. Can you not find the advertisement, Mr. Wilson?"

"Yes, I have got it now," he answered, with his thick, red finger planted half-way down the column. "Here it is. This is what began it all. You just read it for yourself, sir."

I took the paper from him and read as follows:

To the Red-headed League:
On account of the bequest of the late Ezekiah Hopkins, of Lebanon, Penn., U.S.A., there is now another vacancy open which entitles a member of the League to a salary of four pounds a week for purely nominal services. All red-headed men who are sound in body and mind, and above the age of twenty-one years, are eligible. Apply in person on Monday, at eleven o'clock, to Duncan Ross, at the offices of the League, 7 Pope's Court, Fleet Street.

"What on earth does this mean?" I ejaculated, after I had twice read over the extraordinary announcement.

Holmes chuckled, and wriggled in his chair, as was his habit when in high spirits. "It is a little off the beaten track, isn't it?" said he. "And now, Mr. Wilson, off you go at scratch, and tell us all about yourself, your household, and the effect which this advertisement had upon your fortunes. You will first make a note, Doctor, of the paper and the date."

"It is *The Morning Chronicle,* of April 27, 1890. Just two months ago."

"Very good. Now, Mr. Wilson?"

"Well, it is just as I have been telling you, Mr. Sherlock Holmes," said Jabez Wilson, mopping his forehead, "I have a small pawnbroker's

---

[1] *Omne . . . magnifico*: "Everything unknown passes for something grand."

business at Coburg Square, near the City. It's not a very large affair, and of late years it has not done more than just give me a living. I used to be able to keep two assistants, but now I only keep one; and I would have a job to pay him, but that he is willing to come for half wages, so as to learn the business."

"What is the name of this obliging youth?" asked Sherlock Holmes.

"His name is Vincent Spaulding, and he's not such a youth either. It's hard to say his age. I should not wish a smarter assistant, Mr. Holmes; and I know very well that he could better himself, and earn twice what I am able to give him. But after all, if he is satisfied, why should I put ideas in his head?"

"Why, indeed? You seem most fortunate in having an employé who comes under the full market price. It is not a common experience among employers in this age. I don't know that your assistant is not as remarkable as your advertisement."

"Oh, he has his faults, too," said Mr. Wilson. "Never was such a fellow for photography. Snapping away with a camera when he ought to be improving his mind, and then diving down into the cellar like a rabbit into its hole to develop his pictures. That is his main fault; but on the whole, he's a good worker. There's no vice in him."

"He is still with you, I presume?"

"Yes, sir. He and a girl of fourteen, who does a bit of simple cooking, and keeps the place clean — that's all I have in the house, for I am a widower, and never had any family. We live very quietly, sir, the three of us; and we keep a roof over our heads, and pay our debts, if we do nothing more.

"The first thing that put us out was that advertisement. Spaulding, he came down into the office just this day eight weeks with this very paper in his hand, and he says:

"'I wish to the Lord, Mr. Wilson, that I was a red-headed man.'

"'Why that?' I asks.

"'Why,' says he, 'here's another vacancy on the League of the Red-headed Men. It's worth quite a little fortune to any man who gets it, and I understand that there are more vacancies than there are men, so that the trustees are at their wits' end what to do with the money. If my hair would only change colour, here's a nice little crib all ready for me to step into.'

"'Why, what is it, then?' I asked. You see, Mr. Holmes, I am a very stay-at-home man, and, as my business came to me instead of my having to go to it, I was often weeks on end without putting my foot over the door-mat. In that way I didn't know much of what was going on outside, and I was always glad of a bit of news.

"'Have you never heard of the League of the Red-headed Men?' he asked, with his eyes open.

"'Never.'

"'Why, I wonder at that, for you are eligible yourself for one of the vacancies.'

"'And what are they worth?' I asked.

"'Oh, merely a couple of hundred a year, but the work is slight, and it need not interfere much with one's other occupations.'

"Well, you can easily think that that made me prick up my ears, for the business has not been over good for some years, and an extra couple of hundred would have been very handy.

"'Tell me all about it,' said I.

"'Well,' said he, showing me the advertisement, 'you can see for yourself that the League has a vacancy, and there is the address where you should apply for particulars. As far as I can make out, the League was founded by an American millionaire, Ezekiah Hopkins, who was very peculiar in his ways. He was himself red-headed, and he had a great sympathy for all red-headed men; so, when he died, it was found that he had left his enormous fortune in the hands of trustees, with instructions to apply the interest to the providing of easy berths to men whose hair is of that colour. From all I hear it is splendid pay, and very little to do.'

"'But,' said I, 'there would be millions of red-headed men who would apply.'

"'Not so many as you might think,' he answered. 'You see, it is really confined to Londoners, and to grown men. This American had started from London when he was young, and he wanted to do the old town a good turn. Then, again, I have heard it is no use your applying if your hair is light red, or dark red, or anything but real, bright, blazing, fiery red. Now, if you cared to apply, Mr. Wilson, you would just walk in; but perhaps it would hardly be worth your while to put yourself out of the way for the sake of a few hundred pounds.'

"Now, it is a fact, gentlemen, as you may see for yourselves, that my hair is of a very full and rich tint, so that it seemed to me that, if there was to be any competition in the matter, I stood as good a chance as any man that I had ever met. Vincent Spaulding seemed to know so much about it that I thought he might prove useful, so I just ordered him to put up the shutters for the day, and to come right away with me. He was very willing to have a holiday, so we shut the business up, and started off for the address that was given us in the advertisement.

"I never hope to see such a sight as that again, Mr. Holmes. From north, south, east, and west every man who had a shade of red in his hair had tramped into the City to answer the advertisement. Fleet Street was choked with red-headed folk, and Pope's Court looked like a coster's orange barrow.[2] I should not have thought there were so many in the whole country as were brought together by that single advertisement. Every shade of colour they were — straw, lemon, orange, brick, Irish-setter, liver, clay; but, as Spaulding said, there were not many who had the real vivid flame-coloured tint. When I saw how many were waiting, I would have given it up in despair; but Spaulding would not hear of it. How he did it I could not imagine, but he pushed and pulled and butted until he got me through the crowd, and right up to the steps which led to the office. There was a double stream upon the stair, some going up in hope, and some coming back dejected; but we wedged in as well as we could, and soon found ourselves in the office."

"Your experience has been a most entertaining one," remarked Holmes, as his client paused and refreshed his memory with a huge pinch of snuff. "Pray continue your very interesting statement."

"There was nothing in the office but a couple of wooden chairs and a deal table, behind which sat a small man, with a head that was even redder than mine. He said a few words to each candidate as he came up, and then he always managed to find some fault in them which would disqualify them. Getting a vacancy did not seem to be such a very easy matter after all. However, when our turn came, the little man was more favourable to me than to any of the others, and he closed the door as we entered, so that he might have a private word with us.

" 'This is Mr. Jabez Wilson,' said my assistant, 'and he is willing to fill a vacancy in the League.'

" 'And he is admirably suited for it,' the other answered. 'He has every requirement. I cannot recall when I have seen anything so fine.' He took a step backwards, cocked his head on one side, and gazed at my hair until I felt quite bashful. Then suddenly he plunged forward, wrung my hand, and congratulated me warmly on my success.

" 'It would be injustice to hesitate,' said he. 'You will, however, I am sure, excuse me for taking an obvious precaution.' With that he seized my hair in both his hands, and tugged until I yelled with the pain. 'There is water in your eyes,' said he, as he released me. 'I perceive that all is as it should be. But we have to be careful, for we have twice been

---

[2] *coster:* A costermonger; someone who sold fruit, vegetables, or other goods from a barrow in the street.

deceived by wigs and once by paint. I could tell you tales of cobbler's wax which would disgust you with human nature.' He stepped over to the window, and shouted through it at the top of his voice that the vacancy was filled. A groan of disappointment came up from below, and the folk all trooped away in different directions, until there was not a red head to be seen except my own and that of the manager.

"'My name,' said he, 'is Mr. Duncan Ross, and I am myself one of the pensioners upon the fund left by our noble benefactor. Are you a married man, Mr. Wilson? Have you a family?'

"I answered that I had not.

"His face fell immediately.

"'Dear me!' he said gravely, 'that is very serious indeed! I am sorry to hear you say that. The fund was, of course, for the propagation and spread of the red-heads as well as for their maintenance. It is exceedingly unfortunate that you should be a bachelor.'

"My face lengthened at this, Mr. Holmes, for I thought that I was not to have the vacancy after all; but after thinking it over for a few minutes, he said that it would be all right.

"'In the case of another,' said he, 'the objection might be fatal, but we must stretch a point in favour of a man with such a head of hair as yours. When shall you be able to enter upon your new duties?'

"'Well, it is a little awkward, for I have a business already,' said I.

"'Oh, never mind about that, Mr. Wilson!' said Vincent Spaulding. 'I shall be able to look after that for you.'

"'What would be the hours?' I asked.

"'Ten to two.'

"Now a pawnbroker's business is mostly done of an evening, Mr. Holmes, especially Thursday and Friday evening, which is just before pay-day; so it would suit me very well to earn a little in the mornings. Besides, I knew that my assistant was a good man, and that he would see to anything that turned up.

"'That would suit me very well,' said I. 'And the pay?'

"'Is four pounds a week.'

"'And the work?'

"'Is purely nominal.'

"'What do you call purely nominal?'

"'Well, you have to be in the office, or at least in the building, the whole time. If you leave, you forfeit your whole position for ever. The will is very clear upon that point. You don't comply with the conditions if you budge from the office during that time.'

"'It's only four hours a day, and I should not think of leaving,' said I.

"'No excuse will avail,' said Mr. Duncan Ross, 'neither sickness, nor business, nor anything else. There you must stay, or you lose your billet.'

"'And the work?'

"'Is to copy out the *Encyclopædia Britannica*. There is the first volume of it in that press. You must find your own ink, pens, and blotting-paper, but we provide this table and chair. Will you be ready to-morrow?'

"'Certainly,' I answered.

"'Then, good-bye, Mr. Jabez Wilson, and let me congratulate you once more on the important position which you have been fortunate enough to gain.' He bowed me out of the room, and I went home with my assistant, hardly knowing what to say or do, I was so pleased at my own good fortune.

"'Well, I thought over the matter all day, and by evening I was in low spirits again; for I had quite persuaded myself that the whole affair must be some great hoax or fraud, though what its object might be I could not imagine. It seemed altogether past belief that anyone could make such a will, or that they would pay such a sum for doing anything so simple as copying out the *Encyclopædia Britannica*. Vincent Spaulding did what he could to cheer me up, but by bedtime I had reasoned myself out of the whole thing. However, in the morning I determined to have a look at it anyhow, so I bought a penny bottle of ink, and with a quill pen, and seven sheets of foolscap paper, I started off for Pope's Court.

"Well, to my surprise and delight everything was as right as possible. The table was set out ready for me, and Mr. Duncan Ross was there to see that I got fairly to work. He started me off upon the letter A, and then he left me; but he would drop in from time to time to see that all was right with me. At two o'clock he bade me good day, complimented me upon the amount that I had written, and locked the door of the office after me.

"This went on day after day, Mr. Holmes, and on Saturday the manager came in and planked down four golden sovereigns for my week's work. It was the same next week, and the same the week after. Every morning I was there at ten, and every afternoon I left at two. By degrees Mr. Duncan Ross took to coming in only once of a morning, and then, after a time, he did not come in at all. Still, of course, I never dared to leave the room for an instant, for I was not sure when he might come, and the billet was such a good one, and suited me so well, that I would not risk the loss of it.

"Eight weeks passed away like this, and I had written about Abbots, and Archery, and Armour, and Architecture, and Attica, and hoped with diligence that I might get on to the B's before very long. It cost me something in foolscap, and I had pretty nearly filled a shelf with my writings. And then suddenly the whole business came to an end."

"To an end?"

"Yes, sir. And no later than this morning. I went to my work as usual at ten o'clock, but the door was shut and locked, with a little square of cardboard hammered on to the middle of the panel with a tack. Here it is, and you can read for yourself."

He held up a piece of white cardboard, about the size of a sheet of note-paper. It read in this fashion:

THE RED-HEADED LEAGUE IS DISSOLVED.
OCT. 9, 1890.

Sherlock Holmes and I surveyed this curt announcement and the rueful face behind it, until the comical side of the affair so completely over-topped every other consideration that we both burst out into a roar of laughter.

"I cannot see that there is anything very funny," cried our client, flushing up to the roots of his flaming head. "If you can do nothing better than laugh at me, I can go elsewhere."

"No, no," cried Holmes, shoving him back into the chair from which he had half risen. "I really wouldn't miss your case for the world. It is most refreshingly unusual. But there is, if you will excuse me saying so, something just a little funny about it. Pray what steps did you take when you found the card upon the door?"

"I was staggered, sir. I did not know what to do. Then I called at the offices round, but none of them seemed to know anything about it. Finally, I went to the landlord, who is an accountant living on the ground floor, and I asked him if he could tell me what had become of the Red-headed League. He said that he had never heard of any such body. Then I asked him who Mr. Duncan Ross was. He answered that the name was new to him.

"'Well,' said I, 'the gentleman at No. 4.'

"'What, the red-headed man?'

"'Yes.'

"'Oh,' said he, 'his name was William Morris. He was a solicitor, and was using my room as a temporary convenience until his new premises were ready. He moved out yesterday.'

"'Where could I find him?'

"'Oh, at his new offices. He did tell me the address. Yes, 17 King Edward Street, near St. Paul's.'

"I started off, Mr. Holmes, but when I got to that address it was a manufactory of artificial knee-caps, and no one in it had ever heard of either Mr. William Morris, or Mr. Duncan Ross."

"And what did you do then?" asked Holmes.

"I went home to Saxe-Coburg Square, and I took the advice of my assistant. But he could not help me in any way. He could only say that if I waited I should hear by post. But that was not quite good enough, Mr. Holmes. I did not wish to lose such a place without a struggle, so, as I had heard that you were good enough to give advice to poor folk who were in need of it, I came right away to you."

"And you did very wisely," said Holmes. "Your case is an exceedingly remarkable one, and I shall be happy to look into it. From what you have told me I think that it is possible that graver issues hang from it than might at first sight appear."

"Grave enough!" said Mr. Jabez Wilson. "Why, I have lost four pounds a week."

"As far as you are personally concerned," remarked Holmes, "I do not see that you have any grievance against this extraordinary league. On the contrary, you are, as I understand, richer by some thirty pounds, to say nothing of the minute knowledge which you have gained on every subject which comes under the letter A. You have lost nothing by them."

"No, sir. But I want to find out about them, and who they are, and what their object was in playing this prank — if it was a prank — upon me. It was a pretty expensive joke for them, for it cost them two-and-thirty pounds."

"We shall endeavour to clear up these points for you. And, first, one or two questions, Mr. Wilson. This assistant of yours who first called your attention to the advertisement — how long had he been with you?"

"About a month then."

"How did he come?"

"In answer to an advertisement."

"Was he the only applicant?"

"No, I had a dozen."

"Why did you pick him?"

"Because he was handy, and would come cheap."

"At half wages, in fact."

"Yes."

"What is he like, this Vincent Spaulding?"

"Small, stout-built, very quick in his ways, no hair on his face, though he's not short of thirty. Has a white splash of acid upon his forehead."

Holmes sat up in his chair in considerable excitement.

"I thought as much," said he. "Have you ever observed that his ears are pierced for ear-rings?"

"Yes, sir. He told me that a gipsy had done it for him when he was a lad."

"Hum!" said Holmes, sinking back in deep thought. "He is still with you?"

"Oh, yes, sir; I have only just left him."

"And has your business been attended to in your absence?"

"Nothing to complain of, sir. There's never very much to do of a morning."

"That will do, Mr. Wilson. I shall be happy to give you an opinion upon the subject in the course of a day or two. To-day is Saturday, and I hope that by Monday we may come to a conclusion."

"Well, Watson," said Holmes, when our visitor had left us, "what do you make of it all?"

"I make nothing of it," I answered, frankly. "It is a most mysterious business."

"As a rule," said Holmes, "the more bizarre a thing is the less mysterious it proves to be. It is your commonplace, featureless crimes which are really puzzling, just as a commonplace face is the most difficult to identify. But I must be prompt over this matter."

"What are you going to do then?" I asked.

"To smoke," he answered. "It is quite a three-pipe problem, and I beg that you won't speak to me for fifty minutes." He curled himself up in his chair, with his thin knees drawn up to his hawk-like nose, and there he sat with his eyes closed and his black clay pipe thrusting out like the bill of some strange bird. I had come to the conclusion that he had dropped asleep, and indeed was nodding myself, when he suddenly sprang out of his chair with the gesture of a man who had made up his mind, and put his pipe down upon the mantelpiece.

"Sarasate plays at the St. James's Hall this afternoon," he remarked. "What do you think, Watson? Could your patients spare you for a few hours?"

"I have nothing to do to-day. My practice is never very absorbing."

"Then put on your hat, and come. I am going through the City first, and we can have some lunch on the way. I observe that there is a good deal of German music on the programme, which is rather more to my taste than Italian or French. It is introspective, and I want to introspect. Come along!"

We travelled by the Underground as far as Aldersgate; and a short walk took us to Saxe-Coburg Square, the scene of the singular story which we had listened to in the morning. It was a pokey, little, shabby-genteel place, where four lines of dingy two-storied brick houses looked out into a small railed-in enclosure, where a lawn of weedy grass and a few clumps of faded laurel bushes made a hard fight against a smoke-laden and uncongenial atmosphere. Three gilt balls and a brown board with "JABEZ WILSON" in white letters, upon a corner house, announced the place where our red-headed client carried on his business. Sherlock Holmes stopped in front of it with his head on one side and looked it all over, with his eyes shining brightly between puckered lids. Then he walked slowly up the street and then down again to the corner, still looking keenly at the houses. Finally he returned to the pawnbroker's, and, having thumped vigorously upon the pavement with his stick two or three times, he went up to the door and knocked. It was instantly opened by a bright-looking, clean-shaven young fellow, who asked him to step in.

"Thank you," said Holmes, "I only wished to ask you how you would go from here to the Strand."

"Third right, fourth left," answered the assistant promptly, closing the door.

"Smart fellow, that," observed Holmes as we walked away. "He is, in my judgment, the fourth smartest man in London, and for daring I am not sure that he has not a claim to be third. I have known something of him before."

"Evidently," said I, "Mr. Wilson's assistant counts for a good deal in this mystery of the Red-headed League. I am sure that you inquired your way merely in order that you might see him."

"Not him."

"What then?"

"The knees of his trousers."

"And what did you see?"

"What I expected to see."

"Why did you beat the pavement?"

"My dear Doctor, this is a time for observation, not for talk. We are spies in an enemy's country. We know something of Saxe-Coburg Square. Let us now explore the paths which lie behind it."

The road in which we found ourselves as we turned round the corner from the retired Saxe-Coburg Square presented as great a contrast to it as the front of a picture does to the back. It was one of the main arteries which convey the traffic of the City to the north and west. The roadway was blocked with the immense stream of commerce flowing in a double tide inwards and outwards, while the footpaths were black with the hurrying swarm of pedestrians. It was difficult to realize as we looked at the line of fine shops and stately business premises that they really abutted on the other side upon the faded and stagnant square which we had just quitted.

"Let me see," said Holmes, standing at the corner, and glancing along the line, "I should like just to remember the order of the houses here. It is a hobby of mine to have an exact knowledge of London. There is Mortimer's, the tobacconist, the little newspaper shop, the Co-burg branch of the City and Suburban Bank, the Vegetarian Restaurant, and McFarlane's carriage-building depôt. That carries us right on to the other block. And now, Doctor, we've done our work, so it's time we had some play. A sandwich, and a cup of coffee, and then off to violin land, where all is sweetness, and delicacy, and harmony, and there are no red-headed clients to vex us with their conundrums."

My friend was an enthusiastic musician, being himself not only a very capable performer, but a composer of no ordinary merit. All the afternoon he sat in the stalls wrapped in the most perfect happiness, gently waving his long thin fingers in time to the music, while his gently smiling face and his languid, dreamy eyes were as unlike those of Holmes the sleuth-hound, Holmes the relentless, keen-witted, ready-handed criminal agent, as it was possible to conceive. In his singular character the dual nature alternately asserted itself, and his extreme ex-actness and astuteness represented, as I have often thought, the reaction against the poetic and contemplative mood which occasionally predom-inated in him. The swing of his nature took him from extreme languor to devouring energy; and, as I knew well, he was never so truly formida-ble as when, for days on end, he had been lounging in his arm-chair amid his improvisations and his black-letter editions. Then it was that the lust of the chase would suddenly come upon him, and that his bril-liant reasoning power would rise to the level of intuition, until those who were unacquainted with his methods would look askance at him as on a man whose knowledge was not that of other mortals. When I saw him that afternoon so enwrapped in the music at St. James's Hall I felt that an evil time might be coming upon those whom he had set himself to hunt down.

"You want to go home, no doubt, Doctor," he remarked, as we emerged.

"Yes, it would be as well."

"And I have some business to do which will take some hours. This business at Coburg Square is serious."

"Why serious?"

"A considerable crime is in contemplation. I have every reason to believe that we shall be in time to stop it. But to-day being Saturday rather complicates matters. I shall want your help to-night."

"At what time?"

"Ten will be early enough."

"I shall be at Baker Street at ten."

"Very well. And, I say, Doctor! there may be some little danger, so kindly put your army revolver in your pocket." He waved his hand, turned on his heel, and disappeared in an instant among the crowd.

I trust that I am not more dense than my neighbours, but I was always oppressed with a sense of my own stupidity in my dealings with Sherlock Holmes. Here I had heard what he had heard, I had seen what he had seen, and yet from his words it was evident that he saw clearly not only what had happened, but what was about to happen, while to me the whole business was still confused and grotesque. As I drove home to my house in Kensington I thought over it all, from the extraordinary story of the red-headed copier of the *Encyclopædia* down to the visit to Saxe-Coburg Square, and the ominous words with which he had parted from me. What was this nocturnal expedition, and why should I go armed? Where were we going, and what were we to do? I had the hint from Holmes that this smooth-faced pawnbroker's assistant was a formidable man — a man who might play a deep game. I tried to puzzle it out, but gave it up in despair, and set the matter aside until night should bring an explanation.

It was a quarter past nine when I started from home and made my way across the Park, and so through Oxford Street to Baker Street. Two hansoms were standing at the door, and, as I entered the passage, I heard the sound of voices from above. On entering his room, I found Holmes in animated conversation with two men, one of whom I recognized as Peter Jones, the official police agent; while the other was a long, thin, sad-faced man, with a very shiny hat and oppressively respectable frock-coat.

"Ha! our party is complete," said Holmes, buttoning up his pea-jacket, and taking his heavy hunting-crop from the rack. "Watson, I think you know Mr. Jones, of Scotland Yard? Let me introduce you to Mr. Merryweather, who is to be our companion in to-night's adventure."

"We're hunting in couples again, Doctor, you see," said Jones in his consequential way. "Our friend here is a wonderful man for starting a chase. All he wants is an old dog to help him to do the running down."

"I hope a wild goose may not prove to be the end of our chase," observed Mr. Merryweather gloomily.

"You may place considerable confidence in Mr. Holmes, sir," said the police agent loftily. "He has his own little methods, which are, if he won't mind my saying so, just a little too theoretical and fantastic, but he has the makings of a detective in him. It is not too much to say that once or twice, as in that business of the Sholto murder and the Agra treasure, he has been more nearly correct than the official force."

"Oh, if you say so, Mr. Jones, it is all right!" said the stranger, with deference. "Still, I confess that I miss my rubber. It is the first Saturday night for seven-and-twenty years that I have not had my rubber."

"I think you will find," said Sherlock Holmes, "that you will play for a higher stake to-night than you have ever done yet, and that the play will be more exciting. For you, Mr. Merryweather, the stake will be some thirty thousand pounds; and for you, Jones, it will be the man upon whom you wish to lay your hands."

"John Clay, the murderer, thief, smasher, and forger. He's a young man, Mr. Merryweather, but he is at the head of his profession, and I would rather have my bracelets on him than on any criminal in London. He's a remarkable man, is young John Clay. His grandfather was a Royal Duke, and he himself has been to Eton and Oxford. His brain is as cunning as his fingers, and though we meet signs of him at every turn, we never know where to find the man himself. He'll crack a crib in Scotland one week, and be raising money to build an orphanage in Cornwall the next. I've been on his track for years, and have never set eyes on him yet."

"I hope that I may have the pleasure of introducing you to-night. I've had one or two little turns also with Mr. John Clay, and I agree with you that he is at the head of his profession. It is past ten, however, and quite time that we started. If you two will take the first hansom, Watson and I will follow in the second."

Sherlock Holmes was not very communicative during the long drive, and lay back in the cab humming the tunes which he had heard in the afternoon. We rattled through an endless labyrinth of gas-lit streets until we emerged into Farringdon Street.

"We are close there now," my friend remarked. "This fellow Merryweather is a bank director and personally interested in the matter. I thought it as well to have Jones with us also. He is not a bad fellow, though an absolute imbecile in his profession. He has one positive virtue. He is as brave as a bulldog, and as tenacious as a lobster if he gets his claws upon anyone. Here we are, and they are waiting for us."

We had reached the same crowded thoroughfare in which we had found ourselves in the morning. Our cabs were dismissed, and, following the guidance of Mr. Merryweather, we passed down a narrow passage, and through a side door, which he opened for us. Within there was a small corridor, which ended in a very massive iron gate. This also was opened, and led down a flight of winding stone steps, which terminated at another formidable gate. Mr. Merryweather stopped to light a lantern, and then conducted us down a dark, earth-smelling passage, and so, after opening a third door, into a huge vault or cellar, which was piled all round with crates and massive boxes.

"You are not very vulnerable from above," Holmes remarked, as he held up the lantern and gazed about him.

"Nor from below," said Mr. Merryweather, striking his stick upon the flags which lined the floor. "Why, dear me, it sounds quite hollow!" he remarked, looking up in surprise.

"I must really ask you to be a little more quiet," said Holmes severely. "You have already imperilled the whole success of our expedition. Might I beg that you would have the goodness to sit down upon one of those boxes, and not to interfere?"

The solemn Mr. Merryweather perched himself upon a crate, with a very injured expression upon his face, while Holmes fell upon his knees upon the floor, and, with the lantern and a magnifying lens, began to examine minutely the cracks between the stones. A few seconds sufficed to satisfy him, for he sprang to his feet again, and put his glass in his pocket.

"We have at least an hour before us," he remarked, "for they can hardly take any steps until the good pawnbroker is safely in bed. Then they will not lose a minute, for the sooner they do their work the longer time they will have for their escape. We are at present, Doctor — as no doubt you have divined — in the cellar of the City branch of one of the principal London banks. Mr. Merryweather is the chairman of directors, and he will explain to you that there are reasons why the more daring criminals of London should take a considerable interest in this cellar at present."

"It is our French gold," whispered the director. "We have had several warnings that an attempt might be made upon it."

"Your French gold?"

"Yes. We had occasion some months ago to strengthen our resources, and borrowed, for that purpose, thirty thousand napoleons from the Bank of France. It has become known that we have never had occasion to unpack the money, and that it is still lying in our cellar. The

crate upon which I sit contains two thousand napoleons packed between layers of lead foil. Our reserve of bullion is much larger at present
than is usually kept in a single branch office, and the directors have had
misgivings upon the subject."

"Which were very well justified," observed Holmes. "And now it is
time that we arranged our little plans. I expect that within an hour matters will come to a head. In the meantime, Mr. Merryweather, we must
put the screen over that dark lantern."

"And sit in the dark?"

"I am afraid so. I had brought a pack of cards in my pocket, and I
thought that, as we were a *partie carrée*,[3] you might have your rubber
after all. But I see that the enemy's preparations have gone so far that we
cannot risk the presence of a light. And, first of all, we must choose our
positions. These are daring men, and, though we shall take them at a
disadvantage they may do us some harm, unless we are careful. I shall
stand behind this crate, and do you conceal yourself behind those.
Then, when I flash a light upon them, close in swiftly. If they fire, Watson, have no compunction about shooting them down."

I placed my revolver, cocked, upon the top of the wooden case behind which I crouched. Holmes shot the slide across the front of his
lantern, and left us in pitch darkness — such an absolute darkness as I
have never before experienced. The smell of hot metal remained to assure us that the light was still there, ready to flash out at a moment's
notice. To me, with my nerves worked up to a pitch of expectancy, there
was something depressing and subduing in the sudden gloom, and in
the cold, dank air of the vault.

"They have but one retreat," whispered Holmes. "That is back
through the house into Saxe-Coburg Square. I hope that you have done
what I asked you, Jones?"

"I have an inspector and two officers waiting at the front door."

"Then we have stopped all the holes. And now we must be silent
and wait."

What a time it seemed! From comparing notes afterwards it was but
an hour and a quarter, yet it appeared to me that the night must have
almost gone, and the dawn be breaking above us. My limbs were weary
and stiff, for I feared to change my position, yet my nerves were worked
up to the highest pitch of tension, and my hearing was so acute that I
could not only hear the gentle breathing of my companions, but I could
distinguish the deeper, heavier in-breath of the bulky Jones from the

---

[3] *partie carrée:* "Square party," or party of four.

thin sighing note of the bank director. From my position I could look over the case in the direction of the floor. Suddenly my eyes caught the glint of a light.

At first it was but a lurid spark upon the stone pavement. Then it lengthened out until it became a yellow line, and then, without any warning or sound, a gash seemed to open and a hand appeared, a white, almost womanly hand, which felt about in the centre of the little area of light. For a minute or more the hand, with its writhing fingers, protruded out of the floor. Then it was withdrawn as suddenly as it appeared, and all was dark again save the single lurid spark, which marked a chink between the stones.

Its disappearance, however, was but momentary. With a rending, tearing sound, one of the broad, white stones turned over upon its side, and left a square, gaping hole, through which streamed the light of a lantern. Over the edge there peeped a clean-cut, boyish face, which looked keenly about it, and then, with a hand on either side of the aperture, drew itself shoulder high and waist high, until one knee rested upon the edge. In another instant he stood at the side of the hole, and was hauling after him a companion, lithe and small like himself, with a pale face and a shock of very red hair.

"It's all clear," he whispered. "Have you the chisel, and the bags? Great Scott! Jump, Archie, jump, and I'll swing for it!"

Sherlock Holmes had sprung out and seized the intruder by the collar. The other dived down the hole, and I heard the sound of rending cloth as Jones clutched at his skirts. The light flashed upon the barrel of a revolver, but Holmes's hunting-crop came down on the man's wrist, and the pistol clinked upon the stone floor.

"It's no use, John Clay," said Holmes blandly; "you have no chance at all."

"So I see," the other answered with the utmost coolness. "I fancy that my pal is all right, though I see you have got his coat-tails."

"There are three men waiting for him at the door," said Holmes.

"Oh, indeed. You seem to have done the thing very completely. I must compliment you."

"And I you," Holmes answered. "Your red-headed idea was very new and effective."

"You'll see your pal again presently," said Jones. "He's quicker at climbing down holes than I am. Just hold out while I fix the derbies."[4]

"I beg that you will not touch me with your filthy hands," remarked

---

[4]*derbies:* Handcuffs (usually "darbies").

our prisoner, as the handcuffs clattered upon his wrists. "You may not be aware that I have royal blood in my veins. Have the goodness also when you address me always to say 'sir' and 'please.'"

"All right," said Jones, with a stare and a snigger. "Well, would you please, sir, march upstairs, where we can get a cab to carry your highness to the police station."

"That is better," said John Clay serenely. He made a sweeping bow to the three of us, and walked quietly off in the custody of the detective.

"Really, Mr. Holmes," said Mr. Merryweather, as we followed them from the cellar, "I do not know how the bank can thank you or repay you. There is no doubt that you have detected and defeated in the most complete manner one of the most determined attempts at bank robbery that have ever come within my experience."

"I have had one or two little scores of my own to settle with Mr. John Clay," said Holmes. "I have been at some small expense over this matter, which I shall expect the bank to refund, but beyond that I am amply repaid by having had an experience which is in many ways unique, and by hearing the very remarkable narrative of the Red-headed League."

"You see, Watson," he explained in the early hours of the morning, as we sat over a glass of whisky-and-soda in Baker Street, "it was perfectly obvious from the first that the only possible object of this rather fantastic business of the advertisement of the League, and the copying of the *Encyclopædia,* must be to get this not over-bright pawnbroker out of the way for a number of hours every day. It was a curious way of managing it, but really it would be difficult to suggest a better. The method was no doubt suggested to Clay's ingenious mind by the colour of his accomplice's hair. The four pounds a week was a lure which must draw him, and what was it to them, who were playing for thousands? They put in the advertisement; one rogue has the temporary office, the other rogue incites the man to apply for it, and together they manage to secure his absence every morning in the week. From the time that I heard of the assistant having come for half-wages, it was obvious to me that he had some strong motive for securing the situation."

"But how could you guess what the motive was?"

"Had there been women in the house, I should have suspected a mere vulgar intrigue. That, however, was out of the question. The man's business was a small one, and there was nothing in his house which could account for such elaborate preparations and such an expenditure as they were at. It must then be something out of the house.

What could it be? I thought of the assistant's fondness for photography, and his trick of vanishing into the cellar. The cellar! There was the end of this tangled clue. Then I made inquiries as to this mysterious assistant, and found that I had to deal with one of the coolest and most daring criminals in London. He was doing something in the cellar — something which took many hours a day for months on end. What could it be, once more? I could think of nothing save that he was running a tunnel to some other building.

"So far I had got when we went to visit the scene of action. I surprised you by beating upon the pavement with my stick. I was ascertaining whether the cellar stretched out in front or behind. It was not in front. Then I rang the bell, and, as I hoped, the assistant answered it. We have had some skirmishes, but we had never set eyes on each other before. I hardly looked at his face. His knees were what I wished to see. You must yourself have remarked how worn, wrinkled and stained they were. They spoke of those hours of burrowing. The only remaining point was what they were burrowing for. I walked round the corner, saw that the City and Suburban Bank abutted on our friend's premises, and felt that I had solved my problem. When you drove home after the concert I called upon Scotland Yard, and upon the chairman of the bank directors, with the result that you have seen."

"And how could you tell that they would make their attempt tonight?" I asked.

"Well, when they closed their League offices that was a sign that they cared no longer about Mr. Jabez Wilson's presence; in other words, that they had completed their tunnel. But it was essential that they should use it soon, as it might be discovered, or the bullion might be removed. Saturday would suit them better than any other day, as it would give them two days for their escape. For all these reasons I expected them to come to-night."

"You reasoned it out beautifully," I exclaimed in unfeigned admiration. "It is so long a chain, and yet every link rings true."

"It saved me from ennui," he answered, yawning. "Alas, I already feel it closing in upon me! My life is spent in one long effort to escape from the commonplaces of existence. These little problems help me to do so."

"And you are a benefactor of the race," said I.

He shrugged his shoulders. "Well, perhaps, after all, it is of some little use," he remarked. "'*L'homme c'est rien — l'œuvre c'est tout*,'[5] as Gustave Flaubert wrote to George Sand."

---

[5] "*L'homme ... tout*": "The man is nothing — the work is all."

## AFTERWORD

Jabez Wilson, the red-headed gull of this story, makes a particularly effective foil for Holmes. Even Watson, who can make out nothing that is not immediately obvious about "this not over-bright pawnbroker" (Holmes's later phrase for him), perceives that Wilson is "slow." Wilson epitomizes the ordinary, unobservant person so easily amazed by Holmes's inferences while quick to dismiss them as "absurdly simple" (Watson's phrase in "The Dancing Men") when explained. But with his newly acquired minute and encyclopedic knowledge about "every subject which comes under the letter A" — "Abbots, and Archery, and Armour, and Architecture, and Attica" — Wilson also parodically mimics a sliver of Holmes's own encyclopedic knowledge of minutiae. Holmes, however, keeps his intellectual resources accessible and orderly, whereas Wilson's knowledge is a jumbled storeroom of information, of no practical use or (apparently) aesthetic value to him — a brilliant realization of the fool's cluttered "brain-attic" Holmes describes in Chapter 2 of *A Study in Scarlet* (p. 25).

Of an earlier antagonist Holmes had said, "I knew that this man Small had a certain degree of low cunning, but I did not think him capable of anything in the nature of delicate finesse. That is usually a product of higher education" (*The Sign of Four*). John Clay, in contrast, is eminently capable of that: "His grandfather was a Royal Duke, and he himself has been to Eton and Oxford." As the bank director's lament for his missed rubber of whist and Holmes's reply that "you will play for a higher stake to-night than you have ever done yet, and . . . the play will be more exciting" suggest, Clay's strategem is indeed a finesse, and his game (if not his conduct) a gentlemanly one. At the other end of his tunnel to the vault of a bank in the City (the financial district of London; the world of businessmen and gentlemen), though, is a shabby, declining little pawnshop, a poor man's bank of sorts, where Jabez Wilson can afford only a single assistant at half-wages. This is a London not usually seen by readers of the *Strand* (significantly, Holmes's ruse for meeting Wilson's assistant is a disoriented gentleman's request for directions to the Strand), even as the back of a picture is not usually seen by gallery-goers (cf. pp. 65–66), or as John Clay is not seen by the authorities (neither Jones, the police detective, nor Holmes has ever seen him before, though both have had troublesome dealings with him).

# A Case of Identity

"My dear fellow," said Sherlock Holmes, as we sat on either side of the fire in his lodgings at Baker Street, "life is infinitely stranger than anything which the mind of man could invent. We would not dare to conceive the things which are really mere commonplaces of existence. If we could fly out of that window hand in hand, hover over this great city, gently remove the roofs, and peep in at the queer things which are going on, the strange coincidences, the plannings, the cross-purposes, the wonderful chains of events, working through generations, and leading to the most *outré* results, it would make all fiction with its conventionalities and foreseen conclusions most stale and unprofitable."

"And yet I am not convinced of it," I answered. "The cases which come to light in the papers are, as a rule, bald enough, and vulgar enough. We have in our police reports realism pushed to its extreme limits, and yet the result is, it must be confessed, neither fascinating nor artistic."

"A certain selection and discretion must be used in producing a realistic effect," remarked Holmes. "This is wanting in the police report, where more stress is laid perhaps upon the platitudes of the magistrate than upon the details, which to an observer contain the vital essence of the whole matter. Depend upon it, there is nothing so unnatural as the commonplace."

I smiled and shook my head. "I can quite understand your thinking so," I said. "Of course, in your position of unofficial adviser and helper to everybody who is absolutely puzzled, throughout three continents, you are brought in contact with all that is strange and bizarre. But here" — I picked up the morning paper from the ground — "let us put it to a practical test. Here is the first heading upon which I come. 'A husband's cruelty to his wife.' There is half a column of print, but I know without reading it that it is all perfectly familiar to me. There is, of course, the other woman, the drink, the push, the blow, the bruise, the sympathetic sister or landlady. The crudest of writers could invent nothing more crude."

"Indeed, your example is an unfortunate one for your argument," said Holmes, taking the paper, and glancing his eye down it. "This is the Dundas separation case, and, as it happens, I was engaged in clearing up some small points in connection with it. The husband was a teetotaller,

From *The Adventures of Sherlock Holmes* (1892). First published in the *Strand*, September 1891.

there was no other woman, and the conduct complained of was that he had drifted into the habit of winding up every meal by taking out his false teeth and hurling them at his wife, which you will allow is not an action likely to occur to the imagination of the average story-teller. Take a pinch of snuff, Doctor, and acknowledge that I have scored over you in your example."

He held out his snuff-box of old gold, with a great amethyst in the centre of the lid. Its splendour was in such contrast to his homely ways and simple life that I could not help commenting upon it.

"Ah," said he, "I forgot that I had not seen you for some weeks. It is a little souvenir from the King of Bohemia in return for my assistance in the case of the Irene Adler papers."

"And the ring?" I asked, glancing at a remarkable brilliant which sparkled upon his finger.

"It was from the reigning family of Holland, though the matter in which I served them was of such delicacy that I cannot confide it even to you, who have been good enough to chronicle one or two of my little problems."

"And have you any on hand just now?" I asked with interest.

"Some ten or twelve, but none which presents any feature of interest. They are important, you understand, without being interesting. Indeed, I have found that it is usually in unimportant matters that there is a field for observation, and for the quick analysis of cause and effect which gives the charm to an investigation. The larger crimes are apt to be the simpler, for the bigger the crime, the more obvious, as a rule, is the motive. In these cases, save for one rather intricate matter which has been referred to me from Marseilles, there is nothing which presents any features of interest. It is possible, however, that I may have something better before very many minutes are over, for this is one of my clients, or I am much mistaken."

He had risen from his chair, and was standing between the parted blinds, gazing down into the dull, neutral-tinted London street. Looking over his shoulder I saw that on the pavement opposite there stood a large woman with a heavy fur boa round her neck, and a large curling red feather in a broad-brimmed hat which was tilted in a coquettish Duchess-of-Devonshire fashion over her ear. From under this great panoply she peeped up in a nervous, hesitating fashion at our windows, while her body oscillated backwards and forwards, and her fingers fidgeted with her glove buttons. Suddenly, with a plunge, as of the swimmer who leaves the bank, she hurried across the road, and we heard the sharp clang of the bell.

"I have seen those symptoms before," said Holmes, throwing his cigarette into the fire. "Oscillation upon the pavement always means an *affaire du cœur*. She would like advice, but is not sure that the matter is not too delicate for communication. And yet even here we may discriminate. When a woman has been seriously wronged by a man she no longer oscillates, and the usual symptom is a broken bell wire. Here we may take it that there is a love matter, but that the maiden is not so much angry as perplexed, or grieved. But here she comes in person to resolve our doubts."

As he spoke there was a tap at the door, and the boy in buttons entered to announce Miss Mary Sutherland, while the lady herself loomed behind his small black figure like a full-sailed merchantman behind a tiny pilot boat. Sherlock Holmes welcomed her with the easy courtesy for which he was remarkable, and having closed the door, and bowed her into an arm-chair, he looked over her in the minute and yet abstracted fashion which was peculiar to him.

"Do you not find," he said, "that with your short sight it is a little trying to do so much typewriting?"

"I did at first," she answered, "but now I know where the letters are without looking." Then, suddenly realizing the full purport of his words, she gave a violent start, and looked up with fear and astonishment upon her broad, good-humoured face. "You've heard about me, Mr. Holmes," she cried, "else how could you know all that?"

"Never mind," said Holmes, laughing, "it is my business to know things. Perhaps I have trained myself to see what others overlook. If not, why should you come to consult me?"

"I came to you, sir, because I heard of you from Mrs. Etherege, whose husband you found so easy when the police and everyone had given him up for dead. Oh, Mr. Holmes, I wish you would do as much for me. I'm not rich, but still I have a hundred a year in my own right, besides the little that I make by the machine, and I would give it all to know what has become of Mr. Hosmer Angel."

"Why did you come away to consult me in such a hurry?" asked Sherlock Holmes, with his finger-tips together, and his eyes to the ceiling.

Again a startled look came over the somewhat vacuous face of Miss Mary Sutherland. "Yes, I did bang out of the house," she said, "for it made me angry to see the easy way in which Mr. Windibank — that is, my father — took it all. He would not go to the police, and he would not go to you, and so at last, as he would do nothing, and kept on saying that there was no harm done, it made me mad, and I just on with my things and came right away to you."

"Your father?" said Holmes. "Your stepfather, surely, since the name is different?"

"Yes, my stepfather. I call him father, though it sounds funny, too, for he is only five years and two months older than myself."

"And your mother is alive?"

"Oh, yes, mother is alive and well. I wasn't best pleased, Mr. Holmes, when she married again so soon after father's death, and a man who was nearly fifteen years younger than herself. Father was a plumber in the Tottenham Court Road, and he left a tidy business behind him, which mother carried on with Mr. Hardy, the foreman, but when Mr. Windibank came he made her sell the business, for he was very superior, being a traveller in wines. They got four thousand seven hundred for the goodwill and interest, which wasn't near as much as father could have got if he had been alive."

I had expected to see Sherlock Holmes impatient under this rambling and inconsequential narrative, but, on the contrary, he had listened with the greatest concentration of attention.

"Your own little income," he asked, "does it come out of the business?"

"Oh, no, sir, it is quite separate, and was left me by my Uncle Ned in Auckland. It is in New Zealand Stock, paying 4½ per cent. Two thousand five hundred pounds was the amount, but I can only touch the interest."

"You interest me extremely," said Holmes. "And since you draw so large a sum as a hundred a year, with what you earn into the bargain, you no doubt travel a little and indulge yourself in every way. I believe that a single lady can get on very nicely upon an income of about sixty pounds."

"I could do with much less than that, Mr. Holmes, but you understand that as long as I live at home I don't wish to be a burden to them, and so they have the use of the money just while I am staying with them. Of course that is only just for the time. Mr. Windibank draws my interest every quarter, and pays it over to mother, and I find that I can do pretty well with what I earn at typewriting. It brings me twopence a sheet, and I can often do from fifteen to twenty sheets in a day."

"You have made your position very clear to me," said Holmes. "This is my friend, Dr. Watson, before whom you can speak as freely as before myself. Kindly tell us now all about your connection with Mr. Hosmer Angel."

A flush stole over Miss Sutherland's face, and she picked nervously at the fringe of her jacket. "I met him first at the gasfitters' ball," she said. "They used to send father tickets when he was alive, and then afterwards they remembered us, and sent them to mother. Mr. Windibank did not wish us to go. He never did wish us to go anywhere. He would get quite mad if I wanted so much as to join a Sunday school treat. But this time I was set on going, and I would go, for what right had he to prevent? He said the folk were not fit for us to know, when all father's friends were to be there. And he said that I had nothing fit to wear, when I had my purple plush that I had never so much as taken out of the drawer. At last, when nothing else would do, he went off to France upon the business of the firm, but we went, mother and I, with Mr. Hardy, who used to be our foreman, and it was there I met Mr. Hosmer Angel."

"I suppose," said Holmes, "that when Mr. Windibank came back from France, he was very annoyed at your having gone to the ball."

"Oh, well, he was very good about it. He laughed, I remembered, and shrugged his shoulders, and said there was no use denying anything to a woman, for she would have her way."

"I see. Then at the gasfitters' ball you met, as I understand, a gentleman called Mr. Hosmer Angel."

"Yes, sir. I met him that night, and he called next day to ask if we had got home all safe, and after that we met him — that is to say, Mr. Holmes, I met him twice for walks, but after that father came back again, and Mr. Hosmer Angel could not come to the house any more."

"No?"

"Well, you know, father didn't like anything of the sort. He wouldn't have any visitors if he could help it, and he used to say that a woman should be happy in her own family circle. But then, as I used to say to mother, a woman wants her own circle to begin with, and I had not got mine yet."

"But how about Mr. Hosmer Angel? Did he make no attempt to see you?"

"Well, father was going off to France again in a week, and Hosmer wrote and said that it would be safer and better not to see each other until he had gone. We could write in the meantime, and he used to write every day. I took the letters in in the morning so there was no need for father to know."

"Were you engaged to the gentleman at this time?"

"Oh yes, Mr. Holmes. We were engaged after the first walk that we took. Hosmer — Mr. Angel — was a cashier in an office in Leadenhall Street — and——"

"What office?"

"That's the worst of it, Mr. Holmes, I don't know."

"Where did he live then?"

"He slept on the premises."

"And you don't know his address?"

"No — except that it was Leadenhall Street."

"Where did you address your letters, then?"

"To the Leadenhall Street Post Office, to be left till called for. He said that if they were sent to the office he would be chaffed by all the other clerks about having letters from a lady, so I offered to typewrite them, like he did his, but he wouldn't have that, for he said that when I wrote them they seemed to come from me but when they were type-written he always felt that the machine had come between us. That will just show you how fond he was of me, Mr. Holmes, and the little things that he would think of."

"It was most suggestive," said Holmes. "It has long been an axiom of mine that the little things are infinitely the most important. Can you remember any other little things about Mr. Hosmer Angel?"

"He was a very shy man, Mr. Holmes. He would rather walk with me in the evening than in the daylight, for he said that he hated to be conspicuous. Very retiring and gentlemanly he was. Even his voice was gentle. He'd had the quinsy and swollen glands when he was young, he told me, and it had left him with a weak throat, and a hesitating, whis-pering fashion of speech. He was always well-dressed, very neat and plain, but his eyes were weak, just as mine are, and he wore tinted glasses against the glare."

"Well, and what happened when Mr. Windibank, your stepfather, returned to France?"

"Mr. Hosmer Angel came to the house again, and proposed that we should marry before father came back. He was in dreadful earnest, and made me swear, with my hands on the Testament, that whatever hap-pened I would always be true to him. Mother said he was quite right to make me swear, and that it was a sign of his passion. Mother was all in his favour from the first, and was even fonder of him than I was. Then, when they talked of marrying within the week, I began to ask about father; but they both said never to mind about father, but just to tell him afterwards, and mother said she would make it all right with him. I didn't quite like that, Mr. Holmes. It seemed funny that I should ask his leave, as he was only a few years older than me; but I didn't want to do anything on the sly, so I wrote to father at Bordeaux, where the Com-pany has its French offices, but the letter came back to me on the very morning of the wedding."

"It missed him then?"

"Yes, sir, for he had started to England just before it arrived."

"Ha! that was unfortunate. Your wedding was arranged, then, for the Friday. Was it to be in church?"

"Yes, sir, but very quietly. It was to be at St. Saviour's, near King's Cross, and we were to have breakfast afterwards at the St. Pancras Hotel. Hosmer came for us in a hansom, but as there were two of us, he put us both into it, and stepped himself into a four-wheeler which happened to be the only other cab in the street. We got to the church first, and when the four-wheeler drove up we waited for him to step out, but he never did, and when the cabman got down from the box and looked, there was no one there! The cabman said he could not imagine what had become of him, for he had seen him get in with his own eyes. That was last Friday, Mr. Holmes, and I have never seen or heard anything since then to throw any light upon what became of him."

"It seems to me that you have been very shamefully treated," said Holmes.

"Oh no, sir! He was too good and kind to leave me so. Why, all the morning he was saying to me that, whatever happened, I was to be true; and that even if something quite unforeseen occurred to separate us, I was always to remember that I was pledged to him, and that he would claim his pledge sooner or later. It seemed strange talk for a wedding morning, but what has happened since gives a meaning to it."

"Most certainly it does. Your own opinion is, then, that some unforeseen catastrophe has occurred to him?"

"Yes, sir. I believe that he foresaw some danger, or else he would not have talked so. And then I think that what he foresaw happened."

"But you have no notion as to what it could have been?"

"None."

"One more question. How did your mother take the matter?"

"She was angry, and said that I was never to speak of the matter again."

"And your father? Did you tell him?"

"Yes, and he seemed to think, with me, that something had happened, and that I should hear of Hosmer again. As he said, what interest could anyone have in bringing me to the doors of the church, and then leaving me? Now, if he had borrowed my money, or if he had married me and got my money settled on him, there might be some reason; but Hosmer was very independent about money, and never would look at a shilling of mine. And yet what could have happened? And why could he not write? Oh, it drives me half mad to think of it! and I can't sleep a wink at night." She pulled a little handkerchief out of her muff, and began to sob heavily into it.

"I shall glance into the case for you," said Holmes, rising, "and I have no doubt that we shall reach some definite result. Let the weight of the matter rest upon me now, and do not let your mind dwell upon it further. Above all, try to let Mr. Hosmer Angel vanish from your memory, as he has done from your life."

"Then you don't think I'll see him again?"

"I fear not."

"Then what has happened to him?"

"You will leave that question in my hands. I should like an accurate description of him, and any letters of his which you can spare."

"I advertised for him in last Saturday's *Chronicle*," said she. "Here is the slip, and here are four letters from him."

"Thank you. And your address?"

"31 Lyon Place, Camberwell."

"Mr. Angel's address you never had, I understand. Where is your father's place of business?"

"He travels for Westhouse & Marbank, the great claret importers of Fenchurch Street."

"Thank you. You have made your statement very clearly. You will leave the papers here, and remember the advice which I have given you. Let the whole incident be a sealed book, and do not allow it to affect your life."

"You are very kind, Mr. Holmes, but I cannot do that. I shall be true to Hosmer. He shall find me ready when he comes back."

For all the preposterous hat and the vacuous face, there was something noble in the simple faith of our visitor which compelled our respect. She laid her little bundle of papers upon the table, and went her way, with a promise to come again whenever she might be summoned.

Sherlock Holmes sat silent for a few minutes with his finger-tips still pressed together, his legs stretched out in front of him, and his gaze directed upwards to the ceiling. Then he took down from the rack the old and oily clay pipe, which was to him as a counsellor, and, having lit it he leaned back in his chair, with the thick blue cloud-wreaths spinning up from him, and a look of infinite languor in his face.

"Quite an interesting study, that maiden," he observed. "I found her more interesting than her little problem, which, by the way, is rather a trite one. You will find parallel cases, if you consult my index, in Andover in '77, and there was something of the sort at The Hague last year. Old as is the idea, however, there were one or two details which were new to me. But the maiden herself was most instructive."

"You appeared to read a good deal upon her which was quite invisible to me," I remarked.

"Not invisible, but unnoticed, Watson. You did not know where to look, and so you missed all that was important. I can never bring you to realize the importance of sleeves, the suggestiveness of thumb-nails, or the great issues that may hang from a bootlace. Now what did you gather from that woman's appearance? Describe it."

"Well, she had a slate-coloured, broad-brimmed straw hat, with a feather of a brickish red. Her jacket was black, with black beads sewn upon it, and a fringe of little black jet ornaments. Her dress was brown, rather darker than coffee colour, with a little purple plush at the neck and sleeves. Her gloves were greyish, and were worn through at the right forefinger. Her boots I didn't observe. She had small, round, hanging gold ear-rings, and a general air of being fairly well to do, in a vulgar, comfortable, easy-going way."

Sherlock Holmes clapped his hands softly together and chuckled.

"'Pon my word, Watson, you are coming along wonderfully. You have really done very well indeed. It is true that you have missed everything of importance, but you have hit upon the method, and you have a quick eye for colour. Never trust to general impressions, my boy, but concentrate yourself upon details. My first glance is always at a woman's sleeve. In a man it is perhaps better first to take the knee of the trouser. As you observe, this woman had plush upon her sleeves, which is a most useful material for showing traces. The double line a little above the wrist, where the typewritist presses against the table, was beautifully defined. The sewing-machine, of the hand type, leaves a similar mark, but only on the left arm, and on the side of it farthest from the thumb, instead of being right across the broadest part, as this was. I then glanced at her face, and observing the dint of a pince-nez at either side of her nose, I ventured a remark upon short sight and typewriting, which seemed to surprise her."

"It surprised me."

"But, surely, it was very obvious. I was then much surprised and interested on glancing down to observe that, though the boots which she was wearing were not unlike each other, they were really odd ones, the one having a slightly decorated toe-cap, and the other a plain one. One was buttoned only in the two lower buttons out of five, and the other at the first, third, and fifth. Now, when you see that a young lady, otherwise neatly dressed, has come away from home with odd boots, half buttoned, it is no great deduction to say that she came away in a hurry."

"And what else?" I asked, keenly interested, as I always was, by my friend's incisive reasoning.

"I noted, in passing, that she had written a note before leaving home, but after being fully dressed. You observed that her right glove was torn at the forefinger, but you did not apparently see that both glove and finger were stained with violet ink. She had written in a hurry, and dipped her pen too deep. It must have been this morning, or the mark would not remain clear upon the finger. All this is amusing, though rather elementary, but I must go back to business, Watson. Would you mind reading me the advertised description of Mr. Hosmer Angel?"

I held the little printed slip to the light. "Missing," it said, "on the morning of the 14th, a gentleman named Hosmer Angel. About 5 ft. 7 in. in height; strongly built, sallow complexion, black hair, a little bald in the centre, bushy black side whiskers and moustache; tinted glasses, slight infirmity of speech. Was dressed, when last seen, in black frock-coat faced with silk, black waistcoat, gold Albert chain, and grey Harris tweed trousers, with brown gaiters over elastic-sided boots. Known to have been employed in an office in Leadenhall Street. Anybody bringing," etc. etc.

"That will do," said Holmes. "As to the letters," he continued glancing over them, "they are very commonplace. Absolutely no clue in them to Mr. Angel, save that he quotes Balzac once. There is one remarkable point, however, which will no doubt strike you."

"They are typewritten," I remarked.

"Not only that, but the signature is typewritten. Look at the neat little 'Hosmer Angel' at the bottom. There is a date you see, but no superscription, except Leadenhall Street, which is rather vague. The point about the signature is very suggestive — in fact, we may call it conclusive."

"Of what?"

"My dear fellow, is it possible you do not see how strongly it bears upon the case?"

"I cannot say that I do, unless it were that he wished to be able to deny his signature if an action for breach of promise was instituted."

"No, that was not the point. However, I shall write two letters which should settle the matter. One is to a firm in the City, the other is to the young lady's stepfather, Mr. Windibank, asking him whether he could meet us here at six o'clock to-morrow evening. It is just as well that we should do business with the male relatives. And now, Doctor, we can do nothing until the answers to those letters come, so we may put our little problem upon the shelf for the interim."

I had had so many reasons to believe in my friend's subtle powers of reasoning, and extraordinary energy in action, that I felt that he must have some solid grounds for the assured and easy demeanour with which he treated the singular mystery which he had been called upon to fathom. Only once had I known him to fail, in the case of the King of Bohemia and of the Irene Adler photograph, but when I looked back to the weird business of the Sign of Four, and the extraordinary circumstances connected with the Study in Scarlet, I felt that it would be a strange tangle indeed which he could not unravel.

I left him then, still puffing at his black clay pipe, with the conviction that when I came again on the next evening I would find that he held in his hands all the clues which would lead up to the identity of the disappearing bridegroom of Miss Mary Sutherland.

A professional case of great gravity was engaging my own attention at the time, and the whole of next day I was busy at the bedside of the sufferer. It was not until close upon six o'clock that I found myself free, and was able to spring into a hansom and drive to Baker Street, half afraid that I might be too late to assist at the *dénouement* of the little mystery. I found Sherlock Holmes alone, however, half asleep, with his long, thin form curled up in the recesses of his arm-chair. A formidable array of bottles and test-tubes, with the pungent cleanly smell of hydrochloric acid, told me that he had spent his day in the chemical work which was so dear to him.

"Well, have you solved it?" I asked as I entered.

"Yes. It was the bisulphate of baryta."

"No, no, the mystery!" I cried.

"Oh, that! I thought of the salt that I have been working upon. There was never any mystery in the matter, though, as I said yesterday, some of the details are of interest. The only drawback is that there is no law, I fear, that can touch the scoundrel."

"Who was he, then, and what was his object in deserting Miss Sutherland?"

The question was hardly out of my mouth, and Holmes had not yet opened his lips to reply, when we heard a heavy footfall in the passage, and a tap at the door.

"This is the girl's stepfather, Mr. James Windibank," said Holmes. "He has written to me to say that he would be here at six. Come in!"

The man who entered was a sturdy middle-sized fellow, some thirty years of age, clean shaven, and sallow skinned, with a bland, insinuating manner, and a pair of wonderfully sharp and penetrating grey eyes. He shot a questioning glance at each of us, placed his shiny top-hat upon the sideboard, and, with a slight bow, sidled down into the nearest chair.

"Good evening, Mr. James Windibank," said Holmes. "I think that this typewritten letter is from you, in which you made an appointment with me for six o'clock?"

"Yes, sir. I am afraid that I am a little late, but I am not quite my own master, you know. I am sorry that Miss Sutherland has troubled you about this little matter, for I think it is far better not to wash linen of this sort in public. It was quite against my wishes that she came, but she is a very excitable, impulsive girl, as you may have noticed, and she is not easily controlled when she has made up her mind on a point. Of course, I do not mind you so much, as you are not connected with the official police, but it is not pleasant to have a family misfortune like this noised abroad. Besides, it is a useless expense, for how could you possibly find this Hosmer Angel?"

"On the contrary," said Holmes quietly; "I have every reason to believe that I will succeed in discovering Mr. Hosmer Angel."

Mr. Windibank gave a violent start, and dropped his gloves. "I am delighted to hear it," he said.

"It is a curious thing," remarked Holmes, "that a typewriter has really quite as much individuality as a man's handwriting. Unless they are quite new, no two of them write exactly alike. Some letters get more worn than others, and some wear only on one side. Now, you remark in this note of yours, Mr. Windibank, that in every case there is some little slurring over of the 'e,' and a slight defect in the tail of the 'r.' There are fourteen other characteristics, but those are the more obvious."

"We do all our correspondence with this machine at the office, and no doubt it is a little worn," our visitor answered, glancing keenly at Holmes with his bright little eyes.

"And now I will show you what is really a very interesting study, Mr. Windibank," Holmes continued. "I think of writing another little monograph some of these days on the typewriter and its relation to crime. It is a subject to which I have devoted some little attention. I have here four letters which purport to come from the missing man. They are all typewritten. In each case, not only are the 'e's' slurred and the 'r's' tailless, but you will observe, if you care to use my magnifying lens, that the fourteen other characteristics to which I have alluded are there as well."

Mr. Windibank sprang out of his chair, and picked up his hat. "I cannot waste time over this sort of fantastic talk, Mr. Holmes," he said. "If you can catch the man, catch him, and let me know when you have done it."

"Certainly," said Holmes, stepping over and turning the key in the door. "I let you know, then, that I have caught him!"

"What! where?" shouted Mr. Windibank, turning white to his lips, and glancing about him like a rat in a trap.

"Oh, it won't do — really it won't," said Holmes suavely. "There is no possible getting out of it, Mr. Windibank. It is quite too transparent, and it was a very bad compliment when you said it was impossible for me to solve so simple a question. That's right! Sit down, and let us talk it over."

Our visitor collapsed into a chair with a ghastly face and a glitter of moisture on his brow. "It — it's not actionable," he stammered.

"I am very much afraid that it is not. But between ourselves, Windibank, it was as cruel, and selfish, and heartless a trick in a petty way as ever came before me. Now, let me just run over the course of events, and you will contradict me if I go wrong."

The man sat huddled up in his chair, with his head sunk upon his breast, like one who is utterly crushed. Holmes stuck his feet up on the corner of the mantelpiece, and leaning back with his hands in his pockets, began talking, rather to himself, as it seemed, than to us.

"The man married a woman very much older than himself for her money," said he, "and he enjoyed the use of the money of the daughter as long as she lived with them. It was a considerable sum for people in their position, and the loss of it would have made a serious difference. It was worth an effort to preserve it. The daughter was of a good, amiable disposition, but affectionate and warm-hearted in her ways, so that it was evident that with her fair personal advantages, and her little income, she would not be allowed to remain single long. Now her marriage would mean, of course, the loss of a hundred a year, so what does her stepfather do to prevent it? He takes the obvious course of keeping her at home, and forbidding her to seek the company of people of her own age. But soon he found that that would not answer for ever. She became restive, insisted upon her rights, and finally announced her positive intention of going to a certain ball. What does her clever stepfather do then? He conceives an idea more creditable to his head than to his heart. With the connivance and assistance of his wife he disguised himself, covered those keen eyes with tinted glasses, masked the face with a moustache and a pair of bushy whiskers, sunk that clear voice into an insinuating whisper, and, doubly secure on account of the girl's short sight, he appears as Mr. Hosmer Angel, and keeps off other lovers by making love himself."

"It was only a joke at first," groaned our visitor. "We never thought that she would have been so carried away."

"Very likely not. However that may be, the young lady was very decidedly carried away, and having quite made up her mind that her stepfather was in France, the suspicion of treachery never for an instant entered her mind. She was flattered by the gentleman's attentions, and the effect was increased by the loudly expressed admiration of her mother. Then Mr. Angel began to call, for it was obvious that the matter should be pushed as far as it would go, if a real effect were to be produced. There were meetings, and an engagement, which would finally secure the girl's affections from turning towards anyone else. But the deception could not be kept up for ever. These pretended journeys to France were rather cumbrous. The thing to do was clearly to bring the business to an end in such a dramatic manner that it would leave a permanent impression upon the young lady's mind, and prevent her from looking upon any other suitor for some time to come. Hence those vows of fidelity exacted upon a Testament, and hence also the allusions to a possibility of something happening on the very morning of the wedding. James Windibank wished Miss Sutherland to be so bound to Hosmer Angel, and so uncertain as to his fate, that for ten years to come, at any rate, she would not listen to another man. As far as the church door he brought her, and then, as he could go no further, he conveniently vanished away by the old trick of stepping in at one door of a four-wheeler, and out at the other. I think that that was the chain of events, Mr. Windibank!"

Our visitor had recovered something of his assurance while Holmes had been talking, and he rose from his chair now with a cold sneer upon his pale face.

"It may be so, or it may not, Mr. Holmes," said he, "but if you are so very sharp you ought to be sharp enough to know that it is you who are breaking the law now, and not me. I have done nothing actionable from the first, but as long as you keep that door locked you lay yourself open to an action for assault and illegal constraint."

"The law cannot, as you say, touch you," said Holmes, unlocking and throwing open the door, "yet there never was a man who deserved punishment more. If the young lady has a brother or a friend he ought to lay a whip across your shoulders. By Jove!" he continued, flushing up at the sight of the bitter sneer upon the man's face, "it is not part of my duties to my client, but here's a hunting-crop handy, and I think I shall just treat myself to——" He took two swift steps to the whip, but before he could grasp it there was a wild clatter of steps upon the stairs, the heavy hall door banged, and from the window we could see Mr. James Windibank running at the top of his speed down the road.

"There's a cold-blooded scoundrel!" said Holmes, laughing, as he threw himself down into his chair once more. "That fellow will rise from crime to crime until he does something very bad, and ends on a gallows. The case has, in some respects, been not entirely devoid of interest."

"I cannot now entirely see all the steps of your reasoning," I re-marked.

"Well, of course it was obvious from the first that this Mr. Hosmer Angel must have some strong object for his curious conduct, and it was equally clear that the only man who really profited by the incident, as far as we could see, was the stepfather. Then the fact that the two men were never together, but that the one always appeared when the other was away, was suggestive. So were the tinted spectacles and the curious voice, which both hinted at a disguise, as did the bushy whiskers. My suspicions were all con-firmed by his peculiar action in typewriting his signature, which of course inferred that his handwriting was so familiar to her that she would recog-nize even the smallest sample of it. You see all these isolated facts, together with many minor ones, all pointed in the same direction."

"And how did you verify them?"

"Having once spotted my man, it was easy to get corroboration. I knew the firm for which this man worked. Having taken the printed description, I eliminated everything from it which could be the result of a disguise — the whiskers, the glasses, the voice, and I sent it to the firm, with a request that they would inform me whether it answered the description of any of their travellers. I had already noticed the peculiar-ities of the typewriter, and I wrote to the man himself at his business address, asking him if he would come here. As I expected, his reply was typewritten, and revealed the same trivial but characteristic defects. The same post brought me a letter from Westhouse & Marbank, of Fenchurch Street, to say that the description tallied in every respect with that of their employé, James Windibank. *Voilà tout!*"

"And Miss Sutherland?"

"If I tell her she will not believe me. You may remember the old Per-sian saying, 'There is danger for him who taketh the tiger cub, and danger also for whoso snatches a delusion from a woman.' There is as much sense in Hafiz as in Horace, and as much knowledge of the world."

## AFTERWORD

Mary Sutherland's nearsighted gullibility, the scoundrel's plea that "It was only a joke at first," Holmes's laughing if contemptuous dis-missal of him at the end, and the fact that the case is "entirely free of any legal crime" (see "The Blue Carbuncle," p. 134) all conspire to lend this story an air of bizarre humor and domestic comedy entirely in keeping with the morning newspaper story ("A husband's cruelty to his wife") to which Holmes and Watson initially allude: "the conduct complained of was that he had drifted into the habit of winding up every meal by taking out his false teeth and hurling them at his wife." But as a tale of a tyrannical man's attempt to control his daughter's or stepdaughter's money by preventing her from marrying, it has strong affinities with such grim and deadly tales as "The Speckled Band" and "The Copper Beeches"; and the hint of incest in the man's courting of his stepdaughter ("Mother was all in his favour from the first, and was even fonder of him than I was") also anticipates a theme figuratively present in "The Speckled Band."

What defines and characterizes an identity? What distinguishes the remarkable and the specific from the anonymous and the ordinary? "A Case of Identity," with its careful awareness of both individuals and their types (the emphasis on "typewriters" is both significant and punning), raises these fundamental questions throughout. Challenged by Holmes to read Mary Sutherland's appearance, Watson offers specifics of costume plus "general impressions." But such specifics and impressions are precisely the sorts of "typings" that Holmes eliminates from the description of Hosmer Angel so that he may infer something about the actual appearance of Miss Sutherland's fiancé: they describe, but do not characterize. While the essentially undistinguished Hosmer Angel disappears by stepping through a carriage door back into the anonymity of the city's masses, however, Holmes by his attentiveness to "trivial but characteristic" details of Angel's typewritten love letters recovers the identity of a unique typewriter (and so of a particular typist) from the anonymity of a mechanical and mass-produced medium.


## The Boscombe Valley Mystery

We were seated at breakfast one morning, my wife and I, when the maid brought in a telegram. It was from Sherlock Holmes, and ran in this way:

"Have you a couple of days to spare? Have just been wired for from the West of England in connection with Boscombe Valley tragedy. Shall be glad if you will come with me. Air and scenery perfect. Leave Paddington by the 11:15."

From *The Adventures of Sherlock Holmes* (1892). First published in the *Strand*, October 1891.

"What do you say, dear?" said my wife, looking across at me. "Will you go?"

"I really don't know what to say. I have a fairly long list at present."

"Oh, Anstruther would do your work for you. You have been looking a little pale lately. I think that the change would do you good, and you are always so interested in Mr. Sherlock Holmes's cases."

"I should be ungrateful if I were not, seeing what I gained through one of them,"[1] I answered. "But if I am to go I must pack at once, for I have only half an hour."

My experience of camp life in Afghanistan had at least had the effect of making me a prompt and ready traveller. My wants were few and simple, so that in less than the time stated I was in a cab with my valise, rattling away to Paddington Station. Sherlock Holmes was pacing up and down the platform, his tall, gaunt figure made even gaunter and taller by his long grey travelling-cloak and close-fitting cloth cap.

"It is really very good of you to come, Watson," said he. "It makes a considerable difference to me, having someone with me on whom I can thoroughly rely. Local aid is always either worthless or else biased. If you will keep the two corner seats I shall get the tickets."

We had the carriage to ourselves save for an immense litter of papers which Holmes had brought with him. Among these he rummaged and read, with intervals of note-taking and of meditation, until we were past Reading. Then he suddenly rolled them all into a gigantic ball, and tossed them up on to the rack.

"Have you heard anything of the case?" he asked.

"Not a word. I have not seen a paper for some days."

"The London press has not had very full accounts. I have just been looking through all the recent papers in order to master the particulars. It seems, from what I gather, to be one of those simple cases which are so extremely difficult."

"That sounds a little paradoxical."

"But it is profoundly true. Singularity is almost invariably a clue. The more featureless and commonplace a crime is, the more difficult is it to bring it home. In this case, however, they have established a very serious case against the son of the murdered man."

"It is a murder, then?"

"Well, it is conjectured to be so. I shall take nothing for granted until I have the opportunity of looking personally into it. I will explain

[1] *what I gained through one of them:* His wife herself, the former Mary Morstan, whom Watson met when she came to Holmes as a client in *The Sign of Four.*

the state of things to you, as far as I have been able to understand it, in a very few words.

"Boscombe Valley is a country district not very far from Ross, in Herefordshire. The largest landed proprietor in that part is a Mr. John Turner, who made his money in Australia, and returned some years ago to the old country. One of the farms which he held, that of Hatherley, was let to Mr. Charles McCarthy, who was also an ex-Australian. The men had known each other in the Colonies, so that it was not unnatural that when they came to settle down they should do so as near each other as possible. Turner was apparently the richer man, so McCarthy became his tenant, but still remained, it seems, upon terms of perfect equality, as they were frequently together. McCarthy had one son, a lad of eighteen, and Turner had an only daughter of the same age, but neither of them had wives living. They appear to have avoided the society of the neighbouring English families, and to have led retired lives, though both the McCarthys were fond of sport, and were frequently seen at the race meetings of the neighbourhood. McCarthy kept two servants — a man and a girl. Turner had a considerable household, some half-dozen at the least. That is as much as I have been able to gather about the families. Now for the facts.

"On June 3 — that is, on Monday last — McCarthy left his house at Hatherley about three in the afternoon, and walked down to the Boscombe Pool, which is a small lake formed by the spreading out of the stream which runs down the Boscombe Valley. He had been out with his serving-man in the morning at Ross, and he had told the man that he must hurry, as he had an appointment of importance to keep at three. From that appointment he never came back alive.

"From Hatherley Farm-house to the Boscombe Pool is a quarter of a mile, and two people saw him as he passed over this ground. One was an old woman, whose name is not mentioned, and the other was William Crowder, a gamekeeper in the employ of Mr. Turner. Both these witnesses depose that Mr. McCarthy was walking alone. The gamekeeper adds that within a few minutes of his seeing Mr. McCarthy pass he had seen his son, Mr. James McCarthy, going the same way with a gun under his arm. To the best of his belief, the father was actually in sight at the time, and the son was following him. He thought no more of the matter until he heard in the evening of the tragedy that had occurred.

"The two McCarthys were seen after the time when William Crowder, the gamekeeper, lost sight of them. The Boscombe Pool is thickly wooded round, with just a fringe of grass and of reeds round the edge.

A girl of fourteen, Patience Moran, who is the daughter of the lodge-keeper of the Boscombe Valley Estate, was in one of the woods picking flowers. She states that while she was there she saw, at the border of the wood and close by the lake, Mr. McCarthy and his son, and that they appeared to be having a violent quarrel. She heard Mr. McCarthy the elder using very strong language to his son, and she saw the latter raise up his hand as if to strike his father. She was so frightened by their violence that she ran away, and told her mother when she reached home that she had left the two McCarthys quarrelling near Boscombe Pool, and that she was afraid that they were going to fight. She had hardly said the words when young Mr. McCarthy came running up to the lodge to say that he had found his father dead in the wood, and to ask for the help of the lodge-keeper. He was much excited, without either his gun or his hat, and his right hand and sleeve were observed to be stained with fresh blood. On following him they found the dead body of his father stretched out upon the grass beside the Pool. The head had been beaten in by repeated blows of some heavy and blunt weapon. The injuries were such as might very well have been inflicted by the butt-end of his son's gun, which was found lying on the grass within a few paces of the body. Under these circumstances the young man was instantly arrested, and a verdict of 'Wilful Murder' having been returned at the inquest on Tuesday, he was on Wednesday brought before the magistrates at Ross, who have referred the case to the next assizes. Those are the main facts of the case as they came out before the coroner and at the police-court."

"I could hardly imagine a more damning case," I remarked. "If ever circumstantial evidence pointed to a criminal it does so here."

"Circumstantial evidence is a very tricky thing," answered Holmes thoughtfully; "it may seem to point very straight to one thing, but if you shift your own point of view a little, you may find it pointing in an equally uncompromising manner to something entirely different. It must be confessed, however, that the case looks exceedingly grave against the young man, and it is very possible that he is indeed the culprit. There are several people in the neighbourhood, however, and among them Miss Turner, the daughter of the neighbouring land-owner, who believe in his innocence, and who have retained Lestrade, whom you may remember in connection with the Study in Scarlet, to work out the case in his interest. Lestrade, being rather puzzled, has referred the case to me, and hence it is that two middle-aged gentlemen are flying westward at fifty miles an hour, instead of quietly digesting their breakfasts at home."

"I am afraid," said I, "that the facts are so obvious that you will find little credit to be gained out of this case."

"There is nothing more deceptive than an obvious fact," he answered, laughing. "Besides, we may chance to hit upon some other obvious facts which may have been by no means obvious to Mr. Lestrade. You know me too well to think that I am boasting when I say that I shall either confirm or destroy his theory by means which he is quite incapable of employing, or even of understanding. To take the first example to hand, I very clearly perceive that in your bedroom the window is upon the right-hand side, and yet I question whether Mr. Lestrade would have noted even so self-evident a thing as that."

"How on earth——!"

"My dear fellow, I know you well. I know the military neatness which characterizes you. You shave every morning, and in this season you shave by the sunlight, but since your shaving is less and less complete as we get farther back on the left side, until it becomes positively slovenly as we get round the angle of the jaw, it is surely very clear that that side is less well illuminated than the other. I could not imagine a man of your habits looking at himself in an equal light, and being satisfied with such a result. I only quote this as a trivial example of observation and inference. Therein lies my *métier*, and it is just possible that it may be of some service in the investigation which lies before us. There are one or two minor points which were brought out in the inquest, and which are worth considering."

"What are they?"

"It appears that his arrest did not take place at once, but after the return to Hatherley Farm. On the inspector of constabulary informing him that he was a prisoner, he remarked that he was not surprised to hear it, and that it was no more than his deserts. This observation of his had the natural effect of removing any traces of doubt which might have remained in the minds of the coroner's jury."

"It was a confession," I ejaculated.

"No, for it was followed by a protestation of innocence."

"Coming on the top of such a damning series of events, it was at least a most suspicious remark."

"On the contrary," said Holmes, "it is the brightest rift which I can at present see in the clouds. However innocent he might be, he could not be such an absolute imbecile as not to see that the circumstances were very black against him. Had he appeared surprised at his own arrest, or feigned indignation at it, I should have looked upon it as highly suspicious, because such surprise or anger would not be natural under the circumstances, and yet might appear to be the best policy to a scheming man. His frank acceptance of the situation marks him as either an innocent man, or else as a man of considerable self-restraint and firmness. As to his remark about his deserts, it was also not unnatural if you consider that he stood by the dead body of his father, and that there is no doubt that he had that very day so far forgotten his filial duty as to bandy words with him, and even, according to the little girl whose evidence is so important, to raise his hand as if to strike him. The self-reproach and contrition which are displayed in his remark appear to me to be the signs of a healthy mind, rather than of a guilty one."

I shook my head. "Many men have been hanged on far slighter evidence," I remarked.

"So they have. And many men have been wrongfully hanged."

"What is the young man's own account of the matter?"

"It is, I am afraid, not very encouraging to his supporters, though there are one or two points in it which are suggestive. You will find it here, and may read it for yourself."

He picked out from his bundle a copy of the local Herefordshire paper, and having turned down the sheet, he pointed out the paragraph in which the unfortunate young man had given his own statement of what had occurred. I settled myself down in the corner of the carriage, and read it very carefully. It ran in this way:

Mr. James McCarthy, the only son of the deceased, was then called, and gave evidence as follows: "I had been away from home for three days at Bristol, and had only just returned upon the morning of last Monday, the 3rd. My father was absent from home at the time of my arrival, and I was informed by the maid that he had driven over to Ross with John Cobb, the groom. Shortly after my return I heard the wheels of his trap in the yard, and, looking out of my window, I saw him get out and walk rapidly out of the yard, though I was not aware in which direction he was going. I then took my gun, and strolled out in the direction of the Boscombe Pool, with the intention of visiting the rabbit warren which is upon the other side. On my way I saw William Crowder, the gamekeeper, as he has stated in his evidence; but he is mistaken in thinking that I was following my father. I had no idea that he was in front of me. When about a hundred yards from the Pool I heard a cry of "Cooee!" which was a usual signal between my father and myself. I then hurried forward, and found him standing by the Pool. He appeared to be much surprised at seeing me, and asked me rather roughly what I was doing there. A conversation ensued, which led to high words, and almost to

blows, for my father was a man of a very violent temper. Seeing
that his passion was becoming ungovernable, I left him, and returned towards Hatherley Farm. I had not gone more than one
hundred and fifty yards, however, when I heard a hideous outcry
behind me, which caused me to run back again. I found my father
expiring on the ground, with his head terribly injured. I dropped
my gun, and held him in my arms, but he almost instantly ex-
pired. I knelt beside him for some minutes, and then made my
way to Mr. Turner's lodge-keeper, his house being the nearest, to
ask for assistance. I saw no one near my father when I returned,
and I have no idea how he came by his injuries. He was not a popular man, being somewhat cold and forbidding in his manners;
but he had, as far as I know, no active enemies. I know nothing
further of the matter."

The Coroner: Did your father make any statement to you before he died?

Witness: He mumbled a few words, but I could only catch
some allusion to a rat.

The Coroner: What did you understand by that?

Witness: It conveyed no meaning to me. I thought that he was
delirious.

The Coroner: What was the point upon which you and your
father had this final quarrel?

Witness: I should prefer not to answer.

The Coroner: I am afraid that I must press it.

Witness: It is really impossible for me to tell you. I can assure
you that it has nothing to do with the sad tragedy which followed.

The Coroner: That is for the Court to decide. I need not
point out to you that your refusal to answer will prejudice your
case considerably in any future proceedings which may arise.

Witness: I must still refuse.

The Coroner: I understand that the cry of "Cooee" was a
common signal between you and your father?

Witness: It was.

The Coroner: How was it, then, that he uttered it before he
saw you, and before he even knew that you had returned from
Bristol?

Witness (with considerable confusion): I do not know.

A Juryman: Did you see nothing which aroused your suspicions when you returned on hearing the cry, and found your father fatally injured?

Witness: Nothing definite.

The Coroner: What do you mean?

Witness: I was so disturbed and excited as I rushed out into the open, that I could think of nothing except my father. Yet I have a vague impression that as I ran forward something lay upon the ground to the left of me. It seemed to me to be something grey in colour, a coat of some sort, or a plaid perhaps. When I rose from my father I looked round for it, but it was gone.

"Do you mean that it disappeared before you went for help?"

"Yes, it was gone."

"You cannot say what it was?"

"No, I had a feeling something was there."

"How far from the body?"

"A dozen yards or so."

"And how far from the edge of the wood?"

"About the same."

"Then if it was removed it was while you were within a dozen yards of it?"

"Yes, but with my back towards it."

This concluded the examination of the witness.

"I see," said I, as I glanced down the column, "that the coroner in his concluding remarks was rather severe upon young McCarthy. He calls attention, and with reason, to the discrepancy about his father having signalled to him before seeing him, also to his refusal to give details of his conversation with his father, and his singular account of his father's dying words. They are all, as he remarks, very much against the son."

Holmes laughed softly to himself, and stretched himself out upon the cushioned seat. "Both you and the coroner have been at some pains," said he, "to single out the very strongest points in the young man's favour. Don't you see that you alternately give him credit for having too much imagination and too little? Too little, if he could not invent a cause of quarrel which would give him the sympathy of the jury; too much, if he evolved from his own inner consciousness anything so *outré* as a dying reference to a rat, and the incident of the vanishing cloth. No, sir, I shall approach this case from the point of view that what this young man says is true, and we shall see whither that hypothesis will lead us. And now here is my pocket Petrarch, and not another word shall I say of this case until we are on the scene of action. We lunch at Swindon, and I see that we shall be there in twenty minutes."

It was nearly four o'clock when we at last, after passing through the beautiful Stroud Valley and over the broad gleaming Severn, found ourselves at the pretty little country town of Ross. A lean, ferret-like man, furtive and sly-looking, was waiting for us upon the platform. In spite of

the light brown dust-coat and leather leggings which he wore in deference to his rustic surroundings, I had no difficulty in recognizing Lestrade, of Scotland Yard. With him we drove to the Hereford Arms,
where a room had already been engaged for us.

"I have ordered a carriage," said Lestrade, as we sat over a cup of
tea. "I knew your energetic nature, and that you would not be happy
until you had been on the scene of the crime."

"It was very nice and complimentary of you," Holmes answered. "It
is entirely a question of barometric pressure."

Lestrade looked startled. "I do not quite follow," he said.

"How is the glass? Twenty-nine, I see. No wind, and not a cloud in
the sky. I have a caseful of cigarettes here which need smoking, and the
sofa is very much superior to the usual country hotel abomination. I do
not think that it is probable that I shall use the carriage to-night."

Lestrade laughed indulgently. "You have, no doubt, already formed
your conclusions from the newspapers," he said. "The case is as plain as
a pikestaff, and the more one goes into it the plainer it becomes. Still, of
course, one can't refuse a lady, and such a very positive one, too. She
had heard of you, and would have your opinion, though I repeatedly
told her that there was nothing which you could do which I had not
already done. Why, bless my soul! here is her carriage at the door."

He had hardly spoken before there rushed into the room one of the
most lovely young women that I have ever seen in my life. Her violet
eyes shining, her lips parted, a pink flush upon her cheeks, all thought
of her natural reserve lost in her overpowering excitement and concern.

"Oh, Mr. Sherlock Holmes!" she cried, glancing from one to the
other of us, and finally, with a woman's quick intuition, fastening upon
my companion, "I am so glad that you have come. I have driven down
to tell you so. I know that James didn't do it. I know it, and I want you
to start upon your work knowing it, too. Never let yourself doubt upon
that point. We have known each other since we were little children, and
I know his faults as no one else does; but he is too tender-hearted to
hurt a fly. Such a charge is absurd to anyone who really knows him."

"I hope we may clear him, Miss Turner," said Sherlock Holmes.
"You may rely upon my doing all that I can."

"But you have read the evidence. You have formed some conclusion? Do you not see some loophole, some flaw? Do you not yourself
think that he is innocent?"

"I think that it is very probable."

"There now!" she cried, throwing back her head and looking defi-
antly at Lestrade. "You hear! He gives me hope."

Lestrade shrugged his shoulders. "I am afraid that my colleague has been a little quick in forming his conclusions," he said.

"But he is right. Oh! I know that he is right. James never did it. And about his quarrel with his father, I am sure that the reason why he would not speak about it to the coroner was because I was concerned in it."

"In what way?" asked Holmes.

"It is no time for me to hide anything. James and his father had many disagreements about me. Mr. McCarthy was very anxious that there should be a marriage between us. James and I have always loved each other as brother and sister, but of course he is young and has seen very little of life yet, and — and — well, he naturally did not wish to do anything like that yet. So there were quarrels, and this, I am sure, was one of them."

"And your father?" asked Holmes. "Was he in favour of such a union?"

"No, he was averse to it also. No one but Mr. McCarthy was in favour of it." A quick blush passed over her fresh young face as Holmes shot one of his keen, questioning glances at her.

"Thank you for this information," said he. "May I see your father if I call to-morrow?"

"I am afraid the doctor won't allow it."

"The doctor?"

"Yes, have you not heard? Poor father has never been strong for years back, but this has broken him down completely. He has taken to his bed, and Dr. Willows says that he is a wreck, and that his nervous system is shattered. Mr. McCarthy was the only man alive who had known dad in the old days in Victoria."

"Ha! In Victoria! That is important."

"Yes, at the mines."

"Quite so; at the gold mines, where, as I understand, Mr. Turner made his money."

"Yes, certainly."

"Thank you, Miss Turner. You have been of material assistance to me."

"You will tell me if you have any news to-morrow. No doubt you will go to the prison to see James. Oh, if you do, Mr. Holmes, do tell him that I know him to be innocent."

"I will, Miss Turner."

"I must go home now, for dad is very ill, and he misses me so if I leave him. Good-bye, and God help you in your undertaking." She hurried from the room as impulsively as she had entered, and we heard the wheels of her carriage rattle off down the street.

"I am ashamed of you, Holmes," said Lestrade with dignity, after a few minutes' silence. "Why should you raise up hopes which you are bound to disappoint? I am not over-tender of heart, but I call it cruel."

"I think that I see my way to clearing James McCarthy," said Holmes. "Have you an order to see him in prison?"

"Yes, but only for you and me."

"Then I shall reconsider my resolution about going out. We have still time to take a train to Hereford and see him to-night?"

"Ample."

"Then let us do so. Watson, I fear that you will find it very slow, but I shall only be away a couple of hours."

I walked down to the station with them, and then wandered through the streets of the little town, finally returning to the hotel, where I lay upon the sofa and tried to interest myself in a yellow-backed novel. The puny plot of the story was so thin, however, when compared to the deep mystery through which we were groping, and I found my attention wander so constantly from the fiction to the fact, that I at last flung it across the room, and gave myself up entirely to a consideration of the events of the day. Supposing that this unhappy young man's story was absolutely true, then what hellish thing, what absolutely unforeseen and extraordinary calamity, could have occurred between the time when he parted from his father and the moment when, drawn back by his screams, he rushed into the glade? It was something terrible and deadly. What could it be? Might not the nature of the injuries reveal something to my medical instincts? I rang the bell, and called for the weekly county paper, which contained a verbatim account of the inquest. In the surgeon's deposition it was stated that the posterior third of the left parietal bone and the left half of the occipital bone had been shattered by a heavy blow from a blunt weapon. I marked the spot upon my own head. Clearly such a blow must have been struck from behind. That was to some extent in favour of the accused, as when seen quarrelling he was face to face with his father. Still, it did not go for very much, for the older man might have turned his back before the blow fell. Still, it might be worth while to call Holmes's attention to it. Then there was the peculiar dying reference to a rat. What could that mean? It could not be delirium. A man dying from a sudden blow does not commonly become delirious. No, it was more likely to be an attempt to explain how he met his fate. But what could it indicate? I cudgelled my brains to find some possible explanation. And then the incident of the grey cloth, seen by young McCarthy. If that were true, the murderer must have dropped some part of his dress, presumably his overcoat, in his flight, and must have had the hardihood to return and carry it away at the instant when the son was kneeling with his back turned not a dozen paces off. What a tissue of mysteries and improbabilities the whole thing was! I did not wonder at Lestrade's opinion, and yet I had so much faith in Sherlock Holmes's insight that I could not lose hope as long as every fresh fact seemed to strengthen his conviction of young McCarthy's innocence.

It was late before Sherlock Holmes returned. He came back alone, for Lestrade was staying in lodgings in the town.

"The glass still keeps very high," he remarked, as he sat down. "It is of importance that it should not rain before we are able to go over the ground. On the other hand, a man should be at his very best and keenest for such nice work as that, and I did not wish to do it when fagged by a long journey. I have seen young McCarthy."

"And what did you learn from him?"

"Nothing."

"Could he throw no light?"

"None at all. I was inclined to think at one time that he knew who had done it, and was screening him or her, but I am convinced now that he is as puzzled as everyone else. He is not a very quick-witted youth, though comely to look at, and, I should think, sound at heart."

"I cannot admire his taste," I remarked, "if it is indeed a fact that he was averse to a marriage with so charming a young lady as this Miss Turner."

"Ah, thereby hangs a rather painful tale. This fellow is madly, insanely in love with her, but some two years ago, when he was only a lad, and before he really knew her, for she had been away five years at a boarding-school, what does the idiot do but get into the clutches of a barmaid in Bristol, and marry her at a registry office! No one knows a word of the matter, but you can imagine how maddening it must be to him to be upbraided for not doing what he would give his very eyes to do, but what he knows to be absolutely impossible. It was sheer frenzy of this sort which made him throw his hands up into the air when his father, at their last interview, was goading him on to propose to Miss Turner. On the other hand, he had no means of supporting himself, and his father, who was by all accounts a very hard man, would have thrown him over utterly had he known the truth. It was with his barmaid wife that he had spent the last three days in Bristol, and his father did not know where he was. Mark that point. It is of importance. Good has come out of evil, however, for the barmaid, finding from the papers that he is in serious trouble, and likely to be hanged, has thrown him over utterly, and has written to him to say that she has a husband already in the Bermuda Dockyard, so that there is really no tie between them. I think that that bit of news has consoled young McCarthy for all that he has suffered."

"But if he is innocent, who has done it?"

"Ah! who? I would call your attention very particularly to two points. One is that the murdered man had an appointment with someone at the Pool, and that the someone could not have been his son, for his son was away, and he did not know when he would return. The second is that the murdered man was heard to cry 'Cooee!' before he knew that his son had returned. Those are the crucial points upon which the case depends. And now let us talk about George Meredith, if you please, and we shall leave minor points until to-morrow."

There was no rain, as Holmes had foretold, and the morning broke bright and cloudless. At nine o'clock Lestrade called for us with the carriage, and we set off for Hatherley Farm and the Boscombe Pool.

"There is serious news this morning," Lestrade observed. "It is said that Mr. Turner, of the Hall, is so ill that his life is despaired of."

"An elderly man, I presume?" said Holmes.

"About sixty; but his constitution has been shattered by his life abroad, and he has been in failing health for some time. This business has had a very bad effect upon him. He was an old friend of McCarthy's, and, I may add, a great benefactor to him, for I have learned that he gave him Hatherley Farm rent free."

"Indeed! That is interesting," said Holmes.

"Oh, yes! In a hundred other ways he has helped him. Everybody about here speaks of his kindness to him."

"Really! Does it not strike you as a little singular that this McCarthy, who appears to have had little of his own, and to have been under such obligations to Turner, should still talk of marrying his son to Turner's daughter, who is, presumably, heiress to the estate, and that in such a very cocksure manner, as if it was merely a case of a proposal and all else would follow? It is the more strange since we know that Turner himself was averse to the idea. The daughter told us as much. Do you not deduce something from that?"

"We have got to the deductions and the inferences," said Lestrade, winking at me. "I find it hard enough to tackle facts, Holmes, without flying away after theories and fancies."

"You are right," said Holmes demurely; "you do find it very hard to tackle the facts."

"Anyhow, I have grasped one fact which you seem to find it difficult to get hold of," replied Lestrade with some warmth.

"And that is?"

"That McCarthy, senior, met his death from McCarthy, junior, and that all theories to the contrary are the merest moonshine."

"Well, moonshine is a brighter thing than fog," said Holmes, laughing. "But I am very much mistaken if this is not Hatherley Farm upon the left."

"Yes, that is it." It was a widespread, comfortable-looking building, two-storied, slate-roofed, with great yellow blotches of lichen upon the grey walls. The drawn blinds and the smokeless chimneys, however, gave it a stricken look, as though the weight of this horror still lay heavy upon it. We called at the door, when the maid, at Holmes's request, showed us the boots which her master wore at the time of his death, and also a pair of the son's, though not the pair which he had then had. Having measured these very carefully from seven or eight different points, Holmes desired to be led to the courtyard, from which we all followed the winding track which led to Boscombe Pool.

Sherlock Holmes was transformed when he was hot upon such a scent as this. Men who had only known the quiet thinker and logician of Baker Street would have failed to recognize him. His face flushed and darkened. His brows were drawn into two hard, black lines, while his eyes shone out from beneath them with a steely glitter. His face was bent downwards, his shoulders bowed, his lips compressed, and the veins stood out like whip-cord in his long, sinewy neck. His nostrils seemed to dilate with a purely animal lust for the chase, and his mind was so absolutely concentrated upon the matter before him, that a question or remark fell unheeded upon his ears, or at the most only provoked a quick, impatient snarl in reply. Swiftly and silently he made his way along the track which ran through the meadows, and so by way of the woods to the Boscombe Pool. It was damp, marshy ground, as is all that district, and there were marks of many feet, both upon the path and amid the short grass which bounded it on either side. Sometimes Holmes would hurry on, sometimes stop dead, and once he made quite a little *détour* into the meadow. Lestrade and I walked behind him, the detective indifferent and contemptuous, while I watched my friend with the interest which sprang from the conviction that every one of his actions was directed towards a definite end.

The Boscombe Pool, which is a little reed-girt sheet of water some fifty yards across, is situated at the boundary between the Hatherley Farm and the private park of the wealthy Mr. Turner. Above the woods which lined it upon the farther side we could see the red jutting pinnacles which marked the site of the rich landowner's dwelling. On the Hatherley side of the Pool the woods grew very thick, and there was a narrow belt of sodden grass twenty paces across between the edge of the trees and the reeds which lined the lake. Lestrade showed us the exact spot at which the body had been found, and indeed, so moist was the ground, that I could plainly see the traces which had been left by the fall of the stricken man. To Holmes, as I could see by his eager face and peering eyes, very many other things were to be read upon the trampled grass. He ran round, like a dog who is picking up a scent, and then turned upon my companion.

"What did you go into the Pool for?" he asked.

"I fished about with a rake. I thought there might be some weapon or other trace. But how on earth——?"

"Oh, tut, tut! I have no time. That left foot of yours with its inward twist is all over the place. A mole could trace it, and there it vanishes among the reeds. Oh, how simple it would all have been had I been here before they came like a herd of buffalo, and wallowed all over it. Here is where the party with the lodge-keeper came, and they have covered all tracks for six or eight feet round the body. But here are three separate tracks of the same feet." He drew out a lens, and lay down upon his waterproof to have a better view, talking all the time rather to himself than to us. "These are young McCarthy's feet. Twice he was walking, and once he ran swiftly so that the soles are deeply marked, and the heels hardly visible. That bears out his story. He ran when he saw his father on the ground. Then here are the father's feet as he paced up and down. What is this, then? It is the butt end of the gun as the son stood listening. And this? Ha, ha! What have we here? Tip-toes, tip-toes! Square, too, quite unusual boots! They come, they go, they come again — of course that was for the cloak. Now where did they come from?" He ran up and down, sometimes losing, sometimes finding the track, until we were well within the edge of the wood and under the shadow of a great beech, the largest tree in the neighbourhood. Holmes traced his way to the farther side of this, and lay down once more upon his face with a little cry of satisfaction. For a long time he remained there, turning over the leaves and dried sticks, gathering up what seemed to me to be dust into an envelope, and examining with his lens not only the ground, but even the bark of the tree as far as he could reach. A jagged stone was lying among the moss, and this also he carefully examined and retained. Then he followed a pathway through the wood until he came to the high-road, where all traces were lost.

"It has been a case of considerable interest," he remarked, returning to his natural manner. "I fancy that this grey house on the right must be the lodge. I think that I will go in and have a word with Moran, and perhaps write a little note. Having done that, we may drive back to our luncheon. You may walk to the cab, and I shall be with you presently."

It was about ten minutes before we regained our cab, and drove back into Ross, Holmes still carrying with him the stone which he had picked up in the wood.

"This may interest you, Lestrade," he remarked, holding it out. "The murder was done with it."

"I see no marks."

"There are none."

"How do you know, then?"

"The grass was growing under it. It had only lain there a few days. There was no sign of a place whence it had been taken. It corresponds with the injuries. There is no sign of any other weapon."

"And the murderer?"

"Is a tall man, left-handed, limps with the right leg, wears thick-soled shooting-boots and a grey cloak, smokes Indian cigars, uses a cigar-holder, and carries a blunt penknife in his pocket. There are several other indications, but these may be enough to aid us in our search."

Lestrade laughed. "I am afraid that I am still a sceptic," he said. "Theories are all very well, but we have to deal with a hard-headed British jury."

"*Nous verrons,*"[2] answered Holmes calmly. "You work your own method, and I shall work mine. I shall be busy this afternoon, and shall probably return to London by the evening train."

"And leave your case unfinished?"

"No, finished."

"But the mystery?"

"It is solved."

"Who was the criminal, then?"

"The gentleman I describe."

"But who is he?"

"Surely it would not be difficult to find out. This is not such a populous neighbourhood."

Lestrade shrugged his shoulders. "I am a practical man," he said, "and I really cannot undertake to go about the country looking for a

---

[2] *"Nous verrons"*: "We'll see."

left-handed gentleman with a game leg. I should become the laughing-stock of Scotland Yard."

"All right," said Holmes quietly. "I have given you the chance. Here are your lodgings. Good-bye. I shall drop you a line before I leave."

Having left Lestrade at his rooms we drove to our hotel, where we found lunch upon the table. Holmes was silent and buried in thought, with a pained expression upon his face, as one who finds himself in a perplexing position.

"Look here, Watson," he said, when the cloth was cleared; "just sit down in this chair and let me preach to you for a little. I don't quite know what to do, and I should value your advice. Light a cigar, and let me expound."

"Pray do so."

"Well, now, in considering this case there are two points about young McCarthy's narrative which struck us both instantly, although they impressed me in his favour and you against him. One was the fact that his father should, according to his account, cry 'Cooee!' before seeing him. The other was his singular dying reference to a rat. He mumbled several words, you understand, but that was all that caught the son's ear. Now from this double point our research must commence, and we will begin it by presuming that what the lad says is absolutely true."

"What of this 'Cooee!' then?"

"Well, obviously it could not have been meant for the son. The son, as far as he knew, was in Bristol. It was mere chance that he was within earshot. The 'Cooee!' was meant to attract the attention of whoever it was that he had the appointment with. But 'Cooee' is a distinctly Australian cry, and one which is used between Australians. There is a strong presumption that the person whom McCarthy expected to meet him at Boscombe Pool was someone who had been in Australia."

"What of the rat, then?"

Sherlock Holmes took a folded paper from his pocket and flattened it out on the table. "This is a map of the Colony of Victoria," he said. "I wired to Bristol for it last night." He put his hand over part of the map. "What do you read?" he asked.

"ARAT," I read.

"And now?" He raised his hand.

"BALLARAT."

"Quite so. That was the word the man uttered, and of which his son only caught the last two syllables. He was trying to utter the name of his murderer. So-and-so of Ballarat."

"It is wonderful!" I exclaimed.

"It is obvious. And now, you see, I had narrowed the field down considerably. The possession of a grey garment was a third point which, granting the son's statement to be correct, was a certainty. We have come now out of mere vagueness to the definite conception of an Australian from Ballarat with a grey cloak."

"Certainly."

"And one who was at home in the district, for the Pool can only be approached by the farm or by the estate, where strangers could hardly wander."

"Quite so."

"Then comes our expedition of to-day. By an examination of the ground I gained the trifling details which I gave to that imbecile Lestrade, as to the personality of the criminal."

"But how did you gain them?"

"You know my method. It is founded upon the observance of trifles."

"His height I know that you might roughly judge from the length of his stride. His boots, too, might be told from their traces."

"Yes, they were peculiar boots."

"But his lameness?"

"The impression of his right foot was always less distinct than his left. He put less weight upon it. Why? Because he limped — he was lame."

"But his left-handedness?"

"You were yourself struck by the nature of the injury as recorded by the surgeon at the inquest. The blow was struck from immediately behind, and yet was upon the left side. Now, how can that be unless it were by a left-handed man? He had stood behind that tree during the interview between the father and son. He had even smoked there. I found the ash of a cigar, which my special knowledge of tobacco ashes enabled me to pronounce as an Indian cigar. I have, as you know, devoted some attention to this, and written a little monograph on the ashes of 140 different varieties of pipe, cigar, and cigarette tobacco. Having found the ash, I then looked round and discovered the stump among the moss where he had tossed it. It was an Indian cigar, of the variety which are rolled in Rotterdam."

"And the cigar-holder?"

"I could see that the end had not been in his mouth. Therefore he used a holder. The tip had been cut off, not bitten off, but the cut was not a clean one, so I deduced a blunt penknife."

"Holmes," I said, "you have drawn a net round this man from which he cannot escape, and you have saved an innocent human life as truly as if you had cut the cord which was hanging him. I see the direction in which all this points. The culprit is——"

"Mr. John Turner," cried the hotel waiter, opening the door of our sitting-room, and ushering in a visitor.

The man who entered was a strange and impressive figure. His slow, limping step and bowed shoulders gave the appearance of decrepitude, and yet his hard, deep-lined, craggy features, and his enormous limbs showed that he was possessed of unusual strength of body and of character. His tangled beard, grizzled hair, and outstanding, drooping eyebrows combined to give an air of dignity and power to his appearance, but his face was of an ashen white, while his lips and the corners of his nostrils were tinged with a shade of blue. It was clear to me at a glance that he was in the grip of some deadly and chronic disease.

"Pray sit down on the sofa," said Holmes gently. "You had my note?"

"Yes, the lodge-keeper brought it up. You said that you wished to see me here to avoid scandal."

"I thought people would talk if I went to the Hall."

"And why did you wish to see me?" He looked across at my companion with despair in his weary eyes, as though his question were already answered.

"Yes," said Holmes, answering the look rather than the words. "It is so. I know all about McCarthy."

The old man sank his face in his hands. "God help me!" he cried. "But I would not have let the young man come to harm. I give you my word that I would have spoken out if it went against him at the Assizes."

"I am glad to hear you say so," said Holmes gravely.

"I would have spoken now had it not been for my dear girl. It would break her heart — it will break her heart when she hears that I am arrested."

"It may not come to that," said Holmes.

"What!"

"I am no official agent. I understand that it was your daughter who required my presence here, and I am acting in her interests. Young McCarthy must be got off, however."

"I am a dying man," said old Turner. "I have had diabetes for years. My doctor says it is a question whether I shall live a month. Yet I would rather die under my own roof than in a gaol."

Holmes rose and sat down at the table with his pen in his hand and a bundle of paper before him. "Just tell us the truth," he said. "I shall jot down the facts. You will sign it, and Watson here can witness it. Then I could produce your confession at the last extremity to save young McCarthy. I promise you that I shall not use it unless it is absolutely needed."

"It's as well," said the old man; "it's a question whether I shall live to the Assizes, so it matters little to me, but I should wish to spare Alice the shock. And now I will make the thing clear to you; it has been a long time in the acting, but will not take me long to tell.

"You didn't know this dead man, McCarthy. He was a devil incarnate. I tell you that. God keep you out of the clutches of such a man as he. His grip has been upon me these twenty years, and he has blasted my life. I'll tell you first how I came to be in his power.

"It was in the early 'sixties at the diggings. I was a young chap then, hot-blooded and reckless, ready to turn my hand to anything; I got among bad companions, took to drink, had no luck with my claim, took to the bush, and, in a word, became what you would call over here a highway robber. There were six of us, and we had a wild, free life of it, sticking up a station from time to time, or stopping the wagons on the road to the diggings. Black Jack of Ballarat was the name I went under, and our party is still remembered in the colony as the Ballarat Gang.

"One day a gold convoy came down from Ballarat to Melbourne, and we lay in wait for it and attacked it. There were six troopers and six of us, so it was a close thing, but we emptied four of their saddles at the first volley. Three of our boys were killed, however, before we got the swag. I put my pistol to the head of the wagon-driver, who was this very man McCarthy. I wish to the Lord that I had shot him then, but I spared him, though I saw his wicked little eyes fixed on my face, as though to remember every feature. We got away with the gold, became wealthy men, and made our way over to England without being suspected. There I parted from my old pals, and determined to settle down to a quiet and respectable life. I bought this estate, which chanced to be in the market, and I set myself to do a little good with my money, to make up for the way in which I had earned it. I married, too, and though my wife died young, she left me my dear little Alice. Even when she was just a baby her wee hand seemed to lead me down the right path as nothing else had ever done. In a word, I turned over a new leaf, and did my best to make up for the past. All was going well when McCarthy laid his grip upon me.

"I had gone up to town about an investment, and I met him in Regent Street with hardly a coat to his back or a boot to his foot.

"'Here we are, Jack,' says he, touching me on the arm; 'we'll be as good as a family to you. There's two of us, me and my son, and you can have the keeping of us. If you don't — it's a fine, law-abiding country is England, and there's always a policeman within hail.'

"Well, down they came to the West Country, there was no shaking them off, and there they have lived rent free on my best land ever since. There was no rest for me, no peace, no forgetfulness; turn where I would, there was his cunning, grinning face at my elbow. It grew worse as Alice grew up, for he soon saw I was more afraid of her knowing my past than of the police. Whatever he wanted he must have, and whatever it was I gave him without question, land, money, houses, until at last he asked for a thing which I could not give. He asked for Alice.

"His son, you see, had grown up, and so had my girl, and as I was known to be in weak health, it seemed a fine stroke to him that his lad should step into the whole property. But there I was firm. I would not have his cursed stock mixed with mine; not that I had any dislike to the lad, but his blood was in him, and that was enough. I stood firm. McCarthy threatened. I braved him to do his worst. We were to meet at the Pool midway between our houses to talk it over.

"When I went down there I found him talking with his son, so I smoked a cigar, and waited behind a tree until he should be alone. But as I listened to his talk all that was black and bitter in me seemed to come uppermost. He was urging his son to marry my daughter with as little regard for what she might think as if she were a slut from off the streets. It drove me mad to think that I and all that I held most dear should be in the power of such a man as this. Could I not snap the bond? I was already a dying and a desperate man. Though clear of mind and fairly strong of limb, I knew that my own fate was sealed. But my memory and my girl! Both could be saved, if I could but silence that foul tongue. I did it, Mr. Holmes. I would do it again. Deeply as I have sinned, I have led a life of martyrdom to atone for it. But that my girl should be entangled in the same meshes which held me was more than I could suffer. I struck him down with no more compunction than if he had been some foul and venomous beast. His cry brought back his son; but I had gained the cover of the wood, though I was forced to go back to fetch the cloak which I had dropped in my flight. That is the true story, gentlemen, of all that occurred."

"Well, it is not for me to judge you," said Holmes, as the old man signed the statement which had been drawn out. "I pray that we may never be exposed to such a temptation."

"I pray not, sir. And what do you intend to do?"

"In view of your health, nothing. You are yourself aware that you will soon have to answer for your deed at a higher court than the Assizes. I will keep your confession, and, if McCarthy is condemned, I shall be forced to use it. If not, it shall never be seen by mortal eye; and your secret, whether you be alive or dead, shall be safe with us."

"Farewell! then," said the old man solemnly. "Your own death-beds, when they come, will be the easier for the thought of the peace which you have given to mine." Tottering and shaking in all his giant frame, he stumbled slowly from the room.

"God help us!" said Holmes, after a long silence. "Why does Fate play such tricks with poor helpless worms? I never hear of such a case as this that I do not think of Baxter's words, and say: 'There, but for the grace of God, goes Sherlock Holmes.'"

James McCarthy was acquitted at the Assizes, on the strength of a number of objections which had been drawn out by Holmes, and submitted to the defending counsel. Old Turner lived for seven months after our interview, but he is now dead; and there is every prospect that the son and daughter may come to live happily together, in ignorance of the black cloud which rests upon their past.

## AFTERWORD

Like "The Speckled Band," this story hints of the taint of English imperialism brought back to the mother country. For its suggestion of "the crimes of Empire coming home to roost in the respectable heartland," Martin Priestman aptly likens it to Wilkie Collins's novel *The Moonstone* (the prototype of another Doyle work, *The Sign of Four*) but notes Doyle's difference from Collins: now "the booty stays in the mother-country, in the redeeming hands of a new generation." Priestman also calls attention to a certain moral ambiguity in the story: "Holmes allows an innocent man to remain under suspicion of parricide so that he and his rich bride may remain 'in ignorance of the black cloud' of *her* father's record of banditry and murder" (*Detective Fiction and Literature: The Figure on the Carpet* 80).

From a different perspective, "The Boscombe Valley Mystery" interestingly anticipates the moral issues of "Charles Augustus Milverton," with an important gender inversion. In both cases Holmes takes for granted that a prospective marriage (here, James McCarthy with Alice Turner; there, Lady Eva Brackwell with the Earl of Dovercourt) is desirable but is threatened by the potential revelation of some secret from the past (McCarthy's secret supposed marriage to a Bristol barmaid; Lady Eva's "imprudent letters — imprudent, Watson, nothing worse — which were written to an impecunious young squire in the country" [p. 273]). But the gender of the potentially compromised party changes, as, very strikingly, does the kind of imprudence in question. The contrast is heightened all the more by Alice Turner's assumption that McCarthy's reluctance to woo her is the unreadiness of unseasoned youth ("of course he is young and has seen very little of life yet, and — and — well, he naturally did not wish to do anything like that yet"). For McCarthy's reluctance is in fact attributable to his unwillingness to commit bigamy — a threat from which their potential marriage is ultimately spared by McCarthy's "consol[ing]" discovery that he himself is *already* involved in bigamy (his barmaid wife, learning "that he is in serious trouble, and likely to be hanged, has thrown him over utterly and has written to him to say that she has a husband already in the Bermuda Dockyard, so that there is really no tie between them"). The two stories together bring out the double standard of Victorian morality with wonderful starkness.

## The Man with the Twisted Lip

Isa Whitney, brother of the late Elias Whitney, D.D., Principal of the Theological College of St. George's, was much addicted to opium. The habit grew upon him, as I understand, from some foolish freak when he was at college, for having read De Quincey's description of his dreams and sensations,[1] he had drenched his tobacco with laudanum in an attempt to produce the same effects. He found, as so many more have done, that the practice is easier to attain than to get rid of, and for many years he continued to be a slave to the drug, an object of mingled horror and pity to his friends and relatives. I can see him now, with yellow, pasty face, drooping lids and pin-point pupils, all huddled in a chair, the wreck and ruin of a noble man.

From *The Adventures of Sherlock Holmes* (1892). First published in the *Strand*, December 1891.
    [1] *De Quincey:* Thomas De Quincey, author of *Confessions of an English Opium-Eater* (1822).

One night — it was in June, '89 — there came a ring to my bell, about the hour when a man gives his first yawn, and glances at the clock. I sat up in my chair, and my wife laid her needlework down in her lap and made a little face of disappointment.

"A patient!" said she. "You'll have to go out."

I groaned, for I was newly come back from a weary day.

We heard the door open, a few hurried words, and then quick steps upon the linoleum. Our own door flew open, and a lady, clad in some dark-coloured stuff with a black veil, entered the room.

"You will excuse my calling so late," she began, and then, suddenly losing her self-control, she ran forward, threw her arms about my wife's neck, and sobbed upon her shoulder. "Oh! I'm in such trouble!" she cried; "I do so want a little help."

"Why," said my wife, pulling up her veil, "it is Kate Whitney. How you startled me, Kate! I had not an idea who you were when you came in."

"I didn't know what to do, so I came straight to you." That was always the way. Folk who were in grief came to my wife like birds to a lighthouse.

"It was very sweet of you to come. Now, you must have some wine and water, and sit here comfortably and tell us all about it. Or should you rather that I sent James off to bed?"

"Oh, no, no. I want the Doctor's advice and help too. It's about Isa. He has not been home for two days. I am so frightened about him!"

It was not the first time that she had spoken to us of her husband's trouble, to me as a doctor, to my wife as an old friend and school companion. We soothed and comforted her by such words as we could find. Did she know where her husband was? Was it possible that we could bring him back to her?

It seemed that it was. She had the surest information that of late he had, when the fit was on him, made use of an opium den in the furthest east of the City. Hitherto his orgies had always been confined to one day, and he had come back, twitching and shattered, in the evening. But now the spell had been upon him eight-and-forty hours, and he lay there, doubtless, among the dregs of the docks, breathing in the poison or sleeping off the effects. There he was to be found, she was sure of it, at the Bar of Gold, in Upper Swandam Lane. But what was she to do? How could she, a young and timid woman, make her way into such a place, and pluck her husband out from among the ruffians who surrounded him?

There was the case, and of course there was but one way out of it.

Might I not escort her to this place? And, then, as a second thought, why should she come at all? I was Isa Whitney's medical adviser, and as such I had influence over him. I could manage it better if I were alone. I promised her on my word that I would send him home in a cab within two hours if he were indeed at the address which she had given me. And so in ten minutes I had left my arm-chair and cheery sitting-room behind me, and was speeding eastward in a hansom on a strange errand, as it seemed to me at the time, though the future only could show how strange it was to be.

But there was no great difficulty in the first stage of my adventure. Upper Swandam Lane is a vile alley lurking behind the high wharves which line the north side of the river to the east of London Bridge. Between a slop shop[2] and a gin shop, approached by a steep flight of steps leading down to a black gap like the mouth of a cave, I found the den of which I was in search. Ordering my cab to wait, I passed down the steps, worn hollow in the centre by the ceaseless tread of drunken feet, and by the light of a flickering oil lamp above the door I found the latch and made my way into a long, low room, thick and heavy with the brown opium smoke, and terraced with wooden berths, like the forecastle of an emigrant ship.

Through the gloom one could dimly catch a glimpse of bodies lying in strange fantastic poses, bowed shoulders, bent knees, heads thrown back and chins pointing upwards, with here and there a dark, lack-lustre eye turned upon the new-comer. Out of the black shadows there glimmered little red circles of light, now bright, now faint, as the burning poison waxed or waned in the bowls of the metal pipes. The most lay silent, but some muttered to themselves, and others talked together in a strange, low, monotonous voice, their conversation coming in gushes, and then suddenly tailing off into silence, each mumbling out his own thoughts, and paying little heed to the words of his neighbour. At the further end was a small brazier of burning charcoal, beside which on a three-legged wooden stool there sat a tall, thin old man, with his jaw resting upon his two fists, and his elbows upon his knees, staring into the fire.

As I entered, a sallow Malay attendant had hurried up with a pipe for me and a supply of the drug, beckoning me to an empty berth.

"Thank you, I have not come to stay," said I. "There is a friend of mine here, Mr. Isa Whitney, and I wish to speak with him."

---

[2] *slop shop:* A cheap clothing shop; slops were loose trousers, especially those worn by sailors, or cheap, ready-made garments generally.

There was a movement and an exclamation from my right, and, peering through the gloom, I saw Whitney, pale, haggard, and unkempt, staring out at me.

"My God! It's Watson," said he. He was in a pitiable state of reaction, with every nerve in a twitter. "I say, Watson, what o'clock is it?"

"Nearly eleven."

"Of what day?"

"Of Friday, June 19."

"Good heavens! I thought it was Wednesday. It *is* Wednesday. What d'you want to frighten a chap for?" He sank his face on to his arms, and began to sob in a high treble key.

"I tell you that it is Friday, man. Your wife has been waiting this two days for you. You should be ashamed of yourself!"

"So I am. But you've got mixed, Watson, for I have only been here a few hours, three pipes, four pipes — I forget how many. But I'll go home with you. I wouldn't frighten Kate — poor little Kate. Give me your hand! Have you a cab?"

"Yes, I have one waiting."

"Then I shall go in it. But I must owe something. Find what I owe, Watson. I am all off colour. I can do nothing for myself."

I walked down the narrow passage between the double row of sleepers, holding my breath to keep out the vile, stupefying fumes of the drug, and looking about for the manager. As I passed the tall man who sat by the brazier I felt a sudden pluck at my skirt, and a low voice whispered, "Walk past me, and then look back at me." The words fell quite distinctly upon my ear. I glanced down. They could only have come from the old man at my side, and yet he sat now as absorbed as ever, very thin, very wrinkled, bent with age, an opium pipe dangling down from between his knees, as though it had dropped in sheer lassitude from his fingers. I took two steps forward and looked back. It took all my self-control to prevent me from breaking out into a cry of astonishment. He had turned his back so that none could see him but I. His form had filled out, his wrinkles were gone, the dull eyes had regained their fire, and there, sitting by the fire, and grinning at my surprise, was none other than Sherlock Holmes. He made a slight motion to me to approach him, and instantly, as he turned his face half round to the company once more, subsided into a doddering, loose-lipped senility.

"Holmes!" I whispered, "what on earth are you doing in this den?"

"As low as you can," he answered, "I have excellent ears. If you would have the great kindness to get rid of that sottish friend of yours, I should be exceedingly glad to have a little talk with you."

"I have a cab outside."

"Then pray send him home in it. You may safely trust him, for he appears to be too limp to get into any mischief. I should recommend you also to send a note by the cabman to your wife to say that you have thrown in your lot with me. If you will wait outside, I shall be with you in five minutes."

It was difficult to refuse any of Sherlock Holmes's requests, for they were always so exceedingly definite, and put forward with such an air of mastery. I felt, however, that when Whitney was once confined in the cab, my mission was practically accomplished; and for the rest, I could not wish anything better than to be associated with my friend in one of those singular adventures which were the normal condition of his existence. In a few minutes I had written my note, paid Whitney's bill, led him out to the cab, and seen him driven through the darkness. In a very short time a decrepit figure had emerged from the opium den, and I was walking down the street with Sherlock Holmes. For two streets he shuffled along with a bent back and an uncertain foot. Then, glancing quickly round, he straightened himself out and burst into a hearty fit of laughter.

"I suppose, Watson," said he, "that you imagine that I have added opium-smoking to cocaine injections and all the other little weaknesses on which you have favoured me with your medical views."

"I was certainly surprised to find you there."

"But not more so than I to find you."

"I came to find a friend."

"And I to find an enemy!"

"An enemy?"

"Yes, one of my natural enemies, or, shall I say, my natural prey. Briefly, Watson, I am in the midst of a very remarkable inquiry, and I have hoped to find a clue in the incoherent ramblings of these sots, as I have done before now. Had I been recognized in that den my life would not have been worth an hour's purchase, for I have used it before now for my own purposes, and the rascally Lascar who runs it has sworn vengeance upon me. There is a trap-door at the back of that building, near the corner of Paul's Wharf, which could tell some strange tales of what has passed through it upon the moonless nights."

"What! You do not mean bodies?"

"Aye, bodies, Watson. We should be rich men if we had a thousand pounds for every poor devil who has been done to death in that den. It is the vilest murder-trap on the whole river-side, and I fear Neville St. Clair has entered it never to leave it more. But our trap should be here!"

He put his two forefingers between his teeth and whistled shrilly, a signal which was answered by a similar whistle from the distance, followed
shortly by the rattle of wheels and the clink of horse's hoofs.

"Now, Watson," said Holmes, as a tall dog-cart[3] dashed up through
the gloom, throwing out two golden tunnels of yellow light from its
side-lanterns, "you'll come with me, won't you?"

"If I can be of use."

"Oh, a trusty comrade is always of use. And a chronicler still more
so. My room at the Cedars is a double-bedded one."

"The Cedars?"

"Yes; that is Mr. St. Clair's house. I am staying there while I conduct the inquiry."

"Where is it, then?"

"Near Lee, in Kent. We have a seven-mile drive before us."

"But I am all in the dark."

"Of course you are. You'll know all about it presently. Jump up
here! All right, John, we shall not need you. Here's half-a-crown. Look
out for me to-morrow about eleven. Give her her head! So long, then!"

He flicked the horse with his whip, and we dashed away through the
endless succession of somber and deserted streets, which widened gradually, until we were flying across a broad balustraded bridge, with the
murky river flowing sluggishly beneath us. Beyond lay another broad
wilderness of bricks and mortar, its silence broken only by the heavy,
regular footfall of the policeman, or the songs and shouts of some belated party of revellers. A dull wrack was drifting slowly across the sky,
and a star or two twinkled dimly here and there through the rifts of the
clouds. Holmes drove in silence, with his head sunk upon his breast,
and the air of a man who is lost in thought, whilst I sat beside him
curious to learn what this new quest might be which seemed to tax his
powers so sorely, and yet afraid to break in upon the current of his
thoughts. We had driven several miles, and were beginning to get to the
fringe of the belt of suburban villas, when he shook himself, shrugged
his shoulders, and lit up his pipe with the air of a man who has satisfied
himself that he is acting for the best.

"You have a grand gift of silence, Watson," said he. "It makes you
quite invaluable as a companion. 'Pon my word, it is a great thing for
me to have someone to talk to, for my own thoughts are not over-
pleasant. I was wondering what I should say to this dear little woman
to-night when she meets me at the door."

[3] *dog-cart:* A light, two-wheeled open carriage.

"You forget that I know nothing about it."

"I shall just have time to tell you the facts of the case before we get to Lee. It seems absurdly simple, and yet, somehow, I can get nothing to go upon. There's plenty of thread, no doubt, but I can't get the end of it in my hand. Now, I'll state the case clearly and concisely to you, Watson, and maybe you may see a spark where all is dark to me."

"Proceed, then."

"Some years ago — to be definite, in May, 1884 — there came to Lee a gentleman, Neville St. Clair by name, who appeared to have plenty of money. He took a large villa, laid out the grounds very nicely, and lived generally in good style. By degrees he made friends in the neighbourhood, and in 1887 he married the daughter of a local brewer, by whom he has now had two children. He had no occupation, but was interested in several companies, and went into town as a rule in the morning, returning by the 5:14 from Cannon Street every night. Mr. St. Clair is now 37 years of age, is a man of temperate habits, a good husband, a very affectionate father, and a man who is popular with all who know him. I may add that his whole debts at the present moment, as far as we have been able to ascertain, amount to £88 10s., while he has £220 standing to his credit in the Capital and Counties Bank. There is no reason, therefore, to think that money troubles have been weighing upon his mind.

"Last Monday Mr. Neville St. Clair went into town rather earlier than usual, remarking before he started that he had two important commissions to perform, and that he would bring his little boy home a box of bricks. Now, by the merest chance his wife received a telegram upon this same Monday, very shortly after his departure, to the effect that a small parcel of considerable value which she had been expecting was waiting for her at the offices of the Aberdeen Shipping Company. Now, if you are well up in your London, you will know that the office of the company is in Fresno Street, which branches out of Upper Swandam Lane, where you found me to-night. Mrs. St. Clair had her lunch, started for the City, did some shopping, proceeded to the company's office, got her packet, and found herself exactly at 4:35 walking through Swandam Lane on her way back to the station. Have you followed me so far?"

"It is very clear."

"If you remember, Monday was an exceedingly hot day, and Mrs. St. Clair walked slowly, glancing about in the hope of seeing a cab, as she did not like the neighbourhood in which she found herself. While she walked in this way down Swandam Lane she suddenly heard an ejaculation or cry, and was struck cold to see her husband looking down at her, and, as it seemed to her, beckoning to her from a second-floor window. The window was open, and she distinctly saw his face, which she describes as being terribly agitated. He waved his hands frantically to her, and then vanished from the window so suddenly that it seemed to her that he had been plucked back by some irresistible force from behind. One singular point which struck her quick feminine eye was that, although he wore some dark coat, such as he had started to town in, he had on neither collar nor necktie.

"Convinced that something was amiss with him, she rushed down the steps — for the house was none other than the opium den in which you found me to-night — and, running through the front room, she attempted to ascend the stairs which led to the first floor. At the foot of the stairs, however, she met this Lascar scoundrel, of whom I have spoken, who thrust her back, and, aided by a Dane, who acts as assistant there, pushed her out into the street. Filled with the most maddening doubts and fears, she rushed down the lane, and, by rare good fortune, met, in Fresno Street, a number of constables with an inspector, all on their way to their beat. The inspector and two men accompanied her back, and, in spite of the continued resistance of the proprietor, they made their way to the room in which Mr. St. Clair had last been seen. There was no sign of him there. In fact, in the whole of that floor there was no one to be found, save a crippled wretch of hideous aspect, who, it seems, made his home there. Both he and the Lascar stoutly swore that no one else had been in the front room during that afternoon. So determined was their denial that the inspector was staggered, and had almost come to believe that Mrs. St. Clair had been deluded when, with a cry, she sprang at a small deal box which lay upon the table, and tore the lid from it. Out there fell a cascade of children's bricks. It was the toy which he had promised to bring home.

"This discovery, and the evident confusion which the cripple showed, made the inspector realize that the matter was serious. The rooms were carefully examined, and results all pointed to an abominable crime. The front room was plainly furnished as a sitting-room, and led into a small bedroom, which looked out upon the back of one of the wharves. Between the wharf and the bedroom window is a narrow strip, which is dry at low tide, but is covered at high tide with at least four and a half feet of water. The bedroom window was a broad one, and opened from below. On examination traces of blood were to be seen upon the window-sill, and several scattered drops were visible upon the wooden floor of the bedroom. Thrust away behind a curtain in the front room were all the clothes of Mr. Neville St. Clair, with the exception of his coat. His boots, his socks, his hat, and his watch — all were there. There were no signs of violence upon any of these garments, and there were no other traces of Mr. Neville St. Clair. Out of the window he must apparently have gone, for no other exit could be discovered, and the ominous blood-stains upon the sill gave little promise that he could save himself by swimming, for the tide was at its very highest at the moment of the tragedy.

"And now as to the villains who seemed to be immediately implicated in the matter. The Lascar was known to be a man of the vilest antecedents, but as by Mrs. St. Clair's story he was known to have been at the foot of the stair within a few seconds of her husband's appearance at the window, he could hardly have been more than an accessory to the crime. His defence was one of absolute ignorance, and he protested that he had no knowledge as to the doings of Hugh Boone, his lodger, and that he could not account in any way for the presence of the missing gentleman's clothes.

"So much for the Lascar manager. Now for the sinister cripple who lives upon the second floor of the opium den, and who was certainly the last human being whose eyes rested upon Neville St. Clair. His name is Hugh Boone, and his hideous face is one which is familiar to every man who goes much to the City. He is a professional beggar, though in order to avoid the police regulations he pretends to a small trade in wax vestas. Some little distance down Threadneedle Street upon the left-hand side there is, as you may have remarked, a small angle in the wall. Here it is that the creature takes his daily seat, cross-legged, with his tiny stock of matches on his lap, and as he is a piteous spectacle a small rain of charity descends into the greasy leather cap which lies upon the pavement before him. I have watched this fellow more than once, before ever I thought of making his professional acquaintance, and I have been surprised at the harvest which he has reaped in a short time. His appearance, you see, is so remarkable that no one can pass him without observing him. A shock of orange hair, a pale face disfigured by a horrible scar, which, by its contraction, has turned up the outer edge of his upper lip, a bull-dog chin, and a pair of very penetrating dark eyes, which present a singular contrast to the colour of his hair, all mark him out from amid the common crowd of mendicants, and so, too, does his wit, for he is ever ready with a reply to any piece of chaff which may be thrown at him by the passers-by. This is the man whom we now learn to have been the lodger at the opium den, and to have been the last man to see the gentleman of whom we are in quest."

"But a cripple!" said I. "What could he have done single-handed against a man in the prime of life?"

"He is a cripple in the sense that he walks with a limp; but, in other respects, he appears to be a powerful and well-nurtured man. Surely your medical experience would tell you, Watson, that weakness in one limb is often compensated for by exceptional strength in the others."

"Pray continue your narrative."

"Mrs. St. Clair had fainted at the sight of the blood upon the window, and she was escorted home in a cab by the police, as her presence could be of no help to them in their investigations. Inspector Barton, who had charge of the case, made a very careful examination of the premises, but without finding anything which threw any light upon the matter. One mistake had been made in not arresting Boone instantly, as he was allowed some few minutes during which he might have communicated with his friend the Lascar, but this fault was soon remedied, and he was seized and searched, without anything being found which could incriminate him. There were, it is true, some bloodstains upon his right shirt-sleeve, but he pointed to his ring finger, which had been cut near the nail, and explained that the bleeding came from there, adding that he had been to the window not long before, and that the stains which had been observed there came doubtless from the same source. He denied strenuously having ever seen Mr. Neville St. Clair, and swore that the presence of the clothes in his room was as much a mystery to him as to the police. As to Mrs. St. Clair's assertion, that she had actually seen her husband at the window, he declared that she must have been either mad or dreaming. He was removed, loudly protesting, to the police station, while the inspector remained upon the premises in the hope that the ebbing tide might afford some fresh clue.

"And it did, though they hardly found upon the mud-bank what they had feared to find. It was Neville St. Clair's coat, and not Neville St. Clair, which lay uncovered as the tide receded. And what do you think they found in the pockets?"

"I cannot imagine."

"No, I don't think you will guess. Every pocket stuffed with pennies and half-pennies — four hundred and twenty-one pennies, and two hundred and seventy half-pennies. It was no wonder that it had not been swept away by the tide. But a human body is a different matter. There is a fierce eddy between the wharf and the house. It seemed likely enough that the weighted coat had remained when the stripped body had been sucked away into the river."

"But I understand that all the other clothes were found in the room. Would the body be dressed in a coat alone?"

"No, sir, but the facts might be met speciously enough. Suppose that this man Boone had thrust Neville St. Clair through the window, there is no human eye which could have seen the deed. What would he do then? It would of course instantly strike him that he must get rid of the tell-tale garments. He would seize the coat then, and be in the act of throwing it out when it would occur to him that it would swim and not sink. He has little time, for he had heard the scuffle downstairs when the wife tried to force her way up, and perhaps he has already heard from his Lascar confederate that the police are hurrying up the street. There is not an instant to be lost. He rushes to some secret hoard, where he has accumulated the fruits of his beggary, and he stuffs all the coins upon which he can lay his hands into the pockets to make sure of the coat's sinking. He throws it out, and would have done the same with the other garments had not he heard the rush of steps below, and only just had time to close the window when the police appeared."

"It certainly sounds feasible."

"Well, we will take it as a working hypothesis for want of a better. Boone, as I have told you, was arrested and taken to the station, but it could not be shown that there had ever before been anything against him. He had for years been known as a professional beggar, but his life appeared to have been a very quiet and innocent one. There the matter stands at present, and the questions which have to be solved, what Neville St. Clair was doing in the opium den, what happened to him when there, where is he now, and what Hugh Boone had to do with his disappearance, are all as far from a solution as ever. I confess that I cannot recall any case within my experience which looked at the first glance so simple, and yet which presented such difficulties."

Whilst Sherlock Holmes had been detailing this singular series of events we had been whirling through the outskirts of the great town until the last straggling houses had been left behind, and we rattled along with a country hedge upon either side of us. Just as he finished, however, we drove through two scattered villages, where a few lights still glimmered in the windows.

"We are on the outskirts of Lee," said my companion. "We have touched on three English counties in our short drive, starting in Middlesex, passing over an angle of Surrey, and ending in Kent. See that light among the trees? That is the Cedars, and beside that lamp sits a woman whose anxious ears have already, I have little doubt, caught the clink of our horse's feet."

"But why are you not conducting the case from Baker Street?" I asked.

"Because there are many inquiries which must be made out here. Mrs. St. Clair has most kindly put two rooms at my disposal, and you may rest assured that she will have nothing but a welcome for my friend and colleague. I hate to meet her, Watson, when I have no news of her husband. Here we are. Whoa, there, whoa!"

We had pulled up in front of a large villa which stood within its own grounds. A stable-boy had run out to the horse's head, and, springing down, I followed Holmes up the small, winding gravel drive which led to the house. As we approached the door flew open, and a little blonde woman stood in the opening, clad in some sort of light *mousseline-de-soie,* with a touch of fluffy pink chiffon at her neck and wrists. She stood with her figure outlined against the flood of light, one hand upon the door, one half raised in eagerness, her body slightly bent, her head and face protruded, with eager eyes and parted lips, a standing question.

"Well?" she cried, "well?" And then, seeing that there were two of us, she gave a cry of hope which sank into a groan as she saw that my companion shook his head and shrugged his shoulders.

"No good news?"

"None."

"No bad?"

"No."

"Thank God for that. But come in. You must be weary, for you have had a long day."

"This is my friend, Dr. Watson. He has been of most vital use to me in several of my cases, and a lucky chance has made it possible for me to bring him out and associate him with this investigation."

"I am delighted to see you," said she, pressing my hand warmly. "You will, I am sure, forgive anything which may be wanting in our arrangements, when you consider the blow which has come so suddenly upon us."

"My dear madam," said I, "I am an old campaigner, and if I were not, I can very well see that no apology is needed. If I can be of any assistance, either to you or to my friend here, I shall be indeed happy."

"Now, Mr. Sherlock Holmes," said the lady as we entered a well-lit dining-room, upon the table of which a cold supper had been laid out. "I should very much like to ask you one or two plain questions, to which I beg that you will give a plain answer."

"Certainly, madam."

"Do not trouble about my feelings. I am not hysterical, nor given to fainting. I simply wish to hear your real, real opinion."

"Upon what point?"

"In your heart of hearts, do you think that Neville is alive?"

Sherlock Holmes seemed to be embarrassed by the question. "Frankly now!" she repeated, standing upon the rug, and looking keenly down at him, as he leaned back in a basket chair.

"Frankly, then, madam, I do not."

"You think that he is dead?"

"I do."

"Murdered?"

"I don't say that. Perhaps."

"And on what day did he meet his death?"

"On Monday."

"Then perhaps, Mr. Holmes, you will be good enough to explain how it is that I have received this letter from him to-day?"

Sherlock Holmes sprang out of his chair as if he had been galvanized.

"What!" he roared.

"Yes, to-day." She stood smiling, holding up a little slip of paper in the air.

"May I see it?"

"Certainly."

He snatched it from her in his eagerness, and smoothing it out upon the table, he drew over the lamp, and examined it intently. I had left my chair, and was gazing at it over his shoulder. The envelope was a very coarse one, and was stamped with the Gravesend postmark, and with the date of that very day, or rather of the day before, for it was considerably after midnight.

"Coarse writing!" murmured Holmes. "Surely this is not your husband's writing, madam."

"No, but the enclosure is."

"I perceive also that whoever addressed the envelope had to go and inquire as to the address."

"How can you tell that?"

"The name, you see, is in perfectly black ink, which has dried itself. The rest is of the greyish colour which shows that blotting-paper has been used. If it had been written straight off, and then blotted, none would be of a deep black shade. This man has written the name, and there has then been a pause before he wrote the address, which can only mean that he was not familiar with it. It is, of course, a trifle, but there is nothing so important as trifles. Let us now see the letter! Ha! there has been an enclosure here!"

"Yes, there was a ring. His signet ring."

"And you are sure that this is your husband's hand?"

"One of his hands."

"One?"

"His hand when he wrote hurriedly. It is very unlike his usual writing, and yet I know it well."

Dearest, do not be frightened. All will come well. There is a huge error which it may take some little time to rectify. Wait in patience.      — Neville

"Written in pencil upon a fly-leaf of a book, octavo size, no watermark. Posted to-day in Gravesend by a man with a dirty thumb. Ha! And the flap has been gummed, if I am not very much in error, by a person who had been chewing tobacco. And you have no doubt that it is your husband's hand, madam?"

"None. Neville wrote those words."

"And they were posted to-day at Gravesend. Well, Mrs. St. Clair, the clouds lighten, though I should not venture to say that the danger is over."

"But he must be alive, Mr. Holmes."

"Unless this is a clever forgery to put us on the wrong scent. The ring, after all, proves nothing. It may have been taken from him."

"No, no; it is, it is, it is his very own writing!"

"Very well. It may, however, have been written on Monday, and only posted to-day."

"That is possible."

"If so, much may have happened between."

"Oh, you must not discourage me, Mr. Holmes. I know that all is well with him. There is so keen a sympathy between us that I should know if evil came upon him. On the very day that I saw him last he cut himself in the bedroom, and yet I in the dining-room rushed upstairs instantly with the utmost certainty that something had happened. Do you think that I would respond to such a trifle, and yet be ignorant of his death?"

"I have seen too much not to know that the impression of a woman may be more valuable than the conclusion of an analytical reasoner. And in this letter you certainly have a very strong piece of evidence to corroborate your view. But if your husband is alive and able to write letters, why should he remain away from you?"

"I cannot imagine. It is unthinkable."

"And on Monday he made no remarks before leaving you?"

"No."

"And you were surprised to see him in Swandam Lane?"

"Very much so."

"Was the window open?"

"Yes."

"Then he might have called to you?"

"He might."

"He only, as I understand, gave an inarticulate cry?"

"Yes."

"A call for help, you thought?"

"Yes. He waved his hands."

"But it might have been a cry of surprise. Astonishment at the un-expected sight of you might cause him to throw up his hands."

"It is possible."

"And you thought he was pulled back."

"He disappeared so suddenly."

"He might have leaped back. You did not see anyone else in the room?"

"No, but this horrible man confessed to having been there, and the Lascar was at the foot of the stairs."

"Quite so. Your husband, as far as you could see, had his ordinary clothes on?"

"But without his collar or tie. I distinctly saw his bare throat."

"Had he ever spoken of Swandam Lane?"

"Never."

"Had he ever shown any signs of having taken opium?"

"Never."

"Thank you, Mrs. St. Clair. Those are the principal points about which I wished to be absolutely clear. We shall now have a little supper and then retire, for we may have a very busy day to-morrow."

A large and comfortable double-bedded room had been placed at our disposal, and I was quickly between the sheets, for I was weary after my night of adventure. Sherlock Holmes was a man, however, who when he had an unsolved problem upon his mind would go for days, and even for a week, without rest, turning it over, rearranging his facts, looking at it from every point of view, until he had either fathomed it, or convinced himself that his data were insufficient. It was soon evident to me that he was now preparing for an all-night sitting. He took off his coat and waistcoat, put on a large blue dressing-gown, and then wandered about the room collecting pillows from his bed, and cushions from the sofa and arm-chairs. With these he constructed a sort of Eastern divan, upon which he perched himself cross-legged, with an ounce of shag tobacco and a box of matches laid out in front of him. In the dim light of the lamp I saw him sitting there, an old brier pipe between his lips, his eyes fixed vacantly upon the corner of the ceiling, the blue smoke curling up from him, silent, motionless, with the light shining upon his strong-set aquiline features. So he sat as I dropped off to sleep, and so he sat when a sudden ejaculation caused me to wake up, and I found the summer sun shining into the apartment. The pipe was still between his lips, the smoke still curled upwards, and the room was full of a dense tobacco haze, but nothing remained of the heap of shag which I had seen upon the previous night.

"Awake, Watson?" he asked.

"Yes."

"Game for a morning drive?"

"Certainly."

"Then dress. No one is stirring yet, but I know where the stable-boy sleeps, and we shall soon have the trap out." He chuckled to himself as he spoke, his eyes twinkled, and he seemed a different man to the sombre thinker of the previous night.

As I dressed I glanced at my watch. It was no wonder that no one was stirring. It was twenty-five minutes past four. I had hardly finished when Holmes returned with the news that the boy was putting in the horse.

"I want to test a little theory of mine," said he, pulling on his boots. "I think, Watson, that you are now standing in the presence of one of the most absolute fools in Europe. I deserve to be kicked from here to Charing Cross. But I think I have the key of the affair now."

"And where is it?" I asked, smiling.

"In the bath-room," he answered. "Oh, yes, I am not joking," he continued, seeing my look of incredulity. "I have just been there, and I have taken it out, and I have got it in this Gladstone bag. Come on, my boy, and we shall see whether it will not fit the lock."

We made our way downstairs as quickly as possible; and out into the bright morning sunshine. In the road stood our horse and trap, with the half-clad stable-boy waiting at the head. We both sprang in, and away we dashed down the London road. A few country carts were stirring, bearing in vegetables to the metropolis, but the lines of villas on either side were as silent and lifeless as some city in a dream.

"It has been in some points a singular case," said Holmes, flicking the horse on into a gallop. "I confess that I have been as blind as a mole, but it is better to learn wisdom late, than never to learn it at all."

In town, the earliest risers were just beginning to look sleepily from their windows as we drove through the streets of the Surrey side. Passing down the Waterloo Bridge Road we crossed over the river, and dashing up Wellington Street wheeled sharply to the right, and found ourselves in Bow Street. Sherlock Holmes was well known to the Force, and the two constables at the door saluted him. One of them held the horse's head while the other led us in.

"Who is on duty?" asked Holmes.

"Inspector Bradstreet, sir."

"Ah, Bradstreet, how are you?" A tall, stout official had come down the stone-flagged passage, in a peaked cap and frogged jacket. "I wish to have a word with you, Bradstreet."

"Certainly, Mr. Holmes. Step into my room here."

It was a small office-like room, with a huge ledger upon the table, and a telephone projecting from the wall. The inspector sat down at his desk.

"What can I do for you, Mr. Holmes?"

"I called about that beggar-man, Boone — the one who was charged with being concerned in the disappearance of Mr. Neville St. Clair, of Lee."

"Yes. He was brought up and remanded for further inquiries."

"So I heard. You have him here?"

"In the cells."

"Is he quiet?"

"Oh, he gives no trouble. But he is a dirty scoundrel."

"Dirty?"

"Yes, it is all we can do to make him wash his hands, and his face is as black as a tinker's. Well, when once his case has been settled he will have a regular prison bath; and I think, if you saw him, you would agree with me that he needed it."

"I should like to see him very much."

"Would you? That is easily done. Come this way. You can leave your bag."

"No, I think I'll take it."

"Very good. Come this way, if you please." He led us down a passage, opened a barred door, passed down a winding stair, and brought us to a whitewashed corridor with a line of doors on each side.

"The third on the right is his," said the inspector. "Here it is!" He quietly shot back a panel in the upper part of the door, and glanced through.

"He is asleep," said he. "You can see him very well."

We both put our eyes to the grating. The prisoner lay with his face towards us, in a very deep sleep, breathing slowly and heavily. He was a middle-sized man, coarsely clad as became his calling, with a coloured shirt protruding through the rent in his tattered coat. He was, as the inspector had said, extremely dirty, but the grime which covered his face could not conceal its repulsive ugliness. A broad weal from an old scar ran across it from eye to chin, and by its contraction had turned up one side of the upper lip, so that three teeth were exposed in a perpetual snarl. A shock of very bright red hair grew low over his eyes and forehead.

"He's a beauty, isn't he?" said the inspector.

"He certainly needs a wash," remarked Holmes. "I had an idea that he might, and I took the liberty of bringing the tools with me." He opened his Gladstone bag as he spoke, and took out, to my astonishment, a very large bath sponge.

"He! he! You are a funny one," chuckled the inspector.

"Now, if you will have the great goodness to open that door very quietly, we will soon make him cut a much more respectable figure."

"Well, I don't know why not," said the inspector. "He doesn't look a credit to the Bow Street cells, does he?" He slipped his key into the lock, and we all very quietly entered the cell. The sleeper half turned, and then settled down once more into a deep slumber. Holmes stooped to the water jug, moistened his sponge, and then rubbed it twice vigorously across and down the prisoner's face.

"Let me introduce you," he shouted, "to Mr. Neville St. Clair, of Lee, in the county of Kent."

Never in my life have I seen such a sight. The man's face peeled off under the sponge like the bark from a tree. Gone was the coarse brown tint! Gone, too, the horrid scar which had seamed it across, and the twisted lip which had given the repulsive sneer to the face! A twitch brought away the tangled red hair, and there, sitting up in his bed, was a pale, sad-faced, refined-looking man, black-haired and smooth-skinned, rubbing his eyes, and staring about him with sleepy bewilderment. Then suddenly realizing the exposure, he broke into a scream, and threw himself down with his face to the pillow.

"Great heaven!" cried the inspector, "it is, indeed, the missing man. I know him from the photograph."

The prisoner turned with the reckless air of a man who abandons himself to his destiny. "Be it so," said he. "And pray what am I charged with?"

"With making away with Mr. Neville St. —— Oh, come, you can't be charged with that, unless they make a case of attempted suicide of it," said the inspector, with a grin. "Well, I have been twenty-seven years in the Force, but this really takes the cake."

"If I am Mr. Neville St. Clair, then it is obvious that no crime has been committed, and that, therefore, I am illegally detained."

"No crime, but a very great error has been committed," said Holmes. "You would have done better to have trusted your wife."

"It was not the wife, it was the children," groaned the prisoner. "God help me, I would not have them ashamed of their father. My God! What an exposure! What can I do?"

Sherlock Holmes sat down beside him on the couch, and patted him kindly on the shoulder.

"If you leave it to a court of law to clear the matter up," said he, "of course you can hardly avoid publicity. On the other hand, if you convince the police authorities that there is no possible case against you, I do not know that there is any reason that the details should find their way into the papers. Inspector Bradstreet would, I am sure, make notes upon anything which you might tell us, and submit it to the proper authorities. The case would then never go into court at all."

"God bless you!" cried the prisoner passionately. "I would have endured imprisonment, aye, even execution, rather than have left my miserable secret as a family blot to my children.

"You are the first who have ever heard my story. My father was a schoolmaster in Chesterfield, where I received an excellent education. I travelled in my youth, took to the stage, and finally became a reporter on an evening paper in London. One day my editor wished to have a series of articles upon begging in the metropolis, and I volunteered to supply them. There was the point from which all my adventures started. It was only by trying begging as an amateur that I could get the facts upon which to base my articles. When an actor I had, of course, learned all the secrets of making up, and had been famous in the green-room for my skill. I took advantage now of my attainments. I painted my face, and to make myself as pitiable as possible I made a good scar and fixed one side of my lip in a twist by the aid of a small slip of flesh-coloured plaster. Then with a red head of hair, and an appropriate dress, I took my station in the busiest part of the City, ostensibly as a match-seller, but really as a beggar. For seven hours I plied my trade, and when I returned home in the evening I found, to my surprise, that I had received no less than twenty-six shillings and fourpence.

"I wrote my articles, and thought little more of the matter until, some time later, I backed a bill for a friend, and had a writ served upon me for £25. I was at my wits' end where to get the money, but a sudden idea came to me. I begged a fortnight's grace from the creditor, asked for a holiday from my employers, and spent the time in begging in the City under my disguise. In ten days I had the money, and had paid the debt.

"Well, you can imagine how hard it was to settle down to arduous work at two pounds a week, when I knew that I could earn as much in a day by smearing my face with a little paint, laying my cap on the ground, and sitting still. It was a long fight between my pride and the money, but the dollars won at last, and I threw up reporting, and sat day after day in the corner which I had first chosen, inspiring pity by my ghastly face and filling my pockets with coppers. Only one man knew my secret. He was the keeper of a low den in which I used to lodge in Swandam Lane, where I could every morning emerge as a squalid beggar, and in the evenings transform myself into a well-dressed man about town. This fellow, a Lascar, was well paid by me for his rooms, so that I knew that my secret was safe in his possession.

"Well, very soon I found that I was saving considerable sums of money. I do not mean that any beggar in the streets of London could earn seven hundred pounds a year — which is less than my average takings — but I had exceptional advantages in my power of making up, and also in a facility in repartee, which improved by practice, and made me quite a recognized character in the City. All day a stream of pennies, varied by silver, poured in upon me, and it was a very bad day upon which I failed to take two pounds.

"As I grew richer I grew more ambitious, took a house in the country, and eventually married, without anyone having a suspicion as to my real occupation. My dear wife knew that I had business in the City. She little knew what.

"Last Monday I had finished for the day, and was dressing in my room above the opium den, when I looked out of the window, and saw, to my horror and astonishment, that my wife was standing in the street, with her eyes fixed full upon me. I gave a cry of surprise, threw up my arms to cover my face, and rushing to my confidant, the Lascar, entreated him to prevent anyone from coming up to me. I heard her voice downstairs, but I knew that she could not ascend. Swiftly I threw off my clothes, pulled on those of a beggar, and put on my pigments and wig. Even a wife's eyes could not pierce so complete a disguise. But then it occurred to me that there might be a search in the room and that the clothes might betray me. I threw open the window, re-opening by my

violence a small cut which I had inflicted upon myself in the bedroom that morning. Then I seized my coat, which was weighted by
the coppers which I had just transferred to it from the leather bag in
which I carried my takings. I hurled it out of the window, and it
disappeared into the Thames. The other clothes would have followed, but at that moment there was a rush of constables up the
stairs, and a few minutes after I found, rather, I confess, to my relief,
that instead of being identified as Mr. Neville St. Clair, I was arrested
as his murderer.

"I do not know that there is anything else for me to explain. I was
determined to preserve my disguise as long as possible, and hence my
preference for a dirty face. Knowing that my wife would be terribly anxious, I slipped off my ring, and confided it to the Lascar at a moment
when no constable was watching me, together with a hurried scrawl,
telling her that she had no cause to fear."

"That note only reached her yesterday," said Holmes.

"Good God! What a week she must have spent."

"The police have watched this Lascar," said Inspector Bradstreet,
"and I can quite understand that he might find it difficult to post a letter
unobserved. Probably he handed it to some sailor customer of his, who
forgot all about it for some days."

"That was it," said Holmes, nodding approvingly, "I have no doubt
of it. But have you never been prosecuted for begging?"

"Many times; but what was a fine to me?"

"It must stop here, however," said Bradstreet. "If the police are to
hush this thing up, there must be no more of Hugh Boone."

"I have sworn it by the most solemn oaths which a man can take."

"In that case I think that it is probable that no further steps may be
taken. But if you are found again, then all must come out. I am sure,
Mr. Holmes, that we are very much indebted to you for having cleared
the matter up. I wish I knew how you reach your results."

"I reached this one," said my friend, "by sitting upon five pillows
and consuming an ounce of shag. I think, Watson, that if we drive to
Baker Street we shall just be in time for breakfast."

## AFTERWORD

Stephen Knight has suggested that in this story Doyle is "dramatis-
ing his dislike of the Holmes phenomenon": "A respectable writer, for
the sake of gaining large sums of money in a way he has accidentally
discovered, degrades himself and takes profits made in the street from

City workers" (*Form and Ideology in Crime Fiction* 97–98). The opening, recounting Watson's chance meeting with Holmes in an opium den, sets up the story to come with wonderful economy. Watson's mission of charity and mercy (he has gone there to retrieve and send home an addicted friend) parallels Holmes's work ("You are a benefactor of the race," Watson tells Holmes at the conclusion of "The Red-headed League"); the surprise meeting and recognition parallels Mrs. St. Clair's chance discovery of her husband at the same place. Holmes is able to rescue Neville St. Clair from an ignominious life and reform him; Isa Whitney, however, has actually become what St. Clair fears to be, "an object of mingled horror and pity to his friends and relatives," and has apparently slid beyond reform.

When Holmes, on the point of entering the cell of the "dirty scoundrel" Boone with a bath-sponge, offers to "make him cut a much more respectable figure," the inspector is ready enough to have his prisoner, who "doesn't look a credit to the Bow Street cells," cleaned up a bit in advance of a "regular prison bath." But Holmes makes Boone literally respectable by scrubbing his "repulsive" face from the countenance of another social class entirely: beneath the sponge appears not merely a cleaner man but a "refined-looking one," who wakes from his beggar's sleep as if metamorphosed (his "face peeled off under the sponge like the bark from a tree") from a lower order of nature.

# The Blue Carbuncle

I had called upon my friend Sherlock Holmes upon the second morning after Christmas, with the intention of wishing him the compliments of the season. He was lounging upon the sofa in a purple dressing-gown, a pipe-rack within his reach upon the right, and a pile of crumpled morning papers, evidently newly studied, near at hand. Beside the couch was a wooden chair, and on the angle of the back hung a very seedy and disreputable hard felt hat, much the worse for wear, and cracked in several places. A lens and a forceps lying upon the seat of the chair suggested that the hat had been suspended in this manner for the purpose of examination.

From *The Adventures of Sherlock Holmes* (1892). First appeared in the *Strand*, January 1892.

"You are engaged," said I; "perhaps I interrupt you."

"Not at all. I am glad to have a friend with whom I can discuss my results. The matter is a perfectly trivial one" (he jerked his thumb in the direction of the old hat), "but there are points in connection with it which are not entirely devoid of interest, and even of instruction."

I seated myself in his arm-chair, and warmed my hands before his crackling fire, for a sharp frost had set in, and the windows were thick with the ice crystals. "I suppose," I remarked, "that, homely as it looks, this thing has some deadly story linked on to it — that it is the clue which will guide you in the solution of some mystery, and the punishment of some crime."

"No, no. No crime," said Sherlock Holmes, laughing. "Only one of those whimsical little incidents which will happen when you have four million human beings all jostling each other within the space of a few square miles. Amid the action and reaction of so dense a swarm of humanity, every possible combination of events may be expected to take place, and many a little problem will be presented which may be striking and bizarre without being criminal. We have already had experience of such."

"So much so," I remarked, "that, of the last six cases which I have added to my notes, three have been entirely free of any legal crime."

"Precisely. You allude to my attempt to recover the Irene Adler papers, to the singular case of Miss Mary Sutherland, and to the adventure of the man with the twisted lip. Well, I have no doubt that this small matter will fall into the same innocent category. You know Peterson, the commissionaire?"[1]

"Yes."

"It is to him that this trophy belongs."

"It is his hat."

"No, no; he found it. Its owner is unknown. I beg that you will look upon it, not as a battered billycock, but as an intellectual problem. And, first as to how it came here. It arrived upon Christmas morning, in company with a good fat goose, which is, I have no doubt, roasting at this moment in front of Peterson's fire. The facts are these. About four o'clock on Christmas morning, Peterson, who, as you know, is a very honest fellow, was returning from some small jollification, and was making his way homewards down Tottenham Court Road. In front of him

---

[1] *commissionaire:* A member of the Corps of Commissionaires, an association of pensioned soldiers, grandly uniformed, who worked as messengers, porters, and odd-job men.

he saw, in the gaslight, a tallish man, walking with a slight stagger, and carrying a white goose slung over his shoulder. As he reached the corner of Goodge Street a row broke out between this stranger and a little knot of roughs. One of the latter knocked off the man's hat, on which he raised his stick to defend himself, and, swinging it over his head, smashed the shop window behind him. Peterson had rushed forward to protect the stranger from his assailants, but the man, shocked at having broken the window and seeing an official-looking person in uniform rushing towards him, dropped his goose, took to his heels, and vanished amid the labyrinth of small streets which lie at the back of Tottenham Court Road. The roughs had also fled at the appearance of Peterson, so that he was left in possession of the field of battle, and also of the spoils of victory in the shape of this battered hat and a most unimpeachable Christmas goose."

"Which surely he restored to their owner?"

"My dear fellow, there lies the problem. It is true that 'For Mrs. Henry Baker' was printed upon a small card which was tied to the bird's left leg, and it is also true that the initials 'H.B.' are legible upon the lining of this hat; but, as there are some thousands of Bakers, and some hundreds of Henry Bakers in this city of ours, it is not easy to restore lost property to any one of them."

"What, then, did Peterson do?"

"He brought round both hat and goose to me on Christmas morning, knowing that even the smallest problems are of interest to me. The goose we retained until this morning, when there were signs that, in spite of the slight frost, it would be well that it should be eaten without unnecessary delay. Its finder has carried it off therefore to fulfill the ultimate destiny of a goose, while I continue to retain the hat of the unknown gentleman who lost his Christmas dinner."

"Did he not advertise?"

"No."

"Then, what clue could you have as to his identity?"

"Only as much as we can deduce."

"From his hat?"

"Precisely."

"But you are joking. What can you gather from this old battered felt?"

"Here is my lens. You know my methods. What can you gather yourself as to the individuality of the man who has worn this article?"

I took the tattered object in my hands, and turned it over rather ruefully. It was a very ordinary black hat of the usual round shape, hard and much the worse for wear. The lining had been of red silk, but was a good deal discoloured. There was no maker's name; but, as Holmes had remarked, the initials "H.B." were scrawled upon one side. It was pierced in the brim for a hat-securer, but the elastic was missing. For the rest, it was cracked, exceedingly dusty, and spotted in several places, although there seemed to have been some attempt to hide the discoloured patches by smearing them with ink.

"I can see nothing," said I, handing it back to my friend.

"On the contrary, Watson, you can see everything. You fail, however, to reason from what you see. You are too timid in drawing your inferences."

"Then, pray tell me what it is that you can infer from this hat?"

He picked it up, and gazed at it in the peculiar introspective fashion which was characteristic of him. "It is perhaps less suggestive than it might have been," he remarked, "and yet there are a few inferences which are very distinct, and a few others which represent at least a strong balance of probability. That the man was highly intellectual is of course obvious upon the face of it, and also that he was fairly well-to-do within the last three years, although he has now fallen upon evil days. He had foresight, but has less now than formerly, pointing to a moral retrogression, which, when taken with the decline of his fortunes, seems to indicate some evil influence, probably drink, at work upon him. This may account also for the obvious fact that his wife has ceased to love him."

"My dear Holmes!"

"He has, however, retained some degree of self-respect," he continued, disregarding my remonstrance. "He is a man who leads a sedentary life, goes out little, is out of training entirely, is middle-aged, has grizzled hair which he has had cut within the last few days, and which he anoints with lime-cream. These are the more patent facts which are to be deduced from his hat. Also, by the way, that it is extremely improbable that he has gas laid on in his house."

"You are certainly joking, Holmes."

"Not in the least. Is it possible that even now when I give you these results you are unable to see how they are attained?"

"I have no doubt that I am very stupid; but I must confess that I am unable to follow you. For example, how did you deduce that this man was intellectual?"

For answer Holmes clapped the hat upon his head. It came right over the forehead and settled upon the bridge of his nose. "It is a question of cubic capacity," said he: "a man with so large a brain must have something in it."

"The decline of his fortunes, then?"

"This hat is three years old. These flat brims curled at the edge came in then. It is a hat of the very best quality. Look at the band of ribbed silk, and the excellent lining. If this man could afford to buy so expensive a hat three years ago, and has had no hat since, then he has assuredly gone down in the world."

"Well, that is clear enough, certainly. But how about the foresight, and the moral retrogression?"

Sherlock Holmes laughed. "Here is the foresight," said he, putting his finger upon the little disc and loop of the hat-securer. "They are never sold upon hats. If this man ordered one, it is a sign of a certain amount of foresight, since he went out of his way to take this precaution against the wind. But since we see that he has broken the elastic, and has not troubled to replace it, it is obvious that he has less foresight now than formerly, which is a distinct proof of a weakening nature. On the other hand, he has endeavoured to conceal some of these stains upon the felt by daubing them with ink, which is a sign that he has not entirely lost his self-respect."

"Your reasoning is certainly plausible."

"The further points, that he is middle-aged, that his hair is grizzled, that it has been recently cut, and that he uses lime-cream, are all to be gathered from a close examination of the lower part of the lining. The lens discloses a large number of hair-ends, clean cut by the scissors of the barber. They all appear to be adhesive, and there is a distinct odour of lime-cream. This dust, you will observe, is not the gritty, grey dust of the street, but the fluffy brown dust of the house, showing that it has been hung up indoors most of the time; while the marks of moisture upon the inside are proof positive that the wearer perspired very freely, and could, therefore, hardly be in the best of training."

"But his wife — you said that she had ceased to love him."

"This hat has not been brushed for weeks. When I see you, my dear Watson, with a week's accumulation of dust upon your hat, and when your wife allows you to go out in such a state, I shall fear that you also have been unfortunate enough to lose your wife's affection."

"But he might be a bachelor."

"Nay, he was bringing home the goose as a peace-offering to his wife. Remember the card upon the bird's leg."

"You have an answer to everything. But how on earth do you deduce that the gas is not laid on in the house?"

"One tallow stain, or even two, might come by chance; but, when I see no less than five, I think that there can be little doubt that the individual must be brought into frequent contact with burning tallow — walks upstairs at night probably with his hat in one hand and a guttering candle in the other. Anyhow, he never got tallow stains from a gas jet. Are you satisfied?"

"Well, it is very ingenious," said I, laughing; "but since, as you said just now, there has been no crime committed, and no harm done save the loss of a goose, all this seems to be rather a waste of energy."

Sherlock Holmes had opened his mouth to reply, when the door flew open, and Peterson the commissionaire rushed into the compartment with flushed cheeks and the face of a man who is dazed with astonishment.

"The goose, Mr. Holmes! The goose, sir!" he gasped.

"Eh! What of it, then? Has it returned to life, and flapped off through the kitchen window?" Holmes twisted himself round upon the sofa to get a fairer view of the man's excited face.

"See here, sir! See what my wife found in its crop!" He held out his hand, and displayed upon the centre of the palm a brilliantly scintillating blue stone, rather smaller than a bean in size, but of such purity and radiance that it twinkled like an electric point in the dark hollow of his hand.

Sherlock Holmes sat up with a whistle. "By Jove, Peterson," said he, "this is treasure-trove indeed! I suppose you know what you have got?"

"A diamond, sir! A precious stone! It cuts into glass as though it were putty."

"It's more than a precious stone. It's *the* precious stone."

"Not the Countess of Morcar's blue carbuncle?" I ejaculated.

"Precisely so. I ought to know its size and shape, seeing that I have read the advertisement about it in *The Times* every day lately. It is absolutely unique, and its value can only be conjectured, but the reward offered of a thousand pounds is certainly not within a twentieth part of the market price."

"A thousand pounds! Great Lord of mercy!" The commissionaire plumped down into a chair, and stared from one to the other of us.

"That is the reward, and I have reason to know that there are sentimental considerations in the background which would induce the Countess to part with half of her fortune if she could but recover the gem."

"It was lost, if I remember aright, at the Hotel Cosmopolitan," I remarked.

"Precisely so, on the twenty-second of December, just five days ago.

John Horner, a plumber, was accused of having abstracted it from the lady's jewel-case. The evidence against him was so strong that the case has been referred to the Assizes. I have some account of the matter here, I believe." He rummaged amid his newspapers, glancing over the dates, until at last he smoothed one out, doubled it over, and read the following paragraph:

Hotel Cosmopolitan Jewel Robbery. John Horner, 26, plumber, was brought up upon the charge of having upon the 22nd inst., abstracted from the jewel-case of the Countess of Morcar the valuable gem known as the blue carbuncle. James Ryder, upper-attendant at the hotel, gave his evidence to the effect that he had shown Horner up to the dressing-room of the Countess of Morcar upon the day of the robbery, in order that he might solder the second bar of the grate, which was loose. He had remained with Horner some little time but had finally been called away. On returning he found that Horner had disappeared, that the bureau had been forced open, and that the small morocco casket in which, as it afterwards transpired, the Countess was accustomed to keep her jewel, was lying empty upon the dressing-table. Ryder instantly gave the alarm, and Horner was arrested the same evening; but the stone could not be found either upon his person or in his rooms. Catherine Cusack, maid to the Countess, deposed to having heard Ryder's cry of dismay on discovering the robbery, and to having rushed into the room, where she found matters were as described by the last witness. Inspector Bradstreet, B Division, gave evidence as to the arrest of Horner, who struggled frantically, and protested his innocence in the strongest terms. Evidence of a previous conviction for robbery having been given against the prisoner, the magistrate refused to deal summarily with the offence, but referred it to the Assizes. Horner, who had shown signs of intense emotion during the proceedings, fainted away at the conclusion, and was carried out of court.

"Hum! So much for the police-court," said Holmes thoughtfully, tossing aside his paper. "The question for us now to solve is the sequence of events leading from a rifled jewel-case at one end to the crop of a goose in Tottenham Court Road at the other. You see, Watson, our little deductions have suddenly assumed a much more important and less innocent aspect. Here is the stone; the stone came from the goose, and the goose came from Mr. Henry Baker, the gentleman with the bad hat and all the other characteristics with which I have bored you. So now we must set ourselves very seriously to finding this gentleman, and ascertaining what part he has played in this little mystery. To do this, we must try the simplest means first, and these lie undoubtedly in an advertisement in all the evening papers. If this fail, I shall have recourse to other methods."

"What will you say?"

"Give me a pencil, and that slip of paper. Now, then: 'Found at the corner of Goodge Street, a goose and a black felt hat. Mr. Henry Baker can have the same by applying at 6:30 this evening at 221B Baker Street.' That is clear and concise."

"Very. But will he see it?"

"Well, he is sure to keep an eye on the papers, since, to a poor man, the loss was a heavy one. He was clearly so scared by his mischance in breaking the window, and by the approach of Peterson, that he thought of nothing but flight; but since then he must have bitterly regretted the impulse which caused him to drop his bird. Then, again, the introduction of his name will cause him to see it, for every one who knows him will direct his attention to it. Here you are, Peterson, run down to the advertising agency, and have this put in the evening papers."

"In which, sir?"

"Oh, in the *Globe, Star, Pall Mall, St. James's Gazette, Evening News, Standard, Echo,* and any others that occur to you"

"Very well, sir. And this stone?"

"Ah, yes, I shall keep the stone. Thank you. And, I say, Peterson, just buy a goose on your way back, and leave it here with me, for we must have one to give to this gentleman in place of the one which your family is now devouring."

When the commissionaire had gone, Holmes took up the stone and held it against the light. "It's a bonny thing," said he. "Just see how it glints and sparkles. Of course it is a nucleus and focus of crime. Every good stone is. They are the devil's pet baits. In the larger and older jewels every facet may stand for a bloody deed. This stone is not yet twenty years old. It was found in the banks of the Amoy River in Southern China, and is remarkable in having every characteristic of the carbuncle, save that it is blue in shade, instead of ruby red. In spite of its youth, it has already a sinister history. There have been two murders, a vitriol-throwing, a suicide, and several robberies brought about for the sake of this forty-grain weight of crystallized charcoal. Who would think that so pretty a toy would be a purveyor to the gallows and the prison? I'll lock it up in my strong-box now, and drop a line to the Countess to say that we have it."

"Do you think this man Horner is innocent?"

"I cannot tell."

"Well, then, do you imagine that this other one, Henry Baker, had anything to do with the matter?"

"It is, I think, much more likely that Henry Baker is an absolutely innocent man, who had no idea that the bird which he was carrying was of considerably more value than if it were made of solid gold. That, however, I shall determine by a very simple test, if we have an answer to our advertisement."

"And you can do nothing until then?"

"Nothing."

"In that case I shall continue my professional round. But I shall come back in the evening at the hour you have mentioned, for I should like to see the solution of so tangled a business."

"Very glad to see you. I dine at seven. There is a woodcock, I believe. By the way, in view of recent occurrences, perhaps I ought to ask Mrs. Hudson to examine its crop."

I had been delayed at a case, and it was a little after half-past six when I found myself in Baker Street once more. As I approached the house I saw a tall man in a Scotch bonnet, with a coat which was buttoned up to his chin, waiting outside in the bright semicircle which was thrown from the fanlight. Just as I arrived, the door was opened, and we were shown up together to Holmes's room.

"Mr. Henry Baker, I believe," said he, rising from his arm-chair, and greeting his visitor with the easy air of geniality which he could so readily assume. "Pray take this chair by the fire, Mr. Baker. It is a cold night, and I observe that your circulation is more adapted for summer than for winter. Ah, Watson, you have just come at the right time. Is that your hat, Mr. Baker?"

"Yes, sir, that is undoubtedly my hat."

He was a large man, with rounded shoulders, a massive head, and a broad, intelligent face, sloping down to a pointed beard of grizzled brown. A touch of red in nose and cheeks, with a slight tremor of his extended hand, recalled Holmes's surmise as to his habits. His rusty black frock-coat was buttoned right up in front, with the collar turned up, and his lank wrists protruded from his sleeves without a sign of cuff or shirt. He spoke in a low staccato fashion, choosing his words with care, and gave the impression generally of a man of learning and letters who had had ill-usage at the hands of fortune.

"We have retained these things for some days," said Holmes, "because we expected to see an advertisement from you giving your address. I am at a loss to know now why you did not advertise."

Our visitor gave a rather shamefaced laugh. "Shillings have not been so plentiful with me as they once were," he remarked. "I had no doubt that the gang of roughs who assaulted me had carried off both my hat and the bird. I did not care to spend more money in a hopeless attempt at recovering them."

"Very naturally. By the way, about the bird — we were compelled to eat it."

"To eat it!" Our visitor half rose from his chair in his excitement.

"Yes; it would have been no use to anyone had we not done so. But I presume that this other goose upon the sideboard, which is about the same weight and perfectly fresh, will answer your purpose equally well?"

"Oh, certainly, certainly!" answered Mr. Baker, with a sigh of relief.

"Of course, we still have the feathers, legs, crop, and so on of your own bird, if you so wish —— "

The man burst into a hearty laugh. "They might be useful to me as relics of my adventure," said he, "but beyond that I can hardly see what use the *disjecta membra* of my late acquaintance are going to be to me. No, sir, I think that, with your permission, I will confine my attentions to the excellent bird which I perceive upon the sideboard."

Sherlock Holmes glanced sharply across at me with a slight shrug of his shoulders.

"There is your hat, then, and there your bird," said he. "By the way, would it bore you to tell me where you got the other one from? I am somewhat of a fowl fancier, and I have seldom seen a better-grown goose."

"Certainly, sir," said Baker, who had risen and tucked his newly gained property under his arm. "There are a few of us who frequent the Alpha Inn near the Museum — we are to be found in the Museum itself during the day, you understand. This year our good host, Windigate by name, instituted a goose-club, by which, on consideration of some few pence every week, we were to receive a bird at Christmas. My pence were duly paid, and the rest is familiar to you. I am much indebted to you, sir, for a Scotch bonnet is fitted neither to my years nor my gravity." With a comical pomposity of manner he bowed solemnly to both of us, and strode off upon his way.

"So much for Mr. Henry Baker," said Holmes, when he had closed the door behind him. "It is quite certain that he knows nothing whatever about the matter. Are you hungry, Watson?"

"Not particularly."

"Then I suggest that we turn our dinner into a supper, and follow up this clue while it is still hot."

"By all means."

It was a bitter night, so we drew on our ulsters and wrapped cravats about our throats. Outside, the stars were shining coldly in a cloudless sky, and the breath of the passers-by blew out into smoke like so many pistol shots. Our footfalls rang out crisply and loudly as we swung through the doctors' quarter, Wimpole Street, Harley Street, and so through Wigmore Street into Oxford Street. In a quarter of an hour we were in Bloomsbury at the Alpha Inn, which is a small public-house at the corner of one of the streets which runs down into Holborn. Holmes pushed open the door of the private bar, and ordered two glasses of beer from the ruddy-faced, white-aproned landlord.

"Your beer should be excellent if it is as good as your geese," he said.

"My geese!" The man seemed surprised.

"Yes. I was speaking only half an hour ago to Mr. Henry Baker, who was a member of your goose-club."

"Ah! yes, I see. But you see, sir, them's not *our* geese."

"Indeed! Whose, then?"

"Well, I get the two dozen from a salesman in Covent Garden."

"Indeed! I know some of them. Which was it?"

"Breckinridge is his name."

"Ah! I don't know him. Well, here's your good health, landlord, and prosperity to your house. Good night."

"Now for Mr. Breckinridge," he continued, buttoning up his coat, as we came out into the frosty air. "Remember, Watson, that though we have so homely a thing as a goose at one end of this chain, we have at the other a man who will certainly get seven years' penal servitude, unless we can establish his innocence. It is possible that our inquiry may but confirm his guilt; but, in any case, we have a line of investigation which has been missed by the police, and which a singular chance has placed in our hands. Let us follow it out to the bitter end. Faces to the south, then, and quick march!"

We passed across Holborn, down Endell Street, and so through a zigzag of slums to Covent Garden Market. One of the largest stalls bore the name of Breckinridge upon it, and the proprietor, a horsy-looking man, with a sharp face and trim side-whiskers, was helping a boy to put up the shutters.

"Good evening. It's a cold night," said Holmes.

The salesman nodded, and shot a questioning glance at my companion.

"Sold out of geese, I see," continued Holmes, pointing at the bare slabs of marble.

"Let you have five hundred to-morrow morning."

"That's no good."

"Well, there are some on the stall with the gas flare."

"Ah, but I was recommended to you."

"Who by?"

"The landlord of the Alpha."

"Ah, yes; I sent him a couple of dozen."

"Fine birds they were, too. Now where did you get them from?"

To my surprise the question provoked a burst of anger from the salesman.

"Now then, mister," said he, with his head cocked and his arms akimbo, "what are you driving at? Let's have it straight, now."

"It is straight enough. I should like to know who sold you the geese which you supplied to the Alpha."

"Well, then, I shan't tell you. So now!"

"Oh, it is a matter of no importance; but I don't know why you should be so warm over such a trifle."

"Warm! You'd be as warm, maybe, if you were as pestered as I am. When I pay good money for a good article there should be an end of the business; but it's 'Where are the geese?' and 'Who did you sell the geese to?' and 'What will you take for the geese?' One would think they were the only geese in the world, to hear the fuss that is made over them."

"Well, I have no connection with any other people who have been making inquiries," said Holmes carelessly. "If you won't tell us the bet is off, that is all. But I'm always ready to back my opinion on a matter of fowls, and I have a fiver on it that the bird I ate is country bred."

"Well, then, you've lost your fiver, for it's town bred," snapped the salesman.

"It's nothing of the kind."

"I say it is."

"I don't believe you."

"D'you think you know more about fowls than I, who have handled them ever since I was a nipper? I tell you, all those birds that went to the Alpha were town bred."

"You'll never persuade me to believe that."

"Will you bet, then?"

"It's merely taking your money, for I know that I am right. But I'll have a sovereign on with you, just to teach you not to be obstinate."

The salesman chuckled grimly. "Bring me the books, Bill," said he.

The small boy brought round a small thin volume and a great

greasy-backed one, laying them out together beneath the hanging lamp.

"Now then, Mr. Cocksure," said the salesman, "I thought that I was out of geese, but before I finish you'll find that there is still one left in my shop. You see this little book?"

"Well?"

"That's the list of the folk from whom I buy. D'you see? Well, then, here on this page are the country folk, and the numbers after their names are where their accounts are in the big ledger. Now, then! You see this other page in red ink? Well, that is a list of my town suppliers. Now, look at that third name. Just read it out to me."

"Mrs. Oakshott, 117 Brixton Road — 249," read Holmes.

"Quite so. Now turn that up in the ledger."

Holmes turned to the page indicated. "Here you are, 'Mrs. Oakshott, 117 Brixton Road, egg and poultry supplier.'"

"Now, then, what's the last entry?"

"'December 22. Twenty-four geese at 7s. 6d.'"

"Quite so. There you are. And underneath?"

"'Sold to Mr. Windigate of the Alpha at 12s.'"

"What have you to say now?"

Sherlock Holmes looked deeply chagrined. He drew a sovereign from his pocket and threw it down upon the slab, turning away with the air of a man whose digust is too deep for words. A few yards off he stopped under a lamp-post, and laughed in the hearty, noiseless fashion which was peculiar to him.

"When you see a man with whiskers of that cut and the 'Pink 'Un'[2] protruding out of his pocket, you can always draw him by a bet," said he. "I dare say that if I had put a hundred pounds down in front of him that man would not have given me such complete information as was drawn from him by the idea that he was doing me on a wager. Well, Watson, we are, I fancy, nearing the end of our quest, and the only point which remains to be determined is whether we should go on to this Mrs. Oakshott to-night, or whether we should reserve it for to-morrow. It is clear from what that surly fellow said that there are others besides ourselves who are anxious about the matter, and I should ——"

His remarks were suddenly cut short by a loud hubbub which broke out from the stall which we had just left. Turning round we saw a little rat-faced fellow standing in the centre of the circle of yellow light which was thrown by the swinging lamp, while Breckinridge the salesman,

[2] **Pink 'Un:** A sporting journal, printed on pink paper.

framed in the door of his stall, was shaking his fists fiercely at the cringing figure.

"I've had enough of you and your geese," he shouted. "I wish you were all at the devil together. If you come pestering me any more with your silly talk I'll set the dog at you. You bring Mrs. Oakshott here and I'll answer her, but what have you to do with it? Did I buy the geese off you?"

"No; but one of them was mine all the same," whined the little man.

"Well, then, ask Mrs. Oakshott for it."

"She told me to ask you."

"Well, you can ask the King of Proosia, for all I care. I've had enough of it. Get out of this!" He rushed fiercely forward, and the inquirer flitted away into the darkness.

"Ha, this may save us a visit to Brixton Road," whispered Holmes. "Come with me, and we will see what is to be made of this fellow." Striding through the scattered knots of people who lounged round the flaring stalls, my companion speedily overtook the little man and touched him upon the shoulder. He sprang round, and I could see in the gaslight that every vestige of colour had been driven from his face.

"Who are you, then? What do you want?" he asked in a quavering voice.

"You will excuse me," said Holmes blandly, "but I could not help overhearing the questions which you put to the salesman just now. I think that I could be of assistance to you."

"You? Who are you? How could you know anything of the matter?"

"My name is Sherlock Holmes. It is my business to know what other people don't know."

"But you can know nothing of this?"

"Excuse me, I know everything of it. You are endeavouring to trace some geese which were sold by Mrs. Oakshott, of Brixton Road, to a salesman named Breckinridge, by him in turn to Mr. Windigate, of the Alpha, and by him to his club, of which Mr. Henry Baker is a member."

"Oh, sir, you are the very man whom I have longed to meet," cried the little fellow, with outstretched hands and quivering fingers. "I can hardly explain to you how interested I am in this matter."

Sherlock Holmes hailed a four-wheeler which was passing. "In that case we had better discuss it in a cosy room rather than in this windswept market-place," said he. "But pray tell me, before we go further, who it is that I have the pleasure of assisting."

The man hesitated for an instant. "My name is John Robinson," he answered, with a sidelong glance.

"No, no; the real name," said Holmes sweetly. "It is always awkward doing business with an *alias*."

A flush sprang to the white cheeks of the stranger. "Well, then," said he, "my real name is James Ryder."

"Precisely so. Head attendant at the Hotel Cosmopolitan. Pray step into the cab, and I shall soon be able to tell you everything which you would wish to know."

The little man stood, glancing from one to the other of us with half-frightened, half-hopeful eyes, as one who is not sure whether he is on the verge of a windfall or of a catastrophe. Then he stepped into the cab, and in half an hour we were back in the sitting-room at Baker Street. Nothing had been said during our drive, but the high, thin breathings of our new companion, and the claspings and unclaspings of his hands, spoke of the nervous tension within him.

"Here we are!" said Holmes cheerily, as we filed into the room. "The fire looks very seasonable in this weather. You look cold, Mr. Ryder. Pray take the basket chair. I will just put on my slippers before we settle this little matter of yours. Now, then! You want to know what became of those geese?"

"Yes, sir."

"Or rather, I fancy, of that goose. It was one bird, I imagine, in which you were interested — white, with a black bar across the tail."

Ryder quivered with emotion. "Oh, sir," he cried, "can you tell me where it went to?"

"It came here."

"Here?"

"Yes, and a most remarkable bird it proved. I don't wonder that you should take an interest in it. It laid an egg after it was dead — the bonniest, brightest little blue egg that ever was seen. I have it here in my museum."

Our visitor staggered to his feet, and clutched the mantelpiece with his right hand. Holmes unlocked his strong-box, and held up the blue carbuncle, which shone out like a star, with a cold, brilliant, many-pointed radiance. Ryder stood glaring with a drawn face, uncertain whether to claim or to disown it.

"The game's up, Ryder," said Holmes quietly. "Hold up, man, or you'll be into the fire. Give him an arm back into his chair, Watson. He's not got blood enough to go in for felony with impunity. Give him a dash of brandy. So! Now he looks a little more human. What a shrimp it is, to be sure!"

For a moment he had staggered and nearly fallen, but the brandy brought a tinge of colour into his cheeks, and he sat staring with frightened eyes at his accuser.

"I have almost every link in my hands, and all the proofs which I could possibly need, so there is little which you need tell me. Still, that little may as well be cleared up to make the case complete. You had heard, Ryder, of this blue stone of the Countess of Morcar's?"

"It was Catherine Cusack who told me of it," said he, in a crackling voice.

"I see. Her ladyship's waiting-maid. Well, the temptation of sudden wealth so easily acquired was too much for you, as it has been for better men before you; but you were not very scrupulous in the means you used. It seems to me, Ryder, that there is the making of a very pretty villain in you. You knew that this man Horner, the plumber, had been concerned in some such matter before, and that suspicion would rest the more readily upon him. What did you do, then? You made some small job in my lady's room — you and your confederate Cusack — and you managed that he should be the man sent for. Then, when he had left, you rifled the jewel-case, raised the alarm, and had this unfortunate man arrested. You then——"

Ryder threw himself down suddenly upon the rug, and clutched at my companion's knees. "For God's sake, have mercy!" he shrieked. "Think of my father! Of my mother! It would break their hearts. I never went wrong before! I never will again. I swear it. I'll swear it on a Bible. Oh, don't bring it into court! For Christ's sake, don't!"

"Get back into your chair!" said Holmes sternly. "It is very well to cringe and crawl now, but you thought little enough of this poor Horner in the dock for a crime of which he knew nothing."

"I will fly, Mr. Holmes. I will leave the country, sir. Then the charge against him will break down."

"Hum! We will talk about that. And now let us hear a true account of the next act. How came the stone into the goose, and how came the goose into the open market? Tell us the truth, for there lies your only hope of safety."

Ryder passed his tongue over his parched lips. "I will tell you it just as it happened, sir," said he. "When Horner had been arrested, it seemed to me that it would be best for me to get away with the stone at once, for I did not know at what moment the police might not take it into their heads to search me and my room. There was no place about the hotel where it would be safe. I went out, as if on some commission, and I made for my sister's house. She had married a man named Oakshott, and lived in Brixton Road, where she fattened fowls for the market. All the way there every man I met seemed to me to be a police-man or a detective, and for all that it was a cold night, the sweat was pouring down my face before I came to the Brixton Road. My sister asked me what was the matter, and why I was so pale; but I told her that I had been upset by the jewel robbery at the hotel. Then I went into the back-yard, and smoked a pipe, and wondered what it would be best to do.

"I had a friend once called Maudsley, who went to the bad, and has just been serving his time in Pentonville. One day he had met me, and fell into talk about the ways of thieves and how they could get rid of what they stole. I knew that he would be true to me, for I knew one or two things about him, so I made up my mind to go right on to Kilburn, where he lived, and take him into my confidence. He would show me how to turn the stone into money. But how to get to him in safety? I thought of the agonies I had gone through in coming from the hotel. I might at any moment be seized and searched, and there would be the stone in my waistcoat pocket. I was leaning against the wall at the time, and looking at the geese which were waddling about round my feet, and suddenly an idea came into my head which showed me how I could beat the best detective that ever lived.

"My sister had told me some weeks before that I might have the pick of her geese for a Christmas present, and I knew that she was always as good as her word. I would take my goose now, and in it I would carry my stone to Kilburn. There was a little shed in the yard, and behind this I drove one of the birds, a fine big one, white, with a barred tail. I caught it and, prising its bill open, I thrust the stone down its throat as far as my finger could reach. The bird gave a gulp, and I felt the stone pass along its gullet and down into its crop. But the creature flapped and struggled, and out came my sister to know what was the matter. As I turned to speak to her the brute broke loose, and fluttered off among the others.

"'Whatever were you doing with that bird, Jem?' says she.

"'Well,' said I, 'you said you'd give me one for Christmas, and I was feeling which was the fattest.'

"'Oh,' says she, 'we've set yours aside for you. Jem's bird, we call it. It's the big, white one over yonder. There's twenty-six of them, which makes one for you, and one for us, and two dozen for the market.'

"'Thank you, Maggie,' says I; 'but if it is all the same to you I'd rather have that one I was handling just now.'

"'The other is a good three pound heavier,' she said, 'and we fat-tened it expressly for you.'

" 'Never mind. I'll have the other, and I'll take it now,' said I.

" 'Oh, just as you like,' said she, a little huffed. 'Which is it you want, then?'

" 'That white one, with the barred tail, right in the middle of the flock.'

" 'Oh, very well. Kill it and take it with you.'

"Well, I did what she said, Mr. Holmes, and I carried the bird all the way to Kilburn. I told my pal what I had done, for he was a man that it was easy to tell a thing like that to. He laughed until he choked, and we got a knife and opened the goose. My heart turned to water, for there was no sign of the stone, and I knew that some terrible mistake had occurred. I left the bird, rushed back to my sister's, and hurried into the back-yard. There was not a bird to be seen there.

" 'Where are they all, Maggie?' I cried.

" 'Gone to the dealer's.'

" 'Which dealer's?'

" 'Breckinridge, of Covent Garden.'

" 'But was there another with a barred tail?' I asked, 'the same as the one I chose?'

" 'Yes, Jem, there were two barred-tailed ones, and I could never tell them apart.'

"Well, then, of course, I saw it all, and I ran off as hard as my feet would carry me to this man Breckinridge; but he had sold the lot at once, and not one word would he tell me as to where they had gone. You heard him yourselves to-night. Well, he has always answered me like that. My sister thinks that I am going mad. Sometimes I think that I am myself. And now — and now I am myself a branded thief, without ever having touched the wealth for which I sold my character. God help me! God help me!" He burst into convulsive sobbing, with his face buried in his hands.

There was a long silence, broken only by his heavy breathing, and by the measured tapping of Sherlock Holmes's finger-tips upon the edge of the table. Then my friend rose, and threw open the door.

"Get out!" said he.

"What, sir! Oh, Heaven bless you!"

"No more words. Get out!"

And no more words were needed. There was a rush, a clatter upon the stairs, the bang of a door, and the crisp rattle of running footfalls from the street.

"After all, Watson," said Holmes, reaching up his hand for his clay pipe, "I am not retained by the police to supply their deficiencies. If Horner were in danger it would be another thing, but this fellow will not appear against him, and the case must collapse. I suppose that I am commuting a felony, but it is just possible that I am saving a soul. This fellow will not go wrong again. He is too terribly frightened. Send him to gaol now, and you make him a gaolbird for life. Besides, it is the season of forgiveness. Chance has put in our way a most singular and whimsical problem, and its solution is its own reward. If you will have the goodness to touch the bell, Doctor, we will begin another investigation, in which also a bird will be the chief feature."

## AFTERWORD

As a tale about a thief's efforts to recover a stolen jewel hidden in some one outwardly indistinguishable member of a larger set or group, "The Blue Carbuncle" strongly resembles a later story, "The Six Napoleons." Doyle indulges in some fun with his birds here: Holmes comments wryly about the woodcock his landlady has prepared for his dinner ("in view of recent occurrences, perhaps I ought to ask Mrs. Hudson to examine its crop"); Mr. Breckinridge, the Covent Garden fowl salesman, chides Holmes as "Mr. Cocksure" and thinks him a goose (a fool) for challenging Breckinridge's knowledge ("I thought that I was out of geese, but before I finish you'll find that there is still one left in my shop"); and Holmes finally lets James Ryder go rather than make a "gaolbird" of him.

With its final touch of moral and judicial ambiguity (the case against the wrongly accused Horner will break down for the lack of Ryder's testimony against him; but though not convicted, he may remain wrongly suspected of the theft), the story shows a certain affinity with "The Boscombe Valley Mystery." Its conclusion contrasts pointedly, on the other hand, with that of yet another solved but unrevealed mystery, "A Case of Identity." The rush to the passage, the wild clatter of steps upon the stairs, the bang of the hall door, the run down the street — Ryder's precipitous departure from 221B Baker Street specifically recalls Windibank's; but in the earlier story Holmes is offering to whip a scoundrel who "will rise from crime to crime until he does something very bad, and ends on a gallows" (p. 88), whereas now, in allowing a confessed thief to escape, Holmes speculates, "it is just possible that I am saving a soul. This fellow will not go wrong again. He is too terribly frightened. . . . Besides, it is the season of forgiveness."

# The Speckled Band

In glancing over my notes of the seventy odd cases in which I have during the last eight years studied the methods of my friend Sherlock Holmes, I find many tragic, some comic, a large number merely strange, but none commonplace; for, working as he did rather for the love of his art than for the acquirement of wealth, he refused to associate himself with any investigation which did not tend towards the unusual, and even the fantastic. Of all these varied cases, however, I cannot recall any which presented more singular features than that which was associated with the well-known Surrey family of the Roylotts of Stoke Moran. The events in question occurred in the early days of my association with Holmes, when we were sharing rooms as bachelors, in Baker Street. It is possible that I might have placed them upon record before, but a promise of secrecy was made at the time, from which I have only been freed during the last month by the untimely death of the lady to whom the pledge was given. It is perhaps as well that the facts should now come to light, for I have reasons to know there are widespread rumours as to the death of Dr. Grimesby Roylott which tend to make the matter even more terrible than the truth.

It was early in April, in the year '83, that I woke one morning to find Sherlock Holmes standing, fully dressed, by the side of my bed. He was a late riser as a rule, and, as the clock on the mantelpiece showed me that it was only a quarter past seven, I blinked up at him in some surprise, and perhaps just a little resentment, for I was myself regular in my habits.

"Very sorry to knock you up, Watson," said he, "but it's the common lot this morning. Mrs. Hudson has been knocked up, she retorted upon me, and I on you."

"What is it, then? A fire?"

"No, a client. It seems that a young lady has arrived in a considerable state of excitement, who insists upon seeing me. She is waiting now in the sitting-room. Now, when young ladies wander about the metropolis at this hour of the morning, and knock sleepy people up out of their beds, I presume that it is something very pressing which they have to communicate. Should it prove to be an interesting case, you would, I am sure, wish to follow it from the outset. I thought at any rate that I should call you, and give you the chance."

From *The Adventures of Sherlock Holmes* (1892). First published in the *Strand*, February 1892.

"My dear fellow, I would not miss it for anything."

I had no keener pleasure than in following Holmes in his professional investigations, and in admiring the rapid deductions, as swift as intuitions, and yet always founded on a logical basis, with which he unravelled the problems which were submitted to him. I rapidly threw on my clothes, and was ready in a few minutes to accompany my friend down to the sitting-room. A lady dressed in black and heavily veiled, who had been sitting in the window, rose as we entered.

"Good morning, madam," said Holmes cheerily. "My name is Sherlock Holmes. This is my intimate friend and associate, Dr. Watson, before whom you can speak as freely as before myself. Ha, I am glad to see that Mrs. Hudson has had the good sense to light the fire. Pray draw up to it, and I shall order you a cup of hot coffee, for I observe that you are shivering."

"It is not cold which makes me shiver," said the woman in a low voice, changing her seat as requested.

"What then?"

"It is fear, Mr. Holmes. It is terror." She raised her veil as she spoke, and we could see that she was indeed in a pitiable state of agitation, her face all drawn and grey, with restless, frightened eyes, like those of some hunted animal. Her features and figure were those of a woman of thirty, but her hair was shot with premature grey, and her expression was weary and haggard. Sherlock Holmes ran her over with one of his quick, all-comprehensive glances.

"You must not fear," said he soothingly, bending forward and patting her forearm. "We shall soon set matters right, I have no doubt. You have come in by train this morning, I see."

"You know me, then?"

"No, but I observe the second half of a return ticket in the palm of your left glove. You must have started early, and yet you had a good drive in a dog-cart,[1] along heavy roads, before you reached the station."

The lady gave a violent start, and stared in bewilderment at my companion.

"There is no mystery, my dear madam," said he, smiling. "The left arm of your jacket is spattered with mud in no less than seven places. The marks are perfectly fresh. There is no vehicle save a dog-cart which throws up mud in that way, and then only when you sit on the left-hand side of the driver."

"Whatever your reasons may be, you are perfectly correct," said she.

---

[1] *dog-cart:* A light, two-wheeled open carriage.

"I started from home before six, reached Leatherhead at twenty past, and came in by the first train to Waterloo. Sir, I can stand this strain no longer; I shall go mad if it continues. I have no one to turn to — none, save only one, who cares for me, and he, poor fellow, can be of little aid. I have heard of you, Mr. Holmes; I have heard of you from Mrs. Farintosh, whom you helped in the hour of her sore need. It was from her that I had your address. Oh, sir, do you not think you could help me too, and at least throw a little light through the dense darkness which surrounds me? At present it is out of my power to reward you for your services, but in a month or two I shall be married, with the control of my own income, and then at least you shall not find me ungrateful."

Holmes turned to his desk, and unlocking it, drew out a small case-book which he consulted.

"Farintosh," said he. "Ah, yes, I recall the case; it was concerned with an opal tiara. I think it was before your time, Watson. I can only say, madam, that I shall be happy to devote the same care to your case as I did to that of your friend. As to reward, my profession is its reward; but you are at liberty to defray whatever expenses I may be put to, at the time which suits you best. And now I beg that you will lay before us everything that may help us in forming an opinion upon the matter."

"Alas!" replied our visitor. "The very horror of my situation lies in the fact that my fears are so vague, and my suspicions depend so entirely upon small points, which might seem trivial to another, that even he to whom of all others I have a right to look for help and advice looks upon all that I tell him about it as the fancies of a nervous woman. He does not say so, but I can read it from his soothing answers and averted eyes. But I have heard, Mr. Holmes, that you can see deeply into the mani-fold wickedness of the human heart. You may advise me how to walk amid the dangers which encompass me."

"I am all attention, madam."

"My name is Helen Stoner, and I am living with my stepfather, who is the last survivor of one of the oldest Saxon families in England, the Roylotts of Stoke Moran, on the western border of Surrey."

Holmes nodded his head. "The name is familiar to me," said he.

"The family was at one time among the richest in England, and the estate extended over the borders into Berkshire in the north, and Hampshire in the west. In the last century, however, four successive heirs were of a dissolute and wasteful disposition, and the family ruin was eventually completed by a gambler, in the days of the Regency. Nothing was left save a few acres of ground and the two-hundred-year-old house, which is itself crushed under a heavy mortgage. The last squire dragged out his existence there, living the horrible life of an aristocratic pauper; but his only son, my stepfather, seeing that he must adapt himself to the new conditions, obtained an advance from a relative, which enabled him to take a medical degree, and went out to Calcutta, where, by his professional skill and his force of character, he established a large practice. In a fit of anger, however, caused by some robberies which had been perpetrated in the house, he beat his native butler to death, and narrowly escaped a capital sentence. As it was, he suffered a long term of imprisonment, and afterwards returned to England a morose and disappointed man.

"When Dr. Roylott was in India he married my mother, Mrs. Stoner, the young widow of Major-General Stoner, of the Bengal Artillery. My sister Julia and I were twins, and we were only two years old at the time of my mother's re-marriage. She had a considerable sum of money, not less than a thousand a year, and this she bequeathed to Dr. Roylott entirely whilst we resided with him, with a provision that a certain annual sum should be allowed to each of us in the event of our marriage. Shortly after our return to England my mother died — she was killed eight years ago in a railway accident near Crewe. Dr. Roylott then abandoned his attempts to establish himself in practice in London, and took us to live with him in the ancestral house at Stoke Moran. The money which my mother had left was enough for all our wants, and there seemed no obstacle to our happiness.

"But a terrible change came over our stepfather about this time. Instead of making friends and exchanging visits with our neighbours, who had at first been overjoyed to see a Roylott of Stoke Moran back in the old family seat, he shut himself up in his house, and seldom came out save to indulge in ferocious quarrels with whoever might cross his path. Violence of temper approaching to mania has been hereditary in the men of the family, and in my stepfather's case it had, I believe, been intensified by his long residence in the tropics. A series of disgraceful brawls took place, two of which ended in the police-court, until at last he became the terror of the village, and the folks would fly at his approach, for he is a man of immense strength, and absolutely uncontrollable in his anger.

"Last week he hurled the local blacksmith over a parapet into a stream and it was only by paying over all the money that I could gather together that I was able to avert another public exposure. He had no friends at all save the wandering gipsies, and he would give these vagabonds leave to encamp upon the few acres of bramble-covered land which represent the family estate, and would accept in return the hospitality of their tents, wandering away with them sometimes for weeks on end. He has a passion also for Indian animals, which are sent over to him by a correspondent, and he has at this moment a cheetah and a baboon, which wander freely over his grounds, and are feared by the villagers almost as much as their master.

"You can imagine from what I say that my poor sister Julia and I had no great pleasure in our lives. No servant would stay with us, and for a long time we did all the work of the house. She was but thirty at the time of her death, and yet her hair had already begun to whiten, even as mine has."

"Your sister is dead, then?"

"She died just two years ago, and it is of her death that I wish to speak to you. You can understand that, living the life which I have described, we were little likely to see anyone of our own age and position. We had, however, an aunt, my mother's maiden sister, Miss Honoria Westphail, who lives near Harrow, and we were occasionally allowed to pay short visits at this lady's house. Julia went there at Christmas two years ago, and met there a half-pay Major of Marines, to whom she became engaged. My stepfather learned of the engagement when my sister returned, and offered no objection to the marriage; but within a fortnight of the day which had been fixed for the wedding, the terrible event occurred which has deprived me of my only companion."

Sherlock Holmes had been leaning back in his chair with his eyes closed, and his head sunk in a cushion, but he half opened his lids now, and glanced across at his visitor.

"Pray be precise as to details," said he.

"It is easy for me to be so, for every event of that dreadful time is seared into my memory. The manor house is, as I have already said, very old, and only one wing is now inhabited. The bedrooms in this wing are on the ground floor, the sitting-rooms being in the central block of the buildings. Of these bedrooms, the first is Dr. Roylott's, the second my sister's, and the third my own. There is no communication between them, but they all open out into the same corridor. Do I make myself plain?"

"Perfectly so."

"The windows of the three rooms open out upon the lawn. That fatal night Dr. Roylott had gone to his room early, though we knew that he had not retired to rest, for my sister was troubled by the smell of the strong Indian cigars which it was his custom to smoke. She left her room, therefore, and came into mine, where she sat for some time, chatting about her approaching wedding. At eleven o'clock she rose to leave me, but she paused at the door and looked back.

" 'Tell me, Helen,' said she, 'have you ever heard anyone whistle in the dead of the night?'

" 'Never,' said I.

" 'I suppose that you could not possibly whistle yourself in your sleep?'

" 'Certainly not. But why?'

" 'Because during the last few nights I have always, about three in the morning, heard a low clear whistle. I am a light sleeper, and it has awakened me. I cannot tell where it came from — perhaps from the next room, perhaps from the lawn. I thought that I would just ask you whether you had heard it.'

" 'No, I have not. It must be those wretched gipsies in the plantation.'

" 'Very likely. And yet if it were on the lawn I wonder that you did not hear it also.'

" 'Ah, but I sleep more heavily than you.'

" 'Well, it is of no great consequence, at any rate,' she smiled back at me, closed my door, and a few moments later I heard her key turn in the lock."

"Indeed," said Holmes. "Was it your custom always to lock yourselves in at night?"

"Always."

"And why?"

"I think that I mentioned to you that the Doctor kept a cheetah and a baboon. We had no feeling of security unless our doors were locked."

"Quite so. Pray proceed with your statement."

"I could not sleep that night. A vague feeling of impending misfortune impressed me. My sister and I, you will recollect, were twins, and you know how subtle are the links which bind two souls which are so closely allied. It was a wild night. The wind was howling outside, and the rain was beating and splashing against the windows. Suddenly, amidst all the hubbub of the gale, there burst forth the wild scream of a terrified woman. I knew that it was my sister's voice. I sprang from my bed, wrapped a shawl round me, and rushed into the corridor. As I opened my door I seemed to hear a low whistle, such as my sister described, and a few moments later a clanging sound, as if a mass of metal had fallen. As I ran down the passage my sister's door was unlocked, and revolved slowly upon its hinges. I stared at it horror-stricken, not knowing what was about to issue from it. By the light of the corridor lamp I saw my sister appear at the opening, her face blanched with terror, her hands groping for help, her whole figure swaying to and fro like that of a drunkard. I ran to her and threw my arms round her, but at that moment her knees seemed to give way and she fell to the ground. She writhed as one who is in terrible pain, and her limbs were dreadfully convulsed. At first I thought that she had not recognized me, but as I bent over her she suddenly shrieked out in a voice which I shall never forget, 'O, my God! Helen! It was the band! The speckled band!' There was something else which she would fain have said, and she stabbed with her finger into the air in the direction of the Doctor's room, but a fresh convulsion seized her and choked her words. I rushed out, calling loudly for my stepfather, and I met him hastening from his room in his dressing-gown. When he reached my sister's side she was unconscious, and though he poured brandy down her throat, and sent for medical aid from the village, all efforts were in vain, for she slowly sank and died without having recovered her consciousness. Such was the dreadful end of my beloved sister."

"One moment," said Holmes; "are you sure about this whistle and metallic sound? Could you swear to it?"

"That was what the county coroner asked me at the inquiry. It is my strong impression that I heard it, and yet among the crash of the gale, and the creaking of an old house, I may possibly have been deceived."

"Was your sister dressed?"

"No, she was in her nightdress. In her right hand was found the charred stump of a match, and in her left a matchbox."

"Showing that she had struck a light and looked about her when the alarm took place. That is important. And what conclusions did the coroner come to?"

"He investigated the case with great care, for Dr. Roylott's conduct had long been notorious in the county, but he was unable to find any satisfactory cause of death. My evidence showed that the door had been fastened upon the inner side, and the windows were blocked by old-fashioned shutters with broad iron bars, which were secured every night. The walls were carefully sounded, and were shown to be quite solid all round, and the flooring was also thoroughly examined, with the same result. The chimney is wide, but is barred up by four large staples. It is certain, therefore, that my sister was quite alone when she met her end. Besides, there were no marks of any violence upon her."

"How about poison?"

"The doctors examined her for it, but without success."

"What do you think that this unfortunate lady died of, then?"

"It is my belief that she died of pure fear and nervous shock, though what it was which frightened her I cannot imagine."

"Were there gipsies in the plantation at the time?"

"Yes, there are nearly always some there."

"Ah, and what did you gather from this allusion to a band — a speckled band?"

"Sometimes I have thought that it was merely the wild talk of delirium, sometimes that it may have referred to some band of people, perhaps to these very gipsies in the plantation. I do not know whether the spotted handkerchiefs which so many of them wear over their heads might have suggested the strange adjective which she used."

Holmes shook his head like a man who is far from being satisfied.

"These are very deep waters," said he; "pray go on with your narrative."

"Two years have passed since then, and my life has been until lately lonelier than ever. A month ago, however, a dear friend, whom I have known for many years, has done me the honour to ask my hand in marriage. His name is Armitage — Percy Armitage — the second son of Mr. Armitage, of Crane Water, near Reading. My stepfather has offered no opposition to the match, and we are to be married in the course of the spring. Two days ago some repairs were started in the west wing of the building, and my bedroom wall has been pierced, so that I have had to move into the chamber in which my sister died, and to sleep in the very bed in which she slept. Imagine, then, my thrill of terror when last night, as I lay awake, thinking over her terrible fate, I suddenly heard in the silence of the night the low whistle which had been the herald of her own death. I sprang up and lit the lamp, but nothing was to be seen in the room. I was too shaken to go to bed again, however, so I dressed, and as soon as it was daylight I slipped down, got a dog-cart at the Crown Inn, which is opposite, and drove to Leatherhead, from whence I have come on this morning, with the one object of seeing you and asking your advice."

"You have done wisely," said my friend. "But have you told me all?"

"Yes, all."

"Miss Stoner, you have not. You are screening your stepfather."

"Why, what do you mean?"

For answer Holmes pushed back the frill of black lace which fringed the hand that lay upon our visitor's knee. Five little livid spots, the marks of four fingers and a thumb, were printed upon the white wrist.

"You have been cruelly used," said Holmes.

The lady coloured deeply, and covered over her injured wrist. "He is a hard man," she said, "and perhaps he hardly knows his own strength."

There was a long silence, during which Holmes leaned his chin upon his hands and stared into the crackling fire.

"This is very deep business," he said at last. "There are a thousand details which I should desire to know before I decide upon our course of action. Yet we have not a moment to lose. If we were to come to Stoke Moran to-day, would it be possible for us to see over these rooms without the knowledge of your stepfather?"

"As it happens, he spoke of coming into town to-day upon some most important business. It is probable that he will be away all day, and that there would be nothing to disturb you. We have a housekeeper now, but she is old and foolish, and I could easily get her out of the way."

"Excellent. You are not averse to this trip, Watson?"

"By no means."

"Then we shall both come. What are you going to do yourself?"

"I have one or two things which I would wish to do now that I am in town. But I shall return by the twelve o'clock train, so as to be there in time for your coming."

"And you may expect us early in the afternoon. I have myself some small business matters to attend to. Will you not wait and breakfast?"

"No, I must go. My heart is lightened already since I have confided my trouble to you. I shall look forward to seeing you again this afternoon." She dropped her thick black veil over her face, and glided from the room.

"And what do you think of it all, Watson?" asked Sherlock Holmes, leaning back in his chair.

"It seems to me to be a most dark and sinister business."

"Dark enough and sinister enough."

"Yet if the lady is correct in saying that the flooring and walls are sound, and that the door, window, and chimney are impassable, then her sister must have been undoubtedly alone when she met her mysterious end."

"What becomes, then, of these nocturnal whistles, and what of the very peculiar words of the dying woman?"

"I cannot think."

"When you combine the ideas of whistles at night, the presence of a band of gipsies who are on intimate terms with this old doctor, the fact that we have every reason to believe that the doctor has an interest in preventing his stepdaughter's marriage, the dying allusion to a band, and finally, the fact that Miss Helen Stoner heard a metallic clang, which might have been caused by one of those metal bars which secured the shutters falling back into their place, I think there is good ground to think that the mystery may be cleared along those lines."

"But what, then, did the gipsies do?"

"I cannot imagine."

"I see many objections to any such a theory."

"And so do I. It is precisely for that reason that we are going to Stoke Moran this day. I want to see whether the objections are fatal, or if they may be explained away. But what, in the name of the devil!"

The ejaculation had been drawn from my companion by the fact that our door had been suddenly dashed open, and that a huge man framed himself in the aperture. His costume was a peculiar mixture of the professional and of the agricultural, having a black top-hat, a long frock-coat, and a pair of high gaiters, with a hunting-crop swinging in his hand. So tall was he that his hat actually brushed the cross-bar of the doorway, and his breadth seemed to span it across from side to side. A large face, seared with a thousand wrinkles, burned yellow with the sun, and marked with every evil passion, was turned from one to the other of us, while his deep-set, bile-shot eyes, and the high thin fleshless nose, gave him somewhat the resemblance to a fierce old bird of prey.

"Which of you is Holmes?" asked this apparition.

"My name, sir, but you have the advantage of me," said my companion quietly.

"I am Dr. Grimesby Roylott, of Stoke Moran."

"Indeed, Doctor," said Holmes blandly. "Pray take a seat."

"I will do nothing of the kind. My stepdaughter has been here. I have traced her. What has she been saying to you?"

"It is a little cold for the time of the year," said Holmes.

"What has she been saying to you?" screamed the old man furiously.

"But I have heard that the crocuses promise well," continued my companion imperturbably.

"Ha! You put me off, do you?" said our new visitor, taking a step forward, and shaking his hunting-crop. "I know you, you scoundrel! I have heard of you before. You are Holmes the meddler."

My friend smiled.

"Holmes the busybody!"

His smile broadened.

"Holmes the Scotland Yard jack-in-office."

Holmes chuckled heartily. "Your conversation is most entertaining," said he. "When you go out close the door, for there is a decided draught."

"I will go when I have had my say. Don't you dare to meddle with my affairs. I know that Miss Stoner has been here — I traced her! I am a dangerous man to fall foul of! See here." He stepped swiftly forward, seized the poker, and bent it into a curve with his huge brown hands.

"See that you keep yourself out of my grip," he snarled, and hurling the twisted poker into the fireplace, he strode out of the room.

"He seems a very amiable person," said Holmes, laughing. "I am not quite so bulky, but if he had remained I might have shown him that my grip was not much more feeble than his own." As he spoke he picked up the steel poker, and with a sudden effort straightened it out again.

"Fancy his having the insolence to confound me with the official detective force! This incident gives zest to our investigation, however, and I only trust that our little friend will not suffer from her imprudence in allowing this brute to trace her. And now, Watson, we shall order breakfast, and afterwards I shall walk down to Doctors' Commons, where I hope to get some data which may help us in this matter."

It was nearly one o'clock when Sherlock Holmes returned from his excursion. He held in his hand a sheet of blue paper, scrawled over with notes and figures.

"I have seen the will of the deceased wife," said he. "To determine its exact meaning I have been obliged to work out the present prices of the investments with which it is concerned. The total income, which at the time of the wife's death was little short of £1,100, is now through the fall in agricultural prices not more than £750. Each daughter can claim an income of £250, in case of marriage. It is evident, therefore, that if both girls had married this beauty would have had a mere pittance, while even one of them would cripple him to a serious extent. My morning's work has not been wasted, since it has proved that he has the very strongest motives for standing in the way of anything of the sort. And now, Watson, this is too serious for dawdling, especially as the old man is aware that we are interesting ourselves in his affairs, so if you are ready we shall call a cab and drive to Waterloo. I should be very much obliged if you would slip your revolver into your pocket. An Eley's No. 2 is an excellent argument with gentlemen who can twist steel pokers into knots. That and a tooth-brush are, I think, all that we need."

At Waterloo we were fortunate in catching a train for Leatherhead, where we hired a trap at the station inn, and drove for four or five miles through the lovely Surrey lanes. It was a perfect day, with a bright sun and a few fleecy clouds in the heavens. The trees and wayside hedges were just throwing out their first green shoots, and the air was full of the pleasant smell of the moist earth. To me at least there was a strange contrast between the sweet promise of the spring and this sinister quest upon which we were engaged. My companion sat in front of the trap, his arms folded, his hat pulled down over his eyes, and his chin sunk upon his breast, buried in the deepest thought. Suddenly, however, he started, tapped me on the shoulder, and pointed over the meadows.

"Look there!" said he.

A heavily timbered park stretched up in a gentle slope, thickening into a grove at the highest point. From amidst the branches there jutted out the grey gables and high roof-tree of a very old mansion.

"Stoke Moran?" said he.

"Yes, sir, that be the house of Dr. Grimesby Roylott," remarked the driver.

"There is some building going on there," said Holmes; "that is where we are going."

"There's the village," said the driver, pointing to a cluster of roofs some distance to the left; "but if you want to get to the house, you'll find it shorter to go over this stile, and so by the footpath over the fields. There it is, where the lady is walking."

"And the lady, I fancy, is Miss Stoner," observed Holmes, shading his eyes. "Yes, I think we had better do as you suggest."

We got off, paid our fare, and the trap rattled back on its way to Leatherhead.

"I thought it as well," said Holmes, as we climbed the stile, "that this fellow should think we had come here as architects, or on some definite business. It may stop his gossip. Good afternoon, Miss Stoner. You see that we have been as good as our word."

Our client of the morning had hurried forward to meet us with a face which spoke her joy. "I have been waiting so eagerly for you," she cried, shaking hands with us warmly. "All has turned out splendidly. Dr. Roylott has gone to town, and it is unlikely that he will be back before evening."

"We have had the pleasure of making the Doctor's acquaintance," said Holmes, and in a few words he sketched out what had occurred. Miss Stoner turned white to the lips as she listened.

"Good heavens!" she cried, "he has followed me, then."

"So it appears."

"He is so cunning that I never know when I am safe from him. What will he say when he returns?"

"He must guard himself, for he may find that there is someone more cunning than himself upon his track. You must lock yourself from him to-night. If he is violent, we shall take you away to your aunt's at Harrow. Now, we must make the best use of our time, so kindly take us at once to the rooms which we are to examine."

The building was of grey, lichen-blotched stone, with a high central portion, and two curving wings, like the claws of a crab, thrown out on each side. In one of these wings the windows were broken, and blocked with wooden boards, while the roof was partly caved in, a picture of ruin. The central portion was in little better repair, but the right-hand block was comparatively modern, and the blinds in the windows, with the blue smoke curling up from the chimneys, showed that this was where the family resided. Some scaffolding had been erected against the end wall, and the stonework had been broken into, but there were no signs of any workmen at the moment of our visit. Holmes walked slowly up and down the ill-trimmed lawn, and examined with deep attention the outsides of the windows.

"This, I take it, belongs to the room in which you used to sleep, the centre one to your sister's, and the one next to the main building to Dr. Roylott's chamber?"

"Exactly so. But I am now sleeping in the middle one."

"Pending the alterations, as I understand. By the way, there does not seem to be any very pressing need for repairs at that end wall."

"There were none. I believe that it was an excuse to move me from my room."

"Ah! that is suggestive. Now, on the other side of this narrow wing runs the corridor from which these three rooms open. There are windows in it, of course?"

"Yes, but very small ones. Too narrow for anyone to pass through."

"As you both locked your doors at night, your rooms were unapproachable from that side. Now, would you have the kindness to go into your room, and to bar your shutters."

Miss Stoner did so, and Holmes, after a careful examination through the open window, endeavoured in every way to force the shutter open, but without success. There was no slit through which a knife could be passed to raise the bar. Then with his lens he tested the hinges, but they were of solid iron, built firmly into the massive masonry. "Hum!" said he, scratching his chin in some perplexity, "my theory certainly presents some difficulties. No one could pass these shutters if they were bolted. Well, we shall see if the inside throws any light upon the matter."

A small side-door led into the whitewashed corridor from which the three bedrooms opened. Holmes refused to examine the third chamber, so we passed at once to the second, that in which Miss Stoner was now sleeping, and in which her sister had met her fate. It was a homely little room, with a low ceiling and a gaping fireplace, after the fashion of old country houses. A brown chest of drawers stood in one corner, a narrow white-counterpaned bed in another, and a dressing-table on the left-hand side of the window. These articles, with two small wicker-work chairs, made up all the furniture in the room, save for a square of Wilton carpet in the centre. The boards round and the panelling of the walls were brown, worm-eaten oak, so old and discoloured that it may have dated from the original building of the house. Holmes drew one of the chairs into a corner and sat silent, while his eyes travelled round and round and up and down, taking in every detail of the apartment.

"Where does that bell communicate with?" he asked at last, pointing to a thick bell-rope which hung down beside the bed, the tassel actually lying upon the pillow.

"It goes to the housekeeper's room."

"It looks newer than the other things?"

"Yes, it was only put there a couple of years ago."

"Your sister asked for it, I suppose?"

"No, I never heard of her using it. We used always to get what we wanted for ourselves."

"Indeed, it seemed unnecessary to put so nice a bell-pull there. You will excuse me for a few minutes while I satisfy myself as to this floor." He threw himself down upon his face with his lens in his hand, and crawled swiftly backwards and forwards, examining minutely the cracks between the boards. Then he did the same with the woodwork with which the chamber was panelled. Finally he walked over to the bed and spent some time in staring at it, and in running his eye up and down the wall. Finally he took the bell-rope in his hand and gave it a brisk tug.

"Why, it's a dummy," said he.

"Won't it ring?"

"No, it is not even attached to a wire. This is very interesting. You can see now that it is fastened to a hook just above where the little opening of the ventilator is."

"How very absurd! I never noticed that before."

"Very strange!" muttered Holmes, pulling at the rope. "There are one or two very singular points about this room. For example, what a fool a builder must be to open a ventilator into another room, when, with the same trouble, he might have communicated with the outside air!"

"That is also quite modern," said the lady.

"Done about the same time as the bell-rope," remarked Holmes.

"Yes, there were several little changes carried out about that time."

"They seem to have been of a most interesting character — dummy bell-ropes, and ventilators which do not ventilate. With your permission, Miss Stoner, we shall now carry our researches into the inner apartment."

Dr. Grimesby Roylott's chamber was larger than that of his step-daughter, but was as plainly furnished. A camp bed, a small wooden shelf full of books, mostly of a technical character, an arm-chair beside the bed, a plain wooden chair against the wall, a round table, and a large iron safe were the principal things which met the eye. Holmes walked slowly round and examined each and all of them with the keenest interest.

"What's in here?" he asked, tapping the safe.

"My stepfather's business papers."

"Oh! you have seen inside, then?"

"Only once, some years ago. I remember that it was full of papers."

"There isn't a cat in it, for example?"

"No. What a strange idea!"

"Well, look at this!" He took up a small saucer of milk which stood on the top of it.

"No; we don't keep a cat. But there is a cheetah and a baboon."

"Ah, yes, of course! Well, a cheetah is just a big cat, and yet a saucer of milk does not go very far in satisfying its wants, I daresay. There is one point which I should wish to determine." He squatted down in front of the wooden chair, and examined the seat of it with the greatest attention.

"Thank you. That is quite settled," said he, rising and putting his lens in his pocket. "Hullo! here is something interesting!"

The object which had caught his eye was a small dog lash hung on one corner of the bed. The lash, however, was curled upon itself, and tied so as to make a loop of whipcord.

"What do you make of that, Watson?"

"It's a common enough lash. But I don't know why it should be tied."

"That is not quite so common, is it? Ah, me! it's a wicked world, and when a clever man turns his brain to crime it is the worst of all. I think that I have seen enough now, Miss Stoner, and, with your permission, we shall walk out upon the lawn."

I had never seen my friend's face so grim, or his brow so dark, as it was when we turned from the scene of this investigation. We had walked several times up and down the lawn, neither Miss Stoner nor myself liking to break in upon his thoughts before he roused himself from his reverie.

"It is very essential, Miss Stoner," said he, "that you should absolutely follow my advice in every respect."

"I shall most certainly do so."

"The matter is too serious for any hesitation. Your life may depend upon your compliance."

"I assure you that I am in your hands."

"In the first place, both my friend and I must spend the night in your room."

Both Miss Stoner and I gazed at him in astonishment.

"Yes, it must be so. Let me explain. I believe that that is the village inn over there?"

"Yes, that is the Crown."

"Very good. Your windows would be visible from there?"

"Certainly."

"You must confine yourself to your room, on pretence of a headache, when your stepfather comes back. Then when you hear him retire for the night, you must open the shutters of your window, undo the hasp, put your lamp there as a signal to us, and then withdraw with everything which you are likely to want into the room which you used to occupy. I have no doubt that, in spite of the repairs, you could manage there for one night."

"Oh, yes, easily."

"The rest you will leave in our hands."

"But what will you do?"

"We shall spend the night in your room, and we shall investigate the cause of this noise which has disturbed you."

"I believe, Mr. Holmes, that you have already made up your mind," said Miss Stoner, laying her hand upon my companion's sleeve.

"Perhaps I have."

"Then for pity's sake tell me what was the cause of my sister's death."

"I should prefer to have clearer proofs before I speak."

"You can at least tell me whether my own thought is correct, and if she died from some sudden fright."

"No, I do not think so. I think that there was probably some more tangible cause. And now, Miss Stoner, we must leave you, for if Dr. Roylott returned and saw us, our journey would be in vain. Good-bye, and be brave, for if you will do what I have told you, you may rest assured that we shall soon drive away the dangers that threaten you."

Sherlock Holmes and I had no difficulty in engaging a bedroom and sitting-room at the Crown Inn. They were on the upper floor, and from our window we could command a view of the avenue gate, and of the inhabited wing of Stoke Moran Manor House. At dusk we saw Dr. Grimesby Roylott drive past, his huge form looming up beside the little figure of the lad who drove him. The boy had some slight difficulty in undoing the heavy iron gates, and we heard the hoarse roar of the Doctor's voice, and saw the fury with which he shook his clenched fists at him. The trap drove on, and a few minutes later we saw a sudden light spring up among the trees as the lamp was lit in one of the sitting-rooms.

"Do you know, Watson," said Holmes, as we sat together in the gathering darkness, "I have really some scruples as to taking you to-night. There is a distinct element of danger."

"Can I be of assistance?"

"Your presence might be invaluable."

"Then I shall certainly come."

"It is very kind of you."

"You speak of danger. You have evidently seen more in these rooms than was visible to me."

"No, but I fancy that I may have deduced a little more. I imagine that you saw all that I did."

"I saw nothing remarkable save the bell-rope, and what purpose that could answer I confess is more than I can imagine."

"You saw the ventilator, too?"

"Yes, but I do not think that it is such a very unusual thing to have a small opening between two rooms. It was so small that a rat could hardly pass through."

"I knew that we should find a ventilator before ever we came to Stoke Moran."

"My dear Holmes!"

"Oh, yes, I did. You remember in her statement she said that her sister could smell Dr. Roylott's cigar. Now, of course that suggests at once that there must be a communication between the two rooms. It could only be a small one, or it would have been remarked upon at the coroner's inquiry. I deduced a ventilator."

"But what harm can there be in that?"

"Well, there is at least a curious coincidence of dates. A ventilator is made, a cord is hung, and a lady who sleeps in the bed dies. Does not that strike you?"

"I cannot as yet see any connection."

"Did you observe anything very peculiar about that bed?"

"No."

"It was clamped to the floor. Did you ever see a bed fastened like that before?"

"I cannot say that I have."

"The lady could not move her bed. It must always be in the same relative position to the ventilator and to the rope — for so we may call it, since it was clearly never meant for a bell-pull."

"Holmes," I cried, "I seem to see dimly what you are hinting at. We are only just in time to prevent some subtle and horrible crime."

"Subtle enough and horrible enough. When a doctor does go wrong he is the first of criminals. He has nerve and he has knowledge. Palmer and Pritchard were among the heads of their profession. This man strikes even deeper, but I think, Watson, that we shall be able to strike deeper still. But we shall have horrors enough before the night is over; for goodness' sake let us have a quiet pipe, and turn our minds for a few hours to something more cheerful."

About nine o'clock the light among the trees was extinguished, and all was dark in the direction of the Manor House. Two hours passed slowly away, and then, suddenly, just at the stroke of eleven, a single bright light shone out right in front of us.

"That is our signal," said Holmes, springing to his feet; "it comes from the middle window."

As we passed out he exchanged a few words with the landlord, explaining that we were going on a late visit to an acquaintance, and that it was possible that we might spend the night there. A moment later we were out on the dark road, a chill wind blowing in our faces, and one yellow light twinkling in front of us through the gloom to guide us on our sombre errand.

There was little difficulty in entering the grounds, for unrepaired breaches gaped in the old park wall. Making our way among the trees, we reached the lawn, crossed it, and were about to enter through the window, when out from a clump of laurel bushes there darted what seemed to be a hideous and distorted child, who threw itself on the grass with writhing limbs, and then ran swiftly across the lawn into the darkness.

"My God!" I whispered, "did you see it?"

Holmes was for the moment as startled as I. His hand closed like a vice upon my wrist in his agitation. Then he broke into a low laugh, and put his lips to my ear.

"It is a nice household," he murmured. "That is the baboon."

I had forgotten the strange pets which the Doctor affected. There was a cheetah, too; perhaps we might find it upon our shoulders at any moment. I confess that I felt easier in my mind when, after following Holmes's example and slipping off my shoes, I found myself inside the bedroom. My companion noiselessly closed the shutters, moved the lamp on to the table, and cast his eyes round the room. All was as we had seen it in the day-time. Then creeping up to me and making a trumpet of his hand, he whispered into my ear again so gently that it was all that I could do to distinguish the words:

"The least sound would be fatal to our plans."

I nodded to show that I had heard.

"We must sit without a light. He would see it through the ventilator."

I nodded again.

"Do not go to sleep; your very life may depend upon it. Have your pistol ready in case we should need it. I will sit on the side of the bed, and you in that chair."

I took out my revolver and laid it on the corner of the table.

Holmes had brought up a long thin cane, and this he placed upon the bed beside him. By it he laid the box of matches and the stump of a candle. Then he turned down the lamp and we were left in darkness.

How shall I ever forget that dreadful vigil? I could not hear a sound, not even the drawing of a breath, and yet I knew that my companion sat open-eyed, within a few feet of me, in the same state of nervous tension in which I was myself. The shutters cut off the least ray of light, and we waited in absolute darkness. From outside came the occasional cry of a night-bird, and once at our very window a long drawn, cat-like whine, which told us that the cheetah was indeed at liberty. Far away we could hear the deep tones of the parish clock, which boomed out every quarter of an hour. How long they seemed, those quarters! Twelve o'clock, and one, and two, and three, and still we sat waiting silently for whatever might befall.

Suddenly there was the momentary gleam of a light up in the direction of the ventilator, which vanished immediately, but was succeeded by a strong smell of burning oil and heated metal. Someone in the next room had lit a dark lantern. I heard a gentle sound of movement, and then all was silent once more, though the smell grew stronger. For half an hour I sat with straining ears. Then suddenly another sound became audible — a very gentle, soothing sound, like that of a small jet of steam escaping continually from a kettle. The instant that we heard it, Holmes sprang from the bed, struck a match, and lashed furiously with his cane at the bell-pull.

"You see it, Watson?" he yelled. "You see it?"

But I saw nothing. At the moment when Holmes struck the light I heard a low, clear whistle, but the sudden glare flashing into my weary eyes made it impossible for me to tell what it was at which my friend lashed so savagely. I could, however, see that his face was deadly pale, and filled with horror and loathing.

He had ceased to strike, and was gazing up at the ventilator, when suddenly there broke from the silence of the night the most horrible cry to which I have ever listened. It swelled up louder and louder, a hoarse yell of pain and fear and anger all mingled in the one dreadful shriek. They say that away down in the village, and even in the distant parsonage, that cry raised the sleepers from their beds. It struck cold to our hearts, and I stood gazing at Holmes, and he at me, until the last echoes of it had died away into the silence from which it rose.

"What can it mean?" I gasped.

"It means that it is all over," Holmes answered. "And perhaps, after all, it is for the best. Take your pistol, and we shall enter Dr. Roylott's room."

With a grave face he lit the lamp, and led the way down the corridor. Twice he struck at the chamber door without any reply from within. Then he turned the handle and entered, I at his heels, with the cocked pistol in my hand.

It was a singular sight which met our eyes. On the table stood a dark lantern with the shutter half open, throwing a brilliant beam of light upon the iron safe, the door of which was ajar. Beside this table, on the wooden chair, sat Dr. Grimesby Roylott, clad in a long grey dressing-gown, his bare ankles protruding beneath, and his feet thrust into red heelless Turkish slippers. Across his lap lay the short stock with the long lash which we had noticed during the day. His chin was cocked upwards, and his eyes were fixed in a dreadful rigid stare at the corner of the ceiling. Round his brow he had a peculiar yellow band, with brownish speckles, which seemed to be bound tightly round his head. As we entered he made neither sound nor motion.

"The band! the speckled band!" whispered Holmes.

I took a step forward. In an instant his strange headgear began to move, and there reared itself from among his hair the squat diamond-shaped head and puffed neck of a loathsome serpent.

"It is a swamp adder!" cried Holmes — "the deadliest snake in India. He has died within ten seconds of being bitten. Violence does, in truth, recoil upon the violent, and the schemer falls into the pit which he digs for another. Let us thrust this creature back into its den, and we can then remove Miss Stoner to some place of shelter, and let the county police know what has happened."

As he spoke he drew the dog whip swiftly from the dead man's lap, and throwing the noose round the reptile's neck, he drew it from its horrid perch, and, carrying it at arm's length, threw it into the iron safe, which he closed upon it.

Such are the true facts of the death of Dr. Grimesby Roylott, of Stoke Moran. It is not necessary that I should prolong a narrative which has already run to too great a length, by telling how we broke the sad news to the terrified girl, how we conveyed her by the morning train to the care of her good aunt at Harrow, of how the slow process of official inquiry came to the conclusion that the Doctor met his fate while indiscreetly playing with a dangerous pet. The little which I had yet to learn of the case was told me by Sherlock Holmes as we travelled back next day.

"I had," said he, "come to an entirely erroneous conclusion, which shows, my dear Watson, how dangerous it always is to reason from insufficient data. The presence of the gipsies, and the use of the word 'band,' which was used by the poor girl, no doubt, to explain the appearance which she had caught a hurried glimpse of by the light of her match, were sufficient to put me upon an entirely wrong scent. I can only claim the merit that I instantly reconsidered my position when, however, it became clear to me that whatever danger threatened an occupant of the room could not come either from the window or the door. My attention was speedily drawn, as I have already remarked to you, to this ventilator, and to the bell-rope which hung down to the bed. The discovery that this was a dummy, and that the bed was clamped to the floor, instantly gave rise to the suspicion that the rope was there as a bridge for something passing through the hole, and coming to the bed. The idea of a snake instantly occurred to me, and when I coupled it with my knowledge that the Doctor was furnished with a supply of creatures from India, I felt that I was probably on the right track. The idea of using a form of poison which could not possibly be discovered by any chemical test was just such a one as would occur to a clever and ruthless man who had had an Eastern training. The rapidity with which such a poison would take effect would also, from his point of view, be an advantage. It would be a sharp-eyed coroner indeed who could distinguish the two little dark punctures which would show where the poison fangs had done their work. Then I thought of the whistle. Of course, he must recall the snake before the morning light revealed it to the victim. He had trained it, probably by the use of the milk which we saw, to return to him when summoned. He would put it through the ventilator at the hour that he thought best, with the certainty that it would crawl down the rope, and land on the bed. It might or might not bite the occupant, perhaps she might escape every night for a week, but sooner or later she must fall a victim.

"I had come to these conclusions before ever I had entered his room. An inspection of his chair showed me that he had been in the habit of standing on it, which, of course, would be necessary in order that he should reach the ventilator. The sight of the safe, the saucer of milk, and the loop of whipcord were enough to finally dispel any doubts which may have remained. The metallic clang heard by Miss Stoner was obviously caused by her father hastily closing the door of his safe upon its terrible occupant. Having once made up my mind, you know the steps which I took in order to put the matter to the proof. I heard the creature hiss, as I have no doubt that you did also, and I instantly lit the light and attacked it."

"With the result of driving it through the ventilator."

"And also with the result of causing it to turn upon its master at the other side. Some of the blows of my cane came home, and roused its snakish temper, so that it flew upon the first person it saw. In this way I am no doubt indirectly responsible for Dr. Grimesby Roylott's death, and I cannot say that it is likely to weigh very heavily upon my conscience."

## AFTERWORD

As a dark, even grotesque, "locked-room" mystery turning on the murderous agency of a deadly animal, "The Speckled Band" constitutes Doyle's particular homage to the first detective story, Poe's "Murders in the Rue Morgue." Doyle regarded that story as (along with "The Gold-Bug") one of Poe's two best stories and one of "the great short stories of the English language," with a perfect excellence of proportion and perspective, "the horror or weirdness of the idea intensified by the coolness of the narrator and of the principal actor" (*Through the Magic Door* 116–19). In turn he thought "The Speckled Band" the best of his own Sherlock Holmes stories; it is surely the most Poesque. Particular echoes of Poe are perhaps more noticeable in other Holmes stories; but Helen Stoner's opening profession of her "terror," the mental strain and vague suspicions that threaten her with madness even while they seem to her fiancé only "the fancies of a nervous woman," and her appeal to Holmes, as one who "can see deeply into the manifold wickedness of the human heart," to "throw a little light through the dense darkness which surrounds me," all suggest Poe's influence and presence.

## Silver Blaze

"I am afraid, Watson, that I shall have to go," said Holmes, as we sat down together to our breakfast one morning.

"Go! Where to?"

"To Dartmoor — to King's Pyland."

I was not surprised. Indeed, my only wonder was that he had not already been mixed up in this extraordinary case, which was the one topic of conversation through the length and breadth of England. For a whole day my companion had rambled about the room with his chin upon his chest and his brows knitted, charging and re-charging his pipe with the strongest black tobacco, and absolutely deaf to any of my questions or remarks. Fresh editions of every paper had been sent up by our newsagent only to be glanced over and tossed down into a corner. Yet, silent as he was, I knew perfectly well what it was over which he was brooding. There was but one problem before the public which could challenge his powers of analysis, and that was the singular disappearance of the favourite for the Wessex Cup, and the tragic murder of its trainer. When, therefore, he suddenly announced his intention of setting out for the scene of the drama, it was only what I had both expected and hoped for.

"I should be most happy to go down with you if I should not be in the way," said I.

"My dear Watson, you would confer a great favour upon me by coming. And I think that your time will not be mis-spent, for there are points about this case which promise to make it an absolutely unique one. We have, I think, just time to catch our train at Paddington, and I will go further into the matter upon our journey. You would oblige me by bringing with you your very excellent field-glass."

From *The Memoirs of Sherlock Holmes* (1894). First published in the *Strand*, December 1892.

And so it happened that an hour or so later I found myself in the corner of a first-class carriage, flying along, *en route* for Exeter, while Sherlock Holmes, with his sharp, eager face framed in his ear-flapped travelling-cap, dipped rapidly into the bundle of fresh papers which he had procured at Paddington. We had left Reading far behind us before he thrust the last of them under the seat, and offered me his cigar-case.

"We are going well," said he, looking out of the window, and glancing at his watch. "Our rate at present is fifty-three and a half miles an hour."

"I have not observed the quarter-mile posts," said I.

"Nor have I. But the telegraph posts upon this line are sixty yards apart, and the calculation is a simple one. I presume that you have already looked into this matter of the murder of John Straker and the disappearance of Silver Blaze?"

"I have seen what the *Telegraph* and the *Chronicle* have to say."

"It is one of those cases where the art of the reasoner should be used rather for the sifting of details than for the acquiring of fresh evidence. The tragedy has been so uncommon, so complete, and of such personal importance to so many people that we are suffering from a plethora of surmise, conjecture, and hypothesis. The difficulty is to detach the framework of fact — of absolute, undeniable fact — from the embellishments of theorists and reporters. Then, having established ourselves upon this sound basis, it is our duty to see what inferences may be drawn, and which are the special points upon which the whole mystery turns. On Tuesday evening I received telegrams, both from Colonel Ross, the owner of the horse, and from Inspector Gregory, who is looking after the case, inviting my co-operation."

"Tuesday evening!" I exclaimed. "And this is Thursday morning. Why did you not go down yesterday?"

"Because I made a blunder, my dear Watson — which is, I am afraid, a more common occurrence than anyone would think who only knew me through your memoirs. The fact is that I could not believe it possible that the most remarkable horse in England could long remain concealed, especially in so sparsely inhabited a place as the north of Dartmoor. From hour to hour yesterday I expected to hear that he had been found, and that his abductor was the murderer of John Straker. When, however, another morning had come and I found that, beyond the arrest of young Fitzroy Simpson, nothing had been done, I felt that it was time for me to take action. Yet in some ways I feel that yesterday has not been wasted."

"You have formed a theory then?"

"At least I have a grip of the essential facts of the case. I shall enumerate them to you, for nothing clears up a case so much as stating it to another person, and I can hardly expect your co-operation if I do not show you the position from which we start."

I lay back against the cushions, puffing at my cigar, while Holmes, leaning forward, with his long thin forefinger checking off the points upon the palm of his left hand, gave me a sketch of the events which had led to our journey.

"Silver Blaze," said he, "is from the Isonomy stock, and holds as brilliant a record as his famous ancestor. He is now in his fifth year, and has brought in turn each of the prizes of the turf to Colonel Ross, his fortunate owner. Up to the time of the catastrophe he was first favourite for the Wessex Cup, the betting being three to one on him. He has always, however, been a prime favourite with the racing public, and has never yet disappointed them, so that even at short odds enormous sums of money have been laid upon him. It is obvious, therefore, that there were many people who had the strongest interest in preventing Silver Blaze from being there at the fall of the flag next Tuesday.

"This fact was, of course, appreciated at King's Pyland, where the Colonel's training stable is situated. Every precaution was taken to guard the favourite. The trainer, John Straker, is a retired jockey, who rode in Colonel Ross's colours before he became too heavy for the weighing-chair. He has served the Colonel for five years as jockey, and for seven as trainer, and has always shown himself to be a zealous and honest servant. Under him were three lads, for the establishment was a small one, containing only four horses in all. One of these lads sat up each night in the stable, while the others slept in the loft. All three bore excellent characters. John Straker, who is a married man, lived in a small villa about two hundred yards from the stables. He has no children, keeps one maid-servant, and is comfortably off. The country round is very lonely, but about half a mile to the north there is a small cluster of villas which have been built by a Tavistock contractor for the use of invalids and others who may wish to enjoy the pure Dartmoor air. Tavistock itself lies two miles to the west, while across the moor, also about two miles distant, is the larger training establishment of Capleton, which belongs to Lord Backwater, and is managed by Silas Brown. In every other direction the moor is a complete wilderness, inhabited only by a few roaming gipsies. Such was the general situation last Monday night, when the catastrophe occurred.

"On that evening the horses had been exercised and watered as usual, and the stables were locked up at nine o'clock. Two of the lads walked up to the trainer's house, where they had supper in the kitchen, while the third, Ned Hunter, remained on guard. At a few minutes after nine the maid, Edith Baxter, carried down to the stables his supper, which consisted of a dish of curried mutton. She took no liquid, as there was a water-tap in the stables, and it was the rule that the lad on duty should drink nothing else. The maid carried a lantern with her, as it was very dark, and the path ran across the open moor.

"Edith Baxter was within thirty yards of the stables when a man appeared out of the darkness and called to her to stop. As he stepped into the circle of yellow light thrown by the lantern she saw that he was a person of gentlemanly bearing, dressed in a grey suit of tweed with a cloth cap. He wore gaiters, and carried a heavy stick with a knob to it. She was most impressed, however, by the extreme pallor of his face and by the nervousness of his manner. His age, she thought, would be rather over thirty than under it.

" 'Can you tell me where I am?' he asked. 'I had almost made up my mind to sleep on the moor when I saw the light of your lantern.'

" 'You are close to the King's Pyland training stables,' she said.

" 'Oh, indeed! What a stroke of luck!' he cried. 'I understand that a stable boy sleeps there alone every night. Perhaps that is his supper which you are carrying to him. Now I am sure that you would not be too proud to earn the price of a new dress, would you?' He took a piece of white paper folded up out of his waistcoat pocket. 'See that the boy has this to-night, and you shall have the prettiest frock that money can buy.'

"She was frightened by the earnestness of his manner, and ran past him to the window through which she was accustomed to hand the meals. It was already open, and Hunter was seated at the small table inside. She had begun to tell him of what had happened, when the stranger came up again.

" 'Good evening,' said he, looking through the window, 'I wanted to have a word with you.' The girl has sworn that as he spoke she noticed the corner of the little paper packet protruding from his closed hand.

" 'What business have you here?' asked the lad.

" 'It's business that may put something into your pocket,' said the other. 'You've two horses in for the Wessex Cup — Silver Blaze and Bayard. Let me have the straight tip, and you won't be a loser. Is it a fact that at the weights Bayard could give the other a hundred yards in five furlongs, and that the stable have put their money on him?'

" 'So you're one of those damned touts,' cried the lad. 'I'll show you how we serve them in King's Pyland.' He sprang up and rushed across the stable to unloose the dog. The girl fled away to the house, but as she ran she looked back, and saw that the stranger was leaning through the window. A minute later, however, when Hunter rushed out with the hound he was gone, and though the lad ran all round the buildings he failed to find any trace of him."

"One moment!" I asked. "Did the stable boy, when he ran out with the dog, leave the door unlocked behind him?"

"Excellent, Watson; excellent!" murmured my companion. "The importance of the point struck me so forcibly, that I sent a special wire to Dartmoor yesterday to clear the matter up. The boy locked the door before he left it. The window, I may add, was not large enough for a man to get through.

"Hunter waited until his fellow-grooms had returned, when he sent a message up to the trainer and told him what had occurred. Straker was excited at hearing the account, although he does not seem to have quite realized its true significance. It left him, however, vaguely uneasy, and Mrs. Straker, waking at one in the morning, found that he was dressing. In reply to her inquiries, he said that he could not sleep on account of his anxiety about the horses, and that he intended to walk down to the stables to see that all was well. She begged him to remain at home, as she could hear the rain pattering against the windows, but in spite of her entreaties he pulled on his large mackintosh and left the house.

"Mrs. Straker awoke at seven in the morning, to find that her husband had not yet returned. She dressed herself hastily, called the maid, and set off for the stables. The door was open; inside, huddled together upon a chair, Hunter was sunk in a state of absolute stupor, the favourite's stall was empty, and there were no signs of his trainer.

"The two lads who slept in the chaff-cutting loft above the harness-room were quickly roused. They had heard nothing during the night, for they are both sound sleepers. Hunter was obviously under the influence of some powerful drug; and, as no sense could be got out of him, he was left to sleep it off while the two lads and the two women ran out in search of the absentees. They still had hopes that the trainer had for some reason taken out the horse for early exercise, but on ascending the knoll near the house, from which all the neighbouring moors were visible, they not only could see no signs of the favourite, but they perceived something which warned them that they were in the presence of a tragedy.

"About a quarter of a mile from the stables, John Straker's overcoat was flapping from a furze bush. Immediately beyond there was a bowl-shaped depression in the moor, and at the bottom of this was found the dead body of the unfortunate trainer. His head had been shattered by a savage blow from some heavy weapon, and he was wounded in the thigh, where there was a long, clean cut, inflicted evidently by some very sharp instrument. It was clear, however, that Straker had defended himself vigorously against his assailants, for in his right hand he held a small knife, which was clotted with blood up to the handle, while in his left he grasped a red and black silk cravat, which was recognized by the maid as having been worn on the preceding evening by the stranger who had visited the stables.

"Hunter, on recovering from his stupor, was also quite positive as to the ownership of the cravat. He was equally certain that the same stranger had, while standing at the window, drugged his curried mutton, and so deprived the stables of their watchman.

"As to the missing horse, there were abundant proofs in the mud which lay at the bottom of the fatal hollow, that he had been there at the time of the struggle. But from that morning he has disappeared; and although a large reward has been offered, and all the gipsies of Dartmoor are on the alert, no news has come of him. Finally an analysis has shown that the remains of his supper, left by the stable lad, contain an appreciable quantity of powdered opium, while the people of the house partook of the same dish on the same night without any ill effect.

"Those are the main facts of the case stripped of all surmise and stated as baldly as possible. I shall now recapitulate what the police have done in the matter.

"Inspector Gregory, to whom the case has been committed, is an extremely competent officer. Were he but gifted with imagination he might rise to great heights in his profession. On his arrival he promptly found and arrested the man upon whom suspicion naturally rested. There was little difficulty in finding him, for he was thoroughly well known in the neighbourhood. His name, it appears, was Fitzroy Simpson. He was a man of excellent birth and education, who had squandered a fortune upon the turf, and who lived now by doing a little quiet and genteel bookmaking in the sporting clubs of London. An examination of his betting-book shows that bets to the amount of five thousand pounds had been registered by him against the favourite.

"On being arrested he volunteered the statement that he had come down to Dartmoor in the hope of getting some information about the King's Pyland horses, and also about Desborough, the second favourite, which was in charge of Silas Brown, at the Capleton stables. He did not attempt to deny that he had acted as described upon the evening before, but declared that he had no sinister designs, and had simply wished to obtain first-hand information. When confronted with the cravat he turned very pale, and was utterly unable to account for its presence in the hand of the murdered man. His wet clothing showed that he had been out in the storm of the night before, and his stick, which was a Penang lawyer,[1] weighted with lead, was just such a weapon as might, by repeated blows, have inflicted the terrible injuries to which the trainer had succumbed.

"On the other hand, there was no wound upon his person, while the state of Straker's knife would show that one, at least, of his assailants must bear his mark upon him. There you have it all in a nutshell, Watson, and if you can give me any light I shall be infinitely obliged to you."

I had listened with the greatest interest to the statement which Holmes, with characteristic clearness, had laid before me. Though most of the facts were familiar to me, I had not sufficiently appreciated their relative importance, nor their connection with each other.

"Is it not possible," I suggested, "that the incised wound upon Straker may have been caused by his own knife in the convulsive struggles which follow any brain injury?"

"It is more than possible; it is probable," said Holmes. "In that case, one of the main points in favour of the accused disappears."

"And yet," said I, "even now I fail to understand what the theory of the police can be."

"I am afraid that whatever theory we state has very grave objections to it," returned my companion. "The police imagine, I take it, that this Fitzroy Simpson, having drugged the lad, and having in some way obtained a duplicate key, opened the stable door, and took out the horse, with the intention, apparently, of kidnapping him altogether. His bridle is missing, so that Simpson must have put it on. Then, having left the door open behind him, he was leading the horse away over the moor, when he was either met or overtaken by the trainer. A row naturally ensued, Simpson beat out the trainer's brains with his heavy stick without receiving any injury from the small knife which Straker used in self-defence, and then the thief either led the horse on to some secret hiding-place, or else it may have bolted during the struggle, and be now wandering out on the moors. That is the case as it appears to the police, and improbable as it is, all other explanations are more improbable still.

---

[1] *Penang lawyer:* A kind of walking stick, made from the stem of a dwarf palm native to Penang.

However, I shall very quickly test the matter when I am once upon the spot, and until then I really cannot see how we can get much further than our present position."

It was evening before we reached the little town of Tavistock, which lies, like the boss of a shield, in the middle of the huge circle of Dartmoor. Two gentlemen were awaiting us at the station — the one a tall fair man with lion-like hair and beard, and curiously penetrating light blue eyes, the other a small alert person, very neat and dapper, in a frock-coat and gaiters, with trim little side-whiskers and an eye-glass. The latter was Colonel Ross, the well-known sportsman, the other Inspector Gregory, a man who was rapidly making his name in the English detective service.

"I am delighted that you have come down, Mr. Holmes," said the Colonel. "The Inspector here has done all that could possibly be suggested; but I wish to leave no stone unturned in trying to avenge poor Straker, and in recovering my horse."

"Have there been any fresh developments?" asked Holmes.

"I am sorry to say that we have made very little progress," said the Inspector. "We have an open carriage outside, and as you would no doubt like to see the place before the light fails, we might talk it over as we drive."

A minute later we were all seated in a comfortable landau and were rattling through the quaint old Devonshire town. Inspector Gregory was full of his case, and poured out a stream of remarks, while Holmes threw in an occasional question or interjection. Colonel Ross leaned back with his arms folded and his hat tilted over his eyes, while I listened with interest to the dialogue of the two detectives. Gregory was formulating his theory, which was almost exactly what Holmes had foretold in the train.

"The net is drawn pretty close round Fitzroy Simpson," he remarked, "and I believe myself that he is our man. At the same time, I recognize that the evidence is purely circumstantial, and that some new development may upset it."

"How about Straker's knife?"

"We have quite come to the conclusion that he wounded himself in his fall."

"My friend Dr. Watson made that suggestion to me as we came down. If so, it would tell against this man Simpson."

"Undoubtedly. He has neither a knife nor any sign of a wound. The evidence against him is certainly very strong. He had a great interest in the disappearance of the favourite, he lies under the suspicion of having poisoned the stable boy, he was undoubtedly out in the storm, he was armed with a heavy stick, and his cravat was found in the dead man's hand. I really think we have enough to go before a jury."

Holmes shook his head. "A clever counsel would tear it all to rags," said he. "Why should he take the horse out of the stable? If he wished to injure it, why could he not do it there? Has a duplicate key been found in his possession? What chemist sold him the powdered opium? Above all, where could he, a stranger to the district, hide a horse, and such a horse as this? What is his own explanation as to the paper which he wished the maid to give to the stable boy?"

"He says that it was a ten-pound note. One was found in his purse. But your other difficulties are not so formidable as they seem. He is not a stranger to the district. He has twice lodged at Tavistock in the summer. The opium was probably brought from London. The key, having served its purpose, would be hurled away. The horse may lie at the bottom of one of the pits or old mines upon the moor."

"What does he say about the cravat?"

"He acknowledges that it is his, and declares that he had lost it. But a new element has been introduced into the case which may account for his leading the horse from the stable."

Holmes pricked up his ears.

"We have found traces which show that a party of gipsies encamped on Monday night within a mile of the spot where the murder took place. On Tuesday they were gone. Now, presuming that there was some understanding between Simpson and these gipsies, might he not have been leading the horse to them when he was overtaken, and may they not have him now?"

"It is certainly possible."

"The moor is being scoured for these gipsies. I have also examined every stable and outhouse in Tavistock, and for a radius of ten miles."

"There is another training stable quite close, I understand?"

"Yes, and that is a factor which we must certainly not neglect. As Desborough, their horse, was second in the betting, they had an interest in the disappearance of the favourite. Silas Brown, the trainer, is known to have had large bets upon the event, and he was no friend to poor Straker. We have, however, examined the stables, and there is nothing to connect him with the affair."

"And nothing to connect this man Simpson with the interests of the Capleton stable?"

"Nothing at all."

Holmes leaned back in the carriage and the conversation ceased. A few minutes later our driver pulled up at a neat little red-brick villa with overhanging eaves, which stood by the road. Some distance off, across a paddock, lay a long grey-tiled outbuilding. In every other direction the low curves of the moor, bronze-coloured from the fading ferns, stretched away to the skyline, broken only by the steeples of Tavistock, and by a cluster of houses away to the westward, which marked the Capleton stables. We all sprang out with the exception of Holmes, who continued to lean back with his eyes fixed upon the sky in front of him, entirely absorbed in his own thoughts. It was only when I touched his arm that he roused himself with a violent start and stepped out of the carriage.

"Excuse me," said he, turning to Colonel Ross, who had looked at him in some surprise. "I was day-dreaming." There was a gleam in his eyes and a suppressed excitement in his manner which convinced me, used as I was to his ways, that his hand was upon a clue, though I could not imagine where he had found it.

"Perhaps you would prefer at once to go on to the scene of the crime, Mr. Holmes?" said Gregory.

"I think that I should prefer to stay here a little and go into one or two questions of detail. Straker was brought back here, I presume?"

"Yes, he lies upstairs. The inquest is to-morrow."

"He has been in your service some years, Colonel Ross?"

"I have always found him an excellent servant."

"I presume that you made an inventory of what he had in his pockets at the time of his death, Inspector?"

"I have the things themselves in the sitting-room, if you would care to see them."

"I should be very glad."

We all filed into the front room, and sat round the central table, while the Inspector unlocked a square tin box and laid a small heap of things before us. There was a box of vestas,[2] two inches of tallow candle, an A.D.P. briar-root pipe, a pouch of sealskin with half an ounce of long-cut cavendish,[3] a silver watch with a gold chain, five sovereigns in gold, an aluminium pencil-case, a few papers, and an ivory-handled knife with a very delicate inflexible blade marked Weiss & Co., London.

"This is a very singular knife," said Holmes, lifting it up and examining it minutely. "I presume, as I see blood-stains upon it, that it is the one which was found in the dead man's grasp. Watson, this knife is surely in your line."

---

[2] *vestas:* Short friction matches made of wax or wood.
[3] *cavendish:* Smoking tobacco softened and pressed into solid cakes.

"It is what we call a cataract knife," said I.

"I thought so. A very delicate blade devised for very delicate work. A strange thing for a man to carry with him upon a rough expedition, especially as it would not shut in his pocket."

"The tip was guarded by a disc of cork which we found beside his body," said the Inspector. "His wife tells us that the knife had lain for some days upon the dressing-table, and that he had picked it up as he left the room. It was a poor weapon, but perhaps the best that he could lay his hand on at the moment."

"Very possibly. How about these papers?"

"Three of them are receipted hay-dealers' accounts. One of them is a letter of instructions from Colonel Ross. This other is a milliner's account for thirty-seven pounds fifteen, made out by Madame Lesurier, of Bond Street, to William Darbyshire. Mrs. Straker tells us that Darbyshire was a friend of her husband's, and that occasionally his letters were addressed here."

"Madame Darbyshire had somewhat expensive tastes," remarked Holmes, glancing down the account. "Twenty-two guineas is rather heavy for a single costume. However, there appears to be nothing more to learn, and we may now go down to the scene of the crime."

As we emerged from the sitting-room a woman who had been waiting in the passage took a step forward and laid her hand upon the Inspector's sleeve. Her face was haggard, and thin, and eager, stamped with the print of a recent horror.

"Have you got them? Have you found them?" she panted.

"No, Mrs. Straker; but Mr. Holmes, here, has come from London to help us, and we shall do all that is possible."

"Surely I met you in Plymouth, at a garden-party, some little time ago, Mrs. Straker," said Holmes.

"No, sir; you are mistaken."

"Dear me; why, I could have sworn to it. You wore a costume of dove-coloured silk with ostrich feather trimming."

"I never had such a dress, sir," answered the lady.

"Ah, that quite settles it," said Holmes; and, with an apology, he followed the Inspector outside. A short walk across the moor took us to the hollow in which the body had been found. At the brink of it was the furze bush upon which the coat had been hung.

"There was no wind that night, I understand," said Holmes.

"None, but very heavy rain."

"In that case the overcoat was not blown against the furze bushes, but placed there."

"Yes, it was laid across the bush."

"You fill me with interest. I perceive that the ground has been trampled up a good deal. No doubt many feet have been there since Monday
night."

"A piece of matting has been laid here at the side, and we have all
stood upon that."

"Excellent."

"In this bag I have one of the boots which Straker wore, one of
Fitzroy Simpson's shoes, and a cast horseshoe of Silver Blaze."

"My dear Inspector, you surpass yourself!"

Holmes took the bag, and descending into the hollow he pushed
the matting into a more central position. Then stretching himself upon
his face and leaning his chin upon his hands he made a careful study of
the trampled mud in front of him.

"Halloa!" said he, suddenly, "what's this?"

It was a wax vesta, half burned, which was so coated with mud that
it looked at first like a little chip of wood.

"I cannot think how I came to overlook it," said the Inspector, with
an expression of annoyance.

"It was invisible, buried in the mud. I only saw it because I was
looking for it."

"What! You expected to find it?"

"I thought it not unlikely." He took the boots from the bag and
compared the impressions of each of them with marks upon the
ground. Then he clambered up to the rim of the hollow and crawled
about among the ferns and bushes.

"I am afraid that there are no more tracks," said the Inspector. "I
have examined the ground very carefully for a hundred yards in each
direction."

"Indeed!" said Holmes, rising, "I should not have the impertinence
to do it again after what you say. But I should like to take a little walk
over the moors before it grows dark, that I may know my ground to-
morrow, and I think that I shall put this horseshoe into my pocket for
luck."

Colonel Ross, who had shown some signs of impatience at my
companion's quiet and systematic method of work, glanced at his
watch.

"I wish you would come back with me, Inspector," said he. "There
are several points on which I should like your advice, and especially as to
whether we do not owe it to the public to remove our horse's name
from the entries for the Cup."

"Certainly not," cried Holmes, with decision; "I should let the name stand."

The Colonel bowed. "I am very glad to have had your opinion, sir," said he. "You will find us at poor Straker's house when you have finished your walk, and we can drive together into Tavistock."

He turned back with the Inspector, while Holmes and I walked slowly across the moor. The sun was beginning to sink behind the stables of Capleton, and the long sloping plain in front of us was tinged with gold, deepening into rich, ruddy brown where the faded ferns and brambles caught the evening light. But the glories of the landscape were all wasted upon my companion, who was sunk in the deepest thought.

"It's this way, Watson," he said, at last. "We may leave the question of who killed John Straker for the instant, and confine ourselves to finding out what has become of the horse. Now, supposing that he broke away during or after the tragedy, where could he have gone to? The horse is a very gregarious creature. If left to himself, his instincts would have been either to return to King's Pyland or go over to Capleton. Why should he run wild upon the moor? He would surely have been seen by now. And why should gipsies kidnap him? These people always clear out when they hear of trouble, for they do not wish to be pestered by the police. They could not hope to sell such a horse. They would run a great risk and gain nothing by taking him. Surely that is clear."

"Where is he, then?"

"I have already said that he must have gone to King's Pyland or to Capleton. He is not at King's Pyland; therefore he is at Capleton. Let us take that as a working hypothesis, and see what it leads us to. This part of the moor, as the Inspector remarked, is very hard and dry. But it falls away towards Capleton, and you can see from here that there is a long hollow over yonder, which must have been very wet on Monday night. If our supposition is correct, then the horse must have crossed that, and there is the point where we should look for his tracks."

We had been walking briskly during this conversation, and a few more minutes brought us to the hollow in question. At Holmes's request I walked down the bank to the right, and he to the left, but I had not taken fifty paces before I heard him give a shout, and saw him waving his hand to me. The track of a horse was plainly outlined in the soft earth in front of him, and the shoe which he took from his pocket exactly fitted the impression.

"See the value of imagination," said Holmes. "It is the one quality which Gregory lacks. We imagined what might have happened, acted upon the supposition, and find ourselves justified. Let us proceed."

We crossed the marshy bottom and passed over a quarter of a mile of dry, hard turf. Again the ground sloped and again we came on the tracks. Then we lost them for half a mile, but only to pick them up once more quite close to Capleton. It was Holmes who saw them first, and he stood pointing with a look of triumph upon his face. A man's track was visible beside the horse's.

"The horse was alone before," I cried.

"Quite so. It was alone before. Halloa! what is this?"

The double track turned sharp off and took the direction of King's Pyland. Holmes whistled, and we both followed along after it. His eyes were on the trail, but I happened to look a little to one side, and saw to my surprise the same tracks coming back again in the opposite direction.

"One for you, Watson," said Holmes, when I pointed it out; "you have saved us a long walk which would have brought us back on our own traces. Let us follow the return track."

We had not to go far. It ended at the paving of asphalt which led up to the gates of the Capleton stables. As we approached a groom ran out from them.

"We don't want any loiterers about here," said he.

"I only wished to ask a question," said Holmes, with his finger and thumb in his waistcoat pocket. "Should I be too early to see your master, Mr. Silas Brown, if I were to call at five o'clock to-morrow morning?"

"Bless you, sir, if anyone is about he will be, for he is always the first stirring. But here he is, sir, to answer your questions for himself. No, sir, no; it's as much as my place is worth to let him see me touch your money. Afterwards, if you like."

As Sherlock Holmes replaced the half-crown which he had drawn from his pocket, a fierce-looking elderly man strode out from the gate with a hunting-crop swinging in his hand.

"What's this, Dawson?" he cried. "No gossiping! Go about your business! And you — what the devil do you want here?"

"Ten minutes' talk with you, my good sir," said Holmes, in the sweetest of voices.

"I've no time to talk to every gadabout. We want no strangers here. Be off, or you may find a dog at your heels."

Holmes leaned forward and whispered something in the trainer's ear. He started violently and flushed to the temples.

"It's a lie!" he shouted. "An infernal lie!"

"Very good! Shall we argue about it here in public, or talk it over in your parlour?"

"Oh, come in if you wish to."

Holmes smiled. "I shall not keep you more than a few minutes, Watson," he said. "Now, Mr. Brown, I am quite at your disposal."

It was quite twenty minutes, and the reds had all faded into greys before Holmes and the trainer reappeared. Never have I seen such a change as had been brought about in Silas Brown in that short time. His face was ashy pale, beads of perspiration shone upon his brow, and his hands shook until the hunting-crop wagged like a branch in the wind. His bullying, overbearing manner was all gone too, and he cringed along at my companion's side like a dog with its master.

"Your instructions will be done. It shall be done," said he.

"There must be no mistake," said Holmes, looking round at him. The other winced as he read the menace in his eyes.

"Oh, no, there shall be no mistake. It shall be there. Should I change it first or not?"

Holmes thought a little and then burst out laughing. "No, don't," said he. "I shall write to you about it. No tricks now or —— "

"Oh, you can trust me, you can trust me!"

"You must see to it on the day as if it were your own."

"You can rely upon me."

"Yes, I think I can. Well, you shall hear from me to-morrow." He turned upon his heel, disregarding the trembling hand which the other held out to him, and we set off for King's Pyland.

"A more perfect compound of the bully, coward and sneak than Master Silas Brown I have seldom met with," remarked Holmes, as we trudged along together.

"He has the horse, then?"

"He tried to bluster out of it, but I described to him so exactly what his actions had been upon that morning, that he is convinced that I was watching him. Of course, you observed the peculiarly square toes in the impressions, and that his own boots exactly corresponded to them. Again, of course, no subordinate would have dared to have done such a thing. I described to him how when, according to his custom, he was the first down, he perceived a strange horse wandering over the moor; how he went out to it, and his astonishment at recognizing from the white forehead which has given the favourite its name that chance had put in his power the only horse which could beat the one upon which he had put his money. Then I described how his first impulse had been to lead him back to King's Pyland, and how the devil had shown him how he could hide the horse until the race was over, and how he had led it back and concealed it at Capleton. When I told him every detail he gave it up, and thought only of saving his own skin."

"But his stables had been searched."

"Oh, an old horse-faker like him has many a dodge."

"But are you not afraid to leave the horse in his power now, since he has every interest in injuring it?"

"My dear fellow, he will guard it as the apple of his eye. He knows that his only hope of mercy is to produce it safe."

"Colonel Ross did not impress me as a man who would be likely to show much mercy in any case."

"The matter does not rest with Colonel Ross. I follow my own methods, and tell as much or as little as I choose. That is the advantage of being unofficial. I don't know whether you observed it, Watson, but the Colonel's manner has been just a trifle cavalier to me. I am inclined now to have a little amusement at his expense. Say nothing to him about the horse."

"Certainly not without your permission."

"And, of course, this is all quite a minor case compared with the question of who killed John Straker."

"And you will devote yourself to that?"

"On the contrary, we both go back to London by the night train."

I was thunderstruck by my friend's words. We had only been a few hours in Devonshire, and that he should give up an investigation which he had begun so brilliantly was quite incomprehensible to me. Not a word more could I draw from him until we were back at the trainer's house. The Colonel and the Inspector were awaiting us in the parlour.

"My friend and I return to town by the midnight express," said Holmes. "We have had a charming little breath of your beautiful Dartmoor air."

The Inspector opened his eyes, and the Colonel's lips curled in a sneer.

"So you despair of arresting the murderer of poor Straker," said he.

Holmes shrugged his shoulders. "There are certainly grave difficulties in the way," said he. "I have every hope, however, that your horse will start upon Tuesday, and I beg that you will have your jockey in readiness. Might I ask for a photograph of Mr. John Straker?"

The Inspector took one from an envelope in his pocket and handed it to him.

"My dear Gregory, you anticipate all my wants. If I might ask you to wait here for an instant, I have a question which I should like to put to the maid."

"I must say that I am rather disappointed in our London consultant," said Colonel Ross, bluntly, as my friend left the room. "I do not see that we are any further than when he came."

"At least, you have his assurance that your horse will run," said I.

"Yes, I have his assurance," said the Colonel, with a shrug of his shoulders. "I should prefer to have the horse."

I was about to make some reply in defence of my friend, when he entered the room again.

"Now, gentlemen," said he, "I am quite ready for Tavistock."

As we stepped into the carriage one of the stable lads held the door open for us. A sudden idea seemed to occur to Holmes, for he leaned forward and touched the lad upon the sleeve.

"You have a few sheep in the paddock," he said. "Who attends to them?"

"I do, sir."

"Have you noticed anything amiss with them of late?"

"Well, sir, not of much account; but three of them have gone lame, sir."

I could see that Holmes was extremely pleased, for he chuckled and rubbed his hands together.

"A long shot, Watson, a very long shot!" said he, pinching my arm. "Gregory, let me recommend to your attention this singular epidemic among the sheep. Drive on, coachman!"

Colonel Ross still wore an expression which showed the poor opinion which he had formed of my companion's ability, but I saw by the Inspector's face that his attention had been keenly aroused.

"You consider that to be important?" he asked.

"Exceedingly so."

"Is there any other point to which you would wish to draw my attention?"

"To the curious incident of the dog in the night-time."

"The dog did nothing in the night-time."

"That was the curious incident," remarked Sherlock Holmes.

Four days later Holmes and I were again in the train bound for Winchester, to see the race for the Wessex Cup. Colonel Ross met us, by appointment, outside the station, and we drove in his drag[4] to the course beyond the town. His face was grave and his manner was cold in the extreme.

[4] *drag:* A private vehicle similar to a stagecoach, usually drawn by four horses, with seats inside and on top.

"I have seen nothing of my horse," said he.

"I suppose that you would know him when you saw him?" asked Holmes.

The Colonel was very angry. "I have been on the turf for twenty years, and never was asked such a question as that before," said he. "A child would know Silver Blaze with his white forehead and his mottled off foreleg."

"How is the betting?"

"Well, that is the curious part of it. You could have got fifteen to one yesterday, but the price has become shorter and shorter, until you can hardly get three to one now."

"Hum!" said Holmes. "Somebody knows something, that is clear!"

As the drag drew up in the enclosure near the grandstand, I glanced at the card to see the entries. It ran:

Wessex Plate. 50 sovs. each, h ft, with 1,000 sovs. added, for four- and five-year olds. Second £300. Third £200. New course (one mile and five furlongs).
1. Mr. Heath Newton's The Negro (red cap, cinnamon jacket).
2. Colonel Wardlaw's Pugilist (pink cap, blue and black jacket).
3. Lord Backwater's Desborough (yellow cap and sleeves).
4. Colonel Ross's Silver Blaze (black cap, red jacket).
5. Duke of Balmoral's Iris (yellow and black stripes).
6. Lord Singleford's Rasper (purple cap, black sleeves).

"We scratched our other one and put all hopes on your word," said the Colonel. "Why, what is that? Silver Blaze favourite?"

"Five to four against Silver Blaze!" roared the ring. "Five to four against Silver Blaze! Fifteen to five against Desborough! Five to four on the field!"

"There are the numbers up," I cried. "They are all six there."

"All six there! Then my horse is running," cried the Colonel, in great agitation. "But I don't see him. My colours have not passed."

"Only five have passed. This must be he."

As I spoke a powerful bay horse swept out from the weighing enclosure and cantered past us, bearing on its back the well-known black and red of the Colonel.

"That's not my horse," cried the owner. "That beast has not a white hair upon its body. What is this that you have done, Mr. Holmes?"

"Well, well, let us see how he gets on," said my friend, imperturbably. For a few minutes he gazed through my field-glass. "Capital! An excellent start!" he cried suddenly. "There they are, coming round the curve!"

From our drag we had a superb view as they came up the straight. The six horses were so close together that a carpet could have covered them, but half-way up the yellow of the Capleton stable showed to the front. Before they reached us, however, Desborough's bolt was shot, and the Colonel's horse, coming away with a rush, passed the post a good six lengths before its rival, the Duke of Balmoral's Iris making a bad third.

"It's my race anyhow," gasped the Colonel, passing his hand over his eyes. "I confess that I can make neither head not tail of it. Don't you think that you have kept up your mystery long enough, Mr. Holmes?"

"Certainly, Colonel. You shall know everything. Let us all go round and have a look at the horse together. Here he is," he continued, as we made our way into the weighing enclosure where only owners and their friends find admittance. "You have only to wash his face and his leg in spirits of wine and you will find that he is the same old Silver Blaze as ever."

"You take my breath away!"

"I found him in the hands of a faker, and took the liberty of running him just as he was sent over."

"My dear sir, you have done wonders. The horse looks very fit and well. It never went better in its life. I owe you a thousand apologies for having doubted your ability. You have done me a great service by recovering my horse. You would do me a greater still if you could lay your hands on the murderer of John Straker."

"I have done so," said Holmes, quietly.

The Colonel and I stared at him in amazement. "You have got him! Where is he, then?"

"He is here."

"Here! Where?"

"In my company at the present moment."

The Colonel flushed angrily. "I quite recognize that I am under obligations to you, Mr. Holmes," said he, "but I must regard what you have just said as either a very bad joke or an insult."

Sherlock Holmes laughed. "I assure you that I have not associated you with the crime, Colonel," said he; "the real murderer is standing immediately behind you!"

He stepped past and laid his hand upon the glossy neck of the thoroughbred.

"The horse!" cried both the Colonel and myself.

"Yes, the horse. And it may lessen his guilt if I say that it was done in self-defence, and that John Straker was a man who was entirely unworthy of your confidence. But there goes the bell; and as I stand to win a little on this next race, I shall defer a more lengthy explanation until a more fitting time."

We had the corner of a Pullman car to ourselves that evening as we whirled back to London, and I fancy that the journey was a short one to Colonel Ross as well as to myself, as we listened to our companion's narrative of the events which had occurred at the Dartmoor training stables upon that Monday night, and the means by which he had unravelled them.

"I confess," said he, "that any theories which I had formed from the newspaper reports were entirely erroneous. And yet there were indications there, had they not been overlaid by other details which concealed their true import. I went to Devonshire with the conviction that Fitzroy Simpson was the true culprit, although, of course, I saw that the evidence against him was by no means complete.

"It was while I was in the carriage, just as we reached the trainer's house, that the immense significance of the curried mutton occurred to me. You may remember that I was distrait, and remained sitting after you had all alighted. I was marvelling in my own mind how I could possibly have overlooked so obvious a clue."

"I confess," said the Colonel, "that even now I cannot see how it helps us."

"It was the first link in my chain of reasoning. Powdered opium is by no means tasteless. The flavour is not disagreeable, but it is perceptible. Were it mixed with any ordinary dish, the eater would undoubtedly detect it, and would probably eat no more. A curry was exactly the medium which would disguise this taste. By no possible supposition could this stranger, Fitzroy Simpson, have caused curry to be served in the trainer's family that night, and it is surely too monstrous a coincidence to suppose that he happened to come along with powdered opium upon the very night when a dish happened to be served which would disguise the flavour. That is unthinkable. Therefore Simpson becomes eliminated from the case, and our attention centres upon Straker and his wife, the only two people who could have chosen curried mutton for supper that night. The opium was added after the dish was set aside for the stable boy, for the others had the same for supper with no ill effects. Which of them, then, had access to that dish without the maid seeing them?

"Before deciding that question I had grasped the significance of the silence of the dog, for one true inference invariably suggests others. The Simpson incident had shown me that a dog was kept in the stables, and yet, though someone had been in and had fetched out a horse, he had not barked enough to arouse the two lads in the loft. Obviously the midnight visitor was someone whom the dog knew well.

"I was already convinced, or almost convinced, that John Straker went down to the stables in the dead of the night and took out Silver Blaze. For what purpose? For a dishonest one, obviously, or why should he drug his own stable boy? And yet I was at a loss to know why. There have been cases before now where trainers have made sure of great sums of money by laying against their own horses, through agents, and then prevented them from winning by fraud. Sometimes it is a pulling jockey. Sometimes it is some surer and subtler means. What was it here? I hoped that the contents of his pockets might help me to form a conclusion.

"And they did so. You cannot have forgotten the singular knife which was found in the dead man's hand, a knife which certainly no sane man would choose for a weapon. It was, as Dr. Watson told us, a form of knife which is used for the most delicate operations known in surgery. And it was to be used for a delicate operation that night. You must know, with your wide experience of turf matters, Colonel Ross, that it is possible to make a slight nick upon the tendons of a horse's ham, and to do it subcutaneously so as to leave absolutely no trace. A horse so treated would develop a slight lameness which would be put down to a strain in exercise or a touch of rheumatism, but never to foul play."

"Villain! Scoundrel!" cried the Colonel.

"We have here the explanation of why John Straker wished to take the horse out on to the moor. So spirited a creature would have certainly roused the soundest of sleepers when it felt the prick of the knife. It was absolutely necessary to do it in the open air."

"I have been blind!" cried the Colonel. "Of course, that was why he needed the candle, and struck the match."

"Undoubtedly. But in examining his belongings, I was fortunate enough to discover, not only the method of the crime, but even its motives. As a man of the world, Colonel, you know that men do not carry other people's bills about in their pockets. We have most of us quite enough to do to settle our own. I at once concluded that Straker was leading a double life, and keeping a second establishment. The nature of the bill showed that there was a lady in the case, and one who had expensive tastes. Liberal as you are with your servants, one hardly expects that they can buy twenty-guinea walking dresses for their women. I questioned Mrs. Straker as to the dress without her knowing it, and having satisfied myself that it had never reached her, I made a note of the milliner's address, and felt that by calling there with Straker's photograph, I could easily dispose of the mythical Darbyshire.

"From that time on all was plain. Straker had led out the horse to a hollow where his light would be invisible. Simpson, in his flight, had dropped his cravat, and Straker had picked it up with some idea, perhaps, that he might use it in securing the horse's leg. Once in the hollow he had got behind the horse, and had struck a light, but the creature, frightened at the sudden glare, and with the strange instinct of animals feeling that some mischief was intended, had lashed out, and the steel shoe had struck Straker full on the forehead. He had already, in spite of the rain, taken off his overcoat in order to do this delicate task, and so, as he fell, his knife gashed his thigh. Do I make it clear?"

"Wonderful!" cried the Colonel. "Wonderful! You might have been there."

"My final shot was, I confess, a very long one. It struck me that so astute a man as Straker would not undertake this delicate tendon-nicking without a little practice. What could he practise on? My eyes fell upon the sheep, and I asked a question which, rather to my surprise, showed that my surmise was correct."

"You have made it perfectly clear, Mr. Holmes."

"When I returned to London I called upon the milliner, who at once recognized Straker as an excellent customer, of the name of Darbyshire, who had a very dashing wife with a strong partiality for expensive dresses. I have no doubt that this woman had plunged him over head and ears in debt, and so led him into this miserable plot."

"You have explained all but one thing," cried the Colonel. "Where was the horse?"

"Ah, it bolted and was cared for by one of your neighbours. We must have an amnesty in that direction, I think. This is Clapham Junction, if I am not mistaken, and we shall be in Victoria in less than ten minutes. If you care to smoke a cigar in our rooms, Colonel, I shall be happy to give you any other details which might interest you."

## AFTERWORD

Doyle thought highly of this story, but eventually was persuaded that "the racing detail . . . is very faulty." As he wrote in his memoirs,

> Sometimes I have got upon dangerous ground where I have taken risks through my own want of knowledge of the correct atmosphere. I have, for example, never been a racing man, and yet I ventured to write "Silver Blaze," in which the mystery depends upon the laws of training and racing. The story is all right, and Holmes may have been at the top of his form, but my ignorance

cries aloud to heaven. I read an excellent and very damaging criticism of the story in some sporting paper, written clearly by a man who *did* know, in which he explained the exact penalties which would have come upon every one concerned if they had acted as I described. Half would have been in jail and the other half warned off the turf for ever. However, I have never been nervous about details, and one must be masterful sometimes. When an alarmed Editor wrote to me once: "There is no second line of rails at that point," I answered, "I make one." On the other hand, there are cases where accuracy is essential. (*Memories and Adventures* 107–08)

The point at issue here, that of "liberties" versus "errors," matters to some degree in nearly all writing, fiction as well as nonfiction, but within fiction is particularly significant in detective literature.

"Silver Blaze" deserves particular attention as an example of Holmes's detective methodology; the famous line about "the curious incident of the dog in the night-time" only begins to suggest its imaginativeness. But imaginativeness — the ability to hypothesize intelligently, to guess shrewdly — is indeed the detective quality most prominently on display in this story where the evidence, or most of it, has already been gathered by another detective (Gregory) with strong powers of observation. "See the value of imagination," Holmes notes as his investigation begins to come together. "It is the one quality which Gregory lacks. We imagined what might have happened, acted upon the supposition, and find ourselves justified." From a tentative start he can proceed with gradually increasing confidence, "for one true inference invariably suggests others."

"I suppose that you would know him when you saw him?" Holmes asks Colonel Ross of his missing horse. The Colonel is angered by the hinted aspersion on his horse sense; but when an unrecognized horse wins the race for him, he quickly confesses, "I can make neither head nor tail of it." Even to a practiced eye, it seems, one horse, only superficially disguised, looks much like another: a Silver Blaze can vanish into anonymity among his fellow creatures as easily as a John Clay ("The Red-headed League") or a Hugh Boone ("The Man with the Twisted Lip").

In choosing "to have a little amusement at [Col. Ross's] expense" because "the Colonel's manner has been just a trifle cavalier to me," Holmes follows Legrand's example in Poe's story "The Gold-Bug": "I felt somewhat annoyed by your evident suspicions touching my sanity, and so resolved to punish you quietly, in my own way, by a little bit of sober mystification."

# The Musgrave Ritual

An anomaly which often struck me in the character of my friend
Sherlock Holmes was that, although in his methods of thought he was
the neatest and most methodical of mankind, and although also he affected a certain quiet primness of dress, he was none the less in his personal habits one of the most untidy men that ever drove a fellow-lodger
to distraction. Not that I am in the least conventional in that respect
myself. The rough-and-tumble work in Afghanistan, coming on the top
of a natural Bohemianism of disposition, has made me rather more lax
than befits a medical man. But with me there is a limit, and when I find
a man who keeps his cigars in the coal-scuttle, his tobacco in the toe-
end of a Persian slipper, and his unanswered correspondence transfixed
by a jack-knife into the very centre of his wooden mantelpiece, then I
begin to give myself virtuous airs. I have always held, too, that pistol
practice should distinctly be an open-air pastime; and when Holmes in
one of his queer humours would sit in an arm-chair, with his hair-
trigger and a hundred Boxer cartridges, and proceed to adorn the opposite wall with a patriotic V.R.[1] done in bullet-pocks, I felt strongly that
neither the atmosphere nor the appearance of our room was improved
by it.

Our chambers were always full of chemicals and of criminal relics,
which had a way of wandering into unlikely positions, and of turning up
in the butter-dish, or in even less desirable places. But his papers were
my great crux. He had a horror of destroying documents, especially
those which were connected with his past cases, and yet it was only once
in every year or two that he would muster energy to docket and arrange
them, for as I have mentioned somewhere in these incoherent memoirs,
the outbursts of passionate energy when he performed the remarkable
feats with which his name is associated were followed by reactions of
lethargy, during which he would lie about with his violin and his books,
hardly moving, save from the sofa to the table. Thus month after month
his papers accumulated, until every corner of the room was stacked with
bundles of manuscript which were on no account to be burned, and
which could not be put away save by their owner.

One winter's night, as we sat together by the fire, I ventured to
suggest to him that as he had finished pasting extracts into his

From *The Memoirs of Sherlock Holmes* (1894). First published in the *Strand*, May
1893.
  [1] *V.R.:* Victoria Regina, or Queen Victoria.

commonplace book he might employ the next two hours in making our room a little more habitable. He could not deny the justice of my request, so with a rather rueful face he went off to his bedroom, from which he returned presently pulling a large tin box behind him. This he placed in the middle of the floor, and squatting down upon a stool in front of it he threw back the lid. I could see that it was already a third full of bundles of paper tied up with red tape into separate packages.

"There are cases enough here, Watson," said he, looking at me with mischievous eyes. "I think that if you knew all that I had in this box you would ask me to pull some out instead of putting others in."

"These are the records of your early work, then?" I asked. "I have often wished that I had notes of those cases."

"Yes, my boy; these were all done prematurely, before my biographer had come to glorify me." He lifted bundle after bundle in a tender, caressing sort of way. "They are not all successes, Watson," said he, "but there are some pretty little problems among them. Here's the record of the Tarleton murders, and the case of Vamberry, the wine merchant, and the adventure of the old Russian woman, and the singular affair of the aluminium crutch, as well as a full account of Ricoletti of the club foot and his abominable wife. And here — ah, now! this really is something a little *recherché*."

He dived his arm down to the bottom of the chest, and brought up a small wooden box, with a sliding lid, such as children's toys are kept in. From within he produced a crumpled piece of paper, an old-fashioned brass key, a peg of wood with a ball of string attached to it, and three rusty old discs of metal.

"Well, my boy, what do you make of this lot?" he asked, smiling at my expression.

"It is a curious collection."

"Very curious, and the story that hangs round it will strike you as being more curious still."

"These relics have a history, then?"

"So much so that they *are* history."

"What do you mean by that?"

Sherlock Holmes picked them up one by one, and laid them along the edge of the table. Then he re-seated himself in his chair, and looked them over with a gleam of satisfaction in his eyes.

"These," said he, "are all that I have left to remind me of the episode of the Musgrave Ritual."

I had heard him mention the case more than once, though I had never been able to gather the details.

"I should be so glad," said I, "if you would give me an account of it."

"And leave the litter as it is?" he cried, mischievously. "Your tidiness won't bear much strain, after all, Watson. But I should be glad that you should add this case to your annals, for there are points in it which make it quite unique in the criminal records of this or, I believe, of any other country. A collection of my trifling achievements would certainly be incomplete which contained no account of this very singular business.

"You may remember how the affair of the *Gloria Scott,* and my conversation with the unhappy man whose fate I told you of, first turned my attention in the direction of the profession which has become my life's work. You see me now when my name has become known far and wide, and when I am generally recognized both by the public and by the official force as being a final court of appeal in doubtful cases. Even when you knew me first, at the time of the affair which you have commemorated in 'A Study in Scarlet,' I had already established a considerable, though not a very lucrative, connection. You can hardly realize, then, how difficult I found it at first, and how long I had to wait before I succeeded in making any headway.

"When I first came up to London I had rooms in Montague Street, just round the corner from the British Museum, and there I waited, filling in my too abundant leisure time by studying all those branches of science which might make me more efficient. Now and again cases came in my way, principally through the introduction of old fellow-students, for during my last years at the university there was a good deal of talk there about myself and my methods. The third of these cases was that of the Musgrave Ritual, and it is to the interest which was aroused by that singular chain of events, and the large issues which proved to be at stake, that I trace my first stride towards the position which I now hold.

"Reginald Musgrave had been in the same college as myself, and I had some slight acquaintance with him. He was not generally popular among the undergraduates, though it always seemed to me that what was set down as pride was really an attempt to cover extreme natural diffidence. In appearance he was a man of an exceedingly aristocratic type, thin, high-nosed, and large-eyed, with languid and yet courtly manners. He was indeed a scion of one of the very oldest families in the kingdom, though his branch was a cadet[2] one which had separated from the Northern Musgraves some time in the sixteenth century, and had

---

[2] *cadet:* A younger son or brother; here, a branch of a family descended from a younger brother.

established itself in Western Sussex, where the manor house of Hurlstone is perhaps the oldest inhabited building in the county. Something of his birthplace seemed to cling to the man, and I never looked at his pale, keen face, or the poise of his head, without associating him with grey archways and mullioned windows and all the venerable wreckage of a feudal keep. Now and again we drifted into talk, and I can remember that more than once he expressed a keen interest in my methods of observation and inference.

"For four years I had seen nothing of him, until one morning he walked into my room in Montague Street. He had changed little, was dressed like a young man of fashion — he was always a bit of a dandy — and preserved the same quiet, suave manner which had formerly distinguished him.

"'How has all gone with you, Musgrave?' I asked, after we had cordially shaken hands.

"'You probably heard of my poor father's death,' said he. 'He was carried off about two years ago. Since then I have, of course, had the Hurlstone estates to manage, and as I am member for my district as well, my life has been a busy one; but I understand, Holmes, that you are turning to practical ends those powers with which you used to amaze us.'

"'Yes,' said I, 'I have taken to living by my wits.'

"'I am delighted to hear it, for your advice at present would be exceedingly valuable to me. We have had some very strange doings at Hurlstone, and the police have been able to throw no light upon the matter. It is really the most extraordinary and inexplicable business.'

"You can imagine with what eagerness I listened to him, Watson, for the very chance for which I had been panting during all those months of inaction seemed to have come within my reach. In my inmost heart I believed that I could succeed where others failed, and now I had the opportunity to test myself.

"'Pray let me have the details,' I cried.

"Reginald Musgrave sat down opposite to me, and lit the cigarette which I had pushed towards him.

"'You must know,' said he, 'that though I am a bachelor I have to keep up a considerable staff of servants at Hurlstone, for it is a rambling old place, and takes a good deal of looking after. I preserve, too, and in the pheasant months I usually have a house-party, so that it would not do to be short-handed. Altogether there are eight maids, the cook, the butler, two footmen, and a boy. The garden and the stables, of course, have a separate staff.

" 'Of these servants the one who had been longest in our service was Brunton, the butler. He was a young schoolmaster out of place when he was first taken up by my father, but he was a man of great energy and character, and he soon became quite invaluable in the household. He was a well-grown, handsome man, with a splendid forehead, and though he has been with us for twenty years he cannot be more than forty now. With his personal advantages and his extraordinary gifts, for he can speak several languages and play nearly every musical instrument, it is wonderful that he should have been satisfied so long in such a position, but I suppose that he was comfortable and lacked energy to make any change. The butler of Hurlstone is always a thing that is remembered by all who visit us.

" 'But this paragon has one fault. He is a bit of a Don Juan, and you can imagine that for a man like him it is not a very difficult part to play in a quiet country district.

" 'When he was married it was all right, but since he has been a widower we have had no end of trouble with him. A few months ago we were in hopes that he was about to settle down again, for he became engaged to Rachel Howells, our second housemaid, but he has thrown her over since then and taken up with Janet Tregellis, the daughter of the head gamekeeper. Rachel, who is a very good girl, but of an excitable Welsh temperament, had a sharp touch of brain fever, and goes about the house now — or did until yesterday — like a black-eyed shadow of her former self. That was our first drama at Hurlstone, but a second one came to drive it from our minds, and it was prefaced by the disgrace and dismissal of butler Brunton.

" 'This is how it came about. I have said that the man was intelligent, and this very intelligence has caused his ruin, for it seems to have led to an insatiable curiosity about things which did not in the least concern him. I had no idea of the lengths to which this would carry him until the merest accident opened my eyes to it.

" 'I have said that the house is a rambling one. One night last week — on Thursday night, to be more exact — I found that I could not sleep, having foolishly taken a cup of strong *café noir* after my dinner. After struggling against it until two in the morning I felt that it was quite hopeless, so I rose and lit the candle with the intention of continuing a novel which I was reading. The book, however, had been left in the billiard-room, so I pulled on my dressing-gown and started off to get it.

" 'In order to reach the billiard-room I had to descend a flight of stairs, and then to cross the head of the passage which led to the library and the gun-room. You can imagine my surprise when as I looked down this corridor I saw a glimmer of light coming from the open door of the library. I had myself extinguished the lamp and closed the door before coming to bed. Naturally, my first thought was of burglars. The corridors at Hurlstone have their walls largely decorated with trophies of old weapons. From one of these I picked a battle-axe, and then, leaving my candle behind me, I crept on tiptoe down the passage and peeped in at the open door.

"'Brunton, the butler, was in the library. He was sitting, fully dressed, in an easy chair, with a slip of paper, which looked like a map, upon his knee, and his forehead sunk forward upon his hand in deep thought. I stood, dumb with astonishment, watching him from the darkness. A small taper on the edge of the table shed a feeble light, which sufficed to show me that he was fully dressed. Suddenly, as I looked, he rose from his chair, and walking over to a bureau at the side, he unlocked it and drew out one of the drawers. From this he took a paper, and, returning to his seat, he flattened it out beside the taper on the edge of the table, and began to study it with minute attention. My indignation at this calm examination of our family documents overcame me so far that I took a step forward, and Brunton looking up saw me standing in the doorway. He sprang to his feet, his face turned livid with fear, and he thrust into his breast the chart-like paper which he had been originally studying.

"'"So!" said I, "this is how you repay the trust which we have reposed in you! You will leave my service to-morrow."

"'He bowed with the look of a man who is utterly crushed, and slunk past me without a word. The taper was still on the table, and by its light I glanced to see what the paper was which Brunton had taken from the bureau. To my surprise it was nothing of any importance at all, but simply a copy of the questions and answers in the singular old observance called the Musgrave Ritual. It is a sort of ceremony peculiar to our family, which each Musgrave for centuries past has gone through upon his coming of age — a thing of private interest, and perhaps of some little importance to the archaeologist, like our own blazonings and charges, but of no practical use whatever.

"'"We had better come back to the paper afterwards," said I.

"'"If you think it really necessary," he answered, with some hesitation.

"'To continue my statement, however, I re-locked the bureau, using the key which Brunton had left, and I had turned to go, when I was surprised to find that the butler had returned and was standing before me.

" ' "Mr. Musgrave, sir," he cried, in a voice which was hoarse with emotion, "I can't bear disgrace, sir. I've always been proud above my station in life, and disgrace would kill me. My blood will be on your head, sir — it will, indeed — if you drive me to despair. If you cannot keep me after what has passed, then for God's sake let me give you notice and leave in a month, as if of my own free will. I could stand that, Mr. Musgrave, but not to be cast out before all the folk that I know so well."

" ' "You don't deserve much consideration, Brunton," I answered. "Your conduct has been most infamous. However, as you have been a long time in the family, I have no wish to bring public disgrace upon you. A month, however, is too long. Take yourself away in a week, and give what reason you like for going."

" ' "Only a week, sir?" he cried in a despairing voice. "A fortnight — say at least a fortnight."

" ' "A week," I repeated, "and you may consider yourself to have been very leniently dealt with."

" 'He crept away, his face sunk upon his breast, like a broken man, while I put out the light and returned to my room.

" 'For two days after this Brunton was most assiduous in his attention to his duties. I made no allusion to what had passed, and waited with some curiosity to see how he would cover his disgrace. On the third morning, however, he did not appear, as was his custom, after breakfast to receive my instructions for the day. As I left the dining-room I happened to meet Rachel Howells, the maid. I have told you that she had only recently recovered from an illness, and was looking so wretchedly pale and wan that I remonstrated with her for being at work.

" ' "You should be in bed," I said. "Come back to your duties when you are stronger."

" 'She looked at me with so strange an expression that I began to suspect that her brain was affected.

" ' "I am strong enough, Mr. Musgrave," said she.

" ' "We will see what the doctor says," I answered. "You must stop work now, and when you go downstairs just say that I wish to see Brunton."

" ' "The butler is gone," said she.

" ' "Gone! Gone where?"

" ' "He is gone. No one has seen him. He is not in his room. Oh, yes, he is gone — he is gone!" She fell back against the wall with shriek after shriek of laughter, while I, horrified at this sudden hysterical attack, rushed to the bell to summon help. The girl was taken to her room, still screaming and sobbing, while I made inquiries about

Brunton. There was no doubt about it that he had disappeared. His bed had not been slept in; he had been seen by no one since he had retired to his room the night before; and yet it was difficult to see how he could have left the house, as both windows and doors were found to be fastened in the morning. His clothes, his watch, and even his money were in his room — but the black suit which he usually wore was missing. His slippers, too, were gone, but his boots were left behind. Where, then, could butler Brunton have gone in the night, and what could have become of him now?

"'Of course we searched the house from cellar to garret, but there was no trace of him. It is as I have said a labyrinth of an old house, especially the original wing, which is now practically uninhabited, but we ransacked every room and attic without discovering the least sign of the missing man. It was incredible to me that he could have gone away leaving all his property behind him, and yet where could he be? I called in the local police, but without success. Rain had fallen on the night before, and we examined the lawn and the paths all round the house, but in vain. Matters were in this state when a new development quite drew our attention away from the original mystery.

"'For two days Rachel Howells had been so ill, sometimes delirious, sometimes hysterical, that a nurse had been employed to sit up with her at night. On the third night after Brunton's disappearance, the nurse, finding her patient sleeping nicely, had dropped into a nap in the armchair, when she woke in the early morning to find the bed empty, the window open, and no signs of the invalid. I was instantly aroused, and with the two footmen started off at once in search of the missing girl. It was not difficult to tell the direction which she had taken, for, starting from under her window, we could follow her footmarks easily across the lawn to the edge of the mere, where they vanished, close to the gravel path which leads out of the grounds. The lake there is 8 feet deep, and you can imagine our feelings when we saw that the trail of the poor demented girl came to an end at the edge of it.

"'Of course, we had the drags at once, and set to work to recover the remains; but no trace of the body could we find. On the other hand, we brought to the surface an object of a most unexpected kind. It was a linen bag, which contained within it a mass of old rusted and discoloured metal and several dull-coloured pieces of pebble or glass. This strange find was all that we could get from the mere, and although we made every possible search and inquiry yesterday, we know nothing of the fate either of Rachel Howells or Richard Brunton. The county police are at their wits' end, and I have come up to you as a last resource.'

"You can imagine, Watson, with what eagerness I listened to this extraordinary sequence of events, and endeavoured to piece them together, and to devise some common thread upon which they might all hang.

"The butler was gone. The maid was gone. The maid had loved the butler, but had afterwards had cause to hate him. She was of Welsh blood, fiery and passionate. She had been terribly excited immediately after his disappearance. She had flung into the lake a bag containing some curious contents. These were all factors which had to be taken into consideration, and yet none of them got quite to the heart of the matter. What was the starting-point of this chain of events? There lay the end of this tangled line.

"'I must see that paper, Musgrave,' said I, 'which this butler of yours thought it worth his while to consult, even at the risk of the loss of his place.'

"'It is rather an absurd business, this Ritual of ours,' he answered, 'but it has at least the saving grace of antiquity to excuse it. I have a copy of the questions and answers here, if you care to run your eye over them.'

"He handed me the very paper which I have here, Watson, and this is the strange catechism to which each Musgrave had to submit when he came to man's estate. I will read you the questions and answers as they stand:

"'Whose was it?

"'His who is gone.

"'Who shall have it?

"'He who will come.

"'What was the month?

"'The sixth from the first.

"'Where was the sun?

"'Over the oak.

"'Where was the shadow?

"'Under the elm.

"'How was it stepped?

"'North by ten and by ten, east by five and by five, south by two and by two, west by one and by one, and so under.

"'What shall we give for it?

"'All that is ours.

"'Why should we give it?

"'For the sake of the trust.'

"'The original has no date, but is in the spelling of the middle of the

seventeenth century,' remarked Musgrave. 'I am afraid, however, that it
can be of little help to you in solving this mystery.'

"'At least,' said I, 'it gives us another mystery, and one which is even
more interesting than the first. It may be that the solution of the one
may prove to be the solution of the other. You will excuse me,
Musgrave, if I say that your butler appears to me to have been a very
clever man, and to have had a clearer insight than ten generations of his
masters.'

"'I hardly follow you,' said Musgrave. 'The paper seems to me of no
practical importance.'

"'But to me it seems immensely practical, and I fancy that Brunton
took the same view. He had probably seen it before that night on which
you caught him.'

"'It is very possible. We took no pains to hide it.'

"'He simply wished, I should imagine, to refresh his memory upon
that last occasion. He had, as I understand, some sort of map or chart
which he was comparing with the manuscript, and which he thrust into
his pocket when you appeared?'

"'That is true. But what could he have to do with this old family
custom of ours, and what does this rigmarole mean?'

"'I don't think that we should have much difficulty in determining that,' said I. 'With your permission we will take the first train
down to Sussex and go a little more deeply into the matter upon the
spot.'

"The same afternoon saw us both at Hurlstone. Possibly you
have seen pictures and read descriptions of the famous old building,
so I will confine my account of it to saying that it is built in the shape
of an L, the long arm being the more modern portion, and the
shorter the ancient nucleus from which the other has developed.
Over the low, heavy-lintelled door, in the centre of this old part, is
chiselled the date 1607, but experts are agreed that the beams and
stonework are really much older than this. The enormously thick
walls and tiny windows of this part had in the last century driven the
family into building the new wing, and the old one was used now as
a storehouse and a cellar when it was used at all. A splendid park,
with fine old timber, surrounded the house, and the lake, to which
my client had referred, lay close to the avenue, about two hundred
yards from the building.

"I was already firmly convinced, Watson, that there were not three
separate mysteries here, but one only, and that if I could read the
Musgrave Ritual aright, I should hold in my hand the clue which would

lead me to the truth concerning both the butler Brunton, and the maid Howells. To that, then, I turned all my energies. Why should this servant be so anxious to master this old formula? Evidently because he saw something in it which had escaped all those generations of country squires, and from which he expected some personal advantage. What was it, then, and how had it affected his fate?

"It was perfectly obvious to me on reading the Ritual that the measurements must refer to some spot to which the rest of the document alluded, and that if we could find that spot we should be in a fair way towards knowing what the secret was which the old Musgraves had thought it necessary to embalm in so curious a fashion. There were two guides given us to start with, an oak and an elm. As to the oak, there could be no question at all. Right in front of the house, upon the left-hand side of the drive, there stood a patriarch among oaks, one of the most magnificent trees that I have ever seen.

"'That was there when your Ritual was drawn up?' said I, as we drove past it.

"'It was there at the Norman Conquest, in all probability,' he answered. 'It has a girth of 23 feet.'

"Here was one of my fixed points secured.

"'Have you any old elms?' I asked.

"'There used to be a very old one over yonder, but it was struck by lightning ten years ago, and we cut down the stump.'

"'You can see where it used to be?'

"'Oh, yes.'

"'There are no other elms?'

"'No old ones, but plenty of beeches.'

"'I should like to see where it grew.'

"We had driven up in a dog-cart,[3] and my client led me away at once, without our entering the house, to the scar on the lawn where the elm had stood. It was nearly midway between the oak and the house. My investigation seemed to be progressing.

"'I suppose it is impossible to find out how high the elm was?' I asked.

"'I can give you it at once. It was 64 feet.'

"'How do you come to know it?' I asked in surprise.

"'When my old tutor used to give me an exercise in trigonometry it always took the shape of measuring heights. When I was a lad I worked out every tree and building on the estate.'

[3] *dog-cart:* A light, two-wheeled open carriage.

"This was an unexpected piece of luck. My data were coming more quickly than I could have reasonably hoped.

"'Tell me,' I asked, 'did your butler ever ask you such a question?'

"Reginald Musgrave looked at me in astonishment. 'Now that you call it to my mind,' he answered, 'Brunton *did* ask me about the height of the tree some months ago, in connection with some little argument with the groom.'

"This was excellent news, Watson, for it showed me that I was on the right road. I looked up at the sun. It was low in the heavens, and I calculated that in less than an hour it would lie just above the topmost branches of the old oak. One condition mentioned in the Ritual would then be fulfilled. And the shadow of the elm must mean the further end of the shadow, otherwise the trunk would have been chosen as the guide. I had then to find where the far end of the shadow would fall when the sun was just clear of the oak."

"That must have been difficult, Holmes, when the elm was no longer there."

"Well, at least, I knew that if Brunton could do it, I could also. Besides, there was no real difficulty. I went with Musgrave to his study and whittled myself this peg, to which I tied this long string, with a knot at each yard. Then I took two lengths of a fishing-rod, which came to just 6 feet, and I went back with my client to where the elm had been. The sun was just grazing the top of the oak. I fastened the rod on end, marked out the direction of the shadow, and measured it. It was 9 feet in length.

"Of course, the calculation was now a simple one. If a rod of 6 feet threw a shadow of 9 feet, a tree of 64 feet would throw one of 96 feet, and the line of one would of course be the line of the other. I measured out the distance, which brought me almost to the wall of the house, and I thrust a peg into the spot. You can imagine my exultation, Watson, when within 2 inches of my peg I saw a conical depression in the ground. I knew that it was the mark made by Brunton in his measurements, and that I was still upon his trail.

"From this starting-point I proceeded to step, having first taken the cardinal points by my pocket compass. Ten steps with each foot took me along parallel with the wall of the house, and again I marked my spot with a peg. Then I carefully paced off five to the east and two to the south. It brought me to the very threshold of the old door. Two steps to the west meant now that I was to go two paces down the stone-flagged passage, and this was the place indicated by the Ritual.

"Never have I felt such a cold chill of disappointment, Watson. For a moment it seemed to me that there must be some radical mistake in my calculations. The setting sun shone full upon the passage floor, and I could see that the old foot-worn grey stones, with which it was paved, were firmly cemented together, and had certainly not been moved for many a long year. Brunton had not been at work here. I tapped upon the floor, but it sounded the same all over, and there was no sign of any crack or crevice. But fortunately Musgrave, who had begun to appreciate the meaning of my proceedings, and who was now as excited as myself, took out his manuscript to check my calculations.

"'And under,' he cried: 'you have omitted the "and under."'

"I had thought that it meant that we were to dig, but now, of course, I saw at once that I was wrong. 'There is a cellar under this, then?' I cried.

"'Yes, and as old as the house. Down here, through this door.'

"We went down a winding stone stair, and my companion, striking a match, lit a large lantern which stood on a barrel in the corner. In an instant it was obvious that we had at last come upon the true place, and that we had not been the only people to visit the spot recently.

"It had been used for the storage of wood, but the billets, which had evidently been littered over the floor, were now piled at the sides so as to leave a clear space in the middle. In this space lay a large and heavy flagstone, with a rusted iron ring in the centre, to which a thick shepherd's check muffler was attached.

"'By Jove!' cried my client, 'that's Brunton's muffler. I have seen it on him, and could swear to it. What has the villain been doing here?'

"At my suggestion a couple of the county police were summoned to be present, and I then endeavoured to raise the stone by pulling on the cravat. I could only move it slightly, and it was with the aid of one of the constables that I succeeded at last in carrying it to one side. A black hole yawned beneath, into which we all peered, while Musgrave, kneeling at the side, pushed down the lantern.

"A small chamber about 7 feet deep and 4 feet square lay open to us. At one side of this was a squat, brass-bound, wooden box, the lid of which was hinged upwards, with this curious, old-fashioned key projecting from the lock. It was furred outside by a thick layer of dust, and damp and worms had eaten through the wood so that a crop of living fungi was growing on the inside of it. Several discs of metal — old coins apparently — such as I hold here, were scattered over the bottom of the box, but it contained nothing else.

"At the moment, however, we had no thought for the old chest, for our eyes were riveted upon that which crouched beside it. It was the figure of a man, clad in a suit of black, who squatted down upon his hams with his forehead sunk upon the edge of the box and his two arms thrown out on each side of it. The attitude had drawn all the stagnant blood to his face, and no man could have recognized that distorted, liver-coloured countenance; but his height, his dress, and his hair were all sufficient to show my client, when we had drawn the body up, that it was indeed his missing butler. He had been dead some days, but there was no wound or bruise upon his person to show how he had met his dreadful end. When his body had been carried from the cellar we found ourselves still confronted with a problem which was almost as formidable as that with which we had started.

"I confess that so far, Watson, I had been disappointed in my investigation. I had reckoned upon solving the matter when once I had found the place referred to in the Ritual; but now I was there, and was apparently as far as ever from knowing what it was which the family had concealed with such elaborate precautions. It is true that I had thrown a light upon the fate of Brunton, but now I had to ascertain how that fate had come upon him, and what part had been played in the matter by the woman who had disappeared. I sat down upon a keg in the corner and thought the whole matter carefully over.

"You know my methods in such cases, Watson: I put myself in the man's place, and having first gauged his intelligence, I try to imagine how I should myself have proceeded under the same circumstances. In this case the matter was simplified by Brunton's intelligence being quite first rate, so that it was unnecessary to make any allowance for personal equation, as the astronomers have dubbed it. He knew that something valuable was concealed. He had spotted the place. He found that the stone which covered it was just too heavy for a man to move unaided. What would he do next? He could not get help from outside, even if he had someone whom he could trust, without the unbarring of doors, and considerable risk of detection. It was better, if he could, to have his helpmate inside the house. But whom could he ask? This girl had been devoted to him. A man always finds it hard to realize that he may have finally lost a woman's love, however badly he may have treated her. He would try by a few attentions to make his peace with the girl Howells, and then would engage her as his accomplice. Together they would come at night to the cellar, and their united force would suffice to raise the stone. So far I could follow their actions as if I had actually seen them.

"But for two of them, and one a woman, it must have been heavy work, the raising of that stone. A burly Sussex policeman and I had found it no light job. What would they do to assist them? Probably what I should have done myself. I rose and examined carefully the different billets of wood which were scattered round the floor. Almost at once I came upon what I expected. One piece, about 3 feet in length, had a marked indentation at one end, while several were flattened at the sides as if they had been compressed by some considerable weight. Evidently as they had dragged the stone up they had thrust the chunks of wood into the chink, until at last, when the opening was large enough to crawl through, they would hold it open by a billet placed lengthwise, which might very well become indented at the lower end, since the whole weight of the stone would press it down on to the edge of the other slab. So far I was still on safe ground.

"And now, how was I to proceed to reconstruct this midnight drama? Clearly only one could get into the hole, and that one was Brunton. The girl must have waited above. Brunton then unlocked the box, handed up the contents, presumably — since they were not to be found — and then — and then what happened?

"What smouldering fire of vengeance had suddenly sprung into flame in this passionate Celtic woman's soul when she saw the man who had wronged her — wronged her perhaps far more than we suspected — in her power? Was it a chance that the wood had slipped and that the stone had shut Brunton into what had become his sepulchre? Had she only been guilty of silence as to his fate? Or had some sudden blow from her hand dashed the support away and sent the slab crashing down into its place? Be that as it might, I seemed to see that woman's figure, still clutching at her treasure-trove, and flying wildly up the winding stair with her ears ringing perhaps with the muffled screams from behind her, and with the drumming of frenzied hands against the slab of stone which was choking her faithless lover's life out.

"Here was the secret of her blanched face, her shaken nerves, her peals of hysterical laughter on the next morning. But what had been in the box? What had she done with that? Of course, it must have been the old metal and pebbles which my client had dragged from the mere. She had thrown them in there at the first opportunity, to remove the last trace of her crime.

"For twenty minutes I had sat motionless thinking the matter out. Musgrave still stood with a very pale face swinging his lantern and peering down into the hole.

"'These are coins of Charles I,' said he, holding out the few which had been left in the box. 'You see we were right in fixing our date for the Ritual.'

"'We may find something else of Charles I,' I cried, as the probable meaning of the first two questions of the Ritual broke suddenly upon me. 'Let me see the contents of the bag you fished from the mere.'

"We ascended to his study, and he laid the *débris* before me. I could understand his regarding it as of small importance when I looked at it, for the metal was almost black, and the stones lustreless and dull. I rubbed one of them on my sleeve, however, and it glowed afterwards like a spark, in the dark hollow of my hand. The metal-work was in the form of a double-ring, but it had been bent and twisted out of its original shape.

"'You must bear in mind,' said I, 'that the Royal party made head in England even after the death of the King, and that when they at last fled they probably left many of their most precious possessions buried behind them, with the intention of returning for them in more peaceful times.'

"'My ancestor, Sir Ralph Musgrave, was a prominent Cavalier, and the right-hand man of Charles II in his wanderings,' said my friend.

"'Ah, indeed!' I answered. 'Well, now, I think that really should give us the last link that we wanted. I must congratulate you on coming into possession, though in rather a tragic manner, of a relic which is of great intrinsic value, but even of greater importance as an historical curiosity.'

"'What is it, then?' he gasped in astonishment.

"'It is nothing less than the ancient crown of the Kings of England.'

"'The crown!'

"'Precisely. Consider what the Ritual says. How does it run? "Whose was it?" "His who is gone." That was after the execution of Charles. Then, "Who shall have it?" "He who will come." That was Charles II, whose advent was already foreseen. There can, I think, be no doubt that this battered and shapeless diadem once encircled the brows of the Royal Stuarts.'

"'And how came it in the pond?'

"'Ah, that is a question which will take some time to answer,' and with that I sketched out the whole long chain of surmise and of proof which I had constructed. The twilight had closed in and the moon was shining brightly in the sky before my narrative was finished.

"'And how was it, then, that Charles did not get his crown when he returned?' asked Musgrave, pushing back the relic into its linen bag.

"'Ah, there you lay your finger upon the one point which we shall probably never be able to clear up. It is likely that the Musgrave who held the secret died in the interval, and by some oversight left this guide to his descendant without explaining the meaning of it. From that day to this it has been handed down from father to son, until at last it came within reach of a man who tore its secret out of it and lost his life in the venture.'

"And that's the story of the Musgrave Ritual, Watson. They have the crown down at Hurlstone — though they had some legal bother, and a considerable sum to pay before they were allowed to retain it. I am sure that if you mentioned my name they would be happy to show it to you. Of the woman nothing was ever heard, and the probability is that she got away out of England, and carried herself, and the memory of her crime, to some land beyond the seas."

## AFTERWORD

Set at a time before Watson's first meeting with Holmes, this is one of the two Holmes adventures in which Watson plays no part save that of audience and introductory narrator. It originally appeared in May 1893; the first and only other such story, "The *Gloria Scott*," had appeared immediately before, in April 1893. The appearance of these two stories in quick succession suggests that Doyle was experimenting with this particular variation on his chosen narrative form. A similar pattern appears near the end of Doyle's career, when he writes in close succession two Holmes-narrated stories that dispense with Watson entirely ("The Blanched Soldier," November 1926, and "The Lion's Mane," December 1926). (There is also a single third-person story, "The Mazarin Stone" [October 1921], which Doyle rewrote from a one-act Holmes play, *The Crown Diamond* [May 1921].)

As a solution of a long-lost (or long unintelligible) cryptic message directing to hidden treasure, "The Musgrave Ritual" stems directly from Poe's story "The Gold-Bug." It thus merits particular comparison with "The Dancing Men," a very different story stemming from the same original. The "Musgrave Ritual" subplot of a blighted and tragic love affair makes the comparison all the more relevant.

# The Final Problem

It is with a heavy heart that I take up my pen to write these the last words in which I shall ever record the singular gifts by which my friend Mr. Sherlock Holmes was distinguished. In an incoherent and, as I deeply feel, an entirely inadequate fashion, I have endeavoured to give some account of my strange experiences in his company from the chance which first brought us together at the period of the "Study in Scarlet," up to the time of his interference in the matter of the "Naval Treaty" — an interference which had the unquestionable effect of preventing a serious international complication. It was my intention to have stopped there, and to have said nothing of that event which has created a void in my life which the lapse of two years has done little to fill. My hand has been forced, however, by the recent letters in which Colonel James Moriarty defends the memory of his brother, and I have no choice but to lay the facts before the public exactly as they occurred. I alone know the absolute truth of the matter, and I am satisfied that the time has come when no good purpose is to be served by its suppression. As far as I know, there have been only three accounts in the public Press: that in the *Journal de Genève* upon May 6th, 1891, the Reuter's despatch in the English papers upon May 7th, and finally the recent letters to which I have alluded. Of these the first and second were extremely condensed, while the last is, as I shall now show, an absolute perversion of the facts. It lies with me to tell for the first time what really took place between Professor Moriarty and Mr. Sherlock Holmes.

It may be remembered that after my marriage, and my subsequent start in private practice, the very intimate relations which had existed between Holmes and myself became to some extent modified. He still came to me from time to time when he desired a companion in his investigations, but these occasions grew more and more seldom, until I find that in the year 1890 there were only three cases of which I retain any record. During the winter of that year and the early spring of 1891, I saw in the papers that he had been engaged by the French Government upon a matter of supreme importance, and I received two notes from Holmes, dated from Narbonne and from Nîmes, from which I gathered that his stay in France was likely to be a long one. It was with some surprise, therefore, that I saw him walk into my consulting-room upon

From *The Memoirs of Sherlock Holmes* (1894). First appeared in the *Strand*, December 1893.

the evening of the 24th of April. It struck me that he was looking even paler and thinner than usual.

"Yes, I have been using myself up rather too freely," he remarked, in answer to my look rather than to my words; "I have been a little pressed of late. Have you any objection to my closing your shutters?"

The only light in the room came from the lamp upon the table at which I had been reading. Holmes edged his way round the wall, and flinging the shutters together, he bolted them securely.

"You are afraid of something?" I asked.

"Well, I am."

"Of what?"

"Of air-guns."

"My dear Holmes, what do you mean?"

"I think that you know me well enough, Watson, to understand that I am by no means a nervous man. At the same time, it is stupidity rather than courage to refuse to recognize danger when it is close upon you. Might I trouble you for a match?" He drew in the smoke of his cigarette as if the soothing influence was grateful to him.

"I must apologize for calling so late," said he, "and I must further beg you to be so unconventional as to allow me to leave your house presently by scrambling over your back garden wall."

"But what does it all mean?" I asked.

He held out his hand, and I saw in the light of the lamp that two of his knuckles were burst and bleeding.

"It's not an airy nothing, you see," said he, smiling. "On the contrary, it is solid enough for a man to break his hand over. Is Mrs. Watson in?"

"She is away upon a visit."

"Indeed! You are alone?"

"Quite."

"Then it makes it the easier for me to propose that you should come away with me for a week on to the Continent."

"Where?"

"Oh, anywhere. It's all the same to me."

There was something very strange in all this. It was not Holmes's nature to take an aimless holiday, and something about his pale, worn face told me that his nerves were at their highest tension. He saw the question in my eyes, and, putting his finger-tips together and his elbows upon his knees, he explained the situation.

"You have probably never heard of Professor Moriarty?" said he.

"Never."

"Aye, there's the genius and the wonder of the thing!" he cried. "The man pervades London, and no one has heard of him. That's what puts him on a pinnacle in the records of crime. I tell you, Watson, in all seriousness, that if I could beat that man, if I could free society of him, I should feel that my own career had reached its summit, and I should be prepared to turn to some more placid line in life. Between ourselves, the recent cases in which I have been of assistance to the Royal Family of Scandinavia, and to the French Republic, have left me in such a position that I could continue to live in the quiet fashion which is most congenial to me, and to concentrate my attention upon my chemical researches. But I could not rest, Watson, I could not sit quiet in my chair, if I thought that such a man as Professor Moriarty were walking the streets of London unchallenged."

"What has he done, then?"

"His career has been an extraordinary one. He is a man of good birth and excellent education, endowed by Nature with a phenomenal mathematical faculty. At the age of twenty-one he wrote a treatise upon the Binomial Theorem, which has had a European vogue. On the strength of it, he won the Mathematical Chair at one of our smaller Universities, and had, to all appearance, a most brilliant career before him. But the man had hereditary tendencies of the most diabolical kind. A criminal strain ran in his blood, which, instead of being modified, was increased and rendered infinitely more dangerous by his extraordinary mental powers. Dark rumours gathered round him in the University town, and eventually he was compelled to resign his Chair and to come down to London, where he set up as an Army coach. So much is known to the world, but what I am telling you now is what I have myself discovered.

"As you are aware, Watson, there is no one who knows the higher criminal world of London so well as I do. For years past I have continually been conscious of some power behind the malefactor, some deep organizing power which for ever stands in the way of the law, and throws its shield over the wrong-doer. Again and again in cases of the most varying sorts — forgery cases, robberies, murders — I have felt the presence of this force, and I have deduced its action in many of those undiscovered crimes in which I have not been personally consulted. For years I have endeavoured to break through the veil which shrouded it, and at last the time came when I seized my thread and followed it, until it led me, after a thousand cunning windings, to ex-Professor Moriarty of mathematical celebrity.

"He is the Napoleon of crime, Watson. He is the organizer of half that is evil and of nearly all that is undetected in this great city. He is a genius, a philosopher, an abstract thinker. He has a brain of the first order. He sits motionless, like a spider in the centre of its web, but that web has a thousand radiations, and he knows well every quiver of each of them. He does little himself. He only plans. But his agents are numerous and splendidly organized. Is there a crime to be done, a paper to be abstracted, we will say, a house to be rifled, a man to be removed — the word is passed to the Professor, the matter is organized and carried out. The agent may be caught. In that case money is found for his bail or his defence. But the central power which uses the agent is never caught — never so much as suspected. This was the organization which I deduced, Watson, and which I devoted my whole energy to exposing and breaking up.

"But the Professor was fenced round with safeguards so cunningly devised that, do what I would, it seemed impossible to get evidence which could convict in a court of law. You know my powers, my dear Watson, and yet at the end of three months I was forced to confess that I had at last met an antagonist who was my intellectual equal. My horror at his crimes was lost in my admiration at his skill. But at last he made a trip — only a little, little trip — but it was more than he could afford, when I was so close upon him. I had my chance, and, starting from that point, I have woven my net round him until now it is all ready to close. In three days, that is to say on Monday next, matters will be ripe, and the Professor, with all the principal members of his gang, will be in the hands of the police. Then will come the greatest criminal trial of the century, the clearing up of over forty mysteries, and the rope for all of them — but if we move at all prematurely, you understand, they may slip out of our hands even at the last moment.

"Now, if I could have done this without the knowledge of Professor Moriarty, all would have been well. But he was too wily for that. He saw every step which I took to draw my toils round him. Again and again he strove to break away, but I as often headed him off. I tell you, my friend, that if a detailed account of that silent contest could be written, it would take its place as the most brilliant bit of thrust-and-parry work in the history of detection. Never have I risen to such a height, and never have I been so hard pressed by an opponent. He cut deep, and yet I just undercut him. This morning the last steps were taken, and three days only were wanted to complete the business. I was sitting in my room thinking the matter over, when the door opened and Professor Moriarty stood before me.

"My nerves are fairly proof, Watson, but I must confess to a start when I saw the very man who had been so much in my thoughts standing there on my threshold. His appearance was quite familiar to me. He is extremely tall and thin, his forehead domes out in a white curve, and his two eyes are deeply sunken in his head. He is clean-shaven, pale, and ascetic-looking, retaining something of the professor in his features. His shoulders are rounded from much study, and his face protrudes forward, and is for ever slowly oscillating from side to side in a curiously reptilian fashion. He peered at me with great curiosity in his puckered eyes.

"'You have less frontal development than I should have expected,' said he at last. 'It is a dangerous habit to finger loaded firearms in the pocket of one's dressing-gown.'

"The fact is that upon his entrance I had instantly recognized the extreme personal danger in which I lay. The only conceivable escape for him lay in silencing my tongue. In an instant I had slipped the revolver from the drawer into my pocket, and was covering him through the cloth. At his remark I drew the weapon out and laid it cocked upon the table. He still smiled and blinked, but there was something about his eyes which made me feel very glad that I had it there.

"'You evidently don't know me,' said he.

"'On the contrary,' I answered, 'I think it is fairly evident that I do. Pray take a chair. I can spare you five minutes if you have anything to say.'

"'All that I have to say has already crossed your mind,' said he.

"'Then possibly my answer has crossed yours,' I replied.

"'You stand fast?'

"'Absolutely.'

"He clapped his hand into his pocket, and I raised the pistol from the table. But he merely drew out a memorandum-book in which he had scribbled some dates.

"'You crossed my path on the 4th of January,' said he. 'On the 23rd you incommoded me; by the middle of February I was seriously inconvenienced by you; at the end of March I was absolutely hampered in my plans; and now, at the close of April, I find myself placed in such a position through your continual persecution that I am in positive danger of losing my liberty. The situation is becoming an impossible one.'

"'Have you any suggestion to make?' I asked.

"'You must drop it, Mr. Holmes,' said he, swaying his face about. 'You really must, you know.'

"'After Monday,' said I.

"'Tut, tut!' said he. 'I am quite sure that a man of your intelligence will see that there can be but one outcome to this affair. It is necessary that you should withdraw. You have worked things in such a fashion that we have only one resource left. It has been an intellectual treat to me to see the way in which you have grappled with this affair, and I say, unaffectedly, that it would be a grief to me to be forced to take any extreme measure. You smile, sir, but I assure you that it really would.'

" 'Danger is part of my trade,' I remarked.

" 'This is not danger,' said he. 'It is inevitable destruction. You stand in the way not merely of an individual, but of a mighty organization, the full extent of which you, with all your cleverness, have been unable to realize. You must stand clear, Mr. Holmes, or be trodden under foot.'

" 'I am afraid,' said I, rising, 'that in the pleasure of this conversation I am neglecting business of importance which awaits me elsewhere.'

"He rose also and looked at me in silence, shaking his head sadly.

" 'Well, well,' said he at last. 'It seems a pity, but I have done what I could. I know every move of your game. You can do nothing before Monday. It has been a duel between you and me, Mr. Holmes. You hope to place me in the dock. I tell you that I will never stand in the dock. You hope to beat me. I tell you that you will never beat me. If you are clever enough to bring destruction upon me, rest assured that I shall do as much to you.'

" 'You have paid me several compliments, Mr. Moriarty,' said I. 'Let me pay you one in return when I say that if I were assured of the former eventuality I would, in the interests of the public, cheerfully accept the latter.'

" 'I can promise you the one but not the other,' he snarled, and so turned his rounded back upon me and went peering and blinking out of the room.

"That was my singular interview with Professor Moriarty. I confess that it left an unpleasant effect upon my mind. His soft, precise fashion of speech leaves a conviction of sincerity which a mere bully could not produce. Of course, you will say: 'Why not take police precautions against him?' " The reason is that I am well convinced that it is from his agents the blow would fall. I have the best of proofs that it would be so."

"You have already been assaulted?"

"My dear Watson, Professor Moriarty is not a man who lets the grass grow under his feet. I went out about midday to transact some business in Oxford Street. As I passed the corner which leads from Bentinck Street on to the Welbeck Street crossing a two-horse van furiously driven whizzed round and was on me like a flash. I sprang for the footpath and saved myself by the fraction of a second. The van dashed round from Marylebone Lane and was gone in an instant. I kept to the pavement after that, Watson, but as I walked down Vere Street a brick came down from the roof of one of the houses, and was shattered to fragments at my feet. I called the police and had the place examined. There were slates and bricks piled upon the roof preparatory to some repairs, and they would have me believe that the wind had toppled over one of these. Of course I knew better, but I could prove nothing. I took a cab after that and reached my brother's rooms in Pall Mall, where I spent the day. Now I have come round to you, and on my way I was attacked by a rough with a bludgeon. I knocked him down, and the police have him in custody; but I can tell you with the most absolute confidence that no possible connection will ever be traced between the gentleman upon whose front teeth I have barked my knuckles and the retiring mathematical coach, who is, I dare say, working out problems upon a blackboard ten miles away. You will not wonder, Watson, that my first act on entering your rooms was to close your shutters, and that I have been compelled to ask your permission to leave the house by some less conspicuous exit than the front door."

I had often admired my friend's courage, but never more than now, as he sat quietly checking off a series of incidents which must have combined to make up a day of horror.

"You will spend the night here?" I said.

"No, my friend; you might find me a dangerous guest. I have my plans laid, and all will be well. Matters have gone so far now that they can move without my help as far as the arrest goes, though my presence is necessary for a conviction. It is obvious, therefore, that I cannot do better than get away for the few days which remain before the police are at liberty to act. It would be a great pleasure to me, therefore, if you could come on to the Continent with me."

"The practice is quiet," said I, "and I have an accommodating neighbour. I should be glad to come."

"And to start to-morrow morning?"

"If necessary."

"Oh yes, it is most necessary. Then these are your instructions, and I beg, my dear Watson, that you will obey them to the letter, for you are now playing a double-handed game with me against the cleverest rogue and the most powerful syndicate of criminals in Europe. Now listen! You will despatch whatever luggage you intend to take by a trusty messenger unaddressed to Victoria to-night. In the morning you will send for a hansom, desiring your man to take neither the first nor the second which may present itself. Into this hansom you will jump, and you will drive to the Strand end of the Lowther Arcade, handing the address to the cabman upon a slip of paper, with a request that he will not throw it away. Have your fare ready, and the instant that your cab stops, dash through the Arcade, timing yourself to reach the other side at a quarter-past nine. You will find a small brougham waiting close to the kerb, driven by a fellow with a heavy black cloak tipped at the collar with red. Into this you will step, and you will reach Victoria in time for the Continental express."

"Where shall I meet you?"

"At the station. The second first-class carriage from the front will be reserved for us."

"The carriage is our rendezvous, then?"

"Yes."

It was in vain that I asked Holmes to remain for the evening. It was evident to me that he thought he might bring trouble to the roof he was under, and that that was the motive which impelled him to go. With a few hurried words as to our plans for the morrow he rose and came out with me into the garden, clambering over the wall which leads into Mortimer Street, and immediately whistling for a hansom, in which I heard him drive away.

In the morning I obeyed Holmes's injunctions to the letter. A hansom was procured with such precautions as would prevent its being one which was placed ready for us, and I drove immediately after breakfast to the Lowther Arcade, through which I hurried at the top of my speed. A brougham was waiting with a very massive driver wrapped in a dark cloak, who, the instant that I had stepped in, whipped up the horse and rattled off to Victoria Station. On my alighting there he turned the carriage, and dashed away without so much as a look in my direction.

So far all had gone admirably. My luggage was waiting for me, and I had no difficulty in finding the carriage in which Holmes had indicated, the less so as it was the only one in the train which was marked "Engaged." My only source of anxiety now was the non-appearance of Holmes. The station clock marked only seven minutes from the time when we were due to start. In vain I searched among the groups of travellers and leave-takers for the lithe figure of my friend. There was no sign of him. I spent a few minutes in assisting a venerable Italian priest, who was endeavouring to make a porter understand, in his broken English, that his luggage was to be booked through to Paris. Then, having taken another look round, I returned to my carriage, where I found that the porter, in spite of the ticket, had given me my decrepit Italian friend as a travelling companion. It was useless for me to explain to him that his presence was an intrusion, for my Italian was even more limited than his English, so I shrugged my shoulders resignedly and continued to look out anxiously for my friend. A chill of fear had come over me, as I thought that his absence might mean that some blow had fallen during the night. Already the doors had all been shut and the whistle blown, when ——

"My dear Watson," said a voice, "you have not even condescended to say good morning."

I turned in incontrollable astonishment. The aged ecclesiastic had turned his face towards me. For an instant the wrinkles were smoothed away, the nose drew away from the chin, the lower lip ceased to protrude and the mouth to mumble, the dull eyes regained their fire, the drooping figure expanded. The next the whole frame collapsed, and Holmes had gone as quickly as he had come.

"Good heavens!" I cried. "How you startled me!"

"Every precaution is still necessary," he whispered. "I have reason to think that they are hot upon our trail. Ah, there is Moriarty himself."

The train had already begun to move as Holmes spoke. Glancing back I saw a tall man pushing his way furiously through the crowd and waving his hand as if he desired to have the train stopped. It was too late, however, for we were rapidly gathering momentum, and an instant later had shot clear of the station.

"With all our precautions, you see that we have cut it rather fine," said Holmes, laughing. He rose, and throwing off the black cassock and hat which had formed his disguise, he packed them away in a hand-bag.

"Have you seen the morning paper, Watson?"

"No."

"You haven't seen about Baker Street, then?"

"Baker Street?"

"They set fire to our rooms last night. No great harm was done."

"Good heavens, Holmes! This is intolerable."

"They must have lost my track completely after their bludgeon-man was arrested. Otherwise they could not have imagined that I had returned to my rooms. They have evidently taken the precaution of watching you, however, and that is what has brought Moriarty to Victoria. You could not have made any slip in coming?"

"I did exactly what you advised."

"Did you find your brougham?"

"Yes, it was waiting."

"Did you recognize your coachman?"

"No."

"It was my brother Mycroft. It is an advantage to get about in such a case without taking a mercenary into your confidence. But we must plan what we are to do about Moriarty now."

"As this is an express, and as the boat runs in connection with it, I should think we have shaken him off very effectively."

"My dear Watson, you evidently did not realize my meaning when I said that this man may be taken as being quite on the same intellectual plane as myself. You do not imagine that if I were the pursuer I should allow myself to be baffled by so slight an obstacle. Why, then, should you think so meanly of him?"

"What will he do?"

"What I should do."

"What would you do, then?"

"Engage a special."

"But it must be late."

"By no means. This train stops at Canterbury; and there is always at least a quarter of an hour's delay at the boat. He will catch us there."

"One would think that we were the criminals. Let us have him arrested on his arrival."

"It would be to ruin the work of three months. We should get the big fish, but the smaller would dart right and left out of the net. On Monday we should have them all. No, an arrest is inadmissible."

"What then?"

"We shall get out at Canterbury."

"And then?"

"Well, then we must make a cross-country journey to Newhaven, and so over to Dieppe. Moriarty will again do what I should do. He will get on to Paris, mark down our luggage, and wait for two days at the depot. In the meantime we shall treat ourselves to a couple of carpet bags, encourage the manufactures of the countries through which we travel, and make our way at our leisure into Switzerland, via Luxembourg and Basle."

I am too old a traveller to allow myself to be seriously inconvenienced by the loss of my luggage, but I confess that I was annoyed at the idea of being forced to dodge and hide before a man whose record was black with unutterable infamies. It was evident, however, that Holmes understood the situation more clearly than I did. At Canterbury, therefore, we alighted, only to find that we should have to wait an hour before we could get a train to Newhaven.

I was still looking rather ruefully after the rapidly disappearing luggage van which contained my wardrobe, when Holmes pulled my sleeve and pointed up the line.

"Already, you see," said he.

Far away from among the Kentish woods there arose a thin spray of smoke. A minute later a carriage and engine could be seen flying along the open curve which leads to the station. We had hardly time to take our places behind a pile of luggage when it passed with a rattle and a roar, beating a blast of hot air into our faces.

"There he goes," said Holmes, as we watched the carriage swing and rock over the points. "There are limits, you see, to our friend's intelligence. It would have been a *coup de maître* had he deduced what I would deduce and acted accordingly."

"And what would he have done had he overtaken us?"

"There cannot be the least doubt that he would have made a murderous attack upon me. It is, however, a game at which two may play. The question now is whether we should take a premature lunch here, or run our chance of starving before we reach the buffet at Newhaven."

We made our way to Brussels that night and spent two days there, moving on upon the third day as far as Strasburg. On the Monday morning Holmes had telegraphed to the London police, and in the evening we found a reply waiting for us at our hotel. Holmes tore it open, and then with a bitter curse hurled it into the grate.

"I might have known it," he groaned. "He has escaped!"

"Moriarty!"

"They have secured the whole gang with the exception of him. He has given them the slip. Of course, when I had left the country there was no one to cope with him. But I did think that I had put the game in their hands. I think that you had better return to England, Watson."

"Why?"

"Because you will find me a dangerous companion now. This man's occupation is gone. He is lost if he returns to London. If I read his character right he will devote his whole energies to revenging himself upon me. He said as much in our short interview, and I fancy that he meant it. I should certainly recommend you to return to your practice."

It was hardly an appeal to be successful with one who was an old campaigner as well as an old friend. We sat in the Strasburg *salle-à-manger* arguing the question for half an hour, but the same night we had resumed our journey and were well on our way to Geneva.

For a charming week we wandered up the Valley of the Rhone, and then, branching off at Leuk, we made our way over the Gemmi Pass, still deep in snow, and so, by way of Interlaken, to Meiringen. It was a lovely trip, the dainty green of the spring below, the virgin white of the winter above; but it was clear to me that never for one instant did Holmes forget the shadow which lay across him. In the homely Alpine villages or in the lonely mountain passes, I could still tell, by his quick glancing eyes and his sharp scrutiny of every face that passed us, that he was well convinced that, walk where we would, we could not walk ourselves clear of the danger which was dogging our footsteps.

Once, I remember, as we passed over the Gemmi, and walked along the border of the melancholy Daubensee, a large rock which had been dislodged from the ridge upon our right clattered down and roared into the lake behind us. In an instant Holmes had raced up on to the ridge, and, standing upon a lofty pinnacle, craned his neck in every direction. It was in vain that our guide assured him that a fall of stones was a common chance in the spring-time at that spot. He said nothing, but he smiled at me with the air of a man who sees the fulfilment of that which he had expected.

And yet for all his watchfulness he was never depressed. On the contrary, I can never recollect having seen him in such exuberant spirits. Again and again he recurred to the fact that if he could be assured that society was freed from Professor Moriarty, he would cheerfully bring his own career to a conclusion.

"I think that I may go so far as to say, Watson, that I have not lived wholly in vain," he remarked. "If my record were closed to-night I could still survey it with equanimity. The air of London is the sweeter for my presence. In over a thousand cases I am not aware that I have ever used my powers upon the wrong side. Of late I have been tempted to look into the problems furnished by Nature rather than those more superficial ones for which our artificial state of society is responsible. Your memoirs will draw to an end, Watson, upon the day that I crown my career by the capture or extinction of the most dangerous and capable criminal in Europe."

I shall be brief, and yet exact, in the little which remains for me to tell. It is not a subject on which I would willingly dwell, and yet I am conscious that a duty devolves upon me to omit no detail.

It was upon the 3rd of May that we reached the little village of Meiringen, where we put up at the Englischer Hof, then kept by Peter Steiler the elder. Our landlord was an intelligent man, and spoke excellent English, having served for three years as waiter at the Grosvenor Hotel in London. At his advice, upon the afternoon of the 4th we set off together with the intention of crossing the hills and spending the night at the Hamlet of Rosenlaui. We had strict injunctions, however, on no account to pass the falls of Reichenbach, which are about half-way up the hill, without making a small detour to see them.

It is, indeed, a fearful place. The torrent, swollen by the melting snow, plunges into a tremendous abyss, from which the spray rolls up like the smoke from a burning house. The shaft into which the river hurls itself is an immense chasm, lined by glistening, coal-black rock, and narrowing into a creaming, boiling pit of incalculable depth, which brims over and shoots the stream onward over its jagged lip. The long sweep of green water roaring for ever down, and the thick flickering curtain of spray hissing for ever upwards, turn a man giddy with their constant whirl and clamour. We stood near the edge peering down at the gleam of the breaking water far below us against the black rocks, and listening to the half-human shout which came booming up with the spray out of the abyss.

The path has been cut half-way round the fall to afford a complete view, but it ends abruptly, and the traveller has to return as he came. We had turned to do so, when we saw a Swiss lad come running along it with a letter in his hand. It bore the mark of the hotel which we had just left, and was addressed to me by the landlord. It appeared that within a very few minutes of our leaving, an English lady had arrived who was in the last stage of consumption. She had wintered at Davos Platz, and was journeying now to join her friends at Lucerne, when a sudden hæmorrhage had overtaken her. It was thought that she could hardly live a few hours, but it would be a great consolation to her to see an English doctor, and, if I would only return, etc. etc. The good Steiler assured me in a postscript that he would himself look upon my compliance as a very great favour, since the lady absolutely refused to see a Swiss physician, and he could not but feel that he was incurring a great responsibility.

The appeal was one which could not be ignored. It was impossible to refuse the request of a fellow-countrywoman dying in a strange land. Yet I had my scruples about leaving Holmes. It was finally agreed, however, that he should retain the young Swiss messenger with him as guide and companion while I returned to Meiringen. My friend would stay some little time at the fall, he said, and would then walk slowly over the hill to Rosenlaui, where I was to rejoin him in the evening. As I turned away I saw Holmes with his back against a rock and his arms folded, gazing down at the rush of the waters. It was the last that I was ever destined to see of him in this world.

When I was near the bottom of the descent I looked back. It was impossible, from that position, to see the fall, but I could see the curving path which winds over the shoulder of the hill and leads to it. Along this a man was, I remember, walking very rapidly. I could see his black figure clearly outlined against the green behind him. I noted him, and the energy with which he walked, but he passed from my mind again as I hurried on upon my errand.

It may have been a little over an hour before I reached Meiringen. Old Steiler was standing at the porch of his hotel.

"Well," said I, as I came hurrying up, "I trust that she is no worse?"

A look of surprise passed over his face, and at the first quiver of his eyebrows my heart turned to lead in my breast.

"You did not write this?" I said, pulling the letter from my pocket. "There is no sick Englishwoman in the hotel?"

"Certainly not," he cried. "But it has the hotel mark upon it! Ha! it must have been written by that tall Englishman who came in after you had gone. He said—— "

But I waited for none of the landlord's explanations. In a tingle of fear I was already running down the village street, and making for the path which I had so lately descended. It had taken me an hour to come down. For all my efforts, two more had passed before I found myself at the fall of Reichenbach once more. There was Holmes's alpenstock still leaning against the rock by which I had left him. But there was no sign of him, and it was in vain that I shouted. My only answer was my own voice reverberating in a rolling echo from the cliffs around me.

It was the sight of that alpenstock which turned me cold and sick. He had not gone to Rosenlaui, then. He had remained on that three-foot path, with sheer wall on one side and sheer drop upon the other, until his enemy had overtaken him. The young Swiss had gone too. He had probably been in the pay of Moriarty, and had left the two men together. And then what had happened? Who was to tell us what had happened then?

I stood for a minute or two to collect myself, for I was dazed with the horror of the thing. Then I began to think of Holmes's own methods and to try to practise them in reading this tragedy. It was, alas! only too easy to do. During our conversation we had not gone to the end of the path, and the alpenstock marked the place where we had stood. The blackish soil is kept for ever soft by the incessant drift of spray, and a bird would leave its tread upon it. Two lines of footmarks were clearly marked along the further end of the path, both leading away from me. There were none returning. A few yards from the end the soil was all ploughed up into a patch of mud, and the brambles and ferns which fringed the chasm were torn and bedraggled. I lay upon my face and peered over, with the spray spouting up all around me. It had darkened since I had left, and now I could only see here and there the glistening of moisture upon the black walls, and far away down at the end of the shaft the gleam of the broken water. I shouted; but only that same half-human cry of the fall was borne back to my ears.

But it was destined that I should after all have a last word of greeting from my friend and comrade. I have said that his alpenstock had been left leaning against a rock which jutted on to the path. From the top of this boulder the gleam of something bright caught my eye, and, raising my hand, I found that it came from the silver cigarette-case which he used to carry. As I took it up a small square of paper upon which it had lain fluttered down on to the ground. Unfolding it I found that it con-sisted of three pages torn from his notebook and addressed to me. It was characteristic of the man that the direction was as precise, and the writing as firm and clear, as though it had been written in his study.

> MY DEAR WATSON [he said],
> I write these few lines through the courtesy of Mr. Moriarty, who awaits my convenience for the final discussion of those questions which lie between us. He has been giving me a sketch of the meth-ods by which he avoided the English police and kept himself in-formed of our movements. They certainly confirm the very high opinion which I had formed of his abilities. I am pleased to think that I shall be able to free society from any further effects of his presence, though I fear that it is at a cost which will give pain to my friends, and especially, my dear Watson, to you. I have already explained to you, however, that my career had in any case reached its crisis, and that no possible conclusion to it could be more con-genial to me than this. Indeed, if I may make a full confession to you, I was quite convinced that the letter from Meiringen was a hoax, and I allowed you to depart on that errand under the persua-sion that some development of this sort would follow. Tell Inspec-tor Patterson that the papers which he needs to convict the gang are in pigeon-hole M., done up in a blue envelope and inscribed "Moriarty." I made every disposition of my property before leav-ing England, and handed it to my brother Mycroft. Pray give my greetings to Mrs. Watson, and believe me to be, my dear fellow,
>
> Very sincerely yours,
> SHERLOCK HOLMES.

A few words may suffice to tell the little that remains. An examination by experts leaves little doubt that a personal contest between the two men ended, as it could hardly fail to end in such a situation, in their reeling over, locked in each other's arms. Any attempt at recovering the bodies was absolutely hopeless, and there, deep down in that dreadful cauldron of swirling water and seething foam, will lie for all time the most dangerous criminal and the foremost champion of the law of their generation. The Swiss youth was never found again, and there can be no doubt that he was one of the numerous agents whom Moriarty kept in his employ. As to the gang, it will be within the memory of the public how completely the evidence which Holmes had accumulated exposed their organization, and how heavily the hand of the dead man weighed upon them. Of their terrible chief few details came out during the proceeding, and if I have now been compelled to make a clear statement of his career, it is due to those injudicious champions who have endeavoured to clear his memory by attacks upon him whom I shall ever regard as the best and the wisest man whom I have ever known.

## AFTERWORD

"The Final Problem," Doyle's effort to "bring Holmes to an end," pushes the detective story to several other extremes besides that of the detective's mortality. In Moriarty, Doyle introduces the detective's ultimate antagonist, "the Napoleon of crime" whose genius is paradoxically witnessed by his very invisibility ("The man pervades London, and no one has heard of him"). Moriarty is so nearly a match for and an intellectual equal to Holmes that their mode of communication, approaching that of Milton's angels, passes in its subtlety beyond discourse toward the extreme of intuition ("'All that I have to say has already crossed your mind,' said he. 'Then possibly my answer has crossed yours,' I replied"). It is thus richly appropriate that, when their paths again and finally cross, the two should seemingly plunge to their mutual conclusion in an abyss that is itself the extreme home of inarticulate voice, a place of "constant whirl and clamour" where the torrent's "half-human shout . . . came booming up with the spray out of the abyss."

Watson's last words echo Phaedo's as he concludes his account of the death of Socrates in Plato's *Phaedo:* "Such, Echecrates, was the end of our comrade, who was, we may fairly say, of all those whom we knew in our time, the bravest and also the wisest and most upright man."

# The Empty House

It was in the spring of the year 1894 that all London was interested, and the fashionable world dismayed, by the murder of the Honourable Ronald Adair, under most unusual and inexplicable circumstances. The public has already learned those particulars of the crime which came out in the police investigation; but a good deal was suppressed upon that occasion, since the case for the prosecution was so overwhelmingly strong that it was not necessary to bring forward all the facts. Only now, at the end of nearly ten years, am I allowed to supply those missing links which make up the whole of that remarkable chain. The crime was of interest in itself, but that interest was as nothing to me compared to the inconceivable sequel, which afforded me the greatest shock and surprise of any event in my adventurous life. Even now, after this long interval, I find myself thrilling as I think of it, and feeling once more that sudden flood of joy, amazement, and incredulity which utterly submerged my mind. Let me say to that public which has shown some interest in those glimpses which I have occasionally given them of the thoughts and actions of a very remarkable man that they are not to blame me if I have not shared my knowledge with them, for I should have considered it my first duty to have done so had I not been barred by a positive prohibition from his own lips, which was only withdrawn upon the third of last month.

It can be imagined that my close intimacy with Sherlock Holmes had interested me deeply in crime, and that after his disappearance I never failed to read with care the various problems which came before the public, and I even attempted more than once for my own private satisfaction to employ his methods in their solution, though with indifferent success. There was none, however, which appealed to me like this tragedy of Ronald Adair. As I read the evidence at the inquest, which led up to a verdict of wilful murder against some person or persons unknown, I realized more clearly than I had ever done the loss which the community had sustained by the death of Sherlock Holmes. There were points about this strange business which would, I was sure, have specially appealed to him, and the efforts of the police would have been supplemented, or more probably anticipated, by the trained observation and the alert mind of the first criminal agent in Europe. All day as I drove upon my round I turned over the case in my mind, and found no

From *The Return of Sherlock Holmes* (1905). First published in *Collier's*, 26 September 1903; the *Strand*, October 1903.

explanation which appeared to me to be adequate. At the risk of telling a twice-told tale I will recapitulate the facts as they were known to the public at the conclusion of the inquest.

The Honourable Robert Adair was the second son of the Earl of Maynooth, at that time Governor of one of the Australian colonies. Adair's mother had returned from Australia to undergo an operation for cataract, and she, her son Ronald, and her daughter Hilda were living together at 427 Park Lane. The youth moved in the best society, had, so far as was known, no enemies, and no particular vices. He had been engaged to Miss Edith Woodley, of Carstairs, but the engagement had been broken off by mutual consent some months before, and there was no sign that it had left any very profound feeling behind it. For the rest, the man's life moved in a narrow and conventional circle, for his habits were quiet and his nature unemotional. Yet it was upon this easy-going young aristocrat that death came in most strange and unexpected form between the hours of ten and eleven-twenty on the night of March 30, 1894.

Ronald Adair was fond of cards, playing continually, but never for such stakes as would hurt him. He was a member of the Baldwin, the Cavendish, and the Bagatelle Card Clubs. It was shown that after dinner on the day of his death he had played a rubber of whist at the latter club. He had also played there in the afternoon. The evidence of those who had played with him — Mr. Murray, Sir John Hardy, and Colonel Moran — showed that the game was whist, and that there was a fairly equal fall of the cards. Adair might have lost five pounds, but not more. His fortune was a considerable one, and such a loss could not in any way affect him. He had played nearly every day at one club or other, but he was a cautious player, and usually rose a winner. It came out in evidence that in partnership with Colonel Moran he had actually won as much as £420 in a sitting some weeks before from Godfrey Milner and Lord Balmoral. So much for his recent history, as it came out at the inquest.

On the evening of the crime he returned from the club exactly at ten. His mother and sister were out spending the evening with a relation. The servant deposed that she heard him enter the front room on the second floor, generally used as his sitting-room. She had lit a fire there, and as it smoked she had opened the window. No sound was heard from the room until eleven-twenty, the hour of the return of Lady Maynooth and her daughter. Desiring to say good night, she had attempted to enter her son's room. The door was locked on the inside, and no answer could be got to their cries and knocking. Help was obtained, and the door forced. The unfortunate young man was found

lying near the table. His head had been horribly mutilated by an expanding revolver bullet, but no weapon of any sort was to be found in
the room. On the table lay two bank-notes for £10 each and £17 10s. in
silver and gold, the money arranged in little piles of varying amount.
There were some figures also upon a sheet of paper with the names of
some club friends opposite to them, from which it was conjectured that
before his death he was endeavouring to make out his losses or winnings
at cards.

A minute examination of the circumstances served only to make the
case more complex. In the first place, no reason could be given why the
young man should have fastened the door upon the inside. There was
the possibility that the murderer had done this and had afterwards escaped by the window. The drop was at least twenty feet, however, and
a bed of crocuses in full bloom lay beneath. Neither the flowers nor the
earth showed any sign of having been disturbed, nor were there any
marks upon the narrow strip of grass which separated the house from
the road. Apparently, therefore, it was the young man himself who had
fastened the door. But how did he come by his death? No one could
have climbed up to the window without leaving traces. Suppose a man
had fired through the window, it would indeed be a remarkable shot
who could with a revolver inflict so deadly a wound. Again, Park Lane
is a frequented thoroughfare, and there is a cab-stand within a hundred
yards of the house. No one had heard a shot. And yet there was the dead
man, and there the revolver bullet, which had mushroomed out, as soft-
nosed bullets will, and so inflicted a wound which must have caused
instantaneous death. Such were the circumstances of the Park Lane
Mystery, which were further complicated by entire absence of motive,
since, as I have said, young Adair was not known to have any enemy,
and no attempt had been made to remove the money or valuables in the
room.

All day I turned these facts over in my mind, endeavouring to hit
upon some theory which could reconcile them all, and to find that line
of least resistance which my poor friend had declared to be the starting-
point of every investigation. I confess that I made little progress. In the
evening I strolled across the Park, and found myself about six o'clock at
the Oxford Street end of Park Lane. A group of loafers upon the pave-
ments, all staring up at a particular window, directed me to the house
which I had come to see. A tall, thin man with coloured glasses, whom
I strongly suspected of being a plain-clothes detective, was pointing out
some theory of his own, while the others crowded round to listen to
what he said. I got as near as I could, but his observations seemed to me

to be absurd, so I withdrew again in some disgust. As I did so I struck against an elderly deformed man, who had been behind me, and I knocked down several books which he was carrying. I remember that as I picked them up I observed the title of one of them, *The Origin of Tree Worship,* and it struck me that the fellow must be some poor bibliophile who, either as a trade or as a hobby, was a collector of obscure volumes. I endeavoured to apologize for the accident, but it was evident that these books which I had so unfortunately maltreated were very precious objects in the eyes of their owner. With a snarl of contempt he turned upon his heel, and I saw his curved back and white side-whiskers disappear among the throng.

My observations of No. 427 Park Lane did little to clear up the problem in which I was interested. The house was separated from the street by a low wall and railing, the whole not more than five feet high. It was perfectly easy, therefore, for anyone to get into the garden; but the window was entirely inaccessible, since there was no water-pipe or anything which could help the most active man to climb it. More puzzled than ever, I retraced my steps to Kensington. I had not been in my study five minutes when the maid entered to say that a person desired to see me. To my astonishment, it was none other than my strange old book-collector, his sharp, wizened face peering out from a frame of white hair, and his precious volumes, a dozen of them at least, wedged under his right arm.

"You're surprised to see me, sir," said he, in a strange, croaking voice.

I acknowledged that I was.

"Well, I've a conscience, sir, and when I chanced to see you go into this house, as I came hobbling after you, I thought to myself, I'll just step in and see that kind gentleman, and tell him that if I was a bit gruff in my manner there was not any harm meant, and that I am much obliged to him for picking up my books."

"You make too much of a trifle," said I. "May I ask how you knew who I was?"

"Well, sir, if it isn't too great a liberty, I am a neighbour of yours, for you'll find my little bookshop at the corner of Church Street, and very happy to see you, I am sure. Maybe you collect yourself, sir; here's *British Birds,* and *Catullus,* and *The Holy War* — a bargain every one of them. With five volumes you could just fill that gap on that second shelf. It looks untidy, does it not, sir?"

I moved my head to look at the cabinet behind me. When I turned again Sherlock Holmes was standing smiling at me across my study table. I rose to my feet, stared at him for some seconds in utter amazement, and then it appears that I must have fainted for the first and the last time in my life. Certainly a grey mist swirled before my eyes, and when it cleared I found my collar-ends undone and the tingling aftertaste of brandy upon my lips. Holmes was bending over my chair, his flask in his hand.

"My dear Watson," said the well-remembered voice, "I owe you a thousand apologies. I had no idea that you would be so affected."

I gripped him by the arm.

"Holmes!" I cried. "Is it really you? Can it indeed be that you are alive? Is it possible that you succeeded in climbing out of that awful abyss?"

"Wait a moment!" said he. "Are you sure that you are really fit to discuss things? I have given you a serious shock by my unnecessarily dramatic appearance."

"I am all right; but indeed, Holmes, I can hardly believe my eyes. Good heavens, to think that you — you of all men — should be standing in my study!" Again I gripped him by the sleeve and felt the thin, sinewy arm beneath it. "Well, you're not a spirit, anyhow," said I. "My dear chap, I am overjoyed to see you. Sit down, and tell me how you came alive out of that dreadful chasm."

He sat opposite to me and lit a cigarette in his old nonchalant manner. He was dressed in the seedy frock-coat of the book merchant, but the rest of that individual lay in a pile of white hair and old books upon the table. Holmes looked even thinner and keener than of old, but there was a dead-white tinge in his aquiline face which told me that his life recently had not been a healthy one.

"I am glad to stretch myself, Watson," said he. "It is no joke when a tall man has to take a foot off his stature for several hours on end. Now, my dear fellow, in the matter of these explanations we have, if I may ask for your co-operation, a hard and dangerous night's work in front of us. Perhaps it would be better if I gave you an account of the whole situation when that work is finished."

"I am full of curiosity. I should much prefer to hear now."

"You'll come with me to-night?"

"When you like and where you like."

"This is indeed like the old days. We shall have time for a mouthful of dinner before we need go. Well, then, about that chasm. I had no serious difficulty in getting out of it, for the very simple reason that I never was in it."

"You never were in it?"

"No, Watson, I never was in it. My note to you was absolutely genuine. I had little doubt that I had come to the end of my career when I perceived the somewhat sinister figure of the late Professor Moriarty standing upon the narrow pathway which led to safety. I read an inexorable purpose in his grey eyes. I exchanged some remarks with him, therefore, and obtained his courteous permission to write the short note which you afterwards received. I left it with my cigarette-box and my stick, and I walked along the pathway, Moriarty still at my heels. When I reached the end I stood at bay. He drew no weapon, but he rushed at me and threw his long arms around me. He knew that his own game was up, and was only anxious to revenge himself upon me. We tottered together upon the brink of the fall. I have some knowledge, however, of baritsu,[1] or the Japanese system of wrestling, which has more than once been very useful to me. I slipped through his grip, and he with a horrible scream kicked madly for a few seconds and clawed the air with both his hands. But for all his efforts he could not get his balance, and over he went. With my face over the brink I saw him fall for a long way. Then he struck a rock, bounded off, and splashed into the water."

I listened with amazement to this explanation, which Holmes delivered between the puffs of his cigarette.

"But the tracks!" I cried. "I saw with my own eyes that two went down the path and none returned."

"It came about in this way. The instant that the professor had disappeared it struck me what a really extraordinarily lucky chance Fate had placed in my way. I knew that Moriarty was not the only man who had sworn my death. There were at least three others whose desire for vengeance upon me would only be increased by the death of their leader. They were all most dangerous men. One or other would certainly get me. On the other hand, if all the world was convinced that I was dead they would take liberties, these men; they would lay themselves open, and sooner or later I could destroy them. Then it would be time for me to announce that I was still in the land of the living. So rapidly does the brain act that I believe I had thought this all out before Professor Moriarty had reached the bottom of the Reichenbach Fall.

"I stood up and examined the rocky wall behind me. In your picturesque account of the matter, which I read with great interest some months later, you assert that the wall was sheer. This was not literally true. A few small footholds presented themselves, and there was some indication of a ledge. The cliff is so high that to climb it all was an

---

[1] *baritsu:* Probably a mistake for "Bartisu," a European adaptation of jujitsu.

obvious impossibility, and it was equally impossible to make my way along the wet path without leaving some tracks. I might, it is true, have reversed my boots, as I have done on similar occasions, but the sight of three sets of tracks in one direction would certainly have suggested a deception. On the whole, then, it was best that I should risk the climb. It was not a pleasant business, Watson. The fall roared beneath me. I am not a fanciful person, but I give you my word that I seemed to hear Moriarty's voice screaming at me out of the abyss. A mistake would have been fatal. More than once, as tufts of grass came out in my hand or my foot slipped in the wet notches of the rock, I thought that I was gone. But I struggled upwards, and at last I reached a ledge several feet deep and covered with soft green moss, where I could lie unseen in the most perfect comfort. There I was stretched when you, my dear Watson, and all your following were investigating in the most sympathetic and inefficient manner the circumstances of my death.

"At last, when you had all formed your inevitable and totally erro- neous conclusions, you departed for the hotel, and I was left alone. I had imagined that I had reached the end of my adventures, but a very unexpected occurrence showed me that there were surprises still in store for me. A huge rock, falling from above, boomed past me, struck the path, and bounded over into the chasm. For an instant I thought that it was an accident; but a moment later, looking up, I saw a man's head against the darkening sky, and another stone struck the very ledge upon which I was stretched, within a foot of my head. Of course, the meaning of this was obvious. Moriarty had not been alone. A confederate — and even that one glance had told me how dangerous a man that confederate was — had kept guard while the professor had attacked me. From a dis- tance, unseen by me, he had been a witness of his friend's death and of my escape. He had waited, and then, making his way round to the top of the cliff, he had endeavoured to succeed where his comrade had failed.

"I did not take long to think about it, Watson. Again I saw that grim face look over the cliff, and I knew that it was the precursor of another stone. I scrambled down on to the path. I don't think I could have done it in cold blood. It was a hundred times more difficult than getting up. But I had no time to think of the danger, for another stone sang past me as I hung by my hands from the edge of the ledge. Half- way down I slipped, but by the blessing of God I landed, torn and bleeding, upon the path. I took to my heels, did ten miles over the mountains in the darkness, and a week later I found myself in Florence, with the certainty that no one in the world knew what had become of me.

"I had only one confidant — my brother Mycroft. I owe you many apologies, my dear Watson, but it was all-important that it should be thought I was dead, and it is quite certain that you would not have written so convincing an account of my unhappy end had you not yourself thought that it was true. Several times during the last three years I have taken up my pen to write to you, but always I feared lest your affectionate regard for me should tempt you to some indiscretion which would betray my secret. For that reason I turned away from you this evening when you upset my books, for I was in danger at the time, and any show of surprise and emotion upon your part might have drawn attention to my identity and led to the most deplorable and irreparable results. As to Mycroft, I had to confide in him in order to obtain the money which I needed. The course of events in London did not run so well as I had hoped, for the trial of the Moriarty gang left two of its most dangerous members, my own most vindictive enemies, at liberty. I travelled for two years in Tibet, therefore, and amused myself by visiting Lhassa and spending some days with the head Llama. You may have read of the remarkable explorations of a Norwegian named Sigerson, but I am sure that it never occurred to you that you were receiving news of your friend. I then passed through Persia, looked in at Mecca, and paid a short but interesting visit to the Khalifa at Khartoum, the results of which I have communicated to the Foreign Office. Returning to France, I spent some months in a research into the coal-tar derivatives, which I conducted in a laboratory at Montpellier, in the south of France. Having concluded this to my satisfaction, and learning that only one of my enemies was now left in London, I was about to return, when my movements were hastened by the news of this remarkable Park Lane Mystery, which not only appealed to me by its own merits, but which seemed to offer some most peculiar personal opportunities. I came over at once to London, called in my own person at Baker Street, threw Mrs. Hudson into violent hysterics, and found that Mycroft had preserved my rooms and my papers exactly as they had always been. So it was, my dear Watson, that at two o'clock to-day I found myself in my old arm-chair in my own old room, and only wishing that I could have seen my old friend Watson in the other chair which he has so often adorned."

Such was the remarkable narrative to which I listened on that April evening — a narrative which would have been utterly incredible to me had it not been confirmed by the actual sight of the tall, spare figure and the keen, eager face which I had never thought to see again. In some manner he had learned of my own sad bereavement, and his sympathy was shown in his manner rather than in his words. "Work is the best antidote to sorrow, my dear Watson," said he, "and I have a piece of work for us both to-night which, if we can bring it to a successful conclusion, will in itself justify a man's life on this planet." In vain I begged him to tell me more. "You will hear and see enough before morning," he answered. "We have three years of the past to discuss. Let that suffice until half-past nine, when we start upon the notable adventure of the empty house."

It was indeed like old times when, at that hour, I found myself seated beside him in a hansom, my revolver in my pocket and the thrill of adventure in my heart. Holmes was cold and stern and silent. As the gleam of the street-lamps flashed upon his austere features, I saw that his brows were drawn down in thought and his thin lips compressed. I knew not what wild beast we were about to hunt down in the dark jungle of criminal London, but I was well assured from the bearing of this master huntsman that the adventure was a most grave one, while the sardonic smile which occasionally broke through his ascetic gloom boded little good for the object of our quest.

I had imagined that we were bound for Baker Street, but Holmes stopped the cab at the corner of Cavendish Square. I observed that as he stepped out he gave a most searching glance to right and left, and at every subsequent street corner he took the utmost pains to assure that he was not followed. Our route was certainly a singular one. Holmes's knowledge of the by-ways of London was extraordinary, and on this occasion he passed rapidly, and with an assured step, through a network of mews and stables the very existence of which I had never known. We emerged at last into a small road, lined with old, gloomy houses, which led us into Manchester Street, and so to Blandford Street. Here he turned swiftly down a narrow passage, passed through a wooden gate into a deserted yard, and then opened with a key the back door of a house. We entered together, and he closed it behind us.

The place was pitch dark, but it was evident to me that it was an empty house. Our feet creaked and crackled over the bare planking, and my outstretched hand touched a wall from which the paper was hanging in ribbons. Holmes's cold, thin fingers closed round my wrist and led me forward down a long hall, until I dimly saw the murky fanlight over the door. Here Holmes turned suddenly to the right, and we found ourselves in a large, square, empty room, heavily shadowed in the corners, but faintly lit in the centre from the lights of the street beyond. There was no lamp near, and the window was thick with dust, so that we could only just discern each other's figures within. My companion put his hand upon my shoulder, and his lips close to my ear.

"Do you know where we are?" he whispered.

"Surely that is Baker Street," I answered, staring through the dim window.

"Exactly. We are in Camden House, which stands opposite to our own old quarters."

"But why are we here?"

"Because it commands so excellent a view of that picturesque pile. Might I trouble you, my dear Watson, to draw a little nearer to the window, taking every precaution not to show yourself, and then to look up at our old rooms — the starting-point of so many of our little adventures? We will see if my three years of absence have entirely taken away my power to surprise you."

I crept forward and looked across at the familiar window. As my eyes fell upon it I gave a gasp and a cry of amazement. The blind was down, and a strong light was burning in the room. The shadow of a man who was seated in a chair within was thrown in hard, black outline upon the luminous screen of the window. There was no mistaking the poise of the head, the squareness of the shoulders, the sharpness of the features. The face was turned half-round, and the effect was that of one of those black silhouettes which our grandparents loved to frame. It was a perfect reproduction of Holmes. So amazed was I that I threw out my hand to make sure that the man himself was standing beside me. He was quivering with silent laughter.

"Well?" said he.

"Good heavens!" I cried. "It's marvellous."

"I trust that age doth not wither nor custom stale my infinite variety,"[2] said he, and I recognized in his voice the joy and pride which the artist takes in his own creation. "It really is rather like me, is it not?"

"I should be prepared to swear that it was you."

"The credit of the execution is due to Monsieur Oscar Meunier, of Grenoble, who spent some days in doing the moulding. It is a bust in wax. The rest I arranged myself during my visit to Baker Street this afternoon."

"But why?"

"Because, my dear Watson, I had the strongest possible reason for wishing certain people to think that I was there when I was really elsewhere."

---

[2] *age doth not wither . . . variety:* Holmes paraphrases Enobarbus's famous celebration of Cleopatra in Shakespeare's *Antony and Cleopatra:* "Age cannot wither her, nor custom stale / Her infinite variety" (II.ii).

"And you thought the rooms were watched?"

"I *knew* that they were watched."

"By whom?"

"By my old enemies, Watson. By the charming society whose leader lies in the Reichenbach Fall. You must remember that they knew, and only they knew, that I was still alive. Sooner or later they believed that I should come back to my rooms. They watched them continuously, and this morning they saw me arrive."

"How do you know?"

"Because I recognized their sentinel when I glanced out of my window. He is a harmless enough fellow, Parker by name, a garrotter by trade, and a remarkable performer upon the jews' harp. I cared nothing for him. But I cared a great deal for the much more formidable person who was behind him, the bosom friend of Moriarty, the man who dropped the rocks over the cliff, the most cunning and dangerous criminal in London. That is the man who is after me to-night, Watson, and that is the man who is quite unaware that we are after *him*."

My friend's plans were gradually revealing themselves. From this convenient retreat the watchers were being watched and the trackers tracked. That angular shadow up yonder was the bait, and we were the hunters. In silence we stood together in the darkness and watched the hurrying figures who passed and repassed in front of us. Holmes was silent and motionless; but I could tell that he was keenly alert, and that his eyes were fixed intently upon the stream of passers-by. It was a bleak and boisterous night, and the wind whistled shrilly down the long street. Many people were moving to and fro, most of them muffled in their coats and cravats. Once or twice it seemed to me that I had seen the same figure before, and I especially noticed two men who appeared to be sheltering themselves from the wind in the doorway of a house some distance up the street. I tried to draw my companion's attention to them, but he gave a little ejaculation of impatience, and continued to stare into the street. More than once he fidgeted with his feet and tapped rapidly with his fingers upon the wall. It was evident to me that he was becoming uneasy, and that his plans were not working out altogether as he had hoped. At last, as midnight approached and the street gradually cleared, he paced up and down the room in uncontrollable agitation. I was about to make some remark to him, when I raised my eyes to the lighted window, and again experienced almost as great a surprise as before. I clutched Holmes's arm and pointed upwards.

"The shadow has moved!" I cried.

It was, indeed, no longer the profile, but the back, which was turned towards us.

Three years had certainly not smoothed the asperities of his temper, or his impatience with a less active intelligence than his own.

"Of course it has moved," said he. "Am I such a farcical bungler, Watson, that I should erect an obvious dummy and expect that some of the sharpest men in Europe would be deceived by it? We have been in this room two hours, and Mrs. Hudson has made some change in that figure eight times, or once every quarter of an hour. She works it from the front, so that her shadow may never be seen. Ah!" He drew in his breath with a shrill, excited intake. In the dim light I saw his head thrown forward, his whole attitude rigid with attention. Those two men might still be crouching in the doorway, but I could no longer see them. All was still and dark, save only that brilliant yellow screen in front of us with the black figure outlined upon its centre. Again in the utter silence I heard that thin, sibilant note which spoke of intense suppressed excitement. An instant later he pulled me back into the blackest corner of the room, and I felt his warning hand upon my lips. The fingers which clutched me were quivering. Never had I known my friend more moved, and yet the dark street still stretched lonely and motionless before us.

But suddenly I was aware of that which his keener senses had already distinguished. A low, stealthy sound came to my ears, not from the direction of Baker Street, but from the back of the very house in which we lay concealed. A door opened and shut. An instant later steps crept down the passage — steps which were meant to be silent, but which reverberated harshly through the empty house. Holmes crouched back against the wall, and I did the same, my hand closing upon the handle of my revolver. Peering through the gloom, I saw the vague outline of a man a shade blacker than the blackness of the open door. He stood for an instant, and then he crept forward, crouching, menacing, into the room. He was within three yards of us, this sinister figure, and I had braced myself to meet his spring, before I realized that he had no idea of our presence. He passed close beside us, stole over to the window, and very softly and noiselessly raised it for a half a foot. As he sank to the level of this opening the light of the street, no longer dimmed by the dusty glass, fell full upon his face. The man seemed to be beside himself with excitement. His two eyes shone like stars, and his features were working convulsively. He was an elderly man, with a thin projecting nose, a high, bald forehead, and a huge grizzled moustache. An opera-hat was pushed to the back of his head, and an evening dress shirt-front gleamed out through his open overcoat. His face was gaunt and swarthy, scored with deep, savage lines. In his hand he carried what appeared to be a stick, but as he laid it down upon the floor it gave a metallic clang. Then from the pocket of his overcoat he drew a bulky object, and he busied himself in some task which ended with a loud, sharp click, as if a spring or bolt had fallen into its place. Still kneeling upon the floor, he bent forward and threw all his weight and strength upon some lever, with the result that there came a long, whirling, grinding noise, ending once more in a powerful click. He straightened himself then, and I saw that what he held in his hand was a sort of a gun, with a curiously misshapen butt. He opened it at the breech, put something in, and snapped the breech-block. Then, crouching down, he rested the end of the barrel upon the ledge of the open window, and I saw his long moustache droop over the stock and his eye gleam as it peered along the sights. I heard a little sigh of satisfaction as he cuddled the butt into his shoulder, and saw that amazing target, the black man on the yellow ground, standing clear at the end of his foresight. For an instant he was rigid and motionless. Then his finger tightened on the trigger. There was a strange, loud whiz and a long, silvery tinkle of broken glass. At that instant Holmes sprang like a tiger on to the marksman's back and hurled him flat upon his face. He was up again in a moment, and with convulsive strength he seized Holmes by the throat; but I struck him on the head with the butt of my revolver, and he dropped again upon the floor. I fell upon him, and as I held him my comrade blew a shrill call upon a whistle. There was the clatter of running feet upon the pavement, and two policemen in uniform, with one plain-clothes detective, rushed through the front entrance and into the room.

"That you, Lestrade?" said Holmes.

"Yes, Mr. Holmes. I took the job myself. It's good to see you back in London, sir."

"I think you want a little unofficial help. Three undetected murders in one year won't do, Lestrade. But you handled the Molesey Mystery with less than your usual — that's to say, you handled it fairly well."

We had all risen to our feet, our prisoner breathing hard, with a stalwart constable on each side of him. Already a few loiterers had begun to collect in the street. Holmes stepped up to the window, closed it, and dropped the blinds. Lestrade had produced two candles, and the policemen had uncovered their lanterns. I was able at last to have a good look at our prisoner.

It was a tremendously virile and yet sinister face which was turned

towards us. With the brow of a philosopher above and the jaw of a sensu-
alist below, the man must have started with great capacities for good or for
evil. But one could not look upon his cruel blue eyes, with their drooping,
cynical lids, or upon the fierce, aggressive nose and the threatening, deep-
lined brow, without reading Nature's plainest danger-signals. He took no
heed of any of us, but his eyes were fixed upon Holmes's face with an
expression in which hatred and amazement were equally blended. "You
fiend!" he kept on muttering — "you clever, clever fiend!"

"Ah, Colonel," said Holmes, arranging his rumpled collar, "'journeys end in lovers' meetings,' as the old play says.[3] I don't think I have
had the pleasure of seeing you since you favoured me with those attentions as I lay on the ledge above the Reichenbach Fall."

The colonel still stared at my friend like a man in a trance. "You
cunning, cunning fiend!" was all that he could say.

"I have not introduced you yet," said Holmes. "This, gentlemen,
is Colonel Sebastian Moran, once of Her Majesty's Indian Army, and
the best heavy game shot that our Eastern Empire has ever produced.
I believe I am correct, colonel, in saying that your bag of tigers still
remains unrivalled?"

The fierce old man said nothing, but still glared at my companion;
with his savage eyes and bristling moustache, he was wonderfully like a
tiger himself.

"I wonder that my very simple stratagem could deceive so old a
shikari,"[4] said Holmes. "It must be very familiar to you. Have you not
tethered a young kid under a tree, lain above it with your rifle, and
waited for the bait to bring up your tiger? This empty house is my tree,
and you are my tiger. You have possibly had other guns in reserve in
case there should be several tigers, or in the unlikely supposition of your
own aim failing you. These," he pointed around, "are my other guns.
The parallel is exact."

Colonel Moran sprang forward with a snarl of rage, but the constables dragged him back. The fury upon his face was terrible to look at.

"I confess that you had one small surprise for me," said Holmes. "I
did not anticipate that you would yourself make use of this empty house
and this convenient front window. I had imagined you as operating
from the street, where my friend Lestrade and his merry men were
awaiting you. With that exception, all has gone as I expected."

---

[3] *"Journeys end in lovers' meetings"*: Holmes adapts a line from the Clown's song in
Shakespeare's *Twelfth Night*: "Journeys end in lovers meeting" (II.iii).
[4] *shikari*: Anglo-Indian term for a hunter or sportsman.

Colonel Moran turned to the official detective.

"You may or may not have just cause for arresting me," said he, "but at least there can be no reason why I should submit to the gibes of this person. If I am in the hands of the law, let things be done in a legal way."

"Well, that's reasonable enough," said Lestrade. "Nothing further you have to say, Mr. Holmes, before we go?"

Holmes had picked up the powerful air-gun from the floor, and was examining its mechanism.

"An admirable and unique weapon," said he, "noiseless and of tremendous power. I knew Von Herder, the blind German mechanic, who constructed it to the order of the late Professor Moriarty. For years I have been aware of its existence, though I have never before had an opportunity of handling it. I commend it very specially to your attention, Lestrade, and also the bullets which fit it."

"You can trust us to look after that, Mr. Holmes," said Lestrade, as the whole party moved towards the door. "Anything further to say?"

"Only to ask what charge you intend to prefer?"

"What charge, sir? Why, of course, the attempted murder of Mr. Sherlock Holmes."

"Not so, Lestrade. I do not propose to appear in the matter at all. To you, and to you only, belongs the credit of the remarkable arrest which you have effected. Yes, Lestrade, I congratulate you! With your usual happy mixture of cunning and audacity you have got him."

"Got him! Got whom, Mr. Holmes?"

"The man whom the whole Force has been seeking in vain — Colonel Sebastian Moran, who shot the Honourable Ronald Adair with an expanding bullet from an air-gun through the open window of the second-floor front of No. 427 Park Lane, upon the 30th of last month. That's the charge, Lestrade. And now, Watson, if you can endure the draught from a broken window, I think that half an hour in my study over a cigar may afford you some profitable amusement."

Our old chambers had been left unchanged, through the supervision of Mycroft Holmes and the immediate care of Mrs. Hudson. As I entered I saw, it is true, an unwonted tidiness, but the old landmarks were all in their places. There were the chemical corner and the acid-stained deal-topped table. There upon a shelf was the row of formidable scrap-books and books of reference which many of our fellow-citizens would have been so glad to burn. The diagrams, the violin-case, and the pipe-rack — even the Persian slipper which contained the tobacco — all met my eye as I glanced round me. There were two occupants of the room — one Mrs. Hudson, who beamed upon us both as we entered; the other, the strange dummy which had played so important a part in the evening's adventures. It was a wax-coloured model of my friend, so admirably done that it was a perfect facsimile. It stood on a small pedestal table with an old dressing-gown of Holmes's so draped round it that the illusion from the street was absolutely perfect.

"I hope you preserved all precautions, Mrs. Hudson?" said Holmes.

"I went to it on my knees, sir, just as you told me."

"Excellent. You carried the thing out very well. Did you observe where the bullet went?"

"Yes, sir. I'm afraid it has spoilt your beautiful bust, for it passed right through the head and flattened itself on the wall. I picked it up from the carpet. Here it is!"

Holmes held it out to me. "A soft revolver bullet, as you perceive, Watson. There's genius in that — for who would expect to find such a thing fired from an air-gun? All right, Mrs. Hudson, I am much obliged for your assistance. And now, Watson, let me see you in your old seat once more, for there are several points which I should like to discuss with you."

He had thrown off the seedy frock-coat, and now he was the Holmes of old, in the mouse-coloured dressing-gown which he took from his effigy.

"The old shikari's nerves have not lost their steadiness nor his eyes their keenness," said he, with a laugh, as he inspected the shattered forehead of his bust.

"Plumb in the middle of the back of the head and smack through the brain. He was the best shot in India, and I expect that there are few better in London. Have you heard the name?"

"No, I have not."

"Well, well, such is fame! But then, if I remember aright, you had not heard the name of Professor James Moriarty, who had one of the great brains of the century. Just give me down my index of biographies from the shelf."

He turned over the pages lazily, leaning back in his chair and blowing great clouds of smoke from his cigar.

"My collection of M's is a fine one," said he. "Moriarty himself is enough to make any letter illustrious, and here is Morgan the poisoner, and Merridew of abominable memory, and Mathews, who knocked out my left canine in the waiting-room at Charing Cross, and, finally, here is our friend of to-night."

He handed over the book, and I read:

*Moran, Sebastian, Colonel.* Unemployed. Formerly 1st Bengalore
Pioneers. Born London, 1840. Son of Sir Augustus Moran, C.B.,
once British Minister to Persia. Educated Eton and Oxford.
Served in Jowaki Campaign, Afghan Campaign, Charasiab (dis-
patches), Sherpur, and Cabul. Author of *Heavy Game of the West-
ern Himalayas,* 1881; *Three Months in the Jungle,* 1884. Address:
Conduit Street. Clubs: The Anglo-Indian, the Tankerville, the
Bagatelle Card Club.

On the margin was written in Holmes's precise hand: "The second
most dangerous man in London."

"This is astonishing," said I, as I handed back the volume. "The
man's career is that of an honourable soldier."

"It is true," Holmes answered. "Up to a certain point he did well.
He was always a man of iron nerve, and the story is still told in India
how he crawled down a drain after a wounded man-eating tiger. There
are some trees, Watson, which grow to a certain height and then suddenly develop some unsightly eccentricity. You will see it often in hu-
mans. I have a theory that the individual represents in his development
the whole procession of his ancestors, and that such a sudden turn to
good or evil stands for some strong influence which came into the line
of his pedigree. The person becomes, as it were, the epitome of the
history of his own family."

"It is surely rather fanciful."

"Well, I don't insist upon it. Whatever the cause, Colonel Moran
began to go wrong. Without any open scandal, he still made India too
hot to hold him. He retired, came to London, and again acquired an
evil name. It was at this time that he was sought out by Professor
Moriarty, to whom for a time he was chief of the staff. Moriarty supplied
him liberally with money, and used him only in one or two very high-
class jobs which no ordinary criminal could have undertaken. You may
have some recollection of the death of Mrs. Stewart, of Lauder, in 1887.
Not? Well, I am sure Moran was at the bottom of it; but nothing could
be proved. So cleverly was the colonel concealed that even when the
Moriarty gang was broken up we could not incriminate him. You remember at that date, when I called upon you in your rooms, how I put
up the shutters for fear of air-guns? No doubt you thought me fanciful.
I knew exactly what I was doing, for I knew of the existence of this
remarkable gun, and I knew also that one of the best shots in the world
would be behind it. When we were in Switzerland he followed us with
Moriarty, and it was undoubtedly he who gave me that evil five minutes
on the Reichenbach ledge.

"You may think that I read the papers with some attention during my sojourn in France, on the look-out for any chance of laying him by the heels. So long as he was free in London my life would really not have been worth living. Night and day the shadow would have been over me, and sooner or later his chance must have come. What could I do? I could not shoot him at sight, or I should myself be in the dock. There was no use appealing to a magistrate. They cannot interfere on the strength of what would appear to them to be a wild suspicion. So I could do nothing. But I watched the criminal news, knowing that sooner or later I should get him. Then came the death of this Ronald Adair. My chance had come at last! Knowing what I did, was it not certain that Colonel Moran had done it? He had played cards with the lad; he had followed him home from the club; he had shot him through the open window. There was not a doubt of it. The bullets alone are enough to put his head in a noose. I came over at once. I was seen by the sentinel, who would, I knew, direct the colonel's attention to my presence. He could not fail to connect my sudden return with his crime, and to be terribly alarmed. I was sure that he would make an attempt to get me out of the way *at once,* and would bring round his murderous weapon for that purpose. I left him an excellent mark in the window, and, having warned the police that they might be needed — by the way, Watson, you spotted their presence in that doorway with unerring accuracy — I took up what seemed to me to be a judicious post for observation, never dreaming that he would choose the same spot for his attack. Now, my dear Watson, does anything remain for me to explain?"

"Yes," said I. "You have not made it clear what was Colonel Moran's motive in murdering the Honourable Ronald Adair."

"Ah! my dear Watson, there we come into those realms of conjecture where the most logical mind may be at fault. Each may form his own hypothesis upon the present evidence, and yours is as likely to be correct as mine."

"You have formed one, then?"

"I think that is not difficult to explain the facts. It came out in evidence that Colonel Moran and young Adair had between them won a considerable amount of money. Now, Moran undoubtedly played foul — of that I have long been aware. I believe that on the day of the murder, Adair had discovered that Moran was cheating. Very likely he had spoken to him privately, and had threatened to expose him unless he voluntarily resigned his membership of the club and promised not to play cards again. It is unlikely that a youngster like Adair would at once make a hideous scandal by exposing a well-known man so much older than himself. Probably he acted as I suggest. The exclusion from his clubs would mean ruin to Moran, who lived by his ill-gotten card gains. He therefore murdered Adair, who at the time was endeavouring to work out how much money he should himself return, since he could not profit by his partner's foul play. He locked the door, lest the ladies should surprise him and insist upon knowing what he was doing with these names and coins. Will it pass?"

"I have no doubt that you have hit upon the truth."

"It will be verified or disproved at the trial. Meanwhile, come what may, Colonel Moran will trouble us no more, the famous air-gun of Von Herder will embellish the Scotland Yard Museum, and once again Mr. Sherlock Holmes is free to devote his life to examining those interesting little problems which the complex life of London so plentifully presents."

## AFTERWORD

"The Final Problem" seems in so many ways to end the Holmes saga by reducing, not merely duplicity to simplicity (for every detective solution accomplishes this), but doubleness to singleness (protagonist and antagonist join in a single fate; the Holmes-Watson pair is reduced to one). "The Empty House" reverses its predecessor by reviving not merely duality (Watson regains his partner; Holmes bests Moran by repeating one of Moran's old hunting strategems) but also ambivalence. The empty house, for example — which is it? The title refers to the unoccupied Camden House across from 221B Baker Street; but this house already contains Holmes and Watson when Watson recognizes it as "empty," and soon, of course, contains Colonel Moran and then several policemen as well. Ronald Adair's sitting-room at 427 Park Lane is emptied by death; 221B Baker Street itself seems to be occupied, but is not: its resident is a dummy, though the landlady continues in attendance. Holmes's own identity, too, here tempts new extremes of ambivalence: as he returns from absence to presence, he appears not only (as he has oftentimes before) in disguise, but also (for the first time in the stories) in effigy. (Somewhat similarly in *The Hound of the Baskervilles* Holmes had pretended via his correspondence with Watson to be staying at Baker Street while he was secretly living near Watson on the Devon moor.) At both extremes — when Holmes drops the book merchant disguise, and when he reveals the silhouetted effigy — Watson must reassure himself by touch of his companion's present substantiality.

It is in "The Empty House," too, that the fundamental ambivalence of detective fiction's "game" finally becomes explicit. This game is, first of all, a rule-guided contest between opponents. The analogy of detection to a game stems from the genre's very origins: Poe stresses the parallels with draughts and whist ("The Murders in the Rue Morgue") and with the game of "even and odd" ("The Purloined Letter"), the relevance of enigmas and riddles to the recovery of Kidd's treasure, and Legrand's wild confidence, after recovering from a false step, that "the game's not up yet" ("The Gold-Bug"). As the *OED* indicates, "the game is up" was an established nineteenth-century usage meaning "the game is over." But when Shakespeare had originally used the phrase in *Cymbeline,* it referred to the hunter's quarry (here, the deer): "Hark! the game is rous'd. . . . The game is up" (III.iii.98–107). And this sense of "game" is also fundamental in detection, as is particularly obvious in Holmes's frequently literal trackings of his quarry (in *The Sign of Four* he even uses a dog to follow the criminals' scent), and quintessentially in his famous, eager rallying call to Watson at the beginning of "The Abbey Grange" (again taken from Shakespeare, this time *Henry V* III.i.32), "Come, Watson, come! . . . The game is afoot." Now, in "The Empty House," the crime turns on gaming (whist again), while Holmes declares retrospectively of the foiled Moriarty at the Reichenbach Fall, "He knew that his own game was up." But the criminal now is not only a card-cheat but a hunter ("the best heavy game shot that our Eastern Empire has ever produced"), and Holmes's scheme for capturing him is highly analogous, as he points out, to a tiger-hunting strategem.

## The Dancing Men

Holmes had been seated for some hours in silence, with his long, thin back curved over a chemical vessel in which he was brewing a particularly malodorous product. His head was sunk upon his breast, and he looked from my point of view like a strange, lank bird, with dull grey plumage and a black top-knot.

"So, Watson," said he suddenly, "you do not propose to invest in South African securities?"

From *The Return of Sherlock Holmes* (1905). First published in the *Strand,* December 1903.

I gave a start of astonishment. Accustomed as I was to Holmes's curious faculties, this sudden intrusion into my most intimate thoughts was utterly inexplicable.

"How on earth do you know that?" I asked.

He wheeled round upon his stool, with a steaming test-tube in his hand and a gleam of amusement in his deep-set eyes.

"Now, Watson, confess yourself utterly taken aback," said he.

"I am."

"I ought to make you sign a paper to that effect."

"Why?"

"Because in five minutes you will say that it is all so absurdly simple."

"I am sure that I shall say nothing of the kind."

"You see, my dear Watson" — he propped his test-tube in the rack and began to lecture with the air of a professor addressing his class — "it is not really difficult to construct a series of inferences, each dependent upon its predecessor and each simple in itself. If, after doing so, one simply knocks out all the central inferences and presents one's audience with the starting-point and the conclusion, one may produce a startling, though possibly a meretricious, effect. Now, it was not really difficult, by an inspection of the groove between your left forefinger and thumb, to feel sure that you did *not* propose to invest your small capital in the goldfields."

"I see no connection."

"Very likely not; but I can quickly show you a close connection. Here are the missing links of the very simple chain: 1. You had chalk between your left finger and thumb when you returned from the club last night. 2. You put chalk there when you play billiards to steady the cue. 3. You never play billiards except with Thurston. 4. You told me four weeks ago that Thurston had an option on some South African property which would expire in a month, and which he desired you to share with him. 5. Your cheque-book is locked in my drawer, and you have not asked for the key. 6. You do not propose to invest your money in this manner."

"How absurdly simple!" I cried.

"Quite so!" said he, a little nettled. "Every problem becomes very childish when once it is explained to you. Here is an unexplained one. See what you can make of that, friend Watson." He tossed a sheet of paper upon the table, and turned once more to his chemical analysis.

I looked with amazement at the absurd hieroglyphics upon the paper.

"Why, Holmes, it is a child's drawing!" I cried.

"Oh, that's your idea!"

"What else should it be?"

"That is what Mr. Hilton Cubitt, of Ridling Thorpe Manor, Norfolk, is very anxious to know. This little conundrum came by the first post, and he was to follow by the next train. There's a ring at the bell, Watson. I should not be very much surprised if this were he."

A heavy step was heard upon the stairs, and an instant later there entered a tall, ruddy, clean-shaven gentleman, whose clear eyes and florid cheeks told of a life led far from the fogs of Baker Street. He seemed to bring a whiff of his strong, fresh, bracing, east-coast air with him as he entered. Having shaken hands with each of us, he was about to sit down, when his eye rested upon the paper with the curious markings, which I had just examined and left upon the table.

"Well, Mr. Holmes, what do you make of these?" he cried. "They told me that you were fond of queer mysteries, and I don't think you can find a queerer one than that. I sent the paper on ahead so that you might have time to study it before I came."

"It is certainly rather a curious production," said Holmes. "At first sight it would appear to be some childish prank. It consists of a number of absurd little figures dancing across the paper upon which they are drawn. Why should you attribute any importance to so grotesque an object?"

"I never should, Mr. Holmes. But my wife does. It is frightening her to death. She says nothing, but I can see terror in her eyes. That's why I want to sift the matter to the bottom."

Holmes held up the paper so that the sunlight shone full upon it. It was a page torn from a notebook. The markings were done in pencil, and ran in this way:

Holmes examined it for some time, and then, folding it carefully up, he placed it in his pocket-book.

"This promises to be a most interesting and unusual case," said he. "You gave me a few particulars in your letter, Mr. Hilton Cubitt, but I should be very much obliged if you would kindly go over it all again for the benefit of my friend, Dr. Watson."

"I'm not much of a story-teller," said our visitor, nervously clasping and unclasping his great, strong hands. "You'll just ask me anything that I don't make clear. I'll begin at the time of my marriage last year; but I want to say first of all that, though I'm not a rich man, my people have been at Ridling Thorpe for a matter of five centuries, and there is no better-known family in the county of Norfolk. Last year I came up to London for the Jubilee, and I stopped at a boarding-house in Russell Square, because Parker, the vicar of our parish, was staying in it. There was an American young lady there — Patrick was the name — Elsie Patrick. In some way we became friends, until before my month was up I was as much in love as a man could be. We were quietly married at a registry office, and we returned to Norfolk a wedded couple. You'll think it very mad, Mr. Holmes, that a man of a good old family should marry a wife in this fashion, knowing nothing of her past or of her people; but if you saw her and knew her it would help you to understand.

"She was very straight about it, was Elsie. I can't say that she did not give me every chance of getting out of it if I wished to do so. 'I have had some very disagreeable associations in my life,' said she; 'I wish to forget all about them. I would rather never allude to the past, for it is very painful to me. If you take me, Hilton, you will take a woman who has nothing that she need be personally ashamed of; but you will have to be content with my word for it, and to allow me to be silent as to all that passed up to the time when I became yours. If these conditions are too hard, then go back to Norfolk and leave me to the lonely life in which you found me.' It was only the day before our wedding that she said those very words to me. I told her that I was content to take her on her own terms, and I have been as good as my word.

"Well, we have been married now for a year, and very happy we have been. But about a month ago, at the end of June, I saw for the first time signs of trouble. One day my wife received a letter from America. I saw the American stamp. She turned deadly white, read the letter, and threw it into the fire. She made no allusion to it afterwards, and I made none, for a promise is a promise; but she has never known an easy hour from that moment. There is always a look of fear upon her face — a look as if she were waiting and expecting. She would do better to trust me. She would find that I was her best friend. But until she speaks I can say nothing. Mind you, she is a truthful woman, Mr. Holmes, and whatever trouble there may have been in her past life, it has been no fault of hers. I am only a simple Norfolk squire, but there is not a man in England who ranks his family honour more highly than I do. She knows it well, and she knew it well before she married me. She would never bring any stain upon it — of that I am sure.

"Well, now I come to the queer part of my story. About a week ago — it was the Tuesday of last week — I found on one of the window-sills a number of absurd little dancing figures, like these upon the paper. They were scrawled with chalk. I thought that it was the stable-boy who had drawn them, but the lad swore he knew nothing about it. Anyhow, they had come there during the night. I had them washed out, and I only mentioned the matter to my wife afterwards. To my surprise she took it very seriously, and begged me if any more came to let her see them. None did come for a week, and then yesterday morning I found this paper lying on the sundial in the garden. I showed it to Elsie, and down she dropped in a dead faint. Since then she has looked like a woman in a dream, half dazed, and with terror always lurking in her eyes. It was then that I wrote and sent the paper to you, Mr. Holmes. It was not a thing that I could take to the police, for they would have laughed at me, but you will tell me what to do. I am not a rich man; but if there is any danger threatening my little woman, I would spend my last copper to shield her."

He was a fine creature, this man of the old English soil, simple, straight, and gentle, with his great, earnest blue eyes and broad, comely face. His love for his wife and his trust in her shone in his features. Holmes had listened to his story with the utmost attention, and now he sat for some time in silent thought.

"Don't you think, Mr. Cubitt," said he at last, "that your best plan would be to make a direct appeal to your wife, and to ask her to share her secret with you?"

Hilton Cubitt shook his massive head.

"A promise is a promise, Mr. Holmes. If Elsie wished to tell me, she would. If not, it is not for me to force her confidence. But I am justified in taking my own line — and I will."

"Then I will help you with all my heart. In the first place, have you heard of any strangers being seen in your neighbourhood?"

"No."

"I presume that it is a very quiet place. Any fresh face would cause comment?"

"In the immediate neighbourhood, yes. But we have several small watering-places not very far away. And the farmers take in lodgers."

"These hieroglyphics have evidently a meaning. If it is a purely arbitrary one, it may be impossible for us to solve it. If, on the other hand, it is systematic, I have no doubt that we shall get to the bottom of it. But this particular sample is so short that I can do nothing, and the facts which you have brought me are so indefinite that we have no basis for an investigation. I would suggest that you return to Norfolk, that you keep a keen lookout, and that you take an exact copy of any fresh dancing men which may appear. It is a thousand pities that we have not a reproduction of those which were done in chalk upon the window-sill. Make a discreet inquiry, also, as to any strangers in the neighbourhood. When you have collected some fresh evidence, come to me again. That is the best advice which I can give you, Mr. Hilton Cubitt. If there are any pressing fresh developments, I shall be always ready to run down and see you in your Norfolk home."

The interview left Sherlock Holmes very thoughtful, and several times in the next few days I saw him take his slip of paper from his notebook and look long and earnestly at the curious figures inscribed upon it. He made no allusion to the affair, however, until one afternoon a fortnight or so later. I was going out, when he called me back.

"You had better stay here, Watson."

"Why?"

"Because I had a wire from Hilton Cubitt this morning — you remember Hilton Cubitt, of the dancing men? He was to reach Liverpool Street at one-twenty. He may be here at any moment. I gather from his wire that there have been some new incidents of importance."

We had not long to wait, for our Norfolk squire came straight from the station as fast as a hansom could bring him. He was looking worried and depressed, with tired eyes and a lined forehead.

"It's getting on my nerves, this business, Mr. Holmes," said he, as he sank, like a wearied man, into an arm-chair. "It's bad enough to feel that you are surrounded by unseen, unknown folk, who have some kind of design upon you; but when, in addition to that, you know that it is just killing your wife by inches, then it becomes as much as flesh and blood can endure. She's wearing away under it — just wearing away before my eyes."

"Has she said anything yet?"

"No, Mr. Holmes, she has not. And yet there have been times when the poor girl has wanted to speak, and yet could not quite bring herself to take the plunge. I have tried to help her; but I dare say I did it clumsily, and scared her off from it. She has spoken about my old family, and our reputation in the county, and our pride in our unsullied honour, and I always felt it was leading to the point; but somehow it turned off before we got there."

"But you have found out something for yourself?"

"A good deal, Mr. Holmes. I have several fresh dancing men pictures for you to examine, and, what is more important, I have seen the fellow."

"What — the man who draws them?"

"Yes, I saw him at his work. But I will tell you everything in order. When I got back after my visit to you, the very first thing I saw next morning was a fresh crop of dancing men. They had been drawn in chalk upon the black wooden door of the tool-house, which stands beside the lawn in full view of the front windows. I took an exact copy, and here it is." He unfolded a paper and laid it upon the table. Here is a copy of the hieroglyphics:

"Excellent!" said Holmes. "Excellent! Pray continue."

"When I had taken the copy I rubbed out the marks; but two mornings later a fresh inscription had appeared. I have a copy of it here":

Holmes rubbed his hands and chuckled with delight.

"Our material is rapidly accumulating," said he.

"Three days later a message was left scrawled upon paper, and placed under a pebble upon the sundial. Here it is. The characters are, as you see, exactly the same as the last one. After that I determined to lie in wait; so I got out my revolver and I sat up in my study, which overlooks the lawn and garden. About two in the morning I was seated by the window, all being dark save for the moonlight outside, when I heard steps behind me, and there was my wife in her dressing-gown. She implored me to come to bed. I told her frankly that I wished to see who it was who played such absurd tricks upon us. She answered that it was some senseless practical joke, and that I should not take any notice of it.

"'If it really annoys you, Hilton, we might go and travel, you and I, and so avoid this nuisance.'

"'What, be driven out of our own house by a practical joker?' said I. 'Why, we should have the whole county laughing at us!'

"'Well, come to bed,' said she, 'and we can discuss it in the morning.'

"Suddenly, as she spoke, I saw her white face grow whiter yet in the moonlight, and her hand tightened upon my shoulder. Something was moving in the shadow of the tool-house. I saw a dark, creeping figure which crawled round the corner and squatted in front of the door. Seizing my pistol I was rushing out, when my wife threw her arms round me and held me with convulsive strength. I tried to throw her off, but she clung to me most desperately. At last I got clear, but by the time I had opened the door and reached the house the creature was gone. He had left a trace of his presence, however, for there on the door was the very same arrangement of dancing men which had already twice appeared, and which I have copied on that paper. There was no other sign of the fellow anywhere, though I ran all over the grounds. And yet the amazing thing is that he must have been there all the time, for when I examined the door again in the morning he had scrawled some more of his pictures under the line which I had already seen."

"Have you that fresh drawing?"

"Yes; it is very short, but I made a copy of it, and here it is."

Again he produced a paper. The new dance was in this form:

"Tell me," said Holmes — and I could see by his eyes that he was much excited — "was this a mere addition to the first, or did it appear to be entirely separate?"

"It was on a different panel of the door."

"Excellent! This is far the most important of all for our purpose. It fills me with hopes. Now, Mr. Hilton Cubitt, please continue your most interesting statement."

"I have nothing more to say, Mr. Holmes, except that I was angry with my wife that night for having held me back when I might have caught the skulking rascal. She said that she feared that I might come to harm. For an instant it had crossed my mind that perhaps what she really feared was that *he* might come to harm, for I could not doubt that she knew who this man was and what he meant by these strange signals. But there is a tone in my wife's voice, Mr. Holmes, and a look in her eyes which forbid doubt, and I am sure that it was indeed my own safety that was in her mind. There's the whole case, and now I want your advice as to what I ought to do. My own inclination is to put half a dozen of my farm lads in the shrubbery, and when this fellow comes again to give him such a hiding that he will leave us in peace for the future."

"I fear it is too deep a case for such simple remedies," said Holmes. "How long can you stop in London?"

"I must go back to-day. I would not leave my wife alone at night for anything. She is very nervous and begged me to come back."

"I dare say you are right. But if you could have stopped I might possibly have been able to return with you in a day or two. Meanwhile, you will leave me these papers, and I think that it is very likely that I shall be able to pay you a visit shortly and to throw some light upon your case."

Sherlock Holmes preserved his calm professional manner until our visitor had left us, although it was easy for me, who knew him so well, to see that he was profoundly excited. The moment that Hilton Cubitt's broad back had disappeared through the door my comrade rushed to the table, laid out all the slips of paper containing dancing men in front of him, and threw himself into an intricate and elaborate calculation.

For two hours I watched him as he covered sheet after sheet of paper with figures and letters, so completely absorbed in his task that he had evidently forgotten my presence. Sometimes he was making progress, and whistled and sang at his work; sometimes he was puzzled and would sit for a long spell with a furrowed brow and a vacant eye. Finally he sprang from his chair with a cry of satisfaction, and walked up and down the room rubbing his hands together. Then he wrote a long telegram upon a cable form. "If my answer to this is as I hope, you will have a very pretty case to add to your collection, Watson," said he. "I expect that we shall be able to go down to Norfolk to-morrow, and to take our friend some very definite news as to the secret of his annoyance."

I confess that I was filled with curiosity, but I was aware that Holmes liked to make his disclosures at his own time and in his own way; so I waited until it should suit him to take me into his confidence.

But there was a delay in that answering telegram, and two days of impatience followed, during which Holmes pricked up his ears at every ring of the bell. On the evening of the second there came a letter from Hilton Cubitt. All was quiet with him, save that a long inscription had appeared that morning upon the pedestal of the sundial. He enclosed a copy of it, which is here reproduced:

Holmes bent over this grotesque frieze for some minutes and then suddenly sprang to his feet with an exclamation of surprise and dismay. His face was haggard with anxiety.

"We have let this affair go far enough," said he. "Is there a train to North Walsham to-night?"

I turned up the time-table. The last had just gone.

"Then we shall breakfast early and take the very first in the morning," said Holmes. "Our presence is most urgently needed. Ah, here is our expected cablegram. One moment, Mrs. Hudson — there may be an answer. No, that is quite as I expected. This message makes it even more essential that we should not lose an hour in letting Hilton Cubitt know how matters stand, for it is a singular and dangerous web in which our simple Norfolk squire is entangled."

So, indeed, it proved, and as I come to the dark conclusion of a story which had seemed to me to be only childish and bizarre, I experience once again the dismay and horror with which I was filled. Would that I had some brighter ending to communicate to my readers; but these are the chronicles of facts, and I must follow to their dark crisis the strange chain of events which for some days made Ridling Thorpe Manor a household word through the length and breadth of England.

We had hardly alighted at North Walsham, and mentioned the name of our destination, when the station-master hurried towards us. "I suppose that you are the detectives from London?" said he.

A look of annoyance passed over Holmes's face.

"What makes you think such a thing?"

"Because Inspector Martin from Norwich has just passed through. But maybe you are the surgeons. She's not dead — or wasn't by last accounts. You may be in time to save her yet — though it be for the gallows."

Holmes's brow was dark with anxiety.

"We are going to Ridling Thorpe Manor," said he, "but we have heard nothing of what has passed there."

"It's a terrible business," said the station-master. "They are shot, both Mr. Hilton Cubitt and his wife. She shot him and then herself — so the servants say. He's dead, and her life is despaired of. Dear, dear! one of the oldest families in the county of Norfolk, and one of the most honoured."

Without a word Holmes hurried to a carriage, and during the long seven-miles drive he never opened his mouth. Seldom have I seen him so utterly despondent. He had been uneasy during all our journey from town, and I had observed that he had turned over the morning papers with anxious attention; but now this sudden realization of his worst fears left him in a blank melancholy. He leaned back in his seat, lost in gloomy speculation. Yet there was much around us to interest us, for we were passing through as singular a countryside as any in England, where a few scattered cottages represented the population of to-day, while on every hand enormous square-towered churches bristled up from the flat, green landscape and told of the glory and prosperity of old East Anglia. At last the violet rim of the German Ocean appeared over the green edge of the Norfolk coast, and the driver pointed with his whip to two old brick-and-timber gables which projected from a grove of trees. "That's Ridling Thorpe Manor," said he.

As we drove up to the porticoed front door I observed in front of it, beside the tennis lawn, the black tool-house and the pedestalled sundial with which we had such strange associations. A dapper little man, with a quick, alert manner and a waxed moustache, had just descended from a high dog-cart.[1] He introduced himself as Inspector Martin, of the Norfolk Constabulary, and he was considerably astonished when he heard the name of my companion.

"Why, Mr. Holmes, the crime was only committed at three this morning! How could you hear of it in London and get to the spot as soon as I?"

"I anticipated it. I came in the hope of preventing it."

"Then you must have important evidence of which we are ignorant, for they were said to be a most united couple."

"I have only the evidence of the dancing men," said Holmes. "I will explain the matter to you later. Meanwhile, since it is too late to prevent this tragedy, I am very anxious that I should use the knowledge which I possess in order to ensure that justice be done. Will you associate me in your investigation, or will you prefer that I should act independently?"

"I should be proud to feel that we were acting together, Mr. Holmes," said the Inspector earnestly.

"In that case I should be glad to hear the evidence and to examine the premises without an instant of unnecessary delay."

Inspector Martin had the good sense to allow my friend to do things in his own fashion, and contented himself with carefully noting the results. The local surgeon, an old, white-haired man, had just come down from Mrs. Hilton Cubitt's room, and he reported that her injuries were serious, but not necessarily fatal. The bullet had passed through the front of her brain, and it would probably be some time before she could regain consciousness. On the question of whether she had been shot or had shot herself he would not venture to express any decided opinion.

[1] *dog-cart:* A light, two-wheeled open carriage.

Certainly the bullet had been discharged at very close quarters. There was only the one pistol found in the room, two barrels of which had been emptied. Mr. Hilton Cubitt had been shot through the heart. It was equally conceivable that he had shot her and then himself, or that she had been the criminal, for the revolver lay upon the floor midway between them.

"Has he been moved?" asked Holmes.

"We have moved nothing except the lady. We could not leave her lying wounded upon the floor."

"How long have you been here, doctor?"

"Since four o'clock."

"Anyone else?"

"Yes, the constable here."

"And you have touched nothing?"

"Nothing."

"You have acted with great discretion. Who sent for you?"

"The housemaid, Saunders."

"Was it she who gave the alarm?"

"She and Mrs. King, the cook."

"Where are they now?"

"In the kitchen, I believe."

"Then I think we had better hear their story at once."

The old hall, oak-panelled and high-windowed, had been turned into a court of investigation. Holmes sat in a great, old-fashioned chair, his inexorable eyes gleaming out of his haggard face. I could read in them a set purpose to devote his life to this quest until the client whom he had failed to save should at last be avenged. The trim Inspector Martin, the old grey-bearded country doctor, myself, and a stolid village policeman made up the rest of that strange company.

The two women told their story clearly enough. They had been aroused from their sleep by the sound of an explosion, which had been followed a minute later by a second one. They slept in adjoining rooms, and Mrs. King had rushed in to Saunders. Together they had descended the stairs. The door of the study was open and a candle was burning upon the table. Their master lay upon his face in the centre of the room. He was quite dead. Near the window his wife was crouching, her head leaning against the wall. She was horribly wounded, and the side of the face was red with blood. She breathed heavily, but was incapable of saying anything. The passage, as well as the room, was full of smoke and the smell of powder. The window was certainly shut and fastened upon the inside. Both women were positive upon the point. They had at once sent for the doctor and for the constable. Then, with the aid of the groom and the stable-boy, they had conveyed their injured mistress to her room. Both she and her husband had occupied the bed. She was clad in her dress — he in his dressing-gown, over his night-clothes. Nothing had been moved in the study. So far as they knew, there had never been any quarrel between husband and wife. They had always looked upon them as a very united couple.

These were the main points of the servants' evidence. In answer to Inspector Martin they were clear that every door was fastened upon the inside and that no one could have escaped from the house. In answer to Holmes, they both remembered that they were conscious of the smell of powder from the moment that they ran out of their rooms upon the top floor. "I commend that fact very carefully to your attention," said Holmes to his professional colleague. "And now I think that we are in a position to undertake a thorough examination of the room."

The study proved to be a small chamber, lined on three sides with books, and with a writing-table facing an ordinary window, which looked out upon the garden. Our first attention was given to the body of the unfortunate squire, whose huge frame lay stretched across the room. His disordered dress showed that he had been hastily aroused from sleep. The bullet had been fired at him from the front, and had remained in his body after penetrating the heart. His death had certainly been instantaneous and painless. There was no powder-marking either upon his dressing-gown or on his hands. According to the country surgeon, the lady had stains upon her face, but none upon her hand.

"The absence of the latter means nothing, though its presence may mean everything," said Holmes. "Unless the powder from a badly fitting cartridge happens to spurt backwards, one may fire many shots without leaving a sign. I would suggest that Mr. Cubitt's body may now be removed. I suppose, doctor, you have not recovered the bullet which wounded the lady?"

"A serious operation will be necessary before that can be done. But there are still four cartridges in the revolver. Two have been fired and two wounds inflicted, so that each bullet can be accounted for."

"So it would seem," said Holmes. "Perhaps you can account also for the bullet which has so obviously struck the edge of the window?"

He had turned suddenly, and his long, thin finger was pointing to a hole which had been drilled right through the lower window-sash about an inch above the bottom.

"By George!" cried the Inspector. "How ever did you see that?"

"Because I looked for it."

"Wonderful!" said the country doctor. "You are certainly right, sir.

Then a third shot has been fired, and therefore a third person must have been present. But who could that have been, and how could he have got away?"

"That is the problem which we are now about to solve," said Sherlock Holmes. "You remember, Inspector Martin, when the servants said that on leaving their room they were at once conscious of a smell of powder, I remarked that the point was an extremely important one?"

"Yes, sir; but I confess I did not quite follow you."

"It suggested that at the time of the firing the window as well as the door of the room had been open. Otherwise the fumes of powder could not have been blown so rapidly through the house. A draught in the room was necessary for that. Both door and window were only open for a short time, however."

"How do you prove that?"

"Because the candle has not guttered."

"Capital!" cried the Inspector. "Capital!"

"Feeling sure that the window had been open at the time of the tragedy, I conceived that there might have been a third person in the affair, who stood outside this opening and fired through it. Any shot directed at this person might hit the sash. I looked, and there, sure enough, was the bullet mark!"

"But how came the window to be shut and fastened?"

"The woman's first instinct would be to shut and fasten the window. But, halloa! what is this?"

It was a lady's hand-bag which stood upon the study table — a trim little hand-bag of crocodile-skin and silver. Holmes opened it and turned the contents out. There were twenty fifty-pound notes of the Bank of England, held together by an india-rubber band — nothing else.

"This must be preserved, for it will figure in the trial," said Holmes, as he handed the bag with its contents to the Inspector. "It is now necessary that we should try to throw some light upon this third bullet, which has clearly, from the splintering of the wood, been fired from inside the room. I should like to see Mrs. King, the cook, again. . . . You said, Mrs. King, that you were awakened by a *loud* explosion. When you said that, did you mean that it seemed to you to be louder than the second one?"

"Well, sir, it wakened me from my sleep, and so it is hard to judge. But it did seem very loud."

"You don't think that it might have been two shots fired almost at the same instant?"

"I am sure I couldn't say, sir."

"I believe that it was undoubtedly so. I rather think, Inspector Martin, that we have now exhausted all that this room can teach us. If you will kindly step round with me we shall see what fresh evidence the garden has to offer."

A flower-bed extended up to the study window, and we all broke into an exclamation as we approached it. The flowers were trampled down, and the soft soil was imprinted all over with footmarks. Large, masculine feet they were, with peculiarly long, sharp toes. Holmes hunted about among the grass and leaves like a retriever after a wounded bird. Then, with a cry of satisfaction, he bent forward and picked up a little brazen cylinder.

"I thought so," said he; "the revolver had an ejector, and here is the third cartridge. I really think, Inspector Martin, that our case is almost complete."

The country inspector's face had shown his intense amazement at the rapid and masterful progress of Holmes's investigations. At first he had shown some disposition to assert his own position; but now he was overcome with admiration, and ready to follow without question wherever Holmes led.

"Whom do you suspect?" he asked.

"I'll go into that later. There are several points in this problem which I have not been able to explain to you yet. Now that I have got so far I had best proceed on my own lines, and then clear the whole matter up once and for all."

"Just as you wish, Mr. Holmes, so long as we get our man."

"I have no desire to make mysteries, but it is impossible at the moment of action to enter into long and complex explanations. I have the threads of this affair all in my hand. Even if this lady should never recover consciousness we can still reconstruct the events of last night and ensure that justice be done. First of all I wish to know whether there is any inn in this neighbourhood known as 'Elrige's'?"

The servants were cross-questioned, but none of them had heard of such a place. The stable-boy threw a light upon the matter by remembering that a farmer of that name lived miles off in the direction of East Ruston.

"Is it a lonely farm?"

"Very lonely, sir."

"Perhaps they have not heard yet of all that happened here during the night?"

"Maybe not, sir."

Holmes thought for a little, and then a curious smile played over his face.

"Saddle a horse, my lad," said he. "I shall wish you to take a note to Elrige's Farm."

He took from his pocket the various slips of the dancing men. With these in front of him he worked for some time at the study table. Finally he handed a note to the boy, with directions to put it into the hands of the person to whom it was addressed, and especially to answer no questions of any sort which might be put to him. I saw the outside of the note, addressed in straggling, irregular characters, very unlike Holmes's usual precise hand. It was consigned to Mr. Abe Slaney, Elrige's Farm, East Ruston, Norfolk.

"I think, Inspector," Holmes remarked, "that you would do well to telegraph for an escort, as, if my calculations prove to be correct, you may have a particularly dangerous prisoner to convey to the county gaol. The boy who takes this note could no doubt forward your telegram. If there is an afternoon train to town, Watson, I think we should do well to take it, as I have a chemical analysis of some interest to finish, and this investigation draws rapidly to a close."

When the youth had been despatched with the note, Sherlock Holmes gave his instructions to the servants. If any visitor were to call asking for Mrs. Hilton Cubitt no information should be given as to her condition, but he was to be shown at once into the drawing-room. He impressed these points upon them with the utmost earnestness. Finally he led the way into the drawing-room, with the remark that the business was now out of our hands, and that we must while away the time as best we might until we could see what was in store for us. The doctor had departed to his patients, and only the Inspector and myself remained.

"I think I can help you to pass an hour in an interesting and profitable manner," said Holmes, drawing his chair up to the table and spreading out in front of him the various papers upon which were recorded the antics of the dancing men. "As to you, friend Watson, I owe you every atonement for having allowed your natural curiosity to remain so long unsatisfied. To you, Inspector, the whole incident may appeal as a remarkable professional study. I must tell you first of all the interesting circumstances connected with the previous consultations which Mr. Hilton Cubitt has had with me in Baker Street." He then shortly recapitulated the facts which have already been recorded.

"I have here in front of me these singular productions, at which one might smile had they not proved themselves to be the forerunners of so terrible a tragedy. I am fairly familiar with all forms of secret writings, and am myself the author of a trifling monograph upon the subject, in which I analyse one hundred and sixty separate ciphers; but I confess that this is entirely new to me. The object of those who invented the system has apparently been to conceal that these characters convey a message, and to give the idea that they are the mere random sketches of children.

"Having once recognized, however, that the symbols stood for letters, and having applied the rules which guide us in all forms of secret writings, the solution was easy enough. The first message submitted to me was so short that it was impossible for me to do more than to say with some confidence that the symbol     stood for E. As you are aware, E is the most common letter in     the English alphabet and it predominates to so marked an extent that even in a short sentence one would expect to find it most often. Out of fifteen symbols in the first message four were the same, so it was reasonable to set this down as E. It is true that in some cases the figure was bearing a flag, and in some cases not, but it was probable from the way in which the flags were distributed that they were used to break the sentence up into words. I accepted this as an hypothesis, and noted that E was represented by

"But     now came the real difficulty of the inquiry. The order of the English letters after E is by no means well-marked, and any preponderance which may be shown in an average of a printed sheet may be reversed in a single short sentence. Speaking roughly, T, A, O, I, N, S, H, R, D, and L are the numerical order in which letters occur; but T, A, O, and I are very nearly abreast of each other, and it would be an endless task to try each combination until a meaning was arrived at. I, therefore, waited for fresh material. In my second interview with Mr. Hilton Cubitt he was able to give me two other short sentences and one message, which appeared — since there was no flag — to be a single word. Here are the symbols. Now, in the single word I have already got the two E's coming second and fourth in a word of five letters. It might be 'sever,' or 'lever,' or 'never.' There can be no question that the latter as a reply to an appeal is far the most probable, and the circumstances pointed to its being a reply written by the lady. Accepting it as correct, we are now able to say that the symbols     stand respectively for N, V, and R.

"Even now I was in considerable difficulty, but a happy thought put me in possession of several other letters. It occurred to me that if these appeals came, as I expected, from someone who had been intimate with the lady in her early life, a combination which contained two E's with three letters between might very well stand for the name 'ELSIE.' On examination I found that such a combination formed the termination of the message which was three times repeated. It was certainly some appeal to 'Elsie.' In this way I had got my L, S, and I. But what appeal could it be? There were only four letters in the word which preceded 'Elsie,' and it ended in E. Surely the word must be 'COME.' I tried all other four letters ending in E, but could find none to fit the case. So now I was in possession of C, O, and M, and I was in a position to attack the first message once more, dividing it into words and putting dots for each symbol which was still unknown. So treated it worked out in this fashion:

.  M . ERE . . E SL . NE.

"Now, the first letter can only be A, which is a most useful discovery, since it occurs no fewer than three times in this short sentence, and the H is also apparent in the second word. Now it becomes:

AM HERE A . E SLANE.

Or, filling in the obvious vacancies in the name:

AM HERE ABE SLANEY.

I had so many letters now that I could proceed with considerable confidence to the second message, which worked out in this fashion:

A . ELRI . ES.

Here I could only make sense by putting T and G for the missing letters, and supposing that the name was that of some house or inn at which the writer was staying."

Inspector Martin and I had listened with the utmost interest to the full and clear account of how my friend had produced results which had led to so complete a command over our difficulties.

"What did you do then, sir?" asked the Inspector.

"I had every reason to suppose that this Abe Slaney was an American, since Abe is an American contraction, and since a letter from America had been the starting-point of all the trouble. I had also every cause to think that there was some criminal secret in the matter. The lady's allusions to her past and her refusal to take her husband into her confidence both pointed in that direction. I therefore cabled to my friend, Wilson Hargreave, of the New York Police Bureau, who has more than once made use of my knowledge of London crime. I asked him whether the name of Abe Slaney was known to him. Here is his reply: 'The most dangerous crook in Chicago.' On the very evening upon which I had his answer Hilton Cubitt sent me the last message from Slaney. Working with known letters it took this form:

ELSIE . RE . ARE TO MEET THY GO.

The addition of a P and a D completed a message which showed me that the rascal was proceeding from persuasion to threats, and my knowledge of the crooks of Chicago prepared me to find that he might very rapidly put his words into action. I at once came to Norfolk with my friend and colleague, Dr. Watson, but, unhappily, only in time to find that the worst had already occurred."

"It is a privilege to be associated with you in the handling of a case," said the Inspector warmly. "You will excuse me, however, if I speak frankly to you. You are only answerable to yourself, but I have to answer to my superiors. If this Abe Slaney, living at Elrige's, is indeed the murderer, and if he has made his escape while I am seated here, I should certainly get into serious trouble."

"You need not be uneasy. He will not try to escape."

"How do you know?"

"To fly would be a confession of guilt."

"Then let us go to arrest him."

"I expect him here every instant."

"But why should he come?"

"Because I have written and asked him."

"But this is incredible, Mr. Holmes! Why should he come because you have asked him? Would not such a request rather rouse his suspicions and cause him to fly?"

"I think I have known how to frame the letter," said Sherlock Holmes. "In fact, if I am not very much mistaken, here is the gentleman himself coming up the drive."

A man was striding up the path which led to the door. He was a tall, handsome, swarthy fellow, clad in a suit of grey flannel, with a Panama hat, a bristling black beard, and a great, aggressive, hooked nose, and flourishing a cane as he walked. He swaggered up the path as if the place belonged to him, and we heard his loud, confident peal at the bell.

"I think, gentlemen," said Holmes quietly, "that we had best take up our position behind the door. Every precaution is necessary when dealing with such a fellow. You will need your handcuffs, Inspector. You can leave the talking to me."

We waited in silence for a minute — one of those minutes which one can never forget. Then the door opened, and the man stepped in. In an instant Holmes clapped a pistol to his head, and Martin slipped the handcuffs over his wrists. It was all done so swiftly and deftly that the fellow was helpless before he knew that he was attacked. He glared from one to the other of us with a pair of blazing black eyes. Then he burst into a bitter laugh.

"Well, gentlemen, you have the drop on me this time. I seem to have knocked up against something hard. But I came here in answer to a letter from Mrs. Hilton Cubitt. Don't tell me that she is in this? Don't tell me that she helped to set a trap for me?"

"Mrs. Hilton Cubitt was seriously injured, and is at death's door."

The man gave a hoarse cry of grief which rang through the house.

"You're crazy!" he cried fiercely. "It was he that was hurt, not she. Who would have hurt little Elsie? I may have threatened her, God forgive me, but I would not have touched a hair of her pretty head. Take it back — you! Say that she is not hurt!"

"She was found badly wounded by the side of her dead husband."

He sank with a deep groan on to the settee, and buried his face in his manacled hands. For five minutes he was silent. Then he raised his face once more, and spoke with the cold composure of despair.

"I have nothing to hide from you, gentlemen," said he. "If I shot the man he had his shot at me, and there's no murder in that. But if you think I could have hurt that woman, then you don't know either me or her. I tell you there was never a man in this world loved a woman more than I loved her. I had a right to her. She was pledged to me years ago. Who was this Englishman that he should come between us? I tell you that I had the first right to her, and that I was only claiming my own."

"She broke away from your influence when she found the man that you are," said Holmes sternly. "She fled from America to avoid you, and she married an honourable gentleman in England. You dogged her and followed her, and made her life a misery to her in order to induce her to abandon the husband whom she loved and respected in order to fly with you, whom she feared and hated. You have ended by bringing about the death of a noble man and driving his wife to suicide. That is your record in this business, Mr. Abe Slaney, and you will answer for it to the law."

"If Elsie dies I care nothing what becomes of me," said the American. He opened one of his hands and looked at a note crumpled up in his palm. "See here, mister," he cried, with a gleam of suspicion in his eyes, "you're not trying to scare me over this, are you? If the lady is hurt as bad as you say, who was it that wrote this note?" He tossed it forward on to the table.

"I wrote it to bring you here."

"You wrote it? There was no one on earth outside the Joint who knew the secret of the dancing men. How came you to write it?"

"What one man can invent another can discover," said Holmes. "There is a cab coming to convey you to Norwich, Mr. Slaney. But, meanwhile, you have time to make some small reparation for the injury you have wrought. Are you aware that Mrs. Hilton Cubitt has herself lain under grave suspicion of the murder of her husband, and that it was only my presence here and the knowledge which I happened to possess which has saved her from the accusation? The least that you owe her is to make it clear to the whole world that she was in no way directly or indirectly responsible for his tragic end."

"I ask nothing better," said the American. "I guess the very best case I can make for myself is the absolute naked truth."

"It is my duty to warn you that it will be used against you," cried the Inspector, with the magnificent fair-play of the British criminal law.

Slaney shrugged his shoulders.

"I'll chance that," said he. "First of all, I want you gentlemen to understand that I have known this lady since she was a child. There were seven of us in a gang in Chicago, and Elsie's father was the boss of the Joint. He was a clever man, was old Patrick. It was he who invented that writing, which would pass as a child's scrawl unless you just happened to have the key to it. Well, Elsie learned some of our ways; but she couldn't stand the business, and she had a bit of honest money of her own, so she gave us all the slip and got away to London. She had been engaged to me, and she would have married me, I believe, if I had taken over another profession; but she would have nothing to do with anything on the cross. It was only after her marriage to this Englishman that I was able to find out where she was. I wrote to her, but got no answer. After that I came over, and, as letters were of no use, I put my messages where she could read them.

"Well, I have been here a month now. I lived in that farm, where I had a room down below, and could get in and out every night, and no one the wiser. I tried all I could to coax Elsie away. I knew that she read the messages, for once she wrote an answer under one of them. Then my temper got the better of me, and I began to threaten her. She sent me a letter then, imploring me to go away, and saying that it would break her heart if any scandal should come upon her husband. She said that she would come down when her husband was asleep at three in the morning, and speak with me through the end window, if I would go away afterwards and leave her in peace. She came down and brought money with her, trying to bribe me to go. This made me mad, and I caught her arm and tried to pull her through the window. At that moment in rushed the husband with his revolver in his hand. Elsie had sunk down upon the floor, and we were face to face. I was heeled also, and I held up my gun to scare him off and let me get away. He fired and missed me. I pulled off almost at the same instant, and down he dropped. I made away across the garden, and as I went I heard the window shut behind me. That's God's truth, gentlemen, every word of it, and I heard no more about it until that lad came riding up with a note which made me walk in here, like a jay, and give myself into your hands."

A cab had driven up whilst the American had been talking. Two uniformed policemen sat inside. Inspector Martin rose and touched his prisoner on the shoulder.

"It is time for us to go."

"Can I see her first?"

"No, she is not conscious. Mr. Sherlock Holmes, I only hope that if ever again I have an important case I shall have the good fortune to have you by my side."

We stood at the window and watched the cab drive away. As I turned back my eye caught the pellet of paper which the prisoner had tossed upon the table. It was the note with which Holmes had decoyed him.

"See if you can read it, Watson," said he, with a smile.

It contained no word, but this little line of dancing men:

"If you use the code which I have explained," said Holmes, "you will find that it simply means 'Come here at once.' I was convinced that it was an invitation which he would not refuse, since he could never imagine that it could come from anyone but the lady. And so, my dear Watson, we have ended by turning the dancing men to good when they have so often been the agents of evil, and I think that I have fulfilled my promise of giving you something unusual for your notebook. Three-forty is our train, and I fancy we should be back in Baker Street for dinner."

Only one word of epilogue.

The American, Abe Slaney, was condemned to death at the winter assizes at Norwich; but his penalty was changed to penal servitude in consideration of mitigating circumstances, and the certainty that Hilton Cubitt had fired the first shot.

Of Mrs. Hilton Cubitt I only know that I have heard she recovered entirely, and that she still remains a widow, devoting her whole life to the care of the poor and to the administration of her husband's estate.

## AFTERWORD

In "The Dancing Men," like the earlier "The Five Orange Pips," Holmes solves the mystery but fails to avert a tragedy. The plot relates interestingly to those of other Holmes stories in a variety of ways. A returned lover confronting a now apparently happily married woman appears in several Holmes stories, such as "The Noble Bachelor" (Priestman, *Detective Fiction and Literature: The Figure on the Carpet* 78); but Elsie Cubitt's apparent (though ambivalent) rejection of that earlier tie sets this story apart from those. Insofar as she feels Slaney's presence as a threat, she has more in common with all those characters who feel vulnerable to blackmail (cf. "The Boscombe Valley Mystery," "Charles Augustus Milverton," "The Second Stain"). The story is particularly close to one in which the threat proves not to exist after all; in "The Yellow Face" Holmes mistakenly infers that a woman is being pursued by a former husband.

As Fowler notes, simply by virtue of its embedded cryptographic puzzle the story inevitably recalls its great progenitor, Poe's "The Gold-Bug." Indeed, Holmes's reply to Slaney's expressed amazement that Holmes should have broken the cipher, "What one man can invent another can discover," echoes Poe's repeated insistence in his essays on cryptography (somewhat rephrased by Legrand in "The Gold-Bug") that "human ingenuity cannot concoct a cipher which human ingenuity cannot resolve." Holmes's opening trick of reading Watson's train of unspoken thoughts, on the other hand, comes directly from another Poe precedent, "The Murders in the Rue Morgue," even though Holmes (in Chapter 2 of *A Study in Scarlet*) belittles Dupin's demonstration there as "really very showy and superficial.

# Charles Augustus Milverton

It is years since the incidents of which I speak took place, and yet it is with diffidence that I allude to them. For a long time, even with the utmost discretion and reticence, it would have been impossible to make the facts public; but now the principal person concerned is beyond the reach of human law, and with due suppression the story may be told in such fashion as to injure no one. It records an absolutely unique experience in the career both of Mr. Sherlock Holmes and of myself. The reader will excuse me if I conceal the date or any other fact by which he might trace the actual occurrence.

We had been out for one of our evening rambles, Holmes and I, and had returned about six o'clock on a cold, frosty winter's evening. As Holmes turned up the lamp the light fell upon a card on the table. He glanced at it, and then, with an ejaculation of disgust, threw it on the floor. I picked it up and read:

CHARLES AUGUSTUS MILVERTON,
APPLEDORE TOWERS,
HAMPSTEAD.

*Agent.*

"Who is he?" I asked.

"The worst man in London," Holmes answered, as he sat down and stretched his legs before the fire. "Is anything on the back of the card?"

I turned it over.

"Will call at 6:30. — C. A. M.," I read.

"Hum! He's about due. Do you feel a creeping, shrinking sensation, Watson, when you stand before the serpents in the Zoo and see the slithery, gliding, venomous creatures, with their deadly eyes and wicked, flattened faces? Well, that's how Milverton impresses me. I've had to do with fifty murderers in my career, but the worst of them never gave me the repulsion which I have for this fellow. And yet I can't get out of doing business with him — indeed, he is here at my invitation."

"But who is he?"

"I'll tell you, Watson. He is the king of all the blackmailers. Heaven help the man, and still more the woman, whose secret and reputation come into the power of Milverton. With a smiling face and a heart of

From *The Return of Sherlock Holmes* (1905). First published in *Collier's,* 26 March 1904; the *Strand,* April 1904.

marble he will squeeze and squeeze until he has drained them dry. The fellow is a genius in his way, and would have made his mark in some more savoury trade. His method is as follows: He allows it to be known that he is prepared to pay very high sums for letters which compromise people of wealth or position. He receives these wares not only from treacherous valets or maids, but frequently from genteel ruffians who have gained the confidence and affection of trusting women. He deals with no niggard hand. I happen to know that he paid seven hundred pounds to a footman for a note two lines in length, and that the ruin of a noble family was the result. Everything which is in the market goes to Milverton, and there are hundreds in this great city who turn white at his name. No one knows where his grip may fall, for he is far too rich and far too cunning to work from hand to mouth. He will hold a card back for years in order to play it at the moment when the stake is best worth winning. I have said that he is the worst man in London, and I would ask you how could one compare the ruffian who in hot blood bludgeons his mate with this man, who methodically and at his leisure tortures the soul and wrings the nerves in order to add to his already swollen money-bags?"

I had seldom heard my friend speak with such intensity of feeling.

"But surely," said I, "the fellow must be within the grasp of the law?"

"Technically, no doubt, but practically not. What would it profit a woman, for example, to get him a few months' imprisonment if her own ruin must immediately follow? His victims dare not hit back. If ever he blackmailed an innocent person, then, indeed, we should have him; but he is as cunning as the Evil One. No, no; we must find other ways to fight him."

"And why is he here?"

"Because an illustrious client has placed her piteous case in my hands. It is the Lady Eva Brackwell, the most beautiful *débutante* of last season. She is to be married in a fortnight to the Earl of Dovercourt. This fiend has several imprudent letters — imprudent, Watson, nothing worse — which were written to an impecunious young squire in the country. They would suffice to break off the match. Milverton will send the letters to the earl unless a large sum of money is paid him. I have been commissioned to meet him, and — to make the best terms I can."

At that instant there was a clatter and a rattle in the street below. Looking down I saw a stately carriage and pair, the brilliant lamps gleaming on the glossy haunches of the noble chestnuts. A footman opened the door, and a small, stout man in a shaggy astrachan overcoat descended. A minute later he was in the room.

Charles Augustus Milverton was a man of fifty, with a large, intellectual head, a round, plump, hairless face, a perpetual frozen smile, and two keen grey eyes, which gleamed brightly from behind broad, golden-rimmed glasses. There was something of Mr. Pickwick's benevolence in his appearance,[1] marred only by the insincerity of the fixed smile and by the hard glitter of those restless and penetrating eyes. His voice was as smooth and suave as his countenance, as he advanced with a plump little hand extended, murmuring his regret for having missed us at his first visit.

Holmes disregarded the outstretched hand and looked at him with a face of granite. Milverton's smile broadened; he shrugged his shoulders, removed his overcoat, folded it with great deliberation over the back of a chair, and then took a seat.

"This gentleman," said he, with a wave in my direction. "Is it discreet? Is it right?"

"Dr. Watson is my friend and partner."

"Very good, Mr. Holmes. It is only in your client's interests that I protested. The matter is so very delicate —— "

"Dr. Watson has already heard of it."

"Then we can proceed to business. You say that you are acting for Lady Eva. Has she empowered you to accept my terms?"

"What are your terms?"

"Seven thousand pounds."

"And the alternative?"

"My dear sir, it is painful to me to discuss it; but if the money is not paid on the 14th there certainly will be no marriage on the 18th." His insufferable smile was more complacent than ever. Holmes thought for a little.

"You appear to me," he said at last, "to be taking matters too much for granted. I am, of course, familiar with the contents of these letters. My client will certainly do what I may advise. I shall counsel her to tell her future husband the whole story and to trust to his generosity."

Milverton chuckled.

"You evidently do not know the earl," said he.

From the baffled look upon Holmes's face I could clearly see that he did.

"What harm is there in the letters?" he asked.

"They are sprightly — very sprightly," Milverton answered. "The

---

[1] **Mr. Pickwick:** Samuel Pickwick, the comic, benevolent old protagonist of Charles Dickens's *Pickwick Papers* (1836–37).

lady was a charming correspondent. But I can assure you that the Earl of Dovercourt would fail to appreciate them. However, since you think otherwise, we will let it rest at that. It is purely a matter of business. If you think that it is in the best interests of your client that these letters should be placed in the hands of the earl, then you would indeed be foolish to pay so large a sum of money to regain them." He rose and seized his astrachan coat.

Holmes was grey with anger and mortification.

"Wait a little," he said. "You go too fast. We would certainly make every effort to avoid scandal in so delicate a matter."

Milverton relapsed into his chair.

"I was sure that you would see it in that light," he purred.

"At the same time," Holmes continued, "Lady Eva is not a wealthy woman. I assure you that two thousand pounds would be a drain upon her resources, and that the sum you name is utterly beyond her power. I beg, therefore, that you will moderate your demands, and that you will return the letters at the price I indicate, which is, I assure you, the highest that you can get."

Milverton's smile broadened and his eyes twinkled humorously.

"I am aware that what you say is true about the lady's resources," said he. "At the same time, you must admit that the occasion of a lady's marriage is a very suitable time for her friends and relatives to make some little effort upon her behalf. They may hesitate as to an acceptable wedding present. Let me assure them that this little bundle of letters would give more joy than all the candelabra and butter-dishes in London."

"It is impossible," said Holmes.

"Dear me, dear me, how unfortunate!" cried Milverton, taking out a bulky pocket-book. "I cannot help thinking that ladies are ill-advised in not making an effort. Look at this!" He held up a little note with a coat-of-arms upon the envelope. "That belongs to — well, perhaps it is hardly fair to tell the name until to-morrow morning. But at that time it will be in the hands of the lady's husband. And all because she will not find a beggarly sum which she could get in an hour by turning her diamonds into paste. It *is* such a pity. Now, you remember the sudden end of the engagement between the Honourable Miss Miles and Colonel Dorking? Only two days before the wedding there was a paragraph in the *Morning Post* to say that it was all off. And why? It is almost incredible, but the absurd sum of twelve hundred pounds would have settled the whole question. Is it not pitiful? And there I find you, a man of sense, boggling about terms when your client's future and honour are at stake. You surprise me, Mr. Holmes."

"What I say is true," Holmes answered. "The money cannot be found. Surely it is better for you to take the substantial sum which I offer than to ruin this woman's career, which can profit you in no way?"

"There you make a mistake, Mr. Holmes. An exposure would profit me indirectly to a considerable extent. I have eight or ten similar cases maturing. If it was circulated among them that I had made a severe example of the Lady Eva I should find all of them much more open to reason. You see my point?"

Holmes sprang from his chair.

"Get behind him, Watson. Don't let him out! Now, sir, let us see the contents of that notebook."

Milverton had glided as quick as a rat to the side of the room, and stood with his back against the wall.

"Mr. Holmes, Mr. Holmes!" he said, turning the front of his coat and exhibiting the butt of a large revolver, which projected from the inside pocket. "I have been expecting you to do something original. This has been done so often, and what good has ever come from it? I assure you that I am armed to the teeth, and I am perfectly prepared to use my weapon, knowing that the law will support me. Besides, your supposition that I would bring the letters here in a notebook is entirely mistaken. I would do nothing so foolish. And now, gentlemen, I have one or two little interviews this evening, and it is a long drive to Hampstead." He stepped forward, took up his coat, laid his hand on his revolver, and turned to the door. I picked up a chair, but Holmes shook his head, and I laid it down again. With a bow, a smile, and a twinkle Milverton was out of the room, and a few moments after we heard the slam of the carriage door and the rattle of the wheels as he drove away.

Holmes sat motionless by the fire, his hands buried deep in his trouser pockets, his chin sunk upon his breast, his eyes fixed upon the glowing embers. For half an hour he was silent and still. Then, with the gesture of a man who has taken his decision, he sprang to his feet and passed into his bedroom. A little later a rakish young workman with a goatee beard and a swagger lit his clay pipe at the lamp before descending into the street. "I'll be back some time, Watson," said he, and vanished into the night. I understood that he had opened his campaign against Charles Augustus Milverton; but I little dreamed the strange shape which that campaign was destined to take.

For some days Holmes came and went at all hours in this attire, but beyond a remark that his time was spent at Hampstead, and that it was not wasted, I knew nothing of what he was doing. At last, however, on a wild, tempestuous evening, when the wind screamed and rattled against the windows, he returned from his last expedition, and, having removed his disguise, he sat before the fire and laughed heartily in his silent, inward fashion.

"You would not call me a marrying man, Watson?"

"No, indeed!"

"You will be interested to hear that I am engaged."

"My dear fellow! I congrat —— "

"To Milverton's housemaid."

"Good heavens, Holmes!"

"I wanted information, Watson."

"Surely you have gone too far?"

"It was a most necessary step. I am a plumber with a rising business, Escott by name. I have walked out with her each evening, and I have talked with her. Good heavens, those talks! However, I have got all I wanted. I know Milverton's house as I know the palm of my hand."

"But the girl, Holmes?"

He shrugged his shoulders.

"You can't help it, my dear Watson. You must play your cards as best you can when such a stake is on the table. However, I rejoice to say that I have a hated rival who will certainly cut me out the instant that my back is turned. What a splendid night it is!"

"You like this weather?"

"It suits my purpose. Watson, I mean to burgle Milverton's house to-night."

I had a catching of the breath, and my skin went cold at the words, which were slowly uttered in a tone of concentrated resolution. As a flash of lightning in the night shows up in an instant every detail of a wide landscape, so at one glance I seemed to see every possible result of such an action — the detection, the capture, the honoured career ending in irreparable failure and disgrace, my friend himself lying at the mercy of the odious Milverton.

"For Heaven's sake, Holmes, think what you are doing!" I cried.

"My dear fellow, I have given it every consideration. I am never precipitate in my actions, nor would I adopt so energetic and indeed so dangerous a course if any other were possible. Let us look at the matter clearly and fairly. I suppose that you will admit that the action is morally justifiable, though technically criminal. To burgle his house is no more than to forcibly take his pocket-book — an action in which you were prepared to aid me."

I turned it over in my mind.

"Yes," I said, "it is morally justifiable so long as our object is to take no articles save those which are used for an illegal purpose."

"Exactly. Since it is morally justifiable, I have only to consider the question of personal risk. Surely a gentleman should not lay much stress upon this when a lady is in most desperate need of his help?"

"You will be in such a false position."

"Well, that is part of the risk. There is no other possible way of regaining these letters. The unfortunate lady has not the money, and there are none of her people in whom she could confide. To-morrow is the last day of grace, and unless we can get the letters to-night this villain will be as good as his word, and will bring about her ruin. I must, therefore, abandon my client to her fate, or I must play this last card. Between ourselves, Watson, it's a sporting duel between this fellow Milverton and me. He had, as you saw, the best of the first exchanges; but my self-respect and my reputation are concerned to fight it to a finish."

"Well, I don't like it; but I suppose it must be," said I. "When do we start?"

"You are not coming."

"Then you are not going," said I. "I give you my word of honour — and I never broke it in my life — that I will take a cab straight to the police-station and give you away unless you let me share this adventure with you."

"You can't help me."

"How do you know that? You can't tell what may happen. Anyway, my resolution is taken. Other people besides you have self-respect and even reputations."

Holmes had looked annoyed, but his brow cleared, and he clapped me on the shoulder.

"Well, well, my dear fellow, be it so. We have shared the same room for some years, and it would be amusing if we ended by sharing the same cell. You know, Watson, I don't mind confessing to you that I have always had an idea that I would have made a highly efficient criminal. This is the chance of my lifetime in that direction. See here!" He took a neat little leather case out of a drawer, and opening it he exhibited a number of shining instruments. "This is a first-class, up-to-date burgling kit, with nickel-plated jemmy, diamond-tipped glass cutter, adaptable keys, and every modern improvement which the march of civilization demands. Here, too, is my dark lantern. Everything is in order. Have you a pair of silent shoes?"

"I have rubber-soled tennis shoes."

"Excellent. And a mask?"

"I can make a couple out of black silk."

"I can see that you have a strong natural turn for this sort of thing. Very good; do you make the masks. We shall have some cold supper before we start. It is now nine-thirty. At eleven we shall drive as far as Church Row. It is a quarter of an hour's walk from there to Appledore Towers. We shall be at work before midnight. Milverton is a heavy sleeper, and retires punctually at ten-thirty. With any luck we should be back here by two, with the Lady Eva's letters in my pocket."

Holmes and I put on our dress-clothes, so that we might appear to be two theatre-goers homeward bound. In Oxford Street we picked up a hansom and drove to an address in Hampstead. Here we paid off our cab, and with our greatcoats buttoned up — for it was bitterly cold, and the wind seemed to blow through us — we walked along the edge of the Heath.

"It's a business that needs delicate treatment," said Holmes. "These documents are contained in a safe in the fellow's study, and the study is the ante-room of his bedchamber. On the other hand, like all these stout, little men who do themselves well, he is a plethoric sleeper. Agatha — that's my fiancée — says it is a joke in the servants' hall that it's impossible to wake the master. He has a secretary who is devoted to his interests, and never budges from the study all day. That's why we are going at night. Then he has a beast of a dog which roams the garden. I met Agatha late the last two evenings, and she locks the brute up so as to give me a clear run. This is the house, this big one in its own grounds. Through the gate — now to the right among the laurels. We might put on our masks here, I think. You see, there is not a glimmer of light in any of the windows, and everything is working splendidly."

With our black silk face-coverings, which turned us into two of the most truculent figures in London, we stole up to the silent, gloomy house. A sort of tiled veranda extended along one side of it, lined by several windows and two doors.

"That's his bedroom," Holmes whispered. "This door opens straight into the study. It would suit us best, but it is bolted as well as locked, and we should make too much noise getting in. Come round here. There's a greenhouse which opens into the drawing-room."

The place was locked, but Holmes removed a circle of glass and turned the key from the inside. An instant afterwards he had closed the door behind us, and we had become felons in the eyes of the law. The thick warm air of the conservatory and the rich, choking fragrance of exotic plants took us by the throat. He seized my hand in the darkness and led me swiftly past banks of shrubs which brushed against our faces. Holmes had remarkable powers, carefully cultivated, of seeing in the dark. Still holding my hand in one of his, he opened a door, and I was vaguely conscious that we had entered a large room in which a cigar had been smoked not long before. He felt his way among the furniture, opened another door, and closed it behind us. Putting out my hand I felt several coats hanging from the wall, and I understood that I was in a passage. We passed along it, and Holmes very gently opened a door upon the right-hand side. Something rushed out at us, and my heart sprang into my mouth, but I could have laughed when I realized that it was the cat. A fire was burning in this new room, and again the air was heavy with tobacco smoke. Holmes entered on tiptoe, waited for me to follow, and then very gently closed the door. We were in Milverton's study, and a *portière* at the farther side showed the entrance to his bedroom.

It was a good fire, and the room was illuminated by it. Near the door I saw the gleam of an electric switch, but it was unnecessary, even if it had been safe, to turn it on. At one side of the fireplace was a heavy curtain, which covered the bay window we had seen from outside. On the other side was the door which communicated with the veranda. A desk stood in the centre, with a turning chair of shining red leather. Opposite was a large bookcase, with a marble bust of Athene on the top. In the corner between the bookcase and the wall there stood a tall green safe, the firelight flashing back from the polished brass knobs upon its face. Holmes stole across and looked at it. Then he crept to the door of the bedroom, and stood with slanting head listening intently. No sound came from within. Meanwhile it had struck me that it would be wise to secure our retreat through the outer door, so I examined it. To my amazement it was neither locked nor bolted! I touched Holmes on the arm, and he turned his masked face in that direction. I saw him start, and he was evidently as surprised as I.

"I don't like it," he whispered, putting his lips to my very ear. "I can't quite make it out. Anyhow, we have no time to lose."

"Can I do anything?"

"Yes; stand by the door. If you hear anyone come, bolt it on the inside, and we can get away as we came. If they come the other way, we can get through the door if our job is done, or hide behind these window curtains if it is not. Do you understand?"

I nodded and stood by the door. My first feeling of fear had passed away, and I thrilled now with a keener zest than I had ever enjoyed when we were the defenders of the law instead of its defiers. The high object of our mission, the consciousness that it was unselfish and chivalrous, the villainous character of our opponent, all added to the sporting interest of the adventure. Far from feeling guilty, I rejoiced and exulted in our dangers. With a glow of admiration I watched Holmes unrolling his case of instruments and choosing his tool with the calm, scientific accuracy of a surgeon who performs a delicate operation. I knew that the opening of safes was a particular hobby with him, and I understood the joy which it gave him to be confronted with this green and gold monster, the dragon which held in its maw the reputations of many fair ladies. Turning up the cuffs of his dress-coat — he had placed his overcoat on a chair — Holmes laid out two drills, a jemmy, and several skeleton keys. I stood at the centre door with my eyes glancing at each of the others, ready for any emergency; though, indeed, my plans were somewhat vague as to what I should do if we were interrupted. For half an hour Holmes worked with concentrated energy, laying down one tool, picking up another, handling each with the strength and delicacy of the trained mechanic. Finally I heard a click, the broad green door swung open, and inside I had a glimpse of a number of paper packets, each tied, sealed, and inscribed. Holmes picked one out, but it was hard to read by the flickering fire, and he drew out his little dark lantern, for it was too dangerous, with Milverton in the next room, to switch on the electric light. Suddenly I saw him halt, listen intently, and then in an instant he had swung the door of the safe to, picked up his coat, stuffed his tools into the pockets, and darted behind the window curtain, motioning me to do the same.

It was only when I had joined him there that I heard what had alarmed his quicker senses. There was a noise somewhere within the house. A door slammed in the distance. Then a confused, dull murmur broke itself into the measured thud of heavy footsteps rapidly approaching. They were in the passage outside the room. They paused at the door. The door opened. There was a sharp snick as the electric light was turned on. The door closed once more, and the pungent reek of a strong cigar was borne to our nostrils. Then the footsteps continued backwards and forwards, backwards and forwards, within a few yards of us. Finally, there was a creak from a chair, and the footsteps ceased. Then a key clicked in a lock, and I heard the rustle of papers. So far I had not dared to look out, but now I gently parted the division of the curtains in front of me and peeped through. From the pressure of Holmes's shoulder against mine I knew that he was sharing my observations. Right in front of us, and almost within our reach, was the broad, rounded back of Milverton. It was evident that we had entirely miscalculated his movements, that he had never been to his bedroom, but that he had been sitting up in some smoking- or billiard-room in the farther wing of the house, the windows of which we had not seen. His broad, grizzled head, with its shining patch of baldness, was in the immediate foreground of our vision. He was leaning far back in the red leather chair, his legs outstretched, a long black cigar projecting at an angle from his mouth. He wore a semi-military smoking-jacket, claret-coloured, with a black velvet collar. In his hand he held a long legal document, which he was reading in an indolent fashion, blowing rings of tobacco smoke from his lips as he did so. There was no promise of a speedy departure in his composed bearing and his comfortable attitude.

I felt Holmes's hand steal into mine and give me a reassuring shake, as if to say that the situation was within his powers, and that he was easy in his mind. I was not sure whether he had seen what was only too obvious from my position — that the door of the safe was imperfectly closed, and that Milverton might at any moment observe it. In my own mind I had determined that if I were sure, from the rigidity of his gaze, that it had caught his eye, I would at once spring out, throw my great-coat over his head, pinion him, and leave the rest to Holmes. But Milverton never looked up. He was languidly interested by the papers in his hand, and page after page was turned as he followed the argument of the lawyer. At least, I thought, when he has finished the document and the cigar he will go to his room; but before he had reached the end of either there came a remarkable development which turned our thoughts into quite another channel.

Several times I had observed that Milverton looked at his watch, and once he had risen and sat down again, with a gesture of impatience. The idea, however, that he might have an appointment at so strange an hour never occurred to me until a faint sound reached my ears from the veranda outside. Milverton dropped his papers and sat rigid in his chair. The sound was repeated, and then there came a gentle tap at the door. Milverton rose and opened it.

"Well," said he curtly, "you are nearly half an hour late."

So this was the explanation of the unlocked door and of the nocturnal vigil of Milverton. There was the gentle rustle of a woman's dress. I had closed the slit between the curtains as Milverton's face turned in our direction, but now I ventured very carefully to open it once more. He had resumed his seat, the cigar still projecting at an insolent angle from the corner of his mouth. In front of him, in the full glare of the electric light, there stood a tall, slim, dark woman, a veil over her face, a mantle drawn round her chin. Her breath came quick and fast, and every inch of the lithe figure was quivering with strong emotion.

"Well," said Milverton, "you've made me lose a good night's rest, my dear. I hope you'll prove worth it. You couldn't come any other time — eh?"

The woman shook her head.

"Well, if you couldn't you couldn't. If the countess is a hard mistress you have your chance to get level with her now. Bless the girl, what are you shivering about? That's right! Pull yourself together! Now, let us get down to business." He took a note from the drawer of his desk. "You say that you have five letters which compromise the Countess d'Albert. You want to sell them. I want to buy them. So far so good. It only remains to fix a price. I should want to inspect the letters, of course. If they are really good specimens —— Great heavens, is it you?"

The woman without a word had raised her veil and dropped the mantle from her chin. It was a dark, handsome, clear-cut face which confronted Milverton, a face with a curved nose, strong, dark eyebrows shading hard, glittering eyes, and a straight, thin-lipped mouth set in a dangerous smile.

"It is I," she said — "the woman whose life you have ruined."

Milverton laughed, but fear vibrated in his voice. "You were so very obstinate," said he. "Why did you drive me to such extremities? I assure you I wouldn't hurt a fly of my own accord, but every man has his business, and what was I to do? I put the price well within your means. You would not pay."

"So you sent the letters to my husband, and he — the noblest gentleman that ever lived, a man whose boots I was never worthy to lace — he broke his gallant heart and died. You remember that last night when I came through that door I begged and prayed you for mercy, and you laughed in my face as you are trying to laugh now, only your coward heart cannot keep your lips from twitching? Yes, you never thought to see me here again, but it was that night which taught me how I could meet you face to face, and alone. Well, Charles Milverton, what have you to say?"

"Don't imagine that you can bully me," said he, rising to his feet. "I have only to raise my voice, and I could call my servants and have you arrested. But I will make allowance for your natural anger. Leave the room at once as you came, and I will say no more."

The woman stood with her hand buried in her bosom, and the same deadly smile on her thin lips.

"You will ruin no more lives as you ruined mine. You will wring no more hearts as you wrung mine. I will free the world of a poisonous thing. Take that, you hound, and that! — and that! — and that! — and that!"

She had drawn a little gleaming revolver, and emptied barrel after barrel into Milverton's body, the muzzle within two feet of his shirt-front. He shrank away, and then fell forward upon the table, coughing furiously and clawing among the papers. Then he staggered to his feet, received another shot, and rolled upon the floor. "You've done me," he cried, and lay still. The woman looked at him intently and ground her heel into his upturned face. She looked again, but there was no sound or movement. I heard a sharp rustle, the night air blew into the heated room, and the avenger was gone.

No interference upon our part could have saved the man from his fate; but as the woman poured bullet after bullet into Milverton's shrinking body, I was about to spring out, when I felt Holmes's cold, strong grasp upon my wrist. I understood the whole argument of that firm, restraining grip — that it was no affair of ours; that justice had overtaken a villain; that we had our own duties and our own objects which were not to be lost sight of. But hardly had the woman rushed from the room when Holmes, with swift, silent steps, was over at the other door. He turned the key in the lock. At the same instant we heard voices in the house and the sound of hurrying feet. The revolver shots had roused the household. With perfect coolness Holmes slipped across to the safe, filled his two arms with bundles of letters, and poured them all into the fire. Again and again he did it, until the safe was empty. Someone turned the handle and beat upon the outside of the door. Holmes looked swiftly round. The letter which had been the messenger of death for Milverton lay, all mottled with his blood, upon the table. Holmes tossed it in among the blazing papers. Then he drew the key from the outer door, passed through after me, and locked it on the outside. "This way, Watson," said he; "we can scale the garden wall in this direction."

I could not have believed that an alarm could have spread so swiftly. Looking back, the huge house was one blaze of light. The front door was open, and figures were rushing down the drive. The whole garden was alive with people, and one fellow raised a view-halloa as we emerged from the veranda and followed hard at our heels. Holmes seemed to know the ground perfectly, and he threaded his way swiftly among a plantation of small trees, I close at his heels, and our foremost pursuer panting behind us. It was a six-foot wall which barred our path, but he sprang to the top and over. As I did the same I felt the hand of the man behind me grab at my ankle; but I kicked myself free, and scrambled over a glass-strewn coping. I fell upon my face among some bushes; but Holmes had me on my feet in an instant, and together we dashed away across the huge expanse of Hampstead Heath. We had run two miles, I suppose, before Holmes at last halted and listened intently. All was absolute silence behind us. We had shaken off our pursuers, and were safe.

We had breakfasted and were smoking our morning pipe, on the day after the remarkable experience which I have recorded, when Mr. Lestrade, of Scotland Yard, very solemn and impressive, was ushered into our modest sitting-room.

"Good morning, Mr. Holmes," said he — "good morning. May I ask if you are very busy just now?"

"Not too busy to listen to you."

"I thought that, perhaps, if you had nothing particular on hand, you might care to assist us in a most remarkable case which occurred only last night at Hampstead."

"Dear me!" said Holmes. "What was that?"

"A murder — a most dramatic and remarkable murder. I know how keen you are upon these things, and I would take it as a great favour if you would step down to Appledore Towers and give us the benefit of your advice. It is no ordinary crime. We have had our eyes upon this Mr. Milverton for some time, and, between ourselves, he was a bit of a villain. He is known to have held papers which he used for blackmailing purposes. These papers have all been burned by the murderers. No article of value was taken, as it is probable that the criminals were men of good position, whose sole object was to prevent social exposure."

"Criminals!" exclaimed Holmes. "Plural!"

"Yes, there were two of them. They were, as nearly as possible, captured red-handed. We have their footmarks, we have their description; it's ten to one that we trace them. The first fellow was a bit too active, but the second was caught by the under-gardener, and only got away after a struggle. He was a middle-sized, strongly built man — square jaw, thick neck, moustache, a mask over his eyes."

"That's rather vague," said Sherlock Holmes. "Why, it might be a description of Watson!"

"It's true," said the Inspector, with much amusement. "It might be a description of Watson."

"Well, I am afraid I can't help you, Lestrade," said Holmes. "The fact is that I knew this fellow Milverton, that I considered him one of the most dangerous men in London, and that I think there are certain crimes which the law cannot touch, and which therefore, to some extent, justify private revenge. No, it's no use arguing. I have made up my mind. My sympathies are with the criminals rather than with the victim, and I will not handle this case."

Holmes had not said one word to me about the tragedy which we had witnessed, but I observed all the morning that he was in the most thoughtful mood, and he gave me the impression, from his vacant eyes and his abstracted manner, of a man who is striving to recall something to his memory. We were in the middle of our lunch, when he suddenly sprang to his feet. "By Jove, Watson! I've got it!" he cried. "Take your hat! Come with me!" He hurried at his top speed down Baker Street and along Oxford Street, until we had almost reached Regent Circus. Here on the left hand there stands a shop window filled with photographs of the celebrities and beauties of the day. Holmes's eyes fixed themselves upon one of them, and following his gaze I saw the picture of a regal and stately lady in Court dress, with a high diamond tiara upon her noble head. I looked at that delicately curved nose, at the marked eyebrows, at the straight mouth, and the strong little chin beneath it. Then I caught my breath as I read the time-honoured title of the great nobleman and statesman whose wife she had been. My eyes met those of Holmes, and he put his finger to his lips as we turned away from the window.

## AFTERWORD

In this story Doyle finally pushes the detective story to one of its potential, fundamental extremes. Following Dupin's example in Poe's "The Purloined Letter," the detective puts himself in his opponent's place not only imaginatively but actually, and plays the role of a criminal. Moreover, in duplicitously courting Milverton's housemaid in order to gain information about Milverton's house and habits, Holmes repeats and provokes just those roles of unfaithfulness — the ruffian who gains the confidence and affection of a trusting woman, the maid who betrays her master's or mistress's secrets — that Milverton's trade fosters.

With respect to this reversal of the detective's role, the story stands as an interesting comparison to "The Final Problem," where the hunter becomes the hunted. Milverton is in several respects evocative of Moriarty: both are explicitly geniuses of crime, effectively beyond the reach of the law, engaged with Holmes in a duel to the finish. "Milverton" even transposes the scripturally allusive undertone of "The Final Problem" (see Hodgson, p. 345): when Holmes explains the blackmailer's effective invulnerability by asking, "What would it profit a woman . . . to get him a few months' imprisonment if her own ruin must immediately follow?" we hear an echo of Mark 8:36 ("For what shall it profit a man, if he shall gain the whole world, and lose his own soul?").

Although Holmes had never before played a sustained criminal role (he later, in a case of dire national emergency, commits housebreaking and burglary in "The Bruce-Partington Plans"), Doyle sets the stage for this development much earlier. In Chapter 6 of *The Sign of Four,* as Watson watches his friend carefully examine the scene of a crime, he muses, "So swift, silent, and furtive were his movements, like those of a trained bloodhound picking out a scent, that I could not but think what a terrible criminal he would have made had he turned his energy and sagacity against the law instead of exerting them in its defence." Compare also Holmes's extralegal scheme with Watson to trick Irene Adler in "A Scandal in Bohemia."

## The Second Stain

I had intended the "Adventure of the Abbey Grange" to be the last of those exploits of my friend, Mr. Sherlock Holmes, which I should ever communicate to the public. This resolution of mine was not due to any lack of material, since I have notes of many hundreds of cases to which I have never alluded, nor was it caused by any waning interest on the part of my readers in the singular personality and unique methods of this remarkable man. The real reason lay in the reluctance which Mr. Holmes has shown to the continued publication of his experiences. So long as he was in actual professional practice the records of his successes were of some practical value to him; but since he has definitely retired from London and betaken himself to study and bee-farming on the Sussex Downs, notoriety has become hateful to him, and he has peremptorily requested that his wishes in this matter should be strictly observed. It was only upon my representing to him that I had given a promise that

From *The Return of Sherlock Holmes* (1905). First published in the *Strand,* December 1904.

"The Adventure of the Second Stain" should be published when the time was ripe, and pointed out to him that it was only appropriate that this long series of episodes should culminate in the most important international case which he has ever been called upon to handle, that I at last succeeded in obtaining his consent that a carefully guarded account of the incident should at last be laid before the public. If in telling the story I seem to be somewhat vague in certain details the public will readily understand that there is an excellent reason for my reticence.

It was, then, in a year, and even in a decade, that shall be nameless, that upon one Tuesday morning in autumn we found two visitors of European fame within the walls of our humble room in Baker Street. The one, austere, high-nosed, eagle-eyed, and dominant, was none other than the illustrious Lord Bellinger, twice Premier of Britain. The other, dark, clear-cut, and elegant, hardly yet of middle age, and endowed with every beauty of body and of mind, was the Right Honourable Trelawney Hope, Secretary for European Affairs, and the most rising statesman in the country. They sat side by side upon our paper-littered settee, and it was easy to see from their worn and anxious faces that it was business of the most pressing importance which had brought them. The Premier's thin, blue-veined hands were clasped tightly over the ivory head of his umbrella, and his gaunt, ascetic face looked gloomily from Holmes to me. The European Secretary pulled nervously at his moustache and fidgeted with the seals of his watch-chain.

"When I discovered my loss, Mr. Holmes, which was at eight o'clock this morning, I at once informed the Prime Minister. It was at his suggestion that we have both come to you."

"Have you informed the police?"

"No, sir," said the Prime Minister, with the quick, decisive manner for which he was famous. "We have not done so, nor is it possible that we should do so. To inform the police must, in the long run, mean to inform the public. This is what we particularly desire to avoid."

"And why, sir?"

"Because the document in question is of such immense importance that its publication might very easily — I might almost say probably — lead to European complications of the utmost moment. It is not too much to say that peace or war may hang upon the issue. Unless its recovery can be attended with the utmost secrecy, then it may as well not be recovered at all, for all that is aimed at by those who have taken it is that its contents should be generally known."

"I understand. Now, Mr. Trelawney Hope, I should be much obliged if you would tell me exactly the circumstances under which this document disappeared."

"That can be done in a very few words, Mr. Holmes. The letter — for it was a letter from a foreign potentate — was received six days ago. It was of such importance that I have never left it in my safe, but I have taken it across each evening to my house in Whitehall Terrace, and kept it in my bedroom in a locked dispatch-box. It was there last night. Of that I am certain. I actually opened the box while I was dressing for dinner, and saw the document inside. This morning it was gone. The dispatch-box had stood beside the glass upon my dressing-table all night. I am a light sleeper, and so is my wife. We are both prepared to swear that no one could have entered the room during the night. And yet I repeat that the paper is gone."

"What time did you dine?"

"Half-past seven."

"How long was it before you went to bed?"

"My wife had gone to the theatre. I waited up for her. It was half-past eleven before we went to our room."

"Then for four hours the dispatch-box had lain unguarded?"

"No one is ever permitted to enter that room save the housemaid in the morning, and my valet, or my wife's maid, during the rest of the day. They are both trusty servants who have been with us for some time. Besides, neither of them could possibly have known that there was anything more valuable than the ordinary departmental papers in my dispatch-box."

"Who did know of the existence of that letter?"

"No one in the house."

"Surely your wife knew?"

"No, sir; I had said nothing to my wife until I missed the paper this morning."

The Premier nodded approvingly.

"I have long known, sir, how high is your sense of public duty," said he. "I am convinced that in the case of a secret of this importance it would rise superior to the most intimate domestic ties."

The European Secretary bowed.

"You do me no more than justice, sir. Until this morning I have never breathed one word to my wife upon this matter."

"Could she have guessed?"

"No, Mr. Holmes, she could not have guessed — nor could anyone have guessed."

"Have you lost any documents before?"

"No, sir."

"Who is there in England who did know of the existence of this letter?"

"Each member of the Cabinet was informed of it yesterday; but the pledge of secrecy which attends every Cabinet meeting was increased by the solemn warning which was given by the Prime Minister. Good heavens, to think that within a few hours I should myself have lost it!" His handsome face was distorted with a spasm of despair, and his hands tore at his hair. For a moment we caught a glimpse of the natural man — impulsive, ardent, keenly sensitive. The next the aristocratic mask was replaced, and the gentle voice had returned. "Besides the members of the Cabinet there are two, or possibly three, departmental officials who know of the letter. No one else in England, Mr. Holmes, I assure you."

"But abroad?"

"I believe that no one abroad has seen it save the man who wrote it. I am well convinced that his ministers — that the usual official channels have not been employed."

Holmes considered for some little time.

"Now, sir, I must ask you more particularly what this document is, and why its disappearance should have such momentous consequences?"

The two statesmen exchanged a quick glance, and the Premier's shaggy eyebrows gathered in a frown.

"Mr. Holmes, the envelope is a long, thin one of pale blue colour. There is a seal of red wax stamped with a crouching lion. It is addressed in large, bold handwriting to —— "

"I fear," said Holmes, "that, interesting and indeed essential as these details are, my inquiries must go more to the root of things. What *was* the letter?"

"That is a State secret of the utmost importance, and I fear that I cannot tell you, nor do I see that it is necessary. If by the aid of the powers which you are said to possess you can find such an envelope as I describe with its enclosure, you will have deserved well of your country, and earned any reward which it lies in our power to bestow."

Sherlock Holmes rose with a smile.

"You are two of the most busy men in the country," said he, "and in my own small way I have also a good many calls upon me. I regret exceedingly that I cannot help you in this matter, and any continuation of this interview would be a waste of time."

The Premier sprang to his feet with that quick, fierce gleam of his deep-set eyes before which a Cabinet had cowered. "I am not accustomed—— " he began, but mastered his anger and resumed his seat. For a minute or more we all sat in silence. Then the old statesman shrugged his shoulders.

"We must accept your terms, Mr. Holmes. No doubt you are right, and it is unreasonable for us to expect you to act unless we give you our entire confidence."

"I agree with you, sir," said the younger statesman.

"Then I will tell you, relying entirely upon your honour and that of your colleague, Dr. Watson. I may appeal to your patriotism also, for I could not imagine a greater misfortune for the country than that this affair should come out."

"You may safely trust us."

"The letter, then, is from a certain foreign potentate who has been ruffled by some recent colonial developments of this country. It has been written hurriedly and upon his own responsibility entirely. Inquiries have shown that his ministers know nothing of the matter. At the same time it is couched in so unfortunate a manner, and certain phrases in it are of so provocative a character, that its publication would undoubtedly lead to a most dangerous state of feeling in this country. There would be such a ferment, sir, that I do not hesitate to say that within a week of the publication of that letter this country would be involved in a great war."

Holmes wrote a name upon a slip of paper and handed it to the Premier.

"Exactly. It was he. And it is this letter — this letter which may well mean the expenditure of a thousand millions and the lives of a hundred thousand men — which has become lost in this unaccountable fashion."

"Have you informed the sender?"

"Yes, sir, a cipher telegram has been despatched."

"Perhaps he desires the publication of the letter."

"No, sir, we have strong reason to believe that he already understands that he has acted in an indiscreet and hot-headed manner. It would be a greater blow to him and to his country than to us if this letter were to come out."

"If this is so, whose interest is it that the letter should come out? Why should anyone desire to steal it or to publish it?"

"There, Mr. Holmes, you take me into regions of high international politics. But if you consider the European situation you will have no difficulty in perceiving the motive. The whole of Europe is an armed camp. There is a double league which makes a fair balance of military power. Great Britain holds the scales. If Britain were driven into war with one confederacy, it would assure the supremacy of the other confederacy, whether they joined in the war or not. Do you follow?"

"Very clearly. It is then the interest of the enemies of this potentate to secure and publish this letter, so as to make a breach between his country and ours?"

"Yes, sir."

"And to whom would this document be sent if it fell into the hands of an enemy?"

"To any of the great Chancelleries of Europe. It is probably speeding on its way thither at the present instant as fast as steam can take it."

Mr. Trelawney Hope dropped his head on his chest and groaned aloud. The Premier placed his hand kindly upon his shoulder.

"It is your misfortune, my dear fellow. No one can blame you. There is no precaution which you have neglected. Now, Mr. Holmes, you are in full possession of the facts. What course do you recommend?"

Holmes shook his head mournfully.

"You think, sir, that unless this document is recovered there will be war?"

"I think it is very probable."

"Then, sir, prepare for war."

"That is a hard saying, Mr. Holmes."

"Consider the facts, sir. It is inconceivable that it was taken after eleven-thirty at night, since I understand that Mr. Hope and his wife were both in the room from that hour until the loss was found out. It was taken, then, yesterday evening between seven-thirty and eleven-thirty, probably near the earlier hour, since whoever took it evidently knew that it was there, and would naturally secure it as early as possible. Now, sir, if a document of this importance were taken at that hour, where can it be now? No one has any reason to retain it. It has been passed rapidly on to those who need it. What chance have we now to overtake or even to trace it? It is beyond our reach."

The Prime Minister rose from the settee.

"What you say is perfectly logical, Mr. Holmes. I feel that the matter is indeed out of our hands."

"Let us presume, for argument's sake, that the document was taken by the maid or by the valet—— "

"They are both old and tried servants."

"I understand you to say that your room is on the second floor, that there is no entrance from without, and that from within no one could go up unobserved. It must, then, be somebody in the house who has taken it. To whom would the thief take it? To one of several international spies and secret agents, whose names are tolerably familiar to me. There are three who may be said to be the heads of their profession. I will begin my research by going round and finding if each of them is at his post. If one is missing — especially if he has disappeared since last night — we will have some indication as to where the document has gone."

"Why should he be missing?" asked the European Secretary. "He would take the letter to an Embassy in London, as likely as not."

"I fancy not. These agents work independently, and their relations with the Embassies are often strained."

The Prime Minister nodded his acquiescence.

"I believe you are right, Mr. Holmes. He would take so valuable a prize to headquarters with his own hands. I think that your course of action is an excellent one. Meanwhile, Hope, we cannot neglect our other duties on account of this one misfortune. Should there be any fresh developments during the day we shall communicate with you, and you will no doubt let us know the results of your own inquiries."

The two statesmen bowed and walked gravely from the room.

When our illustrious visitors had departed, Holmes lit his pipe in silence, and sat for some time lost in the deepest thought. I had opened the morning paper and was immersed in a sensational crime which had occurred in London the night before, when my friend gave an exclamation, sprang to his feet, and laid his pipe down upon the mantelpiece.

"Yes," said he, "there is no better way of approaching it. The situation is desperate, but not hopeless. Even now, if we could be sure which of them has taken it, it is just possible that it has not yet passed out of his hands. After all, it is a question of money with these fellows, and I have the British Treasury behind me. If it's on the market I'll buy it — if it means another penny on the income tax. It is conceivable that the fellow might hold it back to see what bids come from this side before he tries his luck on the other. There are only those three capable of playing so bold a game; there are Oberstein, La Rothiere, and Eduardo Lucas. I will see each of them."

I glanced at my morning paper.

"Is that Eduardo Lucas of Godolphin Street?"

"Yes."

"You will not see him."

"Why not?"

"He was murdered in his house last night."

My friend has so often astonished me in the course of our adventures that it was with a sense of exultation that I realized how completely I had astonished him. He stared in amazement, and then snatched the paper from my hands. This was the paragraph which I had been engaged in reading when he rose from his chair:

### MURDER IN WESTMINSTER

A crime of a mysterious character was committed last night at 16 Godolphin Street, one of the old-fashioned and secluded rows of eighteenth-century houses which lie between the river and the Abbey, almost in the shadow of the great tower of the Houses of Parliament. This small but select mansion has been inhabited for some years by Mr. Eduardo Lucas, well known in society circles both on account of his charming personality and because he has the well-deserved reputation of being one of the best amateur tenors in the country. Mr. Lucas is an unmarried man, thirty-four years of age, and his establishment consists of Mrs. Pringle, an elderly housekeeper, and of Mitton, his valet. The former retires early and sleeps at the top of the house. The valet was out for the evening, visiting a friend at Hammersmith. From ten o'clock onwards Mr. Lucas had the house to himself. What occurred during that time has not yet transpired, but at a quarter to twelve Police-constable Barrett, passing along Godolphin Street, observed that the door of No. 16 was ajar. He knocked, but received no answer. Perceiving a light in the front room he advanced into the passage and again knocked, but without reply. He then pushed open the door and entered. The room was in a state of wild disorder, the furniture being all swept to one side, and one chair lying on its back in the centre. Beside this chair, and still grasping one of its legs, lay the unfortunate tenant of the house. He had been stabbed to the heart, and must have died instantly. The knife with which the crime had been committed was a curved Indian dagger, plucked down from a trophy of Oriental arms which adorned one of the walls. Robbery does not appear to have been the motive of the crime, for there had been no attempt to remove the valuable contents of the room. Mr. Eduardo Lucas was so well known and popular that his violent and mysterious fate will arouse painful interest and intense sympathy in a widespread circle of friends.

"Well, Watson, what do you make of this?" asked Holmes, after a long pause.

"It is an amazing coincidence."

"A coincidence! Here is one of three men who we had named as possible actors in this drama, and he meets a violent death during the very hours when we know that that drama was being enacted. The odds are enormous against its being coincidence. No figures could express them. No, my dear Watson, the two events are connected — *must* be connected. It is for us to find the connection."

"But now the official police must know all."

"Not at all. They know all they see at Godolphin Street. They know — and shall know — nothing of Whitehall Terrace. Only *we* know of both events, and can trace the relation between them. There is one obvious point which would, in any case, have turned my suspicions against Lucas. Godolphin Street, Westminster, is only a few minutes' walk from Whitehall Terrace. The other secret agents whom I have named live in the extreme West End. It was easier, therefore, for Lucas than for the others to establish a connection or receive a message from the European Secretary's household — a small thing, and yet where events are compressed into a few hours it may prove essential. Halloa! what have we here?"

Mrs. Hudson had appeared with a lady's card upon her salver. Holmes glanced at it, raised his eyebrows, and handed it over to me.

"Ask Lady Hilda Trelawney Hope if she will be kind enough to step up," said he.

A moment later our modest apartment, already so distinguished that morning, was further honoured by the entrance of the most lovely woman in London. I had often heard of the beauty of the youngest daughter of the Duke of Belminster, but no description of it, and no contemplation of colourless photographs, had prepared me for the subtle, delicate charm and the beautiful colouring of that exquisite head. And yet as we saw it that autumn morning it was not its beauty which would be the first thing to impress the observer. The cheek was lovely, but it was paled with emotion; the eyes were bright, but it was the brightness of fever; the sensitive mouth was tight and drawn in an effort after self-command. Terror — not beauty — was what sprang first to the eye as our fair visitor stood framed for an instant in the open door.

"Has my husband been here, Mr. Holmes?"

"Yes, madam, he has been here."

"Mr. Holmes, I implore you not to tell him that I came here." Holmes bowed coldly and motioned the lady to a chair.

"Your ladyship places me in a very delicate position. I beg that you will sit down and tell me what you desire; but I fear that I cannot make any unconditional promise."

She swept across the room and seated herself with her back to the window. It was a queenly presence — tall, graceful, and intensely womanly.

"Mr. Holmes," she said — and her white-gloved hands clasped and unclasped as she spoke — "I will speak frankly to you in the hope that it may induce you to speak frankly in return. There is complete confidence between my husband and me on all matters save one. That one is politics. On this his lips are sealed. He tells me nothing. Now, I am aware that there was a most deplorable occurrence in our house last night. I know that a paper has disappeared. But because the matter is political my husband refuses to take me into his complete confidence. Now it is essential — essential, I say — that I should thoroughly understand it. You are the only other person, save these politicians, who knows the true facts. I beg you, then, Mr. Holmes, to tell me exactly what has happened and what it will lead to. Tell me all, Mr. Holmes. Let no regard for your client's interests keep you silent, for I assure you that his interests, if he would only see it, would be best served by taking me into his complete confidence. What was this paper that was stolen?"

"Madam, what you ask me is really impossible."

She groaned and sank her face in her hands.

"You must see that this is so, madam. If your husband thinks fit to keep you in the dark over this matter, is it for me, who have only learned the true facts under the pledge of professional secrecy, to tell what he has withheld? It is not fair to ask it. It is him whom you must ask."

"I have asked him. I come to you as a last resource. But without your telling me anything definite, Mr. Holmes, you may do a great service if you would enlighten me on one point."

"What is it, madam?"

"Is my husband's political career likely to suffer through this incident?"

"Well, madam, unless it is set right it may certainly have a very unfortunate effect."

"Ah!" She drew in her breath sharply as one whose doubts are resolved.

"One more question, Mr. Holmes. From an expression which my husband dropped in the first shock of this disaster I understood that terrible public consequences might arise from the loss of this document."

"If he said so, I certainly cannot deny it."

"Of what nature are they?"

"Nay, madam, there again you ask me more than I can possibly answer."

"Then I will take up no more of your time. I cannot blame you, Mr. Holmes, for having refused to speak more freely, and you on your side will not, I am sure, think the worse of me because I desire, even against his will, to share my husband's anxieties. Once more I beg that you will say nothing of my visit." She looked back at us from the door, and I had a last impression of that beautiful, haunted face, the startled eyes, and the drawn mouth. Then she was gone.

"Now, Watson, the fair sex is your department," said Holmes, with a smile, when the dwindling *frou-frou* of skirts had ended in the slam of the door. "What was the fair lady's game? What did she really want?"

"Surely her own statement is clear and her anxiety very natural."

"Hum! Think of her appearance, Watson, her manner, her suppressed excitement, her restlessness, her tenacity in asking questions. Remember that she comes of a caste who do not lightly show emotion."

"She was certainly much moved."

"Remember also the curious earnestness with which she assured us that it was best for her husband that she should know all. What did she mean by that? And you must have observed, Watson, how she manœuvred to have the light at her back. She did not wish us to read her expression."

"Yes; she chose the one chair in the room."

"And yet the motives of women are so inscrutable. You remember the woman at Margate whom I suspected for the same reason. No powder on her nose — that proved to be the correct solution. How can you build on such a quicksand? Their most trivial action may mean volumes, or their most extraordinary conduct may depend upon a hairpin or a curling-tongs. Good morning, Watson."

"You are off?"

"Yes; I will while away the morning at Godolphin Street with our friends of the regular establishment. With Eduardo Lucas lies the solution of our problem, though I must admit that I have not an inkling as to what form it may take. It is a capital mistake to theorize in advance of the facts. Do you stay on guard, my good Watson, and receive any fresh visitors. I'll join you at lunch if I am able."

All that day and the next and the next Holmes was in a mood which his friends would call taciturn, and others morose. He ran out and ran in, smoked incessantly, played snatches on his violin, sank into reveries, devoured sandwiches at irregular hours, and hardly answered the casual

questions which I put to him. It was evident to me that things were
not going well with him or his quest. He would say nothing of the
case, and it was from the papers that I learned the particulars of the
inquest, and the arrest with the subsequent release of John Mitton,
the valet of the deceased. The coroner's jury brought in the obvious
"Wilful murder," but the parties remained as unknown as ever. No
motive was suggested. The room was full of articles of value, but
none had been taken. The dead man's papers had not been tampered
with. They were carefully examined, and showed that he was a keen
student of international politics, an indefatigable gossip, a remarkable linguist, and an untiring letter-writer. He had been on intimate
terms with the leading politicians of several countries. But nothing
sensational was discovered among the documents which filled his
drawers. As to his relations with women, they appeared to have been
promiscuous but superficial. He had many acquaintances among
them, but few friends, and no one whom he loved. His habits were
regular, his conduct inoffensive. His death was an absolute mystery,
and likely to remain so.

As to the arrest of John Mitton, the valet, it was a counsel of despair
as an alternative to absolute inaction. But no case could be sustained
against him. He had visited friends in Hammersmith that night. The
*alibi* was complete. It is true that he started home at an hour which
should have brought him to Westminster before the time when the
crime was discovered, but his own explanation that he had walked part
of the way seemed probable enough in view of the fineness of the night.
He had actually arrived at twelve o'clock, and appeared to be over-
whelmed by the unexpected tragedy. He had always been on good
terms with his master. Several of the dead man's possessions — notably
a small case of razors — had been found in the valet's boxes, but he
explained that they had been presents from the deceased, and the
housekeeper was able to corroborate the story. Mitton had been in
Lucas's employment for three years. It was noticeable that Lucas did
not take Mitton on the Continent with him. Sometimes he visited Paris
for three months on end, but Mitton was left in charge of the
Godolphin Street house. As to the housekeeper, she had heard nothing
on the night of the crime. If her master had a visitor, he had himself
admitted him.

So for three mornings the mystery remained, so far as I could follow
it in the papers. If Holmes knew more he kept his own counsel, but, as
he told me that Inspector Lestrade had taken him into his confidence in
the case, I knew that he was in close touch with every development.

Upon the fourth day there appeared a long telegram from Paris which seemed to solve the whole question.

> A discovery has just been made by the Parisian police [said the *Daily Telegraph*] which raises the veil which hung round the tragic fate of Mr. Eduardo Lucas, who met his death by violence last Monday night at Godolphin Street, Westminster. Our readers will remember that the deceased gentleman was found stabbed in his room, and that some suspicion attached to his valet, but that the case broke down on an *alibi*. Yesterday a lady, who has been known as Mme. Henri Fournaye, occupying a small villa in the Rue Austerlitz, was reported to the authorities by her servants as being insane. An examination showed that she had indeed developed mania of a dangerous and permanent form. On inquiry the police have discovered that Mme. Henri Fournaye only returned from a journey to London on Tuesday last, and there is evidence to connect her with the crime at Westminster. A comparison of photographs has proved conclusively that M. Henri Fournaye and Eduardo Lucas were really one and the same person, and that the deceased had for some reason lived a double life in London and Paris. Mme. Fournaye, who is of creole origin, is of an extremely excitable nature, and has suffered in the past from attacks of jealousy which have amounted to frenzy. It is conjectured that it was in one of these that she committed the terrible crime which has caused such a sensation in London. Her movements upon the Monday night have not yet been traced, but it is undoubted that a woman answering to her description attracted much attention at Charing Cross Station on Tuesday morning by the wildness of her appearance and the violence of her gestures. It is probable, therefore, that the crime was either committed when insane, or that its immediate effect was to drive the unhappy woman out of her mind. At present she is unable to give any coherent account of the past, and the doctors hold out no hopes of the re-establishment of her reason. There is evidence that a woman, who might have been Mme. Fournaye, was seen for some hours on Monday night watching the house in Godolphin Street.

"What do you think of that, Holmes?" I had read the account aloud to him, while he finished his breakfast.

"My dear Watson," said he, as he rose from the table and paced up and down the room, "you are most long-suffering, but if I have told you nothing in the last three days it is because there is nothing to tell. Even now this report from Paris does not help us much."

"Surely it is final as regards the man's death."

"The man's death is a mere incident — a trivial episode — in comparison with our real task, which is to trace this document and save a European catastrophe. Only one important thing has happened in the last three days, and that is that nothing has happened. I get reports almost hourly from the Government, and it is certain that nowhere in Europe is there any sign of trouble. Now, if this letter were loose — no, it *can't* be loose — but if it isn't loose, where can it be? Who has it? Why is it held back? That's the question that beats in my brain like a hammer. Was it, indeed, a coincidence that Lucas should meet his death on the night when the letter disappeared? Did the letter ever reach him? If so, why is it not among his papers? Did this mad wife of his carry it off with her? If so, is it in her house in Paris? How could I search for it without the French police having their suspicions aroused? It is a case, my dear Watson, where the law is as dangerous to us as the criminals are. Every man's hand is against us, and yet the interests at stake are colossal. Should I bring it to a successful conclusion, it will certainly represent the crowning glory of my career. Ah, here is my latest from the front!" He glanced hurriedly at the note which had been handed in. "Halloa! Lestrade seems to have observed something of interest. Put on your hat, Watson, and we will stroll down together to Westminster."

It was my first visit to the scene of the crime — a high, dingy, narrow-chested house, prim, formal, and solid, like the century which gave it birth. Lestrade's bulldog features gazed out at us from the front window, and he greeted us warmly when a big constable had opened the door and let us in. The room into which we were shown was that in which the crime had been committed, but no trace of it now remained, save an ugly, irregular stain upon the carpet. This carpet was a small square drugget in the centre of the room, surrounded by a broad expanse of beautiful, old-fashioned, wood flooring in square blocks highly polished. Over the fireplace was a magnificent trophy of weapons, one of which had been used on that tragic night. In the window was a sumptuous writing-desk, and every detail of the apartment, the pictures, the rugs, and the hangings, all pointed to a taste which was luxurious to the verge of effeminacy.

"Seen the Paris news?" asked Lestrade.

Holmes nodded.

"Our French friends seem to have touched the spot this time. No doubt it's just as they say. She knocked at the door — surprise visit, I guess, for he kept his life in watertight compartments. He let her in — couldn't keep her in the street. She told him how she had traced him, reproached him, one thing led to another, and then with that dagger so handy the end soon came. It wasn't all done in an instant, though, for these chairs were all swept over yonder, and he had one in his hand as if he had tried to hold her off with it. We've got it all as clear as if we had seen it."

Holmes raised his eyebrows.

"And yet you have sent for me?"

"Ah, yes, that's another matter — a mere trifle, but the sort of thing you take an interest in — queer, you know, and what you might call freakish. It has nothing to do with the main fact — can't have, on the face of it."

"What is it, then?"

"Well, you know after a crime of this sort we are very careful to keep things in their position. Nothing has been moved. Officer in charge here day and night. This morning, as the man was buried and the investigation over — so far as this room is concerned — we thought we could tidy up a bit. This carpet. You see, it is not fastened down, only just laid there. We had occasion to raise it. We found—— "

"Yes? You found—— "

Holmes's face grew tense with anxiety.

"Well, I'm sure you would never guess in a hundred years what we did find. You see that stain on the carpet? Well, a great deal must have soaked through, must it not?"

"Undoubtedly it must."

"Well, you will be surprised to hear that there is no stain on the white woodwork to correspond."

"No stain! But there must—— "

"Yes; so you would say. But the fact remains that there isn't."

He took the corner of the carpet in his hand and, turning it over, he showed that it was indeed as he said.

"But the under side is as stained as the upper. It must have left a mark."

Lestrade chuckled with delight at having puzzled the famous expert.

"Now I'll show you the explanation. There *is* a second stain, but it does not correspond with the other. See for yourself." As he spoke he turned over another portion of the carpet, and there, sure enough, was a great crimson spill upon the square white facing of the old-fashioned floor. "What do you make of that, Mr. Holmes?"

"Why, it is simple enough. The two stains did correspond, but the carpet has been turned round. As it was square and unfastened, it was easily done."

"The official police don't need you, Mr. Holmes, to tell them that the carpet must have been turned round. That's clear enough, for the stains lie above each other — if you lay it over this way. But what I want to know is, who shifted the carpet, and why?"

I could see from Holmes's rigid face that he was vibrating with inward excitement.

"Look here, Lestrade!" said he. "Has that constable in the passage been in charge of the place all the time?"

"Yes, he has."

"Well, take my advice. Examine him carefully. Don't do it before us. We'll wait here. You take him into the back room. You'll be more likely to get a confession out of him alone. Ask him how he dare to admit people and leave them alone in this room. Don't ask him if he has done it. Take it for granted. Tell him you *know* someone has been here. Press him. Tell him that a full confession is his only chance of forgiveness. Do exactly what I tell you!"

"By George, if he knows I'll have it out of him!" cried Lestrade. He darted into the hall, and a few moments later his bullying voice sounded from the back room.

"Now, Watson, now!" cried Holmes, with frenzied eagerness. All the demoniacal force of the man masked behind that listless manner burst out in a paroxysm of energy. He tore the drugget from the floor, and in an instant was down on his hands and knees clawing at each of the squares of wood beneath it. One turned sideways as he dug his nails into the edge of it. It hinged back like the lid of a box. A small black cavity opened beneath it. Holmes plunged his eager hand into it, and drew it out with a bitter snarl of anger and disappointment. It was empty.

"Quick, Watson, quick! Get it back again!" The wooden lid was replaced, and the drugget had only just been drawn straight, when Lestrade's voice was heard in the passage. He found Holmes leaning languidly against the mantelpiece, resigned and patient, endeavouring to conceal his irrepressible yawns.

"Sorry to keep you waiting, Mr. Holmes. I can see that you are bored to death with the whole affair. Well, he has confessed all right. Come in here, MacPherson. Let these gentlemen hear of your most inexcusable conduct."

The big constable, very hot and penitent, sidled into the room.

"I meant no harm, sir, I'm sure. The young woman came to the door last evening — mistook the house, she did. And then we got talking. It's lonesome, when you're on duty here all day."

"Well, what happened then?"

"She wanted to see where the crime was done — had read about it in the papers, she said. She was a very respectable, well-spoken young woman, sir, and I saw no harm in letting her have a peep. When she saw that mark on the carpet, down she dropped on the floor, and lay as if she were dead. I ran to the back and got some water, but I could not bring her to. Then I went round the corner to the Ivy Plant for some brandy, and by the time I had brought it back the young woman had recovered and was off — ashamed of herself, I dare say, and dared not face me."

"How about moving that drugget?"

"Well, sir, it was a bit rumpled, certainly, when I came back. You see, she fell on it, and it lies on a polished floor with nothing to keep it in place. I straightened it out afterwards."

"It's a lesson to you that you can't deceive me, Constable Mac-Pherson," said Lestrade, with dignity. "No doubt you thought that your breach of duty could never be discovered, and yet a mere glance at that drugget was enough to convince me that someone had been admitted to the room. It's lucky for you, my man, that nothing is missing, or you would find yourself in Queer Street. I'm sorry to have to call you down over such a petty business, Mr. Holmes, but I thought the point of the second stain not corresponding with the first would interest you."

"Certainly it was most interesting. Has this woman only been here once, constable?"

"Yes, sir, only once."

"Who was she?"

"Don't know the name, sir. Was answering an advertisement about typewriting, and came to the wrong number — very pleasant, genteel young woman, sir."

"Tall? Handsome?"

"Yes, sir; she was a well-grown young woman. I suppose you might say she was handsome. Perhaps some would say she was very handsome. 'Oh, officer, do let me have a peep!' says she. She had pretty, coaxing ways, as you might say, and I thought there was no harm in letting her just put her head through the door."

"How was she dressed?"

"Quiet, sir — a long mantle down to her feet."

"What time was it?"

"It was just growing dusk at the time. They were lighting the lamps as I came back with the brandy."

"Very good," said Holmes. "Come, Watson, I think that we have more important work elsewhere."

As we left the house Lestrade remained in the front room, while the repentant constable opened the door to let us out. Holmes turned on the step and held up something in his hand. The constable stared intently.

"Good Lord, sir!" he cried, with amazement on his face. Holmes put his finger on his lips, replaced his hand in his breast-pocket, and burst out laughing as we turned down the street. "Excellent!" said he. "Come, friend Watson, the curtain rings up for the last act. You will be relieved to hear that there will be no war, that the Right Honourable Trelawney Hope will suffer no setback in his brilliant career, that the indiscreet Sovereign will receive no punishment for his indiscretion, that the Prime Minister will have no European complication to deal with, and that with a little tact and management upon our part nobody will be a penny the worse for what might have been a very ugly accident."

My mind filled with admiration for this extraordinary man.

"You have solved it!" I cried.

"Hardly that, Watson. There are some points which are as dark as ever. But we have so much that it will be our own fault if we cannot get the rest. We will go straight to Whitehall Terrace and bring the matter to a head."

When we arrived at the residence of the European Secretary it was for Lady Hilda Trelawney Hope that Sherlock Holmes inquired. We were shown into the morning-room.

"Mr. Holmes!" said the lady, and her face was pink with indignation, "this is surely most unfair and ungenerous upon your part. I desired, as I have explained, to keep my visit to you a secret, lest my husband should think that I was intruding into his affairs. And yet you compromise me by coming here, and so showing that there are business relations between us."

"Unfortunately, madam, I had no possible alternative. I have been commissioned to recover this immensely important paper. I must therefore ask you, madam, to be kind enough to place it in my hands."

The lady sprang to her feet, with the colour all dashed in an instant from her beautiful face. Her eyes glazed — she tottered — I thought that she would faint. Then with a grand effort she rallied from the shock, and a supreme astonishment and indignation chased every other expression from her features.

"You — you insult me, Mr. Holmes."

"Come, come, madam, it is useless. Give up the letter."

She darted to the bell.

"The butler shall show you out."

"Do not ring, Lady Hilda. If you do, then all my earnest efforts to avoid a scandal will be frustrated. Give up the letter, and all will be set right. If you will work with me, I can arrange everything. If you work against me, I must expose you."

She stood grandly defiant, a queenly figure, her eyes fixed upon his as if she would read his very soul. Her hand was on the bell, but she had forborne to ring it.

"You are trying to frighten me. It is not a very manly thing, Mr. Holmes, to come here and browbeat a woman. You say that you know something. What is it that you know?"

"Pray sit down, madam. You will hurt yourself there if you fall. I will not speak until you sit down. Thank you."

"I give you five minutes, Mr. Holmes."

"One is enough, Lady Hilda. I know of your visit to Eduardo Lucas, and of your giving him this document, of your ingenious return to the room last night, and of the manner in which you took the letter from the hiding-place under the carpet."

She stared at him with an ashen face, and gulped twice before she could speak.

"You are mad, Mr. Holmes — you are mad!" she cried at last.

He drew a small piece of cardboard from his pocket. It was the face of a woman cut out of a portrait.

"I have carried this because I thought it might be useful," said he. "The policeman has recognized it."

She gave a gasp, and her head dropped back in her chair.

"Come, Lady Hilda. You have the letter. The matter may still be adjusted. I have no desire to bring trouble to you. My duty ends when I have returned the lost letter to your husband. Take my advice and be frank with me; it is your only chance."

Her courage was admirable. Even now she would not own defeat.

"I tell you again, Mr. Holmes, that you are under some absurd illusion."

Holmes rose from his chair.

"I am sorry for you, Lady Hilda. I have done my best for you; I can see that it is all in vain."

He rang the bell. The butler entered.

"Is Mr. Trelawney Hope at home?"

"He will be home, sir, at a quarter to one."

Holmes glanced at his watch.

"Still a quarter of an hour," said he. "Very good, I shall wait."

The butler had hardly closed the door behind him when Lady Hilda was down on her knees at Holmes's feet, her hands outstretched, her beautiful face upturned and wet with her tears.

"Oh, spare me, Mr. Holmes! Spare me!" she pleaded, in a frenzy of supplication. "For Heaven's sake don't tell him! I love him so! I would not bring one shadow on his life, and this I know would break his noble heart."

Holmes raised the lady. "I am thankful, madam, that you have come to your senses even at this last moment! There is not an instant to lose. Where is the letter?"

She darted across to a writing-desk, unlocked it, and drew out a long blue envelope.

"Here it is, Mr. Holmes. Would to Heaven I had never seen it!"

"How can we return it?" Holmes muttered. "Quick, quick, we must think of some way! Where is the dispatch-box?"

"Still in his bedroom."

"What a stroke of luck! Quick, madam, bring it here."

A moment later she had appeared with a red flat box in her hand.

"How did you open it before? You have a duplicate key? Yes, of course you have. Open it!"

From out of her bosom Lady Hilda had drawn a small key. The box flew open. It was stuffed with papers. Holmes thrust the blue envelope deep down into the heart of them, between the leaves of some other document. The box was shut, locked, and returned to his bedroom.

"Now we are ready for him," said Holmes; "we have still ten minutes. I am going far to screen you, Lady Hilda. In return you will spend the time in telling me frankly the real meaning of this extraordinary affair."

"Mr. Holmes, I will tell you everything," cried the lady. "Oh, Mr. Holmes, I would cut off my right hand before I gave him a moment of sorrow! There is no woman in all London who loves her husband as I do, and yet if he knew how I have acted — how I have been compelled to act — he would never forgive me. For his own honour stands so high that he could not forget or pardon a lapse in another. Help me, Mr. Holmes! My happiness, his happiness, our very lives are at stake!"

"Quick, madam, the time grows short!"

"It was a letter of mine, Mr. Holmes, an indiscreet letter written before my marriage — a foolish letter, a letter of an impulsive, loving girl. I meant no harm, and yet he would have thought it criminal. Had he read that letter his confidence would have been for ever destroyed. It is years since I wrote it. I had thought that the whole matter was forgotten. Then at last I heard from this man, Lucas, that it had passed into his hands, and that he would lay it before my husband. I implored his mercy. He said that he would return my letter if I would return him a certain document which he described in my husband's dispatch-box. He had some spy in the office who had told him of its existence. He assured me that no harm could come to my husband. Put yourself in my position, Mr. Holmes! What was I to do?"

"Take your husband into your confidence."

"I could not, Mr. Holmes, I could not! On the one side seemed certain ruin; on the other, terrible as it seemed to take my husband's papers, still in a matter of politics I could not understand the consequences, while in a matter of love and trust they were only too clear to me. I did it, Mr. Holmes! I took an impression of his key; this man Lucas furnished a duplicate. I opened his dispatch-box, took the paper, and conveyed it to Godolphin Street."

"What happened there, madam?"

"I tapped at the door, as agreed. Lucas opened it. I followed him into his room, leaving the hall door ajar behind me, for I feared to be alone with the man. I remembered that there was a woman outside as I entered. Our business was soon done. He had my letter on his desk; I handed him the document. He gave me the letter. At this instant there was a sound at the door. There were steps in the passage. Lucas quickly turned back the drugget, thrust the document into some hiding-place there, and covered it over.

"What happened after that is like some fearful dream. I have a vision of a dark, frantic face, of a woman's voice, which screamed in French, 'My waiting is not in vain. At last, at last I have found you with her!' There was a savage struggle. I saw him with a chair in his hand, a knife gleamed in hers. I rushed from the horrible scene, ran from the house, and only next morning in the paper did I learn the dreadful result. That night I was happy, for I had my letter, and I had not seen yet what the future would bring.

"It was next morning that I realized that I had only exchanged one trouble for another. My husband's anguish at the loss of his paper went to my heart. I could hardly prevent myself from there and then kneeling down at his feet and telling him what I had done. But that again would mean a confession of the past. I came to you that morning in order to understand the full enormity of my offence. From the instant that I grasped it my whole mind was turned to the one thought of getting back my husband's paper. It must still be where Lucas had placed it, for it was concealed before this dreadful woman entered the room. If it had not been for her coming, I should not have known where his hiding-place was. How was I to get into the room? For two days I watched the place, but the door was never left open. Last night I made a last attempt. What I did and how I succeeded, you have already learned. I brought the paper back with me, and thought of destroying it, since I could see no way of returning it without confessing my guilt to my husband. Heavens, I hear his step upon the stair!"

The European Secretary burst excitedly into the room.

"Any news, Mr. Holmes, any news?" he cried.

"I have some hopes."

"Ah, thank Heaven!" His face became radiant. "The Prime Minister is lunching with me. May he share your hopes? He has nerves of steel, and yet I know that he has hardly slept since this terrible event. Jacobs, will you ask the Prime Minister to come up? As to you, dear, I fear that this is a matter of politics. We will join you in a few minutes in the dining-room."

The Prime Minister's manner was subdued, but I could see by the gleam of his eyes and the twitchings of his bony hands that he shared the excitement of his young colleague.

"I understand that you have something to report, Mr. Holmes?"

"Purely negative as yet," my friend answered. "I have inquired at every point where it might be, and I am sure that there is no danger to be apprehended."

"But that is not enough, Mr. Holmes. We cannot live for ever on such a volcano. We must have something definite."

"I am in hopes of getting it. That is why I am here. The more I think of the matter the more convinced I am that the letter has never left this house."

"Mr. Holmes!"

"If it had it would certainly have been public by now."

"But why should anyone take it in order to keep it in this house?"

"I am not convinced that anyone did take it."

"Then how could it leave the dispatch-box?"

"I am not convinced that it ever did leave the dispatch-box."

"Mr. Holmes, this joking is very ill-timed. You have my assurance that it left the box."

"Have you examined the box since Tuesday morning?"

"No; it was not necessary."

"You may conceivably have overlooked it."

"Impossible, I say."

"But I am not convinced of it; I have known such things happen. I presume there are other papers there. Well, it may have got mixed with them."

"It was on the top."

"Someone may have shaken the box and displaced it."

"No, no; I had everything out."

"Surely it is easily decided, Hope!" said the Premier. "Let us have the dispatch-box brought in."

The Secretary rang the bell.

"Jacobs, bring down my dispatch-box. This is a farcical waste of time, but still, if nothing else will satisfy you, it shall be done. Thank you, Jacobs; put it here. I have always had the key on my watch-chain. Here are the papers, you see. Letter from Lord Merrow, report from Sir Charles Hardy, memorandum from Belgrade, note on the Russo-German grain taxes, letter from Madrid, note from Lord Flowers — good heavens! what is this? Lord Bellinger! Lord Bellinger!"

The Premier snatched the blue envelope from his hand.

"Yes, it is it — and the letter intact. Hope, I congratulate you!"

"Thank you! Thank you! What a weight from my heart! But this is inconceivable — impossible! Mr. Holmes, you are a wizard, a sorcerer! How did you know it was there?"

"Because I knew it was nowhere else."

"I cannot believe my eyes!" He ran wildly to the door. "Where is my wife? I must tell her that all is well. Hilda! Hilda!" we heard his voice on the stairs.

The Premier looked at Holmes with twinkling eyes.

"Come, sir," said he. "There is more in this than meets the eye. How came the letter back in the box?"

Holmes turned away smiling from the keen scrutiny of those wonderful eyes.

"We also have our diplomatic secrets," said he, and picking up his hat he turned to the door.


## AFTERWORD

Doyle himself grouped this story ("one of the neatest of the stories," he judged it) with an earlier one, "The Naval Treaty" (October–November 1893) as his "two stories which deal with high diplomacy and intrigue." Both, he thought, were "among the very best of the series." At the outset of "The Naval Treaty," in fact, Watson alludes to

"The Adventure of the Second Stain" as an associated case of great interest which must, however, for now remain untold:

> The July which immediately succeeded my marriage was made
> memorable by three cases of interest, in which I had the privilege
> of being associated with Sherlock Holmes and of studying his
> methods. I find them recorded in my notes under the headings of
> "The Adventure of the Second Stain," "The Adventure of the
> Naval Treaty," and "The Adventure of the Tired Captain." The
> first of these, however, deals with interests of such importance and
> implicates so many of the first families in the kingdom that for
> many years it will be impossible to make it public. No case, how-
> ever, in which Holmes was engaged has ever illustrated the value
> of his analytical methods so clearly or has impressed those who
> were associated with him so deeply. I still retain an almost *verba-
> tim* report of the interview in which he demonstrated the true
> facts of the case to Monsieur Dubugue of the Paris police, and
> Fritz von Waldbaum, the well-known specialist of Dantzig, both
> of whom had wasted their energies upon what proved to be side-
> issues. The new century will have come, however, before the story
> can be safely told. Meanwhile I pass on to the second on my list. . . .

Thus, "The Second Stain" had to satisfy the characteristics specified by Watson here. In this respect it bears comparison to "The Empty House," which had to explain Holmes's return satisfactorily in accordance with the evidence of his apparent death already provided in "The Final Problem."

Doyle often introduced passing allusions to Holmes's other, unrecorded cases; see, for example, the openings of "A Scandal in Bohemia," "The Speckled Band," and "The Musgrave Ritual." "Heaven knows how many titles I have thrown about in a casual way," he later wrote in his memoirs, "and how many readers have begged me to satisfy their curiosity as to 'Rigoletto and his abominable wife' [imperfectly recalled from "The Musgrave Ritual"], 'The Adventure of the Tired Captain,' or 'The Curious Experience of the Patterson Family in the Island of Uffa.'" "The Second Stain" is one of the few titles for which Doyle later wrote a story to correspond.

Watson sometimes conceals from the reader the identities of some figures in Holmes's cases (as at the conclusion of "Charles Augustus Milverton"). This one time, however, Watson himself is excluded from any knowledge of the potentate's identity — even as the Premier is from any knowledge of the theft of the letter.

# PART TWO

# Contemporary
# Critical Essays

# MARTIN PRIESTMAN

## Sherlock Holmes — The Series

In his book *Detective Fiction and Literature: The Figure on the Carpet* (London: Macmillan, 1990), Martin Priestman examines the social, structural, and psychological implications of the detective fiction genre as a context for reconsidering its relationship — "half-polarity, half-collaboration" (195) — with established, so-called serious literature. In the section of Chapter 5 reprinted here, he calls particular attention to the ways in which the form of the Holmes series, and of its individual stories, itself reflects and characterizes the social content of the stories. His suggestion that we think of the formal tensions organizing the stories in terms of two "axes" of indeterminacy versus determinacy (or anonymity versus identity, or generality versus singularity) recalls, but transforms, the crucial structuralist perception of literature's two fundamental dimensions as axes of diachronic (occurring over time, sequential; metonymic) versus synchronic (simultaneous, immediate; metaphoric) modes. The serial form is indeterminate: presumably it can continue indefinitely. But each story in the serial is quite determinate, a separate, independent, and complete entity; each story, then, imposes form on the potentially formless. At the heart of Priestman's argument is the suggestion that this structural relationship of story to series recapitulates the relationship of many other Holmesian elements. This distinction of singularity from generality, moreover — of the singular clue from the confusing mass of data, of the individual client from the mass of men, of the specific culprit from the bewildering range of potential suspects, of inference from information, of every identity and identification from all anonymity — reflects significantly both important social issues of Doyle's time and the nature of detection itself.

Emile Gaboriau, to whom Priestman refers in his first paragraph, was the creator of the detective novel. He established and popularized the genre in France through five related works: *L'Affaire Lerouge* (1866), *Le Crime d'Orcival* (1867), *Le Dossier No. 113* (1867), *Monsieur Lecoq* (1869), and *Les Esclaves de Paris* (1869). Lecoq (protagonist of the last four and appearing also in the first) is a police detective; Père Tabaret (protagonist of the first and reappearing in later books), Lecoq's elderly mentor, is a civilian, a retired pawnbroker.

Edgar Allan Poe, to whom Priestman several times refers, invented the detective story with his tale "The Murders in the Rue Morgue" (1841), featuring his preeminently analytical detective, Auguste Dupin. He subsequently wrote two more detective stories featuring Dupin, "The Mystery of Marie Rogêt" (1842–43) and "The Purloined Letter" (1845). In addition to these, he wrote two other notable detective stories, "The Gold-Bug" (1843), the prototype of all "treasure-hunting, cryptogram solving yarns," as Doyle called it, and "Thou Art the Man" (1844), the first comic or burlesque detective story. His sketch "The Man of the Crowd" (1840) is not a detective story; but its narrator, like a detective, can read men's professions and occupations in their appearances — except in the case of one fascinatingly unintelligible old man whose only behavior is to blend continually into the city's crowd, and who thereby comes to be identifiable only as "the type and genius of deep crime."

---

Tracing the ways in which Doyle varies source material in individual instances only takes us a short way in determining what, if anything, is new about his handling of the detective genre. I would argue that his real distinctiveness lies in his development of the "series" mode which is only rudimentary in his predecessors. Poe's three Dupin stories certainly suggest the possibility of an infinite series of further cases, but he takes it no further, and Gaboriau's five loosely linked novels featuring Tabaret and Lecoq do not induce the same sense of insistent formulaic repetition as the extended short story series which was really Doyle's invention.[1]

With other fictional developments, such as the rise of the novel, early manifestations of a new form often betray a self-consciousness tending at times to self-destruction (or indeed "self-deconstruction"). In two very different contexts, *Don Quixote* and *Tristram Shandy* dramatically exemplify this as far as the novel is concerned. It is arguable that with the ending of "The Purloined Letter" Poe threatens to kill off the infant detective-series genre by converting it back into something

---

[1]See Doyle's autobiography *Memories and Adventures,* p. 95, for the drily prophetic reasons behind the invention: "considering these various journals with their disconnected stories, it had struck me that a single character running through a series, if it only engaged the attention of the reader, would bind that reader to that particular magazine."

more Gothic and personal in the duel between doubles, and that Gaboriau works (especially at the beginning and end of the Tabaret–Lecoq cycle, in *Lerouge* and *Lecoq*) to make us "doubt the very existence of crime," at least as something that can be adequately solved by detectives.

Coming along at a later stage, Doyle evinces a more workaday faith in his form, although arguably . . . the second Holmes novel virtually contradicts the first and, once established, the series makes the largest such attempt before *Dallas* to kill itself off. But despite such hiccups, Doyle's importance as the creator, not of a single hero but of the epic single-hero short-story *series*, cannot be overemphasized.

The series is by definition indeterminate along the axis which links the separate stories together. But there is also the axis in which each story taken as a unit is necessarily highly determinate and finite: any flow onwards from one unit to another would threaten to undermine the required equivalence of each unit by subordinating some to others. I would like to argue that this structure of the series as a whole, whereby an indeterminate axis repeatedly crosses a single or unitary one, is also a vital element in the structure, and even the subject matter, of each story taken individually. At times other related words perhaps better describe this "indeterminacy": depending on the context these can include anonymity, generality and reproducibility. And whereas the opposing axis on the broad structural level is the particular case or the single story, at the level of subject matter it can be variously represented by the precise clue, the exact name, the "singular" detail. I would argue that some of the most memorable and characteristic stories are memorable precisely because of the persistence with which they juggle these two axes together.

"The Red-headed League," the original "fool's errand" story, concerns a red-headed pawnbroker, Jabez Wilson, who is lured into working for the eponymous league while his innocent-seeming assistant Spaulding and new red-headed "employer" dig a tunnel from his shop to the bank next door. Guessing the truth from the street layout and the mud on the assistant's trousers, Holmes lays an ambush in the bank, where Spaulding is revealed to be the brilliant mastermind John Clay.

What might be called the "indefinite" axis of this story is, as often, imaginatively coterminous with London itself, the sprawling anonymous city perceived as virtually unknowable. The opposite axis, of "singularity," is provided on one level by Holmes's correct identification of the criminals and their intentions, but on another level by the comic specificity of the story's opening imagery to do with the bizarre "red-headed league" which the crooks have invented to decoy Jabez Wilson from his shop. Wilson's experience of the league juxtaposes the countless or anonymous with the singular or specific in a number of ways. Indeed its very name, and hence that of the story, suggestively confuses the two ideas by attaching a grammatically "singular" adjective to a collective noun: there is a paradoxical suggestion, which turns out in one sense to be justified, of an innumerable body with a single head. The point of intersection whereby the strikingly peculiar invades Wilson's hitherto conventional life is the newspaper advertisements column which, like London itself, houses the ultimate in singularity within the ultimate in infinitely reproducible anonymity. The singular item brought to his attention by these means is one which professes all the weight and authority of a general advertisement to the public at large, but has in fact been devised to single him out from the mass by way of his one individual trait, his red hair.

In the comic scenes which follow it turns out that within the vast mass of London even this attempt to bestow the required uniqueness on the otherwise undistinguished Wilson is only the first stage in his blatantly rigged selection from a quasi-apocalyptic horde of other redheaded men "from north, south, east and west. . . . I should not have thought there were so many in the whole country as were brought together by that single advertisement . . . — straw, lemon, orange, brick, Irish-setter, liver, clay" (p. 59). Wilson's reward for his "uniqueness" is to be set to work copying out the *Encyclopædia Britannica* verbatim in an empty room. This task too combines the notion of an endlessly reproducible series (not only Wilson's act of copying but also the Encyclopædia's status as mass-object) with that of the odd and the singular. The jostling juxtaposition of "Abbots, and Archery, and Armour, and Architecture, and Attica" comments equally on the old-world individuality of Wilson's scholastic task and on its mass-produced modern arbitrariness. In a further surreal touch, the contrast between imagined organic whole and actual mechanical part is reinforced in Wilson's eventual discovery that the "league is dissolved," and that an elaborately laid trail of false names and addresses leads only to a "manufactory of artificial knee-caps" (p. 63).

Holmes's intervention begins to resolve the cacophony of the reproducible and the unique, but initially does so by simply extending the methods of the crooks. Thus he individuates Wilson from the start on five counts which distinguish him even more precisely than the obvious red hair which gave the gang their handle: "Beyond the obvious facts that he has at some time done manual labour, that he takes snuff, that he is a Freemason, that he has been in China, and that he has done a considerable amount of writing lately, I can deduce nothing else" (p. 55). By singling Wilson out on these very specific counts, Holmes asserts the same kind of power over him as the crooks have done, and the final "nothing else" expresses the same simultaneous dismissal of him as otherwise utterly undistinguished. This fundamental dismissal of Wilson, returning him to the faceless ranks from which he has been plucked, is expressed by the "league" in the brusque announcement of its dissolution which effectually, since Wilson is its only real member, "dissolves" him. Holmes too (or rather the story itself, if they are distinguishable) abandons Wilson as of no further interest once his most striking claim to singularity, namely the story he has to tell, has been drained from him.

The dénouement revolves round Holmes's awareness that what really makes Wilson singular is the fact that his pawnbroker's shop backs on to a bank. Again this is a knowledge, or a type of knowledge, which Holmes shares only with the gang. It is a knowledge of relationships rather than entities; an ability to discern the hidden connections between Wilson's "faded and stagnant square" and "the line of fine shops and stately business premises" which "present[s] as great a contrast to it as the front of a picture does to the back" (pp. 65–66). Such a knowledge of connections, commonly expressed by Holmes's A-to-Z familiarity with London streets and districts, is the magic solution of the impasse between the ungraspably amorphous and the irreducibly singular from which the problem seems so dramatically to arise. His realisation that the source of Wilson's singularity is not him but his shop, and then only in its relation to the bank, implies a means by which the whole cacophony of London might eventually be comprehended: the apparently singular ceases to be so when juxtaposed correctly to something else (and therefore moved on from, with the hint of callousness by which Holmes moves from client to solution, and then from case to case), and the amorphous ceases to be amorphous when grasped as the sum total of all such juxtapositions.

As we have seen, Holmes shares this knowledge with the crooks, and it is their concealment of the hidden connections underlying the amorphous/singular dichotomy that creates the mystery. One of the most entertaining aspects of the "league" is the solemn mimicry of a large and impersonal organisation by what turns out to be a gang of two; of which, moreover, one member is so clearly the boss that his colleague virtually fades out at the end. The finale's somewhat surprising focus on John Clay as a superstar criminal, a "personality" with some of the makings of a Moriarty, provides the necessary opposite pole to the impersonality so successfully mimicked by the league as well as to the role of harmless underpaid assistant Clay himself has adopted in previous appearances. (Glancing for a moment at that role, the trait which most distinguishes "Spaulding" is the passion for photography which drives him repeatedly into the cellar. He is of course really digging a tunnel, but it is typical that he should mask this *connecting* activity behind a harmless "singularity" involving a mass-reproduction technique.)

The unmasked Clay is shot through with the contradictions he has so ably exploited. Despite his virtual invisibility to his employer he is characterised by effeminate, possibly homosexual traits — a smooth face, pierced ears, a "white, almost womanly hand," and a defiant solicitude for a partner "lithe and small like himself" — which, especially in the 1890s context, could be taken to imply a particularly flamboyant individualism. His noble rank and place "at the head of his profession" imply further claims to distinction, reflected in the idiosyncratic demand that even the arresting police call him "sir." But such marks of singularity are also linked with counteracting elements of chameleonlike variety implying a deeper de-individuation or undistinction: mixed sexual identity; the class mixture expressed in his thieves' slang; even a lack of fixed criminal abode whereby "he'll crack a crib in Scotland one week, and be raising money to build an orphanage in Cornwall the next" (p. 68). His very name, John Clay, in contrast to the far more distinctive names of "ordinary" characters like Jabez Wilson or even his own *alter ego* Vincent Spaulding, implies the common clay of average undistinguishable man (as hinted when "clay" closes the list of decreasingly red hairpigments), and perhaps even the distinction-in-indistinction of Adam[2] himself.

But the simultaneity of the singular with the amorphous can also be read as mastery of the connections between worlds normally conceived of as distinct: seen thus, "Clay" also implies the connecting element on which the walls creating the network of distinctions which is the city are superimposed. Such an undermining of the notion of the city, by burrowing beneath the dividing walls but through the connecting clay, is perhaps the real "essence" of what the Poe of "The Man of the Crowd" calls "deep crime." But as we have seen, Sherlock Holmes is also a master of such connections, as witnessed by his initially exclusive interest in

[2] *Adam:* The Hebrew name of the Biblical first man signifies "red earth." [Editor's note]

the earth on Clay's trousers, and his reading of the ground under the pavement by rapping it with his stick. Holmes also possesses much of his antagonist's chameleonlike versatility-within-singularity: it is in this story that we learn that (in close echo of Dupin) "In his singular character the dual nature alternately asserted itself, and his extreme exactness and astuteness represented, as I have often thought, the reaction against the poetic and contemplative mood which occasionally predominated in him" (p. 66). Holmes's fluctuations from langorous musicianship to bloodhound-like energy, which constitute a major part of his pattern, imply a protean ability to hold disparate aspects of experience in easy connection with each other: to that extent it is like the power of disguise which he exploits in other stories. And again, as with his antagonists here and elsewhere, it is precisely this *doubleness* which constitutes "his singular character."

The structure of the ending, in which the two "singular characters" of the criminal and detective confront each other, represents a struggle for the ultimate singularity to be bestowed by the final spotlight. With his arrest and relegation to the class of prisoners the criminal loses the uniqueness which has briefly challenged that of the detective. But to put it another way, the detective has for the first time forced uniqueness in the form of identification on to the criminal who has hitherto sheltered behind anonymity. The criminal then leaves a trace of his singularity in the sense of providing Holmes with a "singular case" ("one of the most singular which I have listened to for some time," as he calls this one) which affords him a respite from the *ennui* and "conventions and humdrum routine of daily life."

But Holmes's disgust with routine, as well as containing a continuing claim to match the "aesthetic" interest of the criminal, perhaps also expresses a self-reflexive awareness on Doyle's part that within the series structure of which he is the first embodiment, Holmes *is* routine incarnate. It is a paradox of these stories that the great and unique Sherlock Holmes, penetrator of all that anonymous London fog, master of the singular detail and the specific identification, represents in his infinite reproducibility (in stories which resemble each other as closely as the houses of a London terrace) the very spirit of endless sameness against which he seems eternally to battle.

As well as clarifying the underlying structure of the series formula, the notions of reproducibility and singularity can also be helpful in understanding Holmes's famous deductive "methods." Poe's "The Man of the Crowd," written just before "Rue Morgue," already laid down the basic logical lines whereby a generally known fact (such as that all clerks' right ears are bent) is used to spotlight the "unreadable" exception. But where Poe uses this basic dichotomy to highlight the terrifying mystery of urban man, Doyle generally uses it as a reassuring and clarifying mechanism.

A classic instance occurs near the beginning of "The Blue Carbuncle," where Holmes draws an amazing string of deductions from a hat picked up in the street. In its status as an arbitrarily detached fragment from the attire of a man who is himself only an arbitrarily detached fragment of a similarly clad mass, the hat would seem to represent the ultimate in anonymity. But, singled out by Holmes's magical scrutiny and emblematically hung on a chair in the middle of the room, it becomes instead the trumpet of its owner's unique life-history.

The most striking fact, that the owner's wife has ceased to love him, is proved by collating the hat's singularly unbrushed state with collateral general evidence of marriage. In this instance, clearly, the "proof" of singularity assumes a very high degree of its opposite in society in general: hat-brushing only inevitably equals marital affection in the world of ideal conformity which, perhaps, it is one of the subliminal aims of detective fiction to create. A truly singular household in which a wife loved her husband while not caring about his hat would be a monstrosity as "unreadable" as Poe's "Man of the Crowd." This household, on the other hand, offers just enough singularity to be identifiable, but cannot even be imagined to break the more fundamental principle which equates wifely love with hat-brushing.

We can express all this more philosophically by remembering that all deduction depends on the syllogism. In this case the syllogism is: the unbrushed hat's owner has a wife; all loving wives brush their husband's hats; therefore this wife is not loving. A similar middle term or "known rule" is present in all of Holmes's deductions, properly so called, and hence I would argue that wherever these deductions touch on matters of social relationship there are always some very large-scale assumptions about unbreakable social rules implicit in them.[3] Though a lot more could be said, this is perhaps enough to demonstrate the generally conservative swing of the "purely" deductive mode which Doyle bequeathed to most of his English successors.

---

[3]See Umberto Eco and Thomas A. Sebeok (eds), *The Sign of Three: Dupin, Holmes, Peirce* (Bloomington, Ind., 1983), particularly the articles by Eco and Sebeok themselves, on Holmes's relation to the logician Charles S. Peirce's theories of deduction, induction and abduction, each dependent on a different type of syllogism.

# PETER BROOKS

# Reading for the Plot

---

The full title of Peter Brooks's book *Reading for the Plot: Design and Intention in Narrative* (New York: Knopf, 1984), from the introductory chapter of which the selection printed here is taken, indicates an interest in plot simultaneously formal and psychoanalytical. Formally, Brooks's approach owes much to the structuralist-based work on theories of narrative that has come to be known as narratology. Narratology is grounded on a fundamental discrimination between two discrete planes of narrative, usually labeled "story" and "discourse." Story is the basic material of narrative, a series of actions or events, the "what" of a narrative, its content; discourse is the presentation of those actions and events, the "how" of a narrative, its "way" or expression. Brooks is relating his argument directly to this theoretical context when he refers to the distinction made by the Russian Formalists (a group of literary critics who in the 1920s anticipated some of the principles of structuralism and narratology) between *fabula* and *sjužet:* as he explains earlier in this chapter, *fabula* designates "the order of events referred to by the narrative," and *sjužet,* "the order of events presented in the narrative discourse" (Brooks 12). *Fabula* thus corresponds to the English "story," or content; *sjužet,* to "discourse," or expression.

Like his structuralist and narratologist predecessors, Brooks is interested in detective fiction not only because the genre so particularly emphasizes plot but also because it so insistently points up the difference between story and discourse (for in detective fiction the full story, "what happened," is by definition *not known,* and must be discovered). As opposed to a tale of pure adventure, a series of events or episodes recounted in their original sequence, the detective story confronts the *question* of what some original sequence of events had been. The detective story thus constitutes, as Brooks notes, perhaps the clearest and purest example of this other extreme of narrative emphasis, the extreme of questions demanding answers, of suspense and its resolution (Brooks 18) — an extreme that Brooks, following the usage of Roland Barthes in his influential book *S/Z,* calls "hermeneutic" in his first sentence below.

But Brooks is interested in plotting as well as plot, in the dynamics as well as the structures of narrative; he is thus concerned also "with how narratives work on us, as readers, to create models of understanding, and with why we need and want such shaping orders" (Brooks xiii). Plot, he insists, is not merely a static condition, but an active process, an ongoing work of interpretation, whether this be the recovery or the making of meaning. In "reading . . . 'The Musgrave Ritual' as an allegory of plot" (p. 325), then, he is reading it as an allegory not only of narrative structure, but of detection and reading as well.

---

I shall now bring this discussion of how we might talk about narrative plot to bear on [a] brief text[,] . . . located at the hermeneutic end of the spectrum . . . of narrative language. . . . [This] is thus necessarily a detective story, Sir Arthur Conan Doyle's "The Musgrave Ritual," the history of one of Sherlock Holmes's early cases — prior to Watson's arrival on the scene — which Holmes will recount to Watson to satisfy his curiosity concerning the contents of a small wooden box, to wit: "a crumpled piece of paper, an old-fashioned brass key, a peg of wood with a ball of string attached to it, and three rusty old discs of metal" (p. 198). The crumpled paper is a copy of the questions and answers of the ritual referred to in the title, the ritual recited by each male Musgrave at his coming of age. It has been the object of the indiscreet attention of Reginald Musgrave's butler, Brunton, who has been dismissed for his prying — then has disappeared, and shortly after him, the maid Rachel Howells, whom he loved and then jilted, whose footprints led to the edge of the lake, from which the county police recovered a linen bag containing "a mass of old rusted and discolored metal and several dull-colored pieces of pebble or glass." Now all these separate enigmas must — as is ever the case in Holmes's working hypothesis — be related as part of the same "chain of events." Holmes needs, he says, "to devise some common thread upon which they might all hang": precisely the interpretive thread of plot.

The key must lie in the ritual itself, which Musgrave considers "rather an absurd business," a text with no meaning other than its consecration as ritual, as rite of passage. Holmes believes otherwise, and he does so because the other curious outsider, Brunton, has done so. The solution of the case consists in taking the apparently meaningless meta-

phor of the ritual — seen by the Musgraves simply to stand for the antiquity of their house and the continuity of their line — and unpacking
it as metonymy.[1] The central part of the tale displays a problem in trigonometry in action, as Holmes interprets the indications of the ritual as
directions for laying out a path on the ground, following the shadow of
the elm when the sun is over the oak, pacing off measurements, and so
forth: he literally plots out on the lawn the points to which the ritual,
read as directions for plotting points, refers him, thus realizing the geo-
metrical sense of plotting and the archaic sense of plot as a bounded area
of ground. In the process, he repeats the plotting-out already accomplished by Brunton: when he thrusts a peg into the ground, he finds
with "exultation" that within two inches of it a depression marks where
Brunton has set his peg. The work of detection in this story makes particularly clear a condition of all classic detective fiction, that the detective repeat, go over again, the ground that has been covered by his predecessor, the criminal. Tzvetan Todorov has noted that the work of
detection that we witness in the detective story, which is *in praesentia*
for the reader, exists to reveal, to realize the story of the crime, which is
*in absentia* yet also the important narrative since it bears the meaning.[2]
Todorov identifies the two orders of story, inquest and crime, as *sjužet*
and *fabula*. He thus makes the detective story the narrative of narratives, its classical structure a laying-bare of the structure of all narrative
in that it dramatizes the role of *sjužet* and *fabula* and the nature of their
relation. Plot, I would add, once more appears as the active process of
*sjužet* working on *fabula*, the dynamic of its interpretive ordering.

Furthermore, in repeating the steps of the criminal-predecessor,
Holmes is literalizing an act that all narrative claims to perform, since
narrative ever, and inevitably — if only because of its use of the preterite —
presents itself as a repetition and rehearsal (which the French language,
of course, makes the same thing) of what has already happened. This
need not mean that it did in fact happen — we are not concerned with

---

[1] *metonomy:* A figure of speech substituting one word or phrase for another on the
basis of their contiguity or sequence. *Metaphor,* in contrast, substitutes on the basis of
similarity or analogy. [Editor's note]

This use of metaphor and metonymy, as representing the selective or substitutive and
the combinatory poles of language respectively (or the paradigmatic and syntagmatic),
comes from Roman Jakobson's influential essay, "Two Types of Language and Two
Types of Aphasic Disturbances," in Roman Jakobson and Morris Halle, *Fundamentals of
Language* (The Hague: Mouton, 1956).

[2] Tzvetan Todorov, "Typologie du roman policier," in *Poétique de la prose,* (Paris:
Editions du Seuil, 1971), pp. 57–59.

verification — and one can perfectly well reverse the proposition to say that the claim to repeat in fact produces the event presented as prior: the story is after all a construction made by the reader, and the detective, from the implications of the narrative discourse, which is all he ever knows. What is important, whatever our decision about priority here, is the constructive, semiotic role of repetition: the function of plot as the active repetition and reworking of story in and by discourse.

Within the conventions of the detective story — and of many other narratives as well — repetition results in both detection and apprehension of the original plotmaker, the criminal: in this case Brunton, whom Holmes finally finds asphyxiated in a crypt in the cellar, into which he has descended for the treasure, and into which he has been sealed by the fiery Welsh maid Rachel Howells. Nonetheless, this solution, finding the *fabula* and its instigator, involves a considerable measure of hypothetical construction, since Brunton is dead and Rachel Howells has fled: verification of the *fabula* lies in its plausibility, its fitting the needs of explanation. And as soon as this level of the *fabula* — the story of the crime — has been constructed, it produces a further level, as Holmes and Musgrave reexamine the contents of the bag that Howells presumably threw into the lake, and Holmes identifies the dull pieces of metal and glass as the gold and jewels of the crown of the Stuarts. He thus at last designates the meaning of the ritual, which we had been content, for the duration of the inquest, to consider merely a trigonometric puzzle, a guide to plotting, and which at the last is restored to its meaning as rite of passage — but in a more nearly world-historical sense, since it was intended as a mnemonic aid to the Cavalier party, to enable the next Charles to recover the crown of his fathers once he had been restored to the throne. Watson says to Holmes at the start of the tale, "These relics have a history, then?" And Holmes replies, "So much so that they *are* history" (p. 198). Between "having a history" and "being history," we move to a deeper level of *fabula,* and the spatio-temporal realization of the story witnessed as Holmes plots out his points on the lawn at the last opens up a vast temporal, historical recess, another story, the history of regicide and restoration, which is brought to light only because of the attempted usurpation of the servant Brunton. As Holmes says at the end, the ritual, the secret of its meaning lost, was passed down from father to son, "until at last it came within reach of a man who tore its secret out of it and lost his life in the venture" (p. 213). Earlier we were told that Brunton was a "schoolmaster out of place" when he entered service with the Musgraves, which may confirm our feeling that usurpation is the act of an intellectual alert to the explosive creative potential of stories. Usurpation is an infraction of order, an attempted change of place, preeminently what it takes to incite narrative into existence: to pull Holmes from his lethargy — described at the start of the tale, as he lies about with his violin and his books, "hardly moving, save from the sofa to the table" — and to begin the plotted life.

What I most wish to stress, in this reading of "The Musgrave Ritual" as an allegory of plot, is how the incomprehensible metaphor of transmission must be unpacked as a metonymy, literally by plotting its cryptic indications out on the lawn. Narrative is this acting out of the implications of metaphor. In its unpacking, the original metaphor is enacted both spatially (the ground plan established by Holmes) and temporally (as we follow Holmes in his pacings and measurements). If the plotting of a solution leads to a place — the crypt with Brunton's body — this opens up temporal constructions — the drama played out between Brunton and Rachel Howells — which redirect attention to the object of Brunton's search, which then in turn opens up a new temporal recess, onto history. If we take metaphor as the paradigmatic axis that marks a synthetic grasp or presentation of a situation, the terminal points of the narrative offer a blinded metaphor of transmission (the ritual as "absurd business") and an enlightened metaphor of transmission (the ritual as part of the history of English monarchy): beginning and end offer a good example of Todorov's "narrative transformation," where start and finish stand in the relation — itself metaphorical — of "the same-but-different."[3] Todorov, however, says little about the dynamic processes of the transformation. What lies between the two related poles is the enactment of the first metaphor as metonymy — and then, a hypothetical and mental enactment of the results thus obtained — in order to establish the second, more fully semiotic metaphor. We start with an inactive, "collapsed" metaphor and work through to a reactivated, transactive one, a metaphor with its difference restored through metonymic process. . . . In "The Musgrave Ritual," we are made to witness in [great] detail the concerted discourse of the transformation, which is no doubt necessary to the detective story, where what is at stake is a gain in knowledge, a self-conscious creation of meaning. But in every case of narrative, it seems fair to say, there must be enactment in order to produce transformation: the plotting-out of initial givens (the ritual, the impasse of misdirected desire) so that their uses may be transformed. Plot, once again, is the active interpretive work of discourse on story.

---

[3]Todorov, "Les Transformations narratives," in *Poétique de la prose,* pp. 225–40.

One could perhaps claim also that the result aimed at by plotting is in some large sense ever the same: the restoration of the possibility of transmission, a goal achieved by the successful transformation of . . . "The Musgrave Ritual." The nineteenth-century novel in particular will play out repeatedly and at length the problem of transmission, staging over and over again the relations of fathers to sons (and also daughters to mothers, aunts, madwomen, and others), asking where an inheritable wisdom is to be found and how its transmission is to be acted toward. If in Benjamin's thesis, to which I alluded earlier, "Death is the sanction of everything that the storyteller can tell," it is because it is at the moment of death that life becomes *transmissible*.[4] The translations of narrative, its slidings-across in the transformatory process of its plot, its movements forward that recover markings from the past in the play of anticipation and retrospection, lead to a final situation where the claim to understanding is incorporate with the claim to transmissibility. One could find some of the most telling illustrations of this claim in the nineteenth century's frequent use of the framed tale which, dramatizing the relations of tellers and listeners, narrators and narratees, regularly enacts the problematic of transmission, looking for the sign of recognition and the promise to carry on, revealing, too, a deep anxiety about the possibility of transmission, as in Marlow's words to his auditors in *Heart of Darkness:* "Do you see the story? Do you see anything?" Here again are questions that will demand fuller discussion later on.

One further lesson drawn from our reading of Sherlock Holmes's reading of the Musgrave ritual needs consideration here. In an essay called "Story and Discourse in the Analysis of Narrative," Jonathan Culler has argued that we need to recognize that narrative proceeds according to a "double logic," in that at certain problematic moments story events seem to be produced by the requirements of the narrative discourse, its needs of meaning, rather than vice-versa, as we normally assume.[5] In other words, the apparently normal claim that *fabula* precedes *sjužet,* which is a reworking of the givens of *fabula,* must be reversed at problematic, challenging moments of narrative, to show that *fabula* is rather produced by the requirements of *sjužet:* that something must have happened because of the results that we know — that, as

---

[4]Walter Benjamin, "The Storyteller," in *Illuminations,* trans. Harry Zohn (New York: Schocken, 1969), p. 94.

[5]Jonathan Culler, "Story and Discourse in the Analysis of Narrative," in *The Pursuit of Signs* (London: Routledge and Kegan Paul, 1981), p. 178. Culler's discussion here is partly in reference to my essay, "Fictions of the Wolfman," *Diacritics 9,* no. 1 (1979), pp. 72–83, which forms the core of chapter 10 of the present study.

Cynthia Chase puts it about Daniel Deronda's Jewishness, "his origin is the effect of its effects."[6] Culler cautions critics against the assumption that these two perspectives can be synthesized without contradiction. The "contradiction" has, I think, been visible and a worry to some of the most perceptive analysts of narrative, and to novelists themselves, for some time: one can read a number of Henry James's discussions in the Prefaces as concerned with how the artificer hides, or glosses over, the contradiction; and Sartre's reflections on how the finalities of telling transform the told — eventually furnishing a basis for his rejection of the novel — touch on the same problem.

Yet I am not satisfied to see the "contradiction" as a literary aporia[7] triumphantly detected by criticism and left at that. The irreconcilability of the "two logics" points to the peculiar work of understanding that narrative is called upon to perform, and to the paralogical status of its "solutions." Let me restate the problem in this way: prior events, causes, are so only retrospectively, in a reading back from the end. In this sense, the metaphoric work of eventual totalization determines the meaning and status of the metonymic work of sequence — though it must also be claimed that the metonymies of the middle produced, gave birth to, the final metaphor. The contradiction may be in the very nature of narrative, which not only uses but *is* a double logic. The detective story, as a kind of dime-store modern version of "wisdom literature," is useful in displaying the double logic most overtly, using the plot of the inquest to find, or construct, a story of the crime which will offer just those features necessary to the thematic coherence we call a solution, while claiming, of course, that the solution has been made necessary by the crime. To quote Holmes at the end of another of his cases, that of "The Naval Treaty": "The principal difficulty in your case . . . lay in the fact of there being too much evidence. What was vital was overlaid and hidden by what was irrelevant. Of all the facts which were presented to us we had to pick just those which we deemed to be essential, and then piece them together in their order so as to reconstruct this very remarkable chain of events." Here we have a clear *ars poetica*, of the detective and of the novelist, and of the plotting of narrative as an example of the mental operation described by Wallace Stevens as "The poem of the mind in the act of finding / What will suffice."

---

[6] Cynthia Chase, "The Decomposition of the Elephants: Double Reading *Daniel Deronda*," *PMLA* 93, no. 2 (1978), p. 218.

[7] *aporia:* An impasse or gap of thought; a paradox. [Editor's note]

GIAN PAOLO CAPRETTINI

# Sherlock Holmes:
# Ethics, Logic, and the Mask

---

This selection is the concluding section of a longer essay, "Peirce, Holmes, Popper," published in *The Sign of Three: Dupin, Holmes, Peirce,* ed. Umberto Eco and Thomas A. Sebeok (Bloomington: Indiana UP, 1983). "Peirce" is Charles Sanders Peirce, the brilliant American philosopher who was one of the founders of semiotics (the science of signs, whether linguistic or nonlinguistic). "Popper" is Karl Popper, a philosopher of science who has investigated the methodology of scientific investigation. As these associations suggest, Caprettini is particularly concerned with Holmes's detective method. While not denying the ethical (more largely, the social) implications of the stories, he stresses Holmes's own separateness from such concerns: "his aim is not ethical but logical" (p. 334).

There are, however, varieties of logic; and Caprettini (along with other contributors to the Eco and Sebeok collection) is careful to point out that Holmes's claim to special powers of "deduction" is imprecise. Holmes's usual method is technically not deductive nor even inductive, but what Peirce labeled "abductive" — a reasoning from a particular result to a particular precedent, a hypothesizing (Peirce himself alternatively called abductions "hypotheses"). Holmes, like a good scientist, conjectures shrewdly; his skill as a detective is indicative of his shrewdness and imaginativeness as a hypothesizer.

A hypothesis, however, is always subject to verification by further testing and may need to be modified or discarded in response to such testing. Here Caprettini analyzes one of Holmes's rare failures as an instance of his uncharacteristic failure to follow his own method.

---

We can easily compare Sherlock Holmes's inner space to an encyclopedia, not only for its variety and vastness of knowledge, but also for the impossibility of having them all under control to the same degree, from the mnemonic point of view: "I may well have but a vague perception of what was there" ("The Lion's Mane"). On the other hand, we know that Holmes makes a great effort to keep them in order, an order which allows him to limit the number of possible associative chains and to come to a conclusion; for instance, to go back to the *Cyanea capillata*[1] in order to explain McPherson's horrible death (ibid.). In this case, memory too works as a mechanism which produces circumstantial evidence: the detective knows that he read "something on that, in a book" (ibid.) whose title he cannot remember. This is enough for him to check his room and find the book he vaguely remembered. As always, Holmes finds what he is looking for because he knows where to look.

Let us go back to the concept of "encyclopedia," more semiotically, in its relation with the "dictionary."[2] . . . Whereas an encyclopedia shows reality through the enumeration of the cultural variables through which its objects are thought, a dictionary uses much more powerful categorical filters and emphasizes the most abstract networks of knowledge. This is the difference between an "historical" and an "ideal" competence of knowledge. Even if Conan Doyle's texts are not detailed on this subject, we have the impression that Holmes dominates the notorious and proliferating vastness of his thought through dictionary-type filters and divisions.

The exclusion of knowledge, however, which is not oriented toward investigation is not Holmes's only precaution to keep his mind completely efficient. A second barrier, as rigid and insuperable as the first one, must be built up against the risk of passions and particularly of "softer passions." Of course, this is valid only in the case of a personal involvement. "They were admirable things for the observer — excellent for drawing the veil from men's motives and actions" ("A Scandal in Bohemia," p. 32). Passion is therefore a shortcut to knowledge, a possible means of getting to the truth without the obstacle of simulation. It is a utopia of transparent signs which guarantee actual knowledge of and control over a universe of circumstantial evidence. But what is most valuable for the observer is dangerous for the thinker: "for the trained reasoner to admit such intrusions into his own delicate and finely adjusted temperament was to introduce a distracting factor which might throw a doubt upon all his mental results. Grit in a sensitive instrument, or a crack in one of his own high-power lenses, would not be more

[1] *Cyanea capillata:* The lion's mane jellyfish, which kills Fitzroy McPherson in the Sherlock Holmes story "The Lion's Mane." [Editor's note]
[2] As postulated in Umberto Eco's *A Theory of Semiotics* (Bloomington: Indiana UP, 1976) 98–100. Eco expands on the topic in *Semiotics and the Philosophy of Language* (Bloomington: Indiana UP, 1984). [Editor's note]

disturbing than a strong emotion in a nature such as his" (p. 32). We could suppose that emotional participation in somebody else's feelings could increase our knowledge (as supported by a certain philosophical current), but Holmes completely refuses this possibility. Feelings and passions are only the object of knowledge, and never its subject. Their "determinism," which helps interpretation by eliminating the masks, obscures the strategic ability of the researcher. Holmes's misogyny — sometimes interpreted as homosexual — has its basis in a theoretical need: if the detective wants his mind to be the mirror of that sequence of causes and effects which ended in a crime, he must get rid of every subjective element of nuisance. The logical purity of his reason should not be disturbed by feeling and pathos. The woman, who has the power of starting illogical (that is, passionate) mechanisms in man's mind, must be strictly excluded from the sphere of analytical and abductive reasoning.

This is proved *ex negativo* the only time Sherlock Holmes loses: it is to a woman — bound to remain for him "*the* woman" (p. 32) — that he suffers this letdown. To be honest, the story does not explicitly ascribe the failure to the intrusion of a passional element. Holmes's feelings that she could have awakened are hidden under an impersonal formulation: "I only caught a glimpse of her at the moment, but she was a lovely woman, with a face that a man might die for" (p. 43). Should we suppose that the enunciator of these words is unconsciously implied in his enunciation? When he expresses regularities in the collective behavior, Holmes usually appears as a detached man: "When a woman thinks that her house is on fire, her instinct is at once to rush to the thing which she values most" (p. 49).The enunciator is the exception who confirms the truth of his enunciations. And this exception is possible because, as opposed to the common man, Holmes knows how to create inside himself a barrier between *pathos* and *logos,* thanks to which the first one never gets mixed up with the second one. This corresponds to the ideal of investigation as a science; that is, a form of knowledge whose validity does not depend upon the empirical features of the investigators.

It is worthwhile to note that in ["A Scandal in Bohemia"] Sherlock Holmes is not in love, but there is at least one bit of circumstantial evidence from which we could suspect a weakening of his intellectual ability. The evening before the final *coup de théâtre,* a person — "a slim youth in an ulster" — says hello to Holmes near his house. He has a rather strange reaction: "Now, I wonder who the deuce that could have been" (p. 49).

It must be pointed out that Holmes had just told Watson that the Irene Adler case was solved, so that he does not begin any new investigation on that. However, this time he forgets his own rules: he disregards a trifle, the mysterious identity of the person who said hello to him, because he does not consider that pertinent to the case he is taking care of. This is a real transgression of the methodology he has successfully applied up to now: Holmes thinks that his receptacle already has all the necessary data. On another occasion, he would have thought of confronting the already-made hypothesis with the *new* (and unexplainable) *fact* which later emerged. Here he does not behave so differently from Watson or from the police: a premature end to the investigation, the refusal of taking into consideration a detail which spoils the harmony of the explanation, the underestimation of "small facts." Directing the lighthouse lamp onto this enigmatic greeting, that is, accepting it as pertinent, Holmes could still modify the dénouement of the story. Why does it not happen, why this time is Holmes won over by laziness? Because of a woman? Is it because Irene Adler's image gets into mechanisms which do not take into account her presence so that she is invisible to Sherlock Holmes's eyes?

The woman, however, fights the detective by his own means: to his masking she opposes her masking. But how many times Holmes, even at the beginning of this story, has been able to recognize the true identity of a person behind a masking! Here is Irene who acts according to all of Holmes's rules; slightly suspicious of the priest who entered her house, she overcomes the laziness which makes one forget the details, and decides to verify her suspicion, following Holmes under a male masking. The situation is reversed. For Holmes camouflage and metamorphosis are a real necessity: as a mythological hero who must put himself in somebody else's place in order to unmask their actions, he must simulate a false identity in order to move efficiently in a world of circumstantial evidence, fictions, and enigmas. The mask allows him to put into action (or to put more rapidly into action) channels of communication which otherwise would not work. In this case, he splits between the function of data-collector and data-processor, which takes place *in his house*. Only here Holmes can take the liberty of keeping his identity unchanged and transparent.

Irene Adler uses the same methods of Sherlock Holmes, and in doing so she unmasks him. Still, if she wins, it is because Holmes neglects to apply his own methods of knowledge. In the letter she leaves for him, she points this out, maybe with a touch of malice: "But, you know, I have been trained as an actress myself. Male costume is nothing new to me" (p. 51). In fact, Holmes forgot to apply his usual procedure. Let us recall one of Peirce's formulations: "x is extraordinary;

however, if y would be true, x would not be extraordinary anymore; so x is possibly true." Here y is known; it would be enough to remember this fact. Therefore Holmes could have inferred as follows: "an unknown person says hello to me; Irene Adler is an actress, so she knows how to look like an unknown person; the person who said hello to me is possibly Irene Adler."

It is a part of the Holmes-hero status that he can be defeated only by a woman, and only once; both these features make Irene Adler "*the* woman." Therefore the woman represents a kind of taboo, a prohibited, excluded space. On the other hand, Dr. Watson represents the transparent and reliable space of complementarity; but this complementarity is necessary. We find here a fairly diffused literary *topos*,[3] from the myth of Don Juan to Faust to Maupassant's tales. The couple servant/master is based on an inextricable connection, where oppositions and differences, functional divisions and alliances meet. Watson's need must be therefore understood in many respects: first of all, he makes possible a hierarchical articulation of knowledge, in which he obviously occupies the humblest position. On the other hand, there would be no right solution by Holmes without wrong ones by Watson: no good master looks as such if not confronted with a bad student. Many conversations between Holmes and Watson are reminiscent of a Socratic dialogue in which the student does not know how to proceed correctly without the continuous help and suggestions of the master, and has a tendency to put forth wrong opinions each time that he works by himself. We get to know, even if only partially, the right principles applied by Holmes just because of Watson's mistakes. Even Watson's blind stubbornness, his persisting in making the same mistakes, is functional in terms of the search for truth, because it allows a new control on the efficacy of the method.

Watson, even if prone to relapse and to be stubborn, is always submissive and always ready to accept his friend's corrections. This creates in a certain way a swinging back and forth of the space between the two characters. Their distance can range from a maximum extension, when they reason separately or when Holmes acts without telling his friend (who is obliged to stand still, passive, waiting for the other's action), to a minimum extension, represented by moments of a full cooperative agreement (to act, listen, wait together). In this second case, identity and agreement are so full as to make completely useless a physical dis-

---

[3] *topos:* A stable combination of features recurring often in literature; a traditional motif. [Editor's note]

tinction between the two. Therefore Holmes tells the prince who wants to speak privately to him: "You may say before this gentleman anything which you may say to me" (p. 37).

It is an ambiguous sentence. We see a highest expression of estimation, but at the same time, a malicious accent; none of Watson's virtues are enough to eliminate a suspicion of him as a wishy-washy man. Holmes knows Watson at least as well as he knows himself; he will never be surprised or disappointed. The hierarchical relation between the two is so solid as to allow the master every kind of manipulation of his servant. In ["The Dying Detective,"] besides the angst of Holmes's illness, he must bear the bitterness of his insults: "after all, you are only a general practitioner with very limited experience and mediocre qualifications." Even if Watson looks hurt, the presumably ill person does not cease to show him how ignorant he is. In fact, we always find in the servant/master *topos* a certain form of sadism, even if a vague and softened one. But we can distinguish between two forms of this *topos*. In the first one, we see the possibility of an overturning of power relations (see *Don Quixote,* when Sancho emancipates himself from his master and takes advantage of his madness). In the second one, the hierarchical relation is not changed, but subordinated to a whole series of undertones, from cordiality and intimacy to an overbearing and complete exploitation of the partner.

From another point of view, Holmes and Watson do not appear in a relation of subordination and apparent complementarity, but in a relation of alternance and compensation. Watson's aspiration is to a quiet family ménage; when he decides to marry, his happiness and his home-centered interests constitute all his problems. Holmes does not look for a moral integration into the society he protects from crime:

> Holmes, who loathed every form of society with his whole Bohemian soul, remained in our lodgings in Baker Street, buried among his old books, and alternating from week to week between cocaine and ambition, the drowsiness of the drug, and the fierce energy of his own keen nature. He was still, as ever, deeply attracted by the study of crime, and occupied his immense faculties and extraordinary powers of observation in following out those clues, and clearing up those mysteries, which had been abandoned as hopeless by the official police. ("A Scandal in Bohemia," p. 33)

But the features "Bohemian soul" and "every form of society" are not to be opposed conflictually, but are to be intended as complementary. Both characters represent a reconciliation of opposites: Holmes alternates an indomitable energy with periods of apathy, stressed by co-

caine, and Watson alternates quiet family ménage and work to often
dangerous adventures which keep him away from his daily world. But
thanks to their duplicity they often have a reciprocal relation of harmony. When Holmes is apathetic, Watson is found to be active; and
when Holmes puts his extraordinary ability into action, Watson is reduced to a slow, incapable, absentminded but always faithful disciple.
Each is, in his own way, incapable of doing something on his own ini-
tiative: Holmes's relation with the world is always defined by a request
("a lack," according to Russian formalists). Holmes is always called to
play a role of mender or transformer (to use cultural anthropologists'
jargon). He can — as can heroes, semigods, priests, shamans — overcome and eliminate contradictions in reality. He acts only when his ambition and his perspicacious nature are stimulated by some worthy fact.
Watson too is pushed to act by a causality which is not inside him, and
this causality is Holmes, symbolically represented in the beginning of
["A Scandal in Bohemia"]. Watson walks along Baker Street and feels
like seeing his old friend again. When he sees Holmes's silhouette passing over and over energetically behind the window of his room, any
hesitation becomes impossible: "To me, who knew his every mood and
habit, his attitude and manner told their own story. He was at work
again" (p. 33). Here is Watson, involved in a new adventure, recalled to
his function of narrator, that is, the role of passive witness of Holmes's
activity.

The perfect knowledge he shows of his partner is remarkable. As to
knowledge of attitude, Watson is on the same level of Holmes, balancing with that the rigid subordination which is established when we
move on the investigative method's level. This probably recalls another
of Sherlock Holmes's duplicities: his aim is not ethical but logical. To
follow traces, to reveal enigmas, to explain mysteries: to bring back the
chaos of clues to a world of signs. After this, his mission is over, and the
police are the ones to enjoy the moral advantages of success. Holmes
complains of that only to a certain extent. If he never gives himself up
to jealousy, rivalry, narcissism, it is just because he knows that his power
does not go beyond the sphere of *logos*. We can say — as in an admired
sentence by Watson: "You would certainly have been burned had you
lived a few centuries ago" (p. 34) — that Holmes acts as a sorcerer or a
diviner, in charge of unveiling some supposed mysteries. He is the ora-
cle of ancient societies, showing everybody the truth. And his theoretical power ends where the practical one, that of justice, starts.

(Translated from the Italian by Roberto Cagliero)

JOHN A. HODGSON

# The Recoil of "The Speckled Band": Detective Story and Detective Discourse

Like Brooks's essay, Hodgson's owes much to narratology and shows particular interest in the interplay of story and discourse within a plot. But where Brooks stresses the reader's "plottings," Hodgson stresses the writer's. Building upon the analogies between detecting and reading and between criminal and authorial plotting, he suggests that the implicit "game" between the author and reader of detective fiction may be more playful than is usually recognized; and in playfully reading "The Speckled Band" as a particularly provocative "invitation to detection," he puts the two planes of narrative, story and discourse, into play with and against each other as guides to alternative and incompatible readings of the text. This deconstructive procedure, though it involves planes of narrative rather than (as is more usual) competing rhetorical effects or ideologies, relates this essay in important respects to others in this collection, especially those by Catherine Belsey and Audrey Jaffe.

Hodgson's essay originally appeared in *Poetics Today* 13 (1992): 309–24.

"You seem to know a lot about [Sherlock Holmes]."

"On the contrary, any Sherlockian would tell you I know nothing about him, except what I picked up as a child reading. . . . Do you think Charlotte Lucas sleeps below a false vent, and is visited nightly by a dangerous snake who responds to whistles?"

"What a memory you have."

"Everyone remembers that."

–AMANDA CROSS, *No Word from Winifred*, 1986

## I

"If you ask the ordinary reader which of the Sherlock Holmes short stories he likes best," Jacques Barzun observes in *The Delights of Detection*, "the chances are that he will say: 'The Speckled Band'" (Barzun 1980 [1961]: 150). There is much evidence to support Barzun's guess. Perhaps the true Holmes afficionado is no ordinary reader; if you ask this same question, though, the chances are very good that get the same answer. Thus readers of the *Strand* magazine, where the Sherlock Holmes stories originally appeared, ranked "The Adventure of the Speckled Band" first among the forty-four stories by then collected in book form in 1927; in the same year readers of the *Observer* ranked it first among all of the adventures, short stories, and novels; the Baker Street Irregulars, in a 1944 poll of members, also placed it first and, at their 1959 "one hundredth anniversary" dinner, again named the story as far and away their first choice; also in that year, a survey taken by the *Baker Street Journal* produced the same result (Bigelow 1976: 47–50; Baring-Gould 1967: I, 262).

Such enthusiasm for the story is not surprising, for certainly "The Speckled Band" has its power. "The vision of the snake coming down the bell pull is the utmost thrill [the ordinary reader] expects from detection," Barzun sniffs, himself disappointed that in this adventure Doyle let "sensationalism" dominate "the detective interest" (Barzun 1980 [1961]: 150). But this hardly does justice to the story, which has its strong detective interest, too. Still, that detective interest seems remarkably uncharacteristic of Conan Doyle in some unsettling ways. The appeal of Sherlock Holmes, after all, comes from his method and his skillful application of it. Holmes is the master reasoner, diagnostician, interpreter: he not only sees (Watson can do as much), he makes sense of what he sees, thanks to his vast store of useful, if often esoteric, knowledge and his highly developed powers of inference. But in "The Speckled Band" Holmes makes nonsense of what he sees; here, to a degree unmatched elsewhere in the canon, his method is not merely shaky, but overtly and devastatingly flawed.[1] As a recent writer for the popular press only begins to summarize:

> Snakes don't have ears, so they cannot hear a low whistle. Snakes can't climb ropes. Snakes can't survive in an airtight safe. There's no such thing as an Indian swamp adder. No snake poison could have killed a huge man like Grimesby Roylott instantly. (Murphy 1987: 65)

That such extravagances of plot and errors of fact, many of them howlers, should not particularly trouble that poor straw man, the ordinary

---

[1]Thus in a recent, impressive collection of scholarly essays bearing on Conan Doyle's and Holmes's methods, *The Sign of Three: Dupin, Holmes, Peirce* (Eco and Sebeok 1983), "The Speckled Band" goes almost entirely unnoticed. This is rather like the famously "curious incident of the dog in the night-time" recounted in "Silver Blaze" (curious, in that "the dog did nothing in the night-time" [p. 190]): it seems noteworthy that this particularly popular story contributes nothing to the evidence of Holmes's method.

reader, is no surprise. It is mildly surprising, perhaps, that the Irregulars and other Holmes enthusiasts should not balk at them. But that Conan Doyle, who took pride in having created "a scientific detective who solved cases on his own merits and not through the folly of the criminal" (Doyle 1924: 21), should have himself ranked the story as his very best — which he explicitly did, listing it first (both "in popular favor and in my own esteem") on the "twelve best" list he drew up for the June 1927 issue of the *Strand* (Doyle 1980 [1927]: 209) — is very surprising indeed. How could so absurd a solution have pleased so analytical a writer?

The very question, of course, is itself an invitation to detection. As Holmes says in *The Hound of the Baskervilles*, "The more *outré* and grotesque an incident is, the more carefully it deserves to be examined," and, in "The Boscombe Valley Mystery," "Singularity is almost invariably a clue" (p. 91).[2] The singular, exaggerated badness of "The Speckled Band's" solution is worth investigating. And indeed, its incongruities and impossibilities so violate the laws of the detective-story genre as to be criminal. Perhaps they are.

Does not "The Adventure of the Speckled Band" itself warn us of this? "When a doctor does go wrong he is the first of criminals. He has nerve and he has knowledge" (p. 169). So Holmes — whose creator, Conan Doyle, was himself a doctor — suggests of Dr. Grimesby Roylott, the villain of this story (and the only villainous doctor in the Holmes canon). The possible parallel of life with literature here is intriguing. What if a master writer of detective stories should "go wrong"? Perhaps we should not too quickly dismiss as mere bumbling what might well be the work of the first of literary criminals.

## II

When I speak of "The Adventure of the Speckled Band" as criminally violating the laws of its genre, I refer above all to the laws, not merely of detective fiction, but of realism itself. In this story Holmes does not merely diagnose more acutely and interpret more shrewdly than an untrained and less knowledgeable observer, such as Watson, might. Rather, he reasons — illogically — from the available evidence to infer the existence of a deadly serpent that not only does not "in fact" exist, but that cannot even presumably exist. This is a far different case

[2] Here again "The Speckled Band" invites particular attention: of all the cases in which he has studied Holmes's methods, Watson tells us, "I cannot recall any which presented more singular features than that which was associated with the well-known Surrey family of the Roylotts of Stoke Moran" (p. 152).

from the kind of mistake central to Dorothy Sayers's *Documents in the Case*. In Sayers's work the detection turns on the fact that the organic and synthetic versions of poisons occurring naturally in toadstools can be distinguished by their different light-polarizing properties. As "a very polite professor of chemistry" informed Sayers soon after the book's appearance, however, "[her] general theory was quite all right, but Muscarin [the particular poison featured in her plot] was an exception. Natural Muscarin didn't play fair. It didn't twist the ray of the polarised light any more than the synthetic kind" (Guillard 1981: 8). So the crucial act of detection in Sayers's plot is invalid; yet it seems credible, and indeed Sayers herself and her scientific collaborator, Robert Eustace (Dr. Eustace Robert Barton), took pains to make it so. Conan Doyle's deadly serpent, however, is not merely farfetched, but epistemically impossible.[3] Even granting Holmes's (and Roylott's) fantastic knowledge, unshared by all zoologists then and since, of a snake of such unprecedented poisonousness, a snake that can survive (apparently for more than two years, since the time of Julia Stoner's engagement and death) in an iron safe, a snake that drinks from a saucer of milk, still we cannot grant those additional premises upon which all of Holmes's conjecture depends — that the snake could hear a low whistle and could climb back up a Victorian bellpull. No snake, however exotic, could do these things, any more than it could fly. The knowledge of these snakish limitations, moreover, is not esoteric (indeed, the snake's deafness is proverbial: cf. Psalms 58:4–5); even a Watson might well know, at the very least, that snakes don't have external ears and can't hear low whistles.[4]

Thus "The Adventure of the Speckled Band," like its villain, is fatally wounded by its own deadly serpent. But is this wounding a crime, rather than an error? What kind of "going wrong" is it? There are rules for these critical detections, too, and perhaps it will be objected that I am myself behaving unlawfully as a critic by positing the criminality of the author. On the contrary: my analogy lies at the very heart of the detective-story genre.

There are two vitally balanced relationships central to the detective story. The first, central indeed to an even larger range of literature, is that obtaining between detective and criminal, pursuer and pursued. Opposed though they may be, these characters have, as is widely recognized, much in common. At the very least, detection often depends

---

[3]"Epistemically impossible": I recur to Michel Foucault (1970 [1966]: xxii et passim) for the concept, but the phrase is also used by Robert Champigny (1977: 22).
[4]Thus a contemporaneous edition of the *Encyclopædia Britannica* notes: "The structure of the ear in serpents seems to demonstrate that these creatures are dull in their sense of hearing" (8th ed., s.v. "serpents").

upon the detective's imaginative ability to identify with his opponent, if only temporarily. Thus Poe's Auguste Dupin solves the mystery of "The Purloined Letter" by identifying his own intellect with that of his opponent (Poe 1978: III, 984); and Holmes similarly reminds Watson (in "The Musgrave Ritual"), "You know my method in such cases . . . I put myself in the man's place, and having first gauged his intelligence, I try to imagine how I should myself have proceeded under the same circumstances" (p. 210). Toward the extreme — or the epitome — of the genre, detective and criminal approach very close to a shared identity. So it is with Holmes and his great adversary, Professor Moriarty. "What will [Moriarty] do?" Watson asks, in "The Final Problem." Holmes knows the answer: "What I should do. . . . Moriarty will again do what I should do" (p. 223). And so it is in "The Purloined Letter" with Dupin and the villainous Minister D——, who are pointedly doubles of each other, perhaps even brothers (Wilbur 1962: 380; Babener 1987 [1972]: 46–50; Hoffman 1972: 131–32; Derrida 1975: 109). At the very extreme, finally, detective and criminal are one and the same. Although both Ronald Knox, in his "Detective Story Decalogue," and S. S. Van Dine, in his "Twenty Rules for Writing Detective Stories," presumed to forbid this, insisting that "the detective must not himself commit the crime" (Knox 1946 [1929]: 196; cf. Van Dine 1946 [1928]: 190), the commandment has come to seem not only narrow-minded but even misguided; witness Robin Winks's flat statement, "The ideal detective story is one in which the detective hero discovers that he (or she) is the criminal" (Winks 1980: 5).[5] The classic instance of the detective as the criminal, of course, is Oedipus. But even at the beginnings of detection proper, in the *Mémoires* of François Vidocq (the former criminal who became chief of detectives in Paris), the pattern recurs: once Vidocq, as a police spy, was assigned to investigate a crime which he himself had committed.[6] Similarly, in Wilkie Collins's

---

[5]Winks seems to be following Charles Rycroft's 1957 remark: "In the ideal detective story, the detective or hero would discover that he himself is the criminal for whom he has been seeking" (quoted in Symons 1972: 7). See also Helmut Heissenbuttel (1983 [1963]: 91). As early as 1933, Sayers's Peter Wimsey is alluding casually to "those detective stories where the detective turns out to be the villain" (Sayers 1967 [1933]: 185). The prologue to Julian Symons's 1949 *Bland Beginning* suggests how conventional this identification had already become: "Posit Willshard/Glibbery, the great detective, as the murderer. Commonplace? Perhaps — but let his murderous identity stay unrevealed, let him be a schizophrene making the most urgent efforts with Detectial Personality Number 1 to unravel the tangle made for him by Murderous Personality Number 2" (Symons 1987 [1949]: vii).

[6]Cited by Gavin Lambert (1980 [1975]: 50). (This passage does not appear in the heavily revised, 1976 American edition of Lambert's book.) Cf. Ian Ousby (1976: 13, citing in particular Jonathan Wild).

*The Moonstone,* the first English detective novel, Franklin Blake initiates and sustains the search for the stolen moonstone until, to his astonishment, "I had discovered Myself as the Thief" (Collins 1966 [1868]: 359). And in Israel Zangwill's important early detective story *The Big Bow Mystery,* the famous retired detective George Grodman concludes his investigation of the murder by confessing his own guilt, intending that his confession should "form the basis of an appendix to the twenty-fifth edition . . . of my book, *Criminals I Have Caught*" (Zangwill 1986 [1891]: 148). A variation on the pattern also informs "The Purloined Letter," as Dupin solves the original crime by duplicating it — and was perhaps the author of the originally purloined letter, even as he was of its replacement (Hoffman 1972: 131).

The second vital relationship of the detective story exists in a curious equilibrium with the first. This second relationship is that obtaining between the author and the reader. As writers, readers, and critics of classic detective fiction have generally agreed, the detective story is a veritable game between two players, the author and the reader: hence the widespread interest in "the rules of the game" (Haycraft 1946: 187; Van Dine 1946 [1928]: 189; Knox 1946 [1929]: 194; Caillois 1983 [1941]; Heissenbutel 1983 [1963]), and the continual recurrence by critics and apologists to chess and even sporting events to explain the genre's appeal (Nicolson 1946 [1929]: 118–22; Van Dine 1946 [1928]: 189, 191; Knox 1946 [1929]: 194–96). The "game" analogy, of course, comes directly from Poe's "Murders in the Rue Morgue" (on the mere complexity and "elaborate frivolity" of chess versus the profundity of draughts and whist [Poe 1978 [1841]: II, 528–30]) and from "The Purloined Letter" (on the game of "even and odd" [ibid. [1845]: III, 984]) — where it is, however, a model for the relationship of the criminal and the detective. But the transition to the second relationship is a natural one, for reading is itself a form of detection. The analogousness of reader to detective is thus central to any poetics of the genre. As Kathleen Klein and Joseph Keller note,

> The criminal's truth generates a fiction, an allegory whose key is hidden, an illusion of which the alibi is an important if not the most important part. The detective's method results in an interpretation of this fiction, a hermeneutic. (Klein and Keller 1986: 162)

But if the reader is a detective, what is the author? Sherlock Holmes himself insinuates the answer to Watson when he alludes, at the beginning of a case ("The Crooked Man"), to the effect of some of these little sketches of yours, which is entirely meretricious, depending as it does upon your retaining in your own hands some factors in the problem which are never imparted to the reader. Now, at present I am in the position of these same readers, for I hold in this hand several threads of one of the strangest cases which ever perplexed a man's brain, and yet I lack the one or two which are needful to complete my theory.

Dorothy Sayers drove her *Omnibus of Crime* at this point almost sixty years ago when she noted that the seasoned reader of detective stories, "instead of detecting the murderer ... is engaged in detecting the writer" (Sayers 1946 [1929]: 108); Tzvetan Todorov similarly implies it in observing that "we have no need to follow the detective's ingenious logic to discover the killer — we need merely refer to the much simpler law of the author of murder mysteries" (Todorov 1977 [1971]: 86). As Dennis Porter notes, criminal and detective "stand in relation to each other as a problem maker to a problem solver and thus repeat inside the novel the relationship that exists between author and reader" (Porter 1981: 88). The analogy insists on the author's being a type of the criminal.

We tend to regard "bad" writing as simply uncontrolled or inexpert (hence our usual figurative labels for it — "clumsy," "careless," "crude," "awkward," "immature," "inconsistent," "overwrought," "silly"), and we do not usually think of a story as committing a kind of crime. But sometimes it does; and one of our terms for such a crime is "hoax." I hesitate to suggest that "The Adventure of the Speckled Band" is a hoax, exactly. Roylott's speckled serpent is no red herring — although it may be something of a gold bug. Yet neither is it simply that absurd swamp adder, which does not and cannot "really" exist. The story's more significant crime, I would propose, is not the impossible crime that it ostensibly recounts, but the crime that it commits; yet for this crime, too, Doyle offers a resolution, although on an entirely different level of narrative.

### III

The doubleness of "The Adventure of the Speckled Band" — a story about twins — is already implicit in its ambivalent title. Here we find another of those singularities which Holmes himself thinks so important as clues. This is the only story in the canon, I believe, that involves a pun in its title. "O, my God! Helen! It was the band! The speckled band!" are the dying Julia Stoner's last words (p. 158). "What did you gather from this allusion to a band — a speckled band?"

Holmes asks Helen Stoner, and she guesses "that it may have referred to some band of people, perhaps to these very gypsies in the planta-tion," many of whom wear spotted handkerchiefs over their heads (p. 159). Holmes, of course, is dissatisfied; nevertheless, he too is misled:

> I had . . . come to an entirely erroneous conclusion, which shows, my dear Watson, how dangerous it always is to reason from insuffi-cient data. The presence of the gipsies, and the use of the word "band," which was used by the poor girl, no doubt, to explain the appearance which she had caught a hurried glimpse of by the light of her match, were sufficient to put me upon an entirely wrong scent. (p. 172)

Thus "the speckled band" — not the serpent but the phrase — *is* a false scent, a red herring. But, curiously, Helen Stoner's wrong guess is partly righted by the snake's final appearance: bound tightly around Roylott's brow, the snake is indeed a spotted headband. Thus the title is effec-tively, rhetorically misleading; yet the "entirely wrong scent" fortu-itously recrosses "the right track" (p. 172). Just so does it happen with the story itself.

In keeping with its doubly significant title, "The Adventure of the Speckled Band" contains within itself two paradigms — one active, one discursive — for its story. The first of these we may call the story's syn-ecdochic[7] paradigm: it constitutes part of the story itself, rather than of the discourse only. This episode occurs when Dr. Roylott tries to warn Holmes off of the case:

> "I am a dangerous man to fall foul of! See here." He stepped swiftly forward, seized the poker, and bent it into a curve with his huge brown hands.
> "See that you keep yourself out of my grip," he snarled, and hurl-ing the twisted poker into the fireplace, he strode out of the room.
> "He seems a very amiable person," said Holmes, laughing. "I am not quite so bulky, but if he had remained I might have shown him that my grip was not much more feeble than his own." As he spoke he picked up the steel poker, and with a sudden effort straightened it out again. (p. 162)

Here is encapsulated the typical plan of the detective story: the detective counters and reverses the actions of the criminal, restoring matters to their proper state, making straight what the criminal has made crooked. At the same time, though, here is another red herring. Roylott is indeed

---

[7] *synecdochic:* A synecdoche is a figure of speech substituting a part for the whole, or vice versa. [Editor's note]

a violent, fierce-tempered "man of immense strength," who leaves the mark of his grip on his stepdaughter's wrist, who recently "hurled the local blacksmith over a parapet into a stream," and who once, in India, "beat his native butler to death" (p. 155). But he is most dangerous to his stepdaughters not as a brute, but as a doctor; his deepest villainy is not confrontational but subtle. This episode, then, is seriously misleading as a clue to Roylott's dangerousness.

The second paradigm of "The Speckled Band" is not mimetic but metaphoric: it comprises part of the discourse but not of the story. This paradigm takes shape in a number of hints, culminating in Holmes's postmortem summation. After Roylott "trace[s]" Helen Stoner to Holmes's sitting room (p. 161), Holmes reassures her, "He must guard himself, for he may find that there is someone more cunning than himself upon his track" (pp. 163–64). That evening, after investigating Miss Stoner's room and discovering Roylott's plot, Holmes notes, "This man strikes even deeper [than earlier doctor-criminals], but I think, Watson, that we shall be able to strike deeper still" (p. 169). And finally, after Roylott is killed by his own serpent, Holmes moralizes, "Violence does, in truth, recoil upon the violent, and the schemer falls into the pit which he digs for another" (pp. 171–72). Here is the apter paradigm for the story of this particular detection — retaliation by repetition: the crime is not merely undone but redone, the criminal not only defeated but victimized by his own devices. From Poe's "Purloined Letter" (if not, indeed, from Dante), Conan Doyle learned how a detection, no less than a punishment, could duplicate a crime. In "The Adventure of the Speckled Band," he offers his own version of this significant redundancy.

## IV

The breakthrough for Holmes's detection in "The Adventure of the Speckled Band" comes when he tugs on the bellpull in Julia Stoner's bedroom and makes an interesting discovery: "Why, it's a dummy" (p. 165). Roylott's plot involves many such devices: "dummy bell-ropes, and ventilators which do not ventilate" (p. 166), and a safe which contains, rather than excludes, danger. Holmes solves the case when he sees through the figuratively innocuous disguises of these accessories to discern their deadly actual uses. We, in turn, in order to discover the deeper, satisfactory resolution of this apparently flawed story, must read its literal clues figuratively, recognizing them as features not of an actual scene, but of a textual one.

The real dummy of this suspicious story, the apparently murderous device which proves to be only figuratively deadly, is that impossible snake, whose insinuation into the story constitutes Doyle's literary crime. Our recognition of the snake as mere figure enables our own interpretive breakthrough. Once we can realize, "why, *it's* a dummy," we, like Holmes, are finally "on the right track" (p. 172).

That track, like the very different one Holmes follows, soon leads us to "one or two very singular points" (p. 165) about the scene. There is, to begin with, the matter of those oddly unfamiliar names. "Grimesby Roylott," especially: what manner of name is this? Even Donald Redmond, in his exhaustive (nearly 400 pages) source study of "the personal names . . . with which Conan Doyle christened his cast" (Redmond 1982: xiv), draws a rare blank here: "The oddest thing about his name is that neither part of it can be found anywhere" (ibid.: 52). Does "Grimesby" simply suggest "grim"? (In placing "The Speckled Band" first on his top-twelve list for the *Strand,* Doyle called it "a grim snake story" [Doyle 1980 {1927}: 209].) "Grime?" "Crime?" (Grimesby Roylott = "Crimes by Roylott"?) "Stoke Moran," we might also note, contains an anagrammatic "snake" (even a "snake o' mort"). And indeed, Watson's initial presentation of the names, the "Roylotts of Stoke Moran," permutes itself anagrammatically into "snake story tomfool rot."

Such Poesque name games are not typical of Conan Doyle — although we might, after all, sense a faintly Poesque self-reflexiveness in Doyle's emphasis on Holmes's "Bohemian soul" in "A Scandal in Bohemia," or his siting "a manufactory of artificial knee-caps" at one dead end of the story ("The Red-headed League") that stresses the evidence afforded by a suspect's knees. The anagram, accordingly, is by itself more curious than convincing. But similarly subversive hints infuse many other aspects of the story as well. Consider, for example, how the secondary instruments of Roylott's criminal plot figuratively evoke the generic plot of detective fiction itself. Roylott's ventilator does not ventilate, his bellpull will not ring any bell, his safe is dangerous. But Holmes, in figuring out Roylott's real devices, realizes Roylott's figures: the dummy bellpull, although useless for calling the foolish housekeeper who was so easily gotten out of the way, "rings a bell" of summons and alarm in Holmes's mind; he "ventilates" Roylott's scheme; he acts to make all truly "safe." Roylott's dummies are Doyle's truths, just as Roylott's truth (the snake) is Doyle's dummy.

A sense of ambivalent self-awareness also resonates within the narrative's two paradigms of its own action. Both paradigms allude pointedly to biblical contexts. The first, synecdochic paradigm, mimetic but misleading — Roylott threateningly bends and twists the poker, and Holmes "straighten[s] it out again" — sports with a Solomonic aphorism. "That which is crooked cannot be made straight" (Eccles. 1:15), the Preacher of Ecclesiastes insists; more accurately, as both John the Baptist and his antitype Isaiah declare, he who makes crooked things straight is God (Isa. 40:4, 42:16; Luke 3:5). But what if an author himself makes something crooked? The Preacher knows of such things — "Consider the work of God: for who can make that straight, which he hath made crooked?" (Eccles. 7:13). And the Scriptures elsewhere specify "that . . . which he hath made crooked": "his hand hath formed the crooked serpent" (Job 26:13).

For the second, metaphorical paradigm of the story, showing the criminal victimized by his own devices, Holmes himself leads us directly to the biblical source. "The schemer falls into the pit which he digs for another," he moralizes to Watson. The wisdom is again Solomon's: "He that diggeth a pit shall fall into it" (Eccles. 10:8; see also Proverbs 26:27). And here again, the text points to the snake, for the verse from Ecclesiastes continues, "And whoso breaketh a hedge, a serpent shall bite him."

Thus, if "The Adventure of the Speckled Band" commits a literary crime by breaking the laws of its genre, it nevertheless works also to detect this crime and to resolve it — which is to say, it remains true to its genre. But this resolution, appropriately, is itself strictly a literary one. While Conan Doyle has "plotted" against his readers (to read the story literally is to be victimized), he has also dug deeper again than his own deep digging; and at this level he has not, after all, broken the "hedge," the limits and rules, of his chosen genre.

"The Speckled Band" is, then, something like a critical work masquerading as a literary one: it is not about detecting a crime, but about defining a crime-detecting genre. Seeming to violate and thus to undermine that genre, Conan Doyle actually respects it and, at a deeper level, remains true to it. And surely he enjoyed thus cutting deeper than his protagonist's cultists could ever plow. As Holmes says of Moriarty in "The Final Problem," "My horror at his crimes was lost in my admiration at his skill" (p. 217). Conan Doyle had good reason to admire "The Adventure of the Speckled Band" as the best of his stories.

## V

So "The Speckled Band," like certain works by such notable enthusiasts of detective fiction as Borges and Nabokov, tells two very different stories, or rather two very different versions of a single story. It operates to contradictory effect at two different levels, telling alternatively of Roylott's crime or of Doyle's, offering alternatively a narrated or an incompatible "literary" detection and resolution.

These two levels have other names, names that I have already introduced without comment. They correspond exactly to what narratology discriminates as "story" (or *histoire*, or *fabula* — "the content plane of narrative . . . the 'what' of a narrative") versus "discourse" (or *sjužhet* — "the expression plane of narrative . . . the 'how' of a narrative") (Prince 1987: 91, 21; see also Culler 1981: 169–71). Indeed, theorists of narrative have taken a particular interest in detective stories precisely because such fiction isolates these two levels so starkly as "the story of the crime" (story, *fabula*) and "the story of the investigation" (discourse, *sjužhet*) (Todorov 1977 [1971]: 45); as Peter Brooks notes, "Narrative always makes the implicit claim to be in a state of repetition, as a going over again of a ground already covered: a *sjužhet* repeating the *fabula*, as the detective retraces the tracks of the criminal" (Brooks 1985 [1984]: 97). But if detective fiction typically suggests "a laying-bare of the structure of all narrative in that it dramatizes the role of *sjužhet* and *fabula* and the nature of their relation" (ibid.: 25), "The Adventure of the Speckled Band" also particularly dramatizes a complicating and blurring of these roles.

Consider again the tale's two paradigms of its own action. The first of these, the episode of the twisted and untwisted poker, I have labeled "active" and "synecdochic" because it is an enactment that is part of the story itself; we might equally well call it a "story-paradigm." The second paradigm, the motif of retaliation by repetition ("This man strikes even deeper, but I think, Watson, that we shall be able to strike deeper still"; "Violence does, in truth, recoil upon the violent, and the schemer falls into the pit which he digs for another"), is in contrast "discursive" and "metaphoric": it recounts rather than enacts, and it proposes a similarity between different signifieds, this paradigm not being part of the story. We can call this one a "discourse-paradigm." These two particular paradigms of detection are figuratively quite dissimilar, almost opposite — a straightening out versus a doubling under or back or around, reversal versus repetition, the crime undone versus the crime redone — but nonetheless entirely compatible with each other, like the two sides of a single door. Indeed, to some degree the patterns of both paradigms — in the former, reversal; in the latter, repetition — will always be present in detective fiction, since these correspond to the dual movement (backward to causes or origins, forward to effects or conclusions) of detective-fiction hypothesis and hypothesis-testing (Sebeok and Umiker-Sebeok 1983: 19–28, 39–41; Truzzi 1983 [1973]: 61–71; Bonfantini and

Proni 1983: 119–28). But how then can we dismiss the former paradigm as a false trail, a red herring, in "The Speckled Band"? It is false or misleading, we recognize, with reference to the story; with reference to the detection, the discourse, it is apt. The story-paradigm of "The Speckled Band" is paradigmatic of the discourse.

The discourse-paradigm of "The Speckled Band," on the other hand, is paradigmatic of the story. It is not, however, paradigmatic of the discourse, which follows no such pattern of retaliation by repetition — not paradigmatic of the discourse, that is, *unless* we entertain some such notion of that discourse's duplicity as I have been advancing here. To do this is also to read Doyle's (not Watson's) "story" as an exercise in distorting and restoring its genre — a meta-story for which the story-paradigm now becomes fitting.

Jonathan Culler has noted that every narrative involves an "irreconcilable opposition, a conflict between two logics" (Culler 1981: 187) founded alternatively on the assumed precedence of story or of discourse: in one, "the discourse is seen as a representation of events which must be thought of as independent of that particular representation," while in the other, "the so-called events are thought of as the postulates or products of a discourse" (ibid.: 186). "One logic assumes the primacy of events; the other treats the events as the products of meanings" (ibid.: 178). "The Adventure of the Speckled Band" not only illustrates this conflict, but points up some of its deeper implications.

A discourse tells a story in a double sense, Culler is arguing: it recounts or relates a prior and independent sequence of events, but then again it shapes these events by its "demands of signification" (ibid.: 175), "suggesting by its implicit claims to significance that these events are justified by their appropriateness to a thematic structure" (ibid.: 178). This doubleness, we might add, suggests one way of understanding how a story can have many discourses (cf. Chatman 1978: 123): the different tellings advance different claims to significance. But this double logic of narrative also suggests — and a narrative such as "The Adventure of the Speckled Band" confirms — that, just as a story may have more than one discourse, so may a discourse have more than one story. The story of the discourse may not be simply or exclusively identifiable with the discoursed story.

## VI

A final problem: In 1894, so the familiar anecdote goes, feeling that he had fallen into a literary rut and anxious to devote himself to grander fictions, Arthur Conan Doyle decided to put an end to his Sherlock

Holmes tales by killing off his protagonist. Accordingly, he wrote for the *Strand* and for the conclusion of *Memoirs of Sherlock Holmes* a valedictory and epitaphic tale, "The Final Problem," recounting Holmes's to-the-death struggle with his archenemy, Moriarty, at the Falls of Reichenbach. The tale recalls "The Adventure of the Speckled Band" in several interesting respects. Like "The Speckled Band," wherein Watson counters the "widespread rumours as to the death of Dr. Grimesby Roylott which tend to make the matter even more terrible than the truth" (p. 152), "The Final Problem" professes to be an alternative retelling of a story: two "extremely condensed" accounts have appeared in the press, and now, Watson says, "my hand has been forced . . . by the recent letters in which Colonel James Moriarty defends the memory of his brother" through "an absolute perversion of the facts" that "endeavoured to clear his memory by attacks upon" Holmes (pp. 214, 229). While the slender, ascetic-looking Professor Moriarty is superficially quite different from the huge and brutish Dr. Roylott, he is nevertheless what Holmes calls Roylott, "the first of criminals" (p. 169): "He is the Napoleon of crime, Watson," and stands "on a pinnacle in the records of crime" (p. 216). Like Roylott, Moriarty personally calls on Holmes to warn him off. Moriarty's "curiously reptilian fashion" of oscillating his face from side to side (p. 218) and the deadly threat of his presence recall Roylott's serpent; and his warning, "You must stand clear, Mr. Holmes, or be trodden under foot" (p. 219), especially in this context of a final, supreme struggle, invokes (inversely, from Holmes's point of view) the prophecy made to the serpent in Genesis 3:15: "It shall bruise thy head, and thou shalt bruise his heel." The motif of the pursuer pursued also recurs in the later story ("One would think that we were the criminals," Watson grumbles about the precautions that Holmes deems necessary for evading Moriarty [p. 223]), as does the very imagery of retaliatory undercutting ("He cut deep," Holmes says of his intellectual contest with Moriarty, "and yet I just undercut him" [p. 217]).

But the discourse of "The Final Problem," like that of "The Speckled Band," has another story. What appears to be a dead end ("The path has been cut half-way round the [Reichenbach] fall to afford a complete view, but it ends abruptly, and the traveller has to return as he came" [p. 226]) is not.

"I alone know the absolute truth of the matter," Watson announces (p. 214). He has arrived at the dénouement of this truth by following Holmes's example. What had happened, he wonders, when Moriarty overtook Holmes?

I stood for a minute or two to collect myself, for I was dazed with the horror of the thing. Then I began to think of Holmes's own methods and to try to practise them in reading this tragedy. It was, alas! only too easy to do. (p. 227)

All signs of that meeting and struggle, including a brief farewell note from Holmes, indicate that

> a personal contest between the two men ended, as it could hardly fail to end in such a situation, in their reeling over, locked in each other's arms. Any attempt at recovering the bodies was absolutely hopeless, and there, deep down in that dreadful cauldron of swirling water and seething foam, will lie for all time the most dangerous criminal and the foremost champion of the law of their generation. (pp. 228–29)

Nine years later, however, in response to immense and sustained popular demand (and strong financial inducements), Conan Doyle brought Sherlock Holmes back to literary life. As he later commented, "I had fully determined at the conclusion of *The Memoirs* to bring Holmes to an end. . . . I did the deed, but fortunately no coroner had pronounced upon the remains, and so, after a long interval, it was not difficult for me to . . . explain my rash act away." But in doing so he thereby made a mockery of Watson's essay in detection at the end of the story, where Watson reads the signs of Holmes's struggle with Moriarty to mean that his friend is surely dead. The *Memoirs of Sherlock Holmes* thus ends, wittily (although its wittiness may — or may not! — be retroactive), with a false detection. The discourse has more than one story.

## References

Babener, Liahna 1987 [1972] "The Shadow's Shadow: The Motif of the Double in Edgar Allan Poe's 'The Purloined Letter,'" in *Literary Theory in Praxis,* edited by Shirley F. Staton, 42–53 (Philadelphia: University of Pennsylvania Press).

Baring-Gould, William S., ed. 1967 *The Annotated Sherlock Holmes,* 2 vols. (New York: Clarkson N. Potter).

Barzun, Jacques 1980 [1961] "Detection and the Literary Art," from *The Delights of Detection,* in Winks 1980: 144–53.

Bigelow, S. Tupper 1976 "An Assessment and Valuation of the Ten Best Canonical Stories, with Some Observations on Those Somewhat Less Deserving of Praise," in *Beyond Baker Street: A Sherlock-*

*ian Anthology,* edited by Michael Harrison, 45–54 (Indianapolis and New York: Bobbs-Merrill).

Bonfantini, Massimo A., and Giampaolo Proni 1983 "To Guess or Not to Guess?" in Eco and Sebeok 1983: 119–34.

Brooks, Peter 1985 [1984] *Reading for the Plot: Design and Intention in Narrative* (New York: Vintage).

Caillois, Roger 1983 [1941] "The Detective Novel as Game," translated by William W. Stowe, in *The Poetics of Murder: Detective Fiction and Literary Theory,* edited by Glenn W. Most and William W. Stowe, 1–12 (New York: Harcourt Brace Jovanovich).

Champigny, Robert 1977 *What Will Have Happened: A Philosophical and Technical Essay on Mystery Stories* (Bloomington: Indiana University Press).

Chatman, Seymour 1978 *Story and Discourse: Narrative Structure in Fiction and Film* (Ithaca: Cornell University Press).

Collins, Wilkie 1966 [1868] *The Moonstone,* edited by J. I. M. Stewart (London: Penguin).

Culler, Jonathan 1981 "Story and Discourse in the Analysis of Narrative," *The Pursuit of Signs: Semiotics, Literature, Deconstruction,* 169–87 (Ithaca: Cornell University Press).

Derrida, Jacques 1975 "The Purveyor of Truth," translated by Willis Domingo, James Hulbert, Moshe Ron, and Marie-Rose Logan, *Yale French Studies* 52: 31–113.

Doyle, Arthur Conan 1924 *Memories and Adventures* (London: Hodder and Stoughton). 1980 [1927] "The Sherlock Holmes Prize Competition — How I Made My List," in *A Sherlock Holmes Compendium,* edited by Peter Haining, 208–10 (London: W. H. Allen).

Eco, Umberto, and Thomas A. Sebeok, eds. 1983 *The Sign of Three: Dupin, Holmes, Peirce* (Bloomington: Indiana University Press).

Foucault, Michel 1970 [1966] *The Order of Things: An Archaeology of the Human Sciences* (New York: Random House).

Guillard, Dawson 1981 *Dorothy L. Sayers* (New York: Ungar).

Haycraft, Howard, ed. 1946 *The Art of the Mystery Story* (New York: Simon and Schuster).

Heissenbuttel, Helmut 1983 [1963] "Rules of the Game of the Crime Novel," translated by Glenn W. Most and William W. Stowe, in *The Poetics of Murder: Detective Fiction and Literary Theory,* edited by Glenn W. Most and William W. Stowe, 79–92 (New York: Harcourt Brace Jovanovich).

Hoffman, Daniel 1972 *Poe Poe Poe Poe Poe Poe Poe* (Garden City, NY: Doubleday).

Klein, Kathleen Gregory, and Joseph Keller 1986 "Deductive Detective Fiction: The Self-Destructive Genre," *Genre* 19(2): 155–72.

Knox, Ronald A. 1946 [1929] "A Detective Story Decalogue," in Haycraft 1946: 194–96.

Lambert, Gavin 1980 [1975] "Prologue," *The Dangerous Edge,* in Winks 1980: 47–52.

Murphy, Cait 1987 "The Game's Still Afoot," *The Atlantic* 259(3): 58–62, 64–66.

Nicolson, Marjorie 1946 [1929] "The Professor and the Detective," in Haycraft 1946: 110–27.

Ousby, Ian 1976 *Bloodhounds of Heaven: The Detective in English Fiction from Godwin to Doyle* (Cambridge, MA: Harvard University Press).

Poe, Edgar Allan 1978 *Collected Works of Edgar Allan Poe,* edited by Thomas Ollive Mabbott. Vols. 2 and 3, *Tales and Sketches* (Cambridge, MA: Harvard University Press).

Porter, Dennis 1981 *The Pursuit of Crime: Art and Ideology in Detective Fiction* (New Haven: Yale University Press).

Prince, Gerald 1987 *A Dictionary of Narratology* (Lincoln and London: University of Nebraska Press).

Redmond, Donald A. 1982 *Sherlock Holmes: A Study in Sources* (Kingston and Montreal: McGill-Queen's University Press).

Sayers, Dorothy L. 1946 [1929] "Introduction," from *The Omnibus of Crime,* in Haycraft 1946: 71–109. 1967 [1933] *Murder Must Advertise* (New York: Avon).

Sebeok, Thomas A., and Jean Umiker-Sebeok 1983 "'You Know My Method': A Juxtaposition of Charles S. Peirce and Sherlock Holmes," in Eco and Sebeok 1983: 11–54.

Symons, Julian 1972 *Mortal Consequences. A History: From the Detective Story to the Crime Novel* (New York: Schocken). 1987 [1949] *Bland Beginning* (New York: Carroll and Graf).

Todorov, Tzvetan 1977 [1971] *The Poetics of Prose,* translated by Richard Howard (Ithaca: Cornell University Press).

Truzzi, Marcello 1983 [1973] "Sherlock Holmes: Applied Social Psychologist," in Eco and Sebeok 1983: 55–80.

Van Dine, S. S. 1946 [1928] "Twenty Rules for Writing Detective Stories," in Haycraft 1946: 189–93.

Wilbur, Richard 1962 "Edgar Allan Poe," in *Major Writers of Amer-*

*ica,* edited by Perry Miller, 1:369–82 (New York: Harcourt Brace Jovanovich).

Winks, Robin W., ed. 1980 *Detective Fiction: A Collection of Critical Essays* (Englewood Cliffs, NJ: Prentice-Hall).

Zangwill, Israel 1986 [1891] *The Big Bow Mystery* (New York: Carroll and Graf).

ALASTAIR FOWLER

# Sherlock Holmes and the Adventure of the Dancing Men and Women

---

Like Brooks, Fowler begins by investigating the hermeneutic (interpreting, problem-solving) emphasis of detective fiction and its particularly concentrated representation in a single Holmes story. He reads Holmes's "deciphering" in "The Dancing Men" much as Brooks uses Holmes's "plotting" in "The Musgrave Ritual" as "an icon of the investigation as a whole" (p. 355). Holmes's deciphering method, and his detective method generally, Fowler finds, contain curious contradictions: they are professedly rigorous but actually indeterminate and mystifying. And in this gap between the purely intellectual deciphering and the socially implicated detecting — which is also figured by that between the arbitrariness of the dancing men as cipher characters and their "vague menace" (p. 363) as socially symbolic figures — Fowler argues, Doyle develops his fictions not as problem-solving amusements but as "symbolic romance," a subtle but "eloquent means of expressing social ideas" (p. 366). Fowler thus agrees with Catherine Belsey about the presence of a Holmesian undertext while disagreeing with her about Doyle's apparent obliviousness to it.

Fowler's essay originally appeared in *Addressing Frank Kermode: Essays in Criticism and Interpretation,* ed. Margaret Tudeau-Clayton and Martin Warner (London: Macmillan, 1991), pp. 154–68.

---

Modern criticism of the detective story has one starting point in Frank Kermode's W. P. Ker lecture of 1972, which filtered implications of earlier work by Raymond Queneau, Michel Butor and Roland Barthes to a clarified form. Kermode talked of a generic specialisation, whereby one element of narrative undergoes elephantiasis, so that the reader's main object becomes interpreting clues or solving problems — in fact, "hermeneutic activity":

Clearly this emphasis requires, to a degree much greater than in

most stories (though all have hermeneutic aspects), the disposition, in a consecutive narrative, of information which requires us
to ask both how it "fits in," and also how it will all "come out";
and this information bears up an event, usually a murder, that precedes the narrative which bears the clues. (Kermode 1983: 56)[1]

This might be qualified by genre. Crimes usually precede detection
in police fiction; but in "mysteries" like Raymond Chandler's, the detective may be hired first. And Conan Doyle's Sherlock Holmes stories
often begin at a stage when the crime (if any) only impends. These are
hardly classic detective stories; yet the idea of a hermeneutic task proves
valuable to their interpreter in unexpected ways.

Of Conan Doyle's art, the first thing to observe is the degree of
subtlety. It is a far more sophisticated art than has usually been supposed. Even the structure of a Sherlock Holmes story is relatively complex: a recent comparison of Conan Doyle's use of narrators to
Nabokov's by no means exaggerates. (Barolsky 1987: 73) Detective fiction generally involves two interpretative activities, the detective's investigation and the reader's attempts (hampered by narrative subterfuges)
at the same problem. But Conan Doyle commonly has at least three
investigations, since the narrator, Watson, also takes a hand (not all visible); sometimes with more success than the reader, but always with less
than Holmes. Even although Watson may exploit hindsight, his limitations control, for the reader, the pace of hermeneutic activity. For
Holmes often chooses not to confide in him — "I confess that I was
filled with curiosity, but I was aware that Holmes liked to make his disclosures at his own time" ("The Dancing Men," p. 257). Kingsley Amis
has perceptively remarked that Watson's "not quite always unqualified" admiration achieves the result of portraying Holmes "at exactly the right distance and in exactly the right light." (Doyle 1974: Introduction) But
Watson's narration achieves almost as much in another mediation: between
the reader's desultory puzzling and the great detective's intense investigations. And other characters too engage in hermeneutic construction — not
only police detectives like Martin, but stationmasters, doctors, servants.
Holmes's society is one of ordinary people making sense of things.

For Conan Doyle's investigative reader, the problems to be solved
are imaginary and intellectual. Yet part of the pleasure of our association
with Holmes depends on his also enjoying the intellectual problems his

[1]Throughout the present paper, I am indebted for many suggestions to Paul Barolsky
and Wallace Robson.

cases present. He is always on the lookout for "interesting" cases with "unique" features. His seductive theoretical interests can sometimes be detected, indeed, breaking out outrageously. When a fresh example turned up of the dancing men cryptograms that were "killing [Elsie] by inches," Holmes "rubbed his hands and chuckled with delight" (pp. 254–55). Holmes's intellectual interests have to be reconciled, however, with the interests of clients and others. His investigations are not pure enquiries, but interactions of pure and impure, theoretical and practical, technical and human factors.

Much of the tension derives from such conflicts of interest; as when Holmes realises a blunder ("I've been a fool") and must break off research for a suspenseful race against time. And if the race is lost, he feels guilty for pursuing theoretical certainty to the point of endangering his client. I almost said "patient"; for conflict between scientific interest and human solicitude characterises medical "cases," too. There is much in Owen Dudley Edwards's contention that Conan Doyle wrote from a conviction about the inhumanity of contemporary medical practice. (Edwards 1983: 200; cf. Accardo 1987) Certainly Holmes, no less than Dr. Conan Doyle, is a professional — a point repeatedly emphasised: "the whole incident may appeal as a remarkable professional study" (p. 264); "Holmes preserved his calm professional manner" (p. 257). But even this hardly broadens the reference far enough; for reading of symptoms belongs to a more general interpreting of life, and Conan Doyle's readers join Holmes in similar inferences as they compose events into a narrative that makes sense, at each stage forming a provisional domain of assumptions to be revised at the next.

Particularly interesting from this point of view is "The Adventure of the Dancing Men," since it contains the subsidiary hermeneutic task of interpreting cryptograms. Holmes's breaking of the cipher stands, in fact, as an icon of the investigation as a whole. The profusion of texts in the story is remarkable (although by no means without parallel in the Sherlock Holmes canon). Besides Watson's everpresent notebook ("I have fulfilled my promise of giving you something unusual for your notebook" [p. 270]), there is the letter from America burnt by Elsie (p. 252); seven cryptograms (one of composite authorship); an eighth by Holmes himself; Hilton Cubitt's transcriptions (one encapsulated in a letter); a reported letter of Elsie's; three telegrams; Holmes's working papers in solution of the code; and literary subtexts present by allusion, especially Poe's "The Gold-Bug." It is natural to enquire whether the cryptograms may not contain self-reflexive analogies with the story or the investigation.

The source of the dancing men cipher, like the source of the Nile, has had many discoverers. We hear that it was invented by the son of one Cubitt, proprietor of the Hill House Hotel at Happisburgh in Norfolk, where Conan Doyle stayed; that it appeared in the St. Nicholas magazine; or that it came from the "alphabet of Hermes" in Albert Mackey's *Encyclopedia of Freemasonry* (1874) (of interest, surely, to Conan Doyle the occultist). (Baring-Gould 1968: n.16) But the cipher's point lies not in sources so much as a functional relation to the cipher of "The Gold-Bug."

Poe's story is an indispensable subtext of "The Dancing Men." In both tales, decipherment comes in flashback, long after the real-time solution has brought a first denouement (discovery of the treasure; Holmes's attendance at Ridling Thorpe Manor soon after Cubitt's death). Poe conceals Kidd's cryptogram until the flashback; motivating this deception as Legrand's practical joke on the narrator (which the latter repeats on us). But Watson honestly follows the sequence he experienced; since he could not decipher the dancing men cryptograms, and Holmes would not help him (p. 257). The anticlimactic structure obviates suspense, but allows the decipherment to become a retrospective microcosm of the investigation. In both stories, the coda of decoding is like the explanatory recapitulation — the Metamenusis, as Knox calls it (1954: 108) — that completes the classic detective story. At the same time, there are striking contrasts between the two detectives' methods.

Legrand's "rationale" is rigorously deductive, and could be repeated in real life, at least with similarly doctored messages. (Poe 1984: 591) Thus TH.RTEE. is "immediately suggestive of the word 'thirteen.'" By contrast, Holmes's professedly scientific method is in practice notoriously hard to follow. For the five letter word he says "might be 'sever,' or 'lever,' or 'never'," there are actually twenty-seven other alternatives (p. 265; Baring-Gould 1968: n.13); he can justify choosing "never" only on grounds of contextual probability. Context is again relied on for the "combination which contained two E's with three letters between," which, "it occurred" to Holmes, "might very well stand for the name 'ELSIE'." But why assume a name at all? Similarly, Holmes "could only make sense" of A. ELRI.ES (pp. 265–66) by assuming the missing letters to be T and G. Add to these guesses mistakes in encipherment, and it is no wonder that readers emulating Holmes have felt the decipherment to be too like life by half.

Both detectives stress the cipher's simplicity, mixing arrogance with patronising encouragement. Legrand makes out "the very simplest species of cryptograph": he has "solved others of an abstruseness ten thousand times greater" (Poe 1984: 567, 591); while Holmes claims to know "all forms" (!) of secret writings, and boasts authorship "of a trifling monograph upon the subject, in which I analyze one hundred and sixty separate ciphers" — although the dancing men are "entirely new" to him. The dancing men cipher is "easy enough," in fact, for Edward Woodland and Fletcher Pratt to suggest that it is only a simplified version — a token surrogate — of the more high-powered cipher that put the great detective to "intricate and elaborate calculation" (see Baring-Gould 1968: n.13). But if the cipher as Watson gives it is so simple, why should its decipherment elude exposition? Why does Holmes not solve it by steps as repeatable as Legrand's?

Two contrasting answers suggest themselves. One might take its departure from the views of poststructuralists like M. Pouffe. Conan Doyle, an inferior artist to the great Poe, has garbled the cipher; this, like other elusivenesses in his text, betrays an area concerning which his ideology remains aphatic. The other approach might assume that Conan Doyle was as capable of standing on Poe's giant shoulders as Holmes (in "Milverton") on Watson's, and that the descents from the rigour of Legrand are quite likely to have been deliberate. After all, Conan Doyle considered "The Dancing Men" his third best story: for him, at least, it was not casual work.

To pursue this second approach thus involves acknowledging the relevance of Conan Doyle's artistry. It calls for knowledge of his *oeuvre*, and of his place in a tradition — the tradition of Poe and Stevenson — that sanctioned expending the classic resources of authorship on peripheral, unofficial genres. In this view, an artist such as Conan Doyle was not likely to have fallen short of his model unnecessarily. Elsewhere, after all, he seems able at will to construct brilliant arabesques of inference, cadenzas of reasoning, bravura passages of deduction.

Indeed, Sherlock Holmes stories generally begin with a supererogatory demonstration of method, exemplifying deduction through a series of "inferences, each dependent upon its predecessor and each simple in itself" (p. 250). Motivated by Holmes's wish to present his credentials to a new client, the demonstration "really" serves to establish his character to new readers. But it also introduces a paradigm of the "scientific" method with whose inadequacy many of the later Sherlock Holmes stories are concerned. In "The Dancing Men," this theme becomes almost explicit. Not only is the demonstration here to Watson himself (and thus thinly motivated), but it takes the form of the very "trick" of Dupin's that Holmes scorns in *A Study in Scarlet* — "that

trick of his of breaking in on his friends' thoughts with an apropos remark after a quarter of an hour's silence is really very showy and superficial."[2] Here, Holmes contemptuously explains "with the air of a professor addressing his class" how, if "one simply knocks out all the
central inferences and presents one's audience with the starting point
and the conclusion, one may produce a startling, though possibly a meretricious, effect." The effect is nevertheless one he cannot resist repeating.

This homage to Poe by no means implies unqualified admiration for
scientific method on Conan Doyle's part. Holmes may profess the
method, but it is not the way his cases are solved — as Watson, with his
talk of Holmes's "curious faculties," seems aware.

"The Dancing Men" presents extreme instances of this contradiction. Holmes talks, indeed, about his science, and his cryptology is superior to Legrand's as regards adequate samples (p. 265) and the rank
ordering of letters by frequency (ETAOINSHRDL, not EAOIDHNRST
as Legrand supposes). But deductive method hardly dominates his actual practice. As we have seen, he guesses "NEVER," arrives at
"ELSIE" by "a happy thought," and makes sense of "ELRI . ES" "by
supposing." Unlike Legrand's, Holmes's deciphering is a multifaceted
process, combining inference, intuition, inspiration, chance, mistake
and recourse to external knowledge; just as in the larger investigation,
where he draws on "knowledge of the crooks of Chicago" (p. 267).
Throughout Holmes depends on assumptions, so that readers, not always able to draw on the relevant domains of assumption, must sometimes be shut out like Watson. Not being in Holmes's confidence, however, lets them share another aspect of the investigative experience:
confrontation of mystery. Prevented from following the investigation
conspectively, readers are mystified, even if (like Watson) perceptive
here and there. Holmes's exclusion of his faithful friend is thus one of
Conan Doyle's masterly ways of fostering identification with Watson.
And Holmes himself, after all, is often less than triumphant. In "The
Dancing Men," breaking the cipher brings only "surprise and dismay,"
and failure to prevent a tragedy.

Assumptions — especially wrong assumptions — are the stuff of
"The Dancing Men." Its hermeneutic task entails not only making
sense of the facts, but working out from exiguous hints what the right
facts to assume are. Almost as with Hawthorne, narrative bricks must be

---

[2]See Edwards 1983: 141. Accardo (1987: 27) notes that the demonstrations follow
the lecturing style of Conan Doyle's professors at Edinburgh.

made with little factual straw. And always readers have to follow Watson in resisting complete identification with Holmes.

The first construction of the case may be regarded as what "the servants say" (p. 258). On this assumption, two shots were fired, one killing Hilton Cubitt and the other wounding Elsie. To the impartial local surgeon "It was equally conceivable that he had shot her and then himself, or that she had been the criminal, for the revolver lay upon the floor midway between them." But to Martin and the servants it was not equally conceivable. As the stationmaster reports, they assume the foreign lady's guilt: if her life can be saved it will be "for the gallows."

At one stage Holmes himself may have assumed Elsie's guilt. When "It fills [him] with hopes" (p. 256) to hear that Elsie has been replying to Abe Slaney's messages, this is probably because he expects her to give away the "secret" — which he also advises Cubitt to ask her about directly (p. 253). But the cryptograms reveal something of Elsie's innocence and guilt; and Holmes goes to Norfolk with a new assumption. Friend of the establishment and enemy of criminals, he tends to assume the guilt of the latter; and his knowledge of Chicago crooks, in particular, prepares him "to find that [Slaney] might very rapidly put his words [ELSIE PREPARE TO MEET THY GOD] into action." Holmes evidently thinks this expectation fulfilled, to judge by his vague continuation: "I at once came to Norfolk . . . to find that the worst had already occurred." When he notices the bullet hole in the window sash, and deduces the firing of a third shot, Holmes's new assumption seems vindicated: Slaney ("the most dangerous crook in Chicago") must be the murderer.

Inspector Martin, changing front, is eager to make an arrest (p. 267). His new-found assumption of Slaney's guilt may be ironically highlighted, for when the American says "I guess the very best case I can make for myself is the absolute naked truth" (p. 269), he is cautioned (not charged): — "'It is my duty to warn you that it will be used against you,' cried the inspector, with the magnificent fair play of the British criminal law." Legally, "will be used" was as valid as "may be used"; but it was not the customary formula. Martin evidently sees no need to specify a charge of murder, nor to envisage the truth's not all being used against Slaney.[3]

But the case, like the decipherment, turns out to have something of a false bottom. Perhaps maturer consideration, certainly Slaney's sur-

---

[3]The form of the caution itself would have been legally acceptable, but probably not customary (for this information I am indebted to Susan Kreitman).

prise and grief at hearing of Elsie's wounding, qualify Holmes's view of the Chicagoan. He "sternly" charges Slaney not with murder but with "bringing about the death of a noble man and driving his wife to suicide."

With uncharacteristic negligence, Ronald Knox remarks that in Sherlock Holmes stories "all criminals are model criminals" (Knox 1954: 113). In fact almost the reverse is true: they tend to be ordinary people, or at least people with ordinary feelings. Although Conan Doyle was no shallow idealist, as the medical stories show he thought well of human nature. "The deeper strata are good" (Doyle 1903: "The Surgeon Speaks," 243). Here, Slaney is shown as a grieving lover rather than a professional killer. In his own view he has "nothing to hide . . . the man . . . had his shot at me, and there's no murder in that" (p. 268); and in the reader's too, perhaps, Slaney's guilt may be palliated by his passion, and his American valuation of what amounts, after all, to a shootout. Nevertheless, the court finds him guilty of murder, doubtless on grounds of constructive malice; for he is condemned to death (a penalty later commuted). His criminal record will have counted against him — significantly Holmes is made to say "That is your record in this business . . . and you will answer for it to the law" (p. 268).

It is not immediately clear what Holmes means by Slaney's "driving" Elsie to attempted suicide: her motivation must be inferred. How much was guilt at her own part in "bringing about the death of a noble man" by keeping her "guilty" secret? How much, perhaps, at a residual attachment to Slaney? And how much apprehension about English society's probable verdict on one with her pedigree? Although Holmes suppresses this point, an entire social culture conspired against Elsie. When she tried to tell Hilton her secret, she never got beyond talk of the Cubitts' "reputation in the county, and our pride in our unsullied honour" (p. 254). For such pride, and for his share in a society where the truth is hard to tell, Holmes's client seems not entirely blameless. And the story diffuses guilt even further, to the great detective himself. For on reading Cubitt's last letter, Holmes says "we have let this affair go far enough"; implying that he could have intervened sooner. Two motives for delay seem likely, and probably both are to be supplied. Holmes may have refrained out of delicacy, giving Elsie a chance to settle the affair discreetly without harming his client's all-important honour. (Holmes was similarly discreet in the Milverton affair.) Or he may have awaited a full understanding of the case; working as usual towards a theatrical disclosure.

Holmes's comparative failure in "The Dancing Men" contrasts

strikingly with Legrand's total success in the denouement of "The Gold-Bug." Legrand may behave madly — with "a nervous empressement which alarmed me and strengthened the suspicions already entertained. His countenance was pale even to ghastliness, and his deep-set eyes glared with unnatural lustre" (Poe 1984: 567): treasure may seem to have obsessed and "demented" the narrator's "unfortunate companion" (567, 577): but this is a false appearance, created by Legrand as a joke. And the landscape descriptions that assist the erroneous construction? The "dreary" region of melancholy, with crags of guilt impending and "deep ravines" which "gave an air of still sterner solemnity to the scene"? All this evocation of a mood of malaise is the narrator's joke on the reader. The outcome reveals a perfectly rational Legrand, who turns to practical account even the *scarabaeus caput hominis* — the previously unknown death's head beetle that has seemed an obsessing "maggot" (his "whole intellect seemed to be absorbed by 'de bug'"). Dropped through the orbit of the skull — linking it with the remaining, buried parts of the divided skeleton — the beetle of death becomes a means of finding treasure.

The story's anamorphic structure (Legrand mad: Legrand sane) is apparently trivialised, when the suggestions of morbidity turn out to be a pointless joke. Otherwise, one might be inclined to see the search for buried treasure as signifying pursuit of identity, selfhood, or an integrated soul.[4] (Decipherment would be abreaction of what had been repressed with violence.) But deep interpretation seems undercut by Legrand's joke — unless that, too, is to be internalised, as the detective-hermeneut's evasion of the narrator's rationality. Was Poe capable of such symbolism? Details like his insistence on the treasure's (and the bug's) being "real gold," "solid gold," with the gratuitous information that "there was no American money" (580), certainly suggest awareness of a psychological dimension. And recent work suggests that Poe was more aware of unconscious repression than has been supposed (see Wuletich-Brinberg 1988). The story's closure — the sinister question about Kidd's violence in suppressing the truth — surely aims at more than a last frisson of horror. But, writing when he did, Poe felt an overwhelming need for concealment.

"The Dancing Men" arouses fewer doubts as to artistic control. Here, successive assumptions are not mutually destructive, but lead in a consistent direction. And Poe's overt psychologising is avoided. For all his emulation of the farouche Virginian, Conan Doyle thought him

[4]On meanings of "the treasure hard to attain" archetype, see Jung, 1953:113–14.

"not altogether a healthy influence": without "countering qualities"
Poe might become "a dangerous comrade" (Doyle 1912: 121). In his
own less romantic fiction, Conan Doyle follows a more social route,
scouting the "perilous tracks" and "deadly quagmires" of Poe's intro-
spection. But the route need not be that of "classic realism." And if
Conan Doyle thinks Poe "devoid of humour," yet in his own composed
way he takes quite as tragic a view of life. In Sherlock Holmes stories,
appearances of morbidity are not explained away as jokes, but hint at a
reality beyond the control of science.

"The Dancing Men" is not the only case in which Holmes arrives
too late to avert "the worst." Although his method is vindicated theo-
retically, he often enough fails to prevent a tragic outcome. Tragedy,
indeed, commonly supplies the generic mechanism of Conan Doyle's
machines of death. Thus, in "The Dancing Men" Holmes's enquiries
have the inexorability of Oedipus's, as he successively implicates Elsie,
Slaney and Cubitt, while conspicuously failing to admit his own responsibility. At last Holmes triumphantly congratulates himself on "a remarkable professional study" that has left his client dead. Here one may
suspect satire of the callously complacent theorising Conan Doyle hated
in the medical establishment. But to stress this aspect is to miss the
story's complexity; for in another mood (as in the train to Norfolk)
Holmes's guilt, or at least sense of failure, can bring him to "blank melancholy" ("Seldom," says Watson, "have I seen him so utterly despondent"). Such depression has to do with Conan Doyle's own sense of
man's "tragic destiny."[5] Understanding is always an eaten apple — retrospective, belated, inadequate. By contrast with Poe's enquiring closure, therefore, Conan Doyle's presents a final image that transcends
understanding: Elsie's life of expiatory caring.

From this viewpoint, one can understand the eponymity of the
dancing men, the story's most memorable image. These scribbled
"forerunners of so terrible a tragedy" connect guilt with childhood,
through their suggestion of "a child's drawing." The seeming childish-
ness of the cryptograms is stressed so repeatedly as to extend the distri-
bution of evil, while curiously intensifying it. The effect is not merely a
sense of horror at discovering that what "would pass as a child's scrawl"
belongs to Slaney's "dangerous web." Less explicitly, there is a sinister
impression of infantile malice. One recalls that the surgeon in Conan
Doyle's "A Medical Document" was only once frightened: by the "ma-
lignancy"of an ambiguously mature "infant." (Doyle 1903: 154)

[5]See, e.g., "The Third Generation," in Doyle 1903.

The vague menace of the dancing men grows ever more imminent, with the inexorability of night following day, as the chalk-mark sites alternate between bright sundial and black toolhouse. The dancing men dance, it seems, a *Totentanz*.[6] (The secret knowledge of evil that Elsie and Slaney share includes, it seems, knowledge of mortality, the wages of sin.) But the toolhouse and sundial suggests also the interaction of technology and time, art and nature — not merely the *circuit de la parole* round-dance but the whole choresis of man's fatal history. As stories such as "The Third Generation" show, the problem of evil — "the sins of the Creator" — much exercised Conan Doyle. Here, the ancestral origin of the cipher (Elsie's father invented it for "the Joint," his criminal organisation of seven, that is, all of us) indicates one answer unambiguously: evil is inherited. Conan Doyle repudiated the Calvinistic doctrine of total depravity, however; inheritance of social circumstances and tendencies may be more to the point. Elsie, who (like everyone in Conan Doyle's view) is good at heart, tries to repudiate her criminal connections. But she succeeds only temporarily; her origin is not to be denied. Indeed, failure to confess her link with "the Joint" is precisely what falsifies her relationships and precipitates tragedy.

I hope these suggestions have been arrived at without violent decentring. Still, they can hardly be called obvious. Conan Doyle's is an economical, understating art, as his muting modulations of "The Gold-Bug" repeatedly reflect. For Poe's landscape of horror, he substitutes the ordinary wasteland of Norfolk. Holmes in his despondency misses altogether the "few scattered cottages" and "enormous square-towered churches" that interest Watson — signs of depopulation, of former glory. But the reader should not overlook these indications of social change, nor the contrast between the flat landscape and Poe's subjectively horrid crags. Yet if Conan Doyle provides "counteracting qualities," he is by no means mocking Poe. He profoundly admired "the master of all" in the short story, and regarded "The Gold-Bug" as one of Poe's two stories of perfect excellence — for proportion and perspective "I don't see how either of those could be bettered" (Doyle 1912: 114). In fact (a hard fact, perhaps, for some) Conan Doyle thought of Poe, much in the way he thought of Stevenson, as a classic writer. Thus he observes that "all treasure-hunting, cryptogram-solving yarns trace back to . . . 'The Gold-Bug'" (Doyle 1912: 115). In emulating such a "classic" model, finesses, economical allusions, and ironic intertextu-

---

[6] *Totentanz:* A dance of death, typically including Death himself as a skeletal dancer — a dancing stick-figure man indeed. [Editor's note]

alities were appropriate, just as in the canonical "great tradition"; so that "The Dancing Men" also has to be approached through its (extra-canonical) tradition.

So regarded, it may become itself a classic, although perhaps of a distinct type. This warrants treating it seriously, and allows Catherine Belsey [see p. 386] to relate it, quite legitimately, to interests of feminism. It is not deficiency of art in Conan Doyle's stories, nor "the limits of their own project," that opens the door to her particular hermeneutic activity.

Kingsley Amis has pointed out that the Sherlock Holmes tales are properly "adventure stories involving a crime, or an apparent crime, and concentrating attention on a detective, his friend and chronicler, and the relations between the two" (Doyle 1974: Introduction, 8). And one might add that Conan Doyle's best "yarns" (as he called them) are "tertiary" adventures, in which features of the "secondary," or conscious, adventure form are reused as material for symbolic applications, and every clue becomes a potential clew of metaphoric yarn. Allowing for the lower profile of their effects, they resemble in this way the stories of Hawthorne and Stevenson.

The principal features of "The Dancing Men" are symbolic, signifying not so much through the representative action of "classic realism" as through recall of analogues in congeners like "The Gold-Bug," through modulation of the genre's repertoire. A generic frame of reference informs our inferences, and each allusion to Poe is potentially meaningful. Thus the decipherment, paradigmatically, can refer to the investigation at large, and can draw attention to assumptions underlying Holmes's procedure. Again, in "The Gold-Bug" the decipherment reveals a secret of ancient aggression, which remains as an object of enquiry. But Conan Doyle applies this potently vague symbol rather differently. His decipherment leads not to a dead pirate's crime, but a living woman's history of criminal association.

As in Poe, disclosure of the secret reveals conflict — as much internal, in Elsie's case, as social. This conflict, precipitated by the surfacing of her past, is a clash between violently contrasted cultures — as often in Conan Doyle. Here, he dramatises the clash in a gunfight between a noble East Anglian and a Chicago criminal; thus externalising, perhaps, the disparities straining the Cubitts' unlucky marriage. Qualities sundering Elsie and Hilton link her to her former love; it would not be surprising if her feelings were mixed when she restrained her husband "with convulsive strength" from pursuing Slaney. It crossed Cubitt's mind for a moment "that perhaps what she really feared was that he

[Slaney] might come to harm." Yet at the same time he is certain of Elsie's loyalty — as Slaney testifies, "she would have nothing to do with anything on the cross" (p. 269). Cubitt's social standing raises this high moral line of Elsie's still higher: she is fatally incapable of expressing her conflict and telling her secret, because "there is not a man in England who ranks his family honour more highly." The resulting conflict charging their relations is symbolised in the catastrophe. For Conan Doyle renews Poe's question about the unfathomable extent of aggression ("perhaps a couple of blows with a mattock were sufficient . . . — who shall tell?"), by making it an issue how many shots were fired at Ridling Thorpe Manor. Perhaps a couple of shots were sufficient? Well, two sounds of shots were. But contributing to one of these reports was Slaney's third, simultaneous shot, the result of aggression provoked by Elsie's attempt to pay him off. And motivating this, in turn, was her wish to conceal her guilty secret, her criminal father. Holmes's client remained unaware of any fault in himself; and so did Holmes — enough that Cubitt, having promised not to speak, was as good as his word. But Conan Doyle the campaigner for women's rights knew how much wives could be silenced and oppressed by the elevation of "family honour."

A remaining subtextual feature, Kidd's treasure, is utilised less obtrusively still. Gold only surfaces in "The Dancing Men" in connection with Watson's train of thought, deduced by Holmes: "it was not really difficult, by an inspection of the groove between your left forefinger and thumb, to feel sure that you did *not* propose to invest your small capital in the goldfields" (p. 250). Watson's cautious bearishness is perhaps to be contrasted with Cubitt's rash foreign investment, not in the goldfields, but in a wife who might turn out a gold-digger. Cubitt said he "would spend [his] last copper to shield" Elsie (p. 253). And she, for her part, was prepared to pay Slaney notes from her specifically silver purse. (Was it silver of faithfulness, or the reprobate silver of Jeremiah 6: 30?) She herself constitutes the treasure Cubitt and Slaney fight over; whether treasure of pure gold, is one of the story's questions.

She comes, like Kidd's treasure, with a guilty secret; but then buried selves are always partly "evil." Exhumation before renunciation. Is not Elsie's repentance "devoting her whole life to the care of the poor" presented a little perfunctorily? Only in terms of realism. No one can deny the virtual death to her old life that her attempted suicide symbolises. Moreover, she is only partly responsible for the tragic denouement. Inherited ills, as we have seen, played their parts; Slaney; Holmes; and Cubitt with his sense of racial superiority.

Only Watson seems free from the diffused taint of guilty responsibility. But is even his refraining from investment in gold quite innocent? How far was his decision overcautious? How far nationally prejudiced? And how far an indication of Conan Doyle's negative judgement on the British gold-diggers in the Rand?[7]

From this approach, assessments of "The Dancing Men" take on an altered appearance. In particular, Pierre Macherey's conclusion (that Conan Doyle silences the woman's voice involuntarily) loses any attraction it may have had.[8] For in "The Dancing Men" the supporter of the rights of women seems well able to express their perspective. And elsewhere he does so, sometimes, with searing intensity — in the symbolism of stories like "Lady Sannox," for example, or in the anecdote of the policeman's compulsory couvade in "A Medical Document." Like the handcuff on the bleeding policeman, the "woman question" constantly chafed at Conan Doyle. Thus, as early as 1888 Holmes was fascinated by Irene Adler, the careerist with "the mind of the most resolute of men" who excelled him in the art of professional disguise ("A Scandal in Bohemia"). For him she was always "*the* woman." And in "Doctors of Hoyland" the woman question — again posed by a successful woman careerist — receives the realistic treatment Macherey desiderates. Departure from "classic realism" was not forced on Conan Doyle simply by his taking up the woman's point of view.

The Sherlock Holmes stories, written for a somewhat different audience, had to appear amusing detective adventures, and so have come to seem to some a "limited project." Throughout his fiction, however, Conan Doyle wrote symbolic romance; and he developed the form as an eloquent means of expressing social ideas. Admittedly, the surface features leading readers to his serious content have very low profiles. But "The Dancing Men" illustrates how much it was possible for Conan Doyle to convey, even in a detective adventure.

The later Sherlock Holmes stories call for as much critical attention as that demanded by Robert Louis Stevenson's — which is as much (although distinct in mode) as with a canonical Conrad tale. In approaching these stories we cannot sustain the usual division between, on the one hand, a canon of "high" works suitable for literary criticism, on the other "low" uncanonical writing to be quarried for examples supporting social or political generalisation. These are too well-written for that,

---

[7]On Conan Doyle's ambivalence towards the Boers in 1899, see Carr 1949: 146.

[8]Macherey and Balibar 1978. The common error of supposing Conan Doyle ambivalent on the woman question may have arisen from his dislike of the "anarchic" suffragette movement.

and merit attention as literature. Frequently they present additional qualities that have little directly to do with social ideas: that elude, indeed, criticism of existing sorts. It seems almost impossible to approach their pleasures — pleasures of being baffled by bizarre impenetrable puzzles rather than of solving them; of detecting rather than apprehending; of anticipating the unexpected — without curtailing them.

## References

Accardo, P. (1987). *Diagnosis and Detection* (London and Toronto: Associated Universities Press).

Baring-Gould, W. S. (1968). *The Annotated Sherlock Holmes,* 2 vols (London: Murray).

Barolsky, P. (1987). *Walter Pater's Renaissance* (University Park, PA, and London: Pennsylvania State UP).

Belsey, C. (1980). *Critical Practice* (London and New York: Methuen).

Carr, J. D. (1949). *The Life of Sir Arthur Conan Doyle* (London: Murray).

Doyle, A. C. (1903). *The Stark Munro Letters and Round the Red Lamp* (London: Smith, Elder).

———. (1912). *Through the Magic Door* (London: Smith, Elder).

———. (1974). *The Memoirs of Sherlock Holmes,* ed. K. Amis (London: John Murray and Cape).

Edwards, O. D. (1983). *The Quest for Sherlock Holmes* (Edinburgh: Mainstream).

Jung, C. G. (1953). *Psychology and Alchemy,* trans. R. F. C. Hull (London: Routledge and Kegan Paul).

Kermode, F. (1983). *Essays on Fiction: 1971–82* (London: Routledge and Kegan Paul).

Knox, R. A. (1954). "Studies in the Literature of Sherlock Holmes," in his *Essays in Satire* (London and New York: Sheed and Ward).

Macherey, P. and Balibar, E. (1978). "Literature as an ideological form," *Oxford Literary Review* 3.

Poe, E. A. (1984). *Poetry and Tales,* ed. P. F. Quinn (New York: Library of America, Literary Classics of the United States).

Wuletich-Brinberg, S. (1988). *The Rationale of the Uncanny.* Studies in Romantic and Modern Literature 2, ed. W. S. Johnson (New York: Lang).

STEPHEN KNIGHT

# The Case of the Great Detective

---

Why did the Sherlock Holmes stories have such immediate popular success? "To become a best-seller like that," Knight argues, "a writer of crime stories has to embody in the detective a set of values which the audience finds convincing, forces which they can believe will work to contain the disorders of crime." Accordingly he sets out to determine what, for Doyle's audience, those disorders and those values were. The crimes, he finds, are largely "disorders in the respectable bourgeois family" (370), disorders motivated most obviously by selfish greed, more deeply by sexual desires and anxieties (regarding these latter, compare Belsey, below). And these disorders were themselves but the dark side of Doyle's and his readers' world, a world that was largely capitalistic, individualistic, and patriarchal. But Holmes's values, too, "rationalism and individualism" (372), are part of that same world, which thus seems able, if only temporarily and episodically, to reorder itself. The stories thus strikingly serve the needs and purposes of their society's dominant ideology.

Knight's essay originally appeared in the Australian journal *Meanjin* 40.2 (1981): 175–85.

---

Everyone knows the traditional image of Sherlock Holmes. An artist only needs to touch in a deerstalker hat, a checked Inverness cape, large curved pipe and a magnifying glass: then if you just add the words "Elementary, my dear Watson" the world famous icon is complete. It's an epitome of the figure which first seized public attention in 1891, when Arthur Conan Doyle began publishing short stories about Sherlock Holmes in the new London monthly magazine, the *Strand*. To become a best-seller like that a writer of crime stories has to embody in the detective a set of values which the audience finds convincing, forces which they can believe will work to contain the disorders of crime. What then were the values that gave power to the Holmes phenomenon — what does the great detective stand for?

In the first place he stands for science, that exciting new nineteenth-century force in the public mind. Doyle said in his memoirs that contemporary crime fiction disappointed him, because it depended so much on luck for a solution: the detective should be able to work it *all* out. So the overt techniques of science, the careful collection and rational analysis of information, were realised in Sherlock Holmes. He can explain the causes of material evidence either by "the science of deduction" as Doyle calls it, or through his knowledge of forensic facts and criminal history. That was a vividly contemporary and credible force against crime. But it also had its inherent drawbacks, as many people found facts and objective science potentially anti-humane: Charles Dickens's automaton teacher Mr. Gradgrind[1] is a fictional realisation of that fear. Darwin's theory of evolution was a real scientific cause of alarm, insisting as it did that men and animals weren't truly different. Naked science could itself appear to be a disorderly force. Doyle avoided such a bad aura by making the second major value of his great detective that equally potent contemporary force — individualism: the essence of humanity as it seemed to many then, and now. Holmes isn't only a man of objective science: he's also aloof, arrogant, eccentric, even bohemian. His exotic character humanises his scientific skills: a lofty hero, but crucially a human one.

That extreme individualism itself had alarming possibilities: to be too aloof was to be unacceptable. Doyle skilfully mollifies Holmes's individualism by a whole series of subtle shifts. Holmes does take some cocaine in the early stories; like the romantic artists in legend and reality, he needs to liberate his consciousness from the shared, everyday world. But he doesn't isolate himself — it's only a little cocaine, "to relax him," as Watson says. After all, Holmes *is* Watson's friend and fellow-lodger, Watson who represents so plainly the average respectable man, so often puzzled, so often in need of heroic assistance to explain crime and disorder. And all Holmes's eccentricities are qualified — his strange atonal violin playing, the accompaniment to his private thinking, is itself matched by visiting ordinary social concerts in Watson's company. And similarly, Holmes fasts while on the scent of a solution, but at other times there are stout English breakfasts, with a house-keeper to match.

The shape of the stories itself acts in support of this dual characterisation: Doyle's pace and tone don't let his detective become a passive, academic figure like Poe's Chevalier C. Auguste Dupin. Holmes may think all night, but he'll be bustling early in the morning. He may wave the wand of science, but he and the narration have a crisp, ironic tone about them, all the sharper if you read the stories beside the often sen-

[1] ***Mr. Gradgrind:*** Thomas Gradgrind, a character in Dickens's *Hard Times* (1845). [Editor's note]

timental and pompous material that also appeared in the *Strand*. A vigorously modern quality enables Sherlock Holmes to fight disorder in a credible, audience-attracting way.

Those are reasons why the great detective is an effective figure. But what is he effective at? One of the crucial features of crime fiction is that different periods, different audiences, see different crimes as being disturbing. Just as the detective's aura embodies values that the audience holds to be important, so the crimes and criminals realise what the audience most fears. In the Agatha Christie pattern, for example, the feared crime is treacherous murder for gain by a relative or trusted friend. The view of the writer, the view of the audience, can give remarkably different accounts of what is the basic source of disorders in the surrounding world.

We are so used to crime novels dealing with murder, it's a real surprise to many people to find that in the early Holmes stories murder is a rare crime. Stranger still, crime itself is relatively rare, especially in the first twelve stories which were reprinted in one volume as *The Adventures of Sherlock Holmes*. These established the fascination of the great detective, and so they're the ones discussed here. Doyle was well aware of the lack of crime as such in the stories. At the beginning of "The Blue Carbuncle," the seventh story, the authority of Holmes is used to justify that pattern. Watson reports that Holmes said, about his London cases:

> "Amid the action and reaction of so dense a swarm of humanity, every possible combination of events . . . will be presented which may be striking and bizarre without being criminal. We have already had experience of such."
>
> "So much so," I remarked, "that, of the last six cases which I have added to my notes, three have been entirely free of any legal crime." (p. 134)

There was plenty of real crime in late Victorian London, as you might expect, but Doyle didn't introduce professional crime and criminals in these early stories. Nor did he at first present a fantastic master criminal reaching in to disturb ordinary life, not until he created Professor Moriarty to dispose of Holmes at the end of his second dozen of stories. What then were the crimes, the problems in the early stories? Broadly speaking, they deal with disorders in the respectable bourgeois family. There are various threats to established middle-class order, but they come from within the family and the class, not from enemy criminals. One major force is a selfish greed which cuts across normal family responsibility. In "A Case of Identity" and "The Copper Beeches" a father interferes with his daughter's marriage prospects, to keep her money. In "The Speckled Band" the father has actually murdered one step-daughter and tries to kill the other to stop them marrying and taking their money with them. In "The Man with the Twisted Lip" money distorts a man away from his normal, open-faced respectable family life. In "The Beryl Coronet" the greed of an outsider disturbs the family order because of the daughter's love for him. In "The Boscombe Valley Mystery" and "The Five Orange Pips" the greedy crime is in the past and it comes back to haunt what seems a respectable family — but their peaceful prosperity was based on the past crime that is revenged in the present. In three other stories greed leads to a breach of trust just outside family relations. In "The Blue Carbuncle" and "The Red-headed League" a living-in servant betrays his employer's trust for money and joins up with criminals. In "The Engineer's Thumb" the employers themselves are greedy and untrustworthy and betray the engineer they employ.

The remaining two stories of the first dozen are a little different. In them a prospective marriage and a past love affair are shown in ruins. In "The Noble Bachelor" Lord St. Simon's bride disappears because her first husband turns up again; in "A Scandal in Bohemia" the King of Bohemia has to extricate himself from the scandal that may follow a love-affair. Sherlock Holmes's distaste for both these noblemen shows that their arrogant insensitivity to respectable bourgeois values is the selfish disturbance here and they deserve their discomfort. The middle class distaste for noble arrogance is close to home; St. Simon represents those English peers who felt themselves above bourgeois values and the King of Bohemia is a fairly thin disguise for the Prince of Wales, that great antagonist of Victorian respectability.

In these twelve stories those who cause the disturbance act in a selfish way, and all but the two aristocrats are motivated by greed for money. There is another structure of motivation which acts behind and within this one, to be discussed in a while. But the quest for money is a manifest cause of an irresponsibility that leads to disgrace, crime, social breakdown. That path to disgrace and disaster is not just Doyle's concern; it is a major topic in the period. Tennyson called this process "reeling back into the beast." Others, including Doyle, talked about plunging into "the abyss," a measureless chasm where reason, self-control, respectability, the bonds that hold society together, are all loosened, even lost. This fear is so insistent because it is structurally related to the positive values of Victorian society: its evil is a reflex of Victorian good. Total self-indulgence, uncontrolled individualism, moral anarchy, they are no more than unfettered developments of the much praised Victorian, and modern, virtues of self-help, independence and the legitimate practices of acquiring money, pleasure, comfort. You've just gone too far; self-help has become helping yourself to everything.

The disorderly selfishness that Holmes unveils is the dark side of the acquisitive individualism which is basic to the economic world-view of the city workers, clerks and businessmen who patronised the *Strand*. The greed specifies an economic formation, and the individualism is also basic to the religious and personal dynamic of a world that was largely capitalist, protestant, and individualised. But not only the crimes in Doyle are structural to his society: so are the controls that fictionally operate against them. The detective's central values, rationalism and individualism, are themselves authentic to that world. The crimes and their controls realise the fears and the hopes integral to what was then, and still largely is, modern society. The ideological, rather thán truly investigative, nature of the stories lies in this intimate relationship between the threats and the values that foreclose them: both have the same determining conditions. So the threats (covert in any case) are neither realised nor resolved in ways which unmask the contemporary conditions of life, but in ways which actually validate those creators of anxiety. The ideological circle is complete.

I hope this doesn't suggest that Doyle sat down with some graph paper and took one axis for detective methods and the other for the audience's central anxiety. It's conceivable to compose fiction like that, and it may well become a viable method in the future. But Doyle did it the old-fashioned way: his imagination created issues that were of importance in his period. One of the reasons he was able to imagine such effective fables of anxiety and comfort for his audience was that he was himself one of them. The fear that selfish greed could bring disorder is especially evident in the stories without Holmes. There Doyle's anxieties are often more evident, because Holmes was a comforting force for him as well as his audience. In fact the stories Doyle wrote just after he killed Holmes off in 1893 are the most revealing of all: he felt Holmes kept "his mind from better things," but the absence of that comforting figure also left him vulnerable to his anxieties.

The largely autobiographical book he started in 1893 lays out the fear of selfish greed very fully. In *The Stark Munro Letters* there is some concern with religion and politics, but both those areas of doubt are resolved by a mixture of science and optimism. Stark Munro declares himself a Deist, believing at least in a creating force behind the universe, a sort of divine super-scientist. And he also espouses Social Darwinism, the notion that social evils are steadily being evolved away, and that a better world waits for the poor and oppressed — for those who survive, at least. These large public problems are easily enough resolved. The real drama in the novel lies in the struggle between Munro, the image of the young Dr. Doyle, and James Cullingworth. Based on a man Doyle knew well, Cullingworth is vigorous, confident, manic. He's full of ideas to make money, a ruthless aggressive doctor-businessman. In fact he's a "worst case" hypothesis of an individual crazed by money and power, devoted to the quest for them. He and Munro are medical partners, but they fall out and Cullingworth tries to ruin Munro. The threat enacted by Cullingworth is not just a bullying and manipulative dominion. It's his attractiveness that's the key to the worry. Munro at least partly admires him. Vigour, confidence, success, self-help, making your own fortune — Cullingworth stands for these and Munro approves. It's the mad limits he goes to that are too much. Notice the character's name, Cullingworth. There's something there worth culling. But Munro is strong enough to resist him — "stark" enough in the Scottish idiom both he and Doyle grew up with.

Finally, Cullingworth is contained and avoided, not defeated. He goes off to South America at the end, that land of mystery and high speculative profits. Munro himself, and his young wife, die in a rail crash, consumed by the technology of the modern Cullingworth-like world; but Munro is also put to silence gladly by the Doyle who had only just lived through a similar crisis. As he was writing that novel he was rich with money from the Sherlock Holmes stories, a series he felt to be a money-grubbing venture, an improper use of his own impressive powers. He felt he should be writing historical novels, making himself a new, English version of the ultra-respectable bourgeois hero Sir Walter Scott. Even before he had made his Holmes success Doyle had expressed his feelings about sudden wealth. This was in 1891, in a short novel called *The Doings of Raffles Haw*. It's a fable about a man who stumbled, by a scientific accident, on great wealth and found it caused nothing but trouble to him and to the world. But not only science is suggested. Raffles was the great entrepreneur of the eastern colonial and business empire, founder of Singapore. And the surname suggests what Doyle thought you were like morally if you just did things for money. He soon enough found himself a bit like Raffles.

Doyle's distaste for Sherlock Holmes is well known, and it caused him to kill his hero after the second series of a dozen stories. That extreme measure arose from Newnes's determination to buy more and more stories. During the first six Doyle was already tiring of Holmes; so he asked £50 a story for the second batch, hoping Newnes would refuse. Doyle was naive. That was only £15 a story more than the first, and they were strong sellers. Newnes jumped at it. Then, hoping for another stop, Doyle asked £1000 for the next dozen. Newnes accepted readily again, so Doyle put himself beyond purchase by killing Holmes; that story was hopefully entitled "The Final Problem." But writers don't just encounter their problems in business terms. Their anxieties are the material of their work, and Doyle's feelings intrude into at least two of the first dozen stories. As I have argued elsewhere (*Form and Ideology in Crime Fiction*, Macmillan, London, 1980, pp. 99–101), in "The Man with the Twisted Lip" and "The Engineer's Thumb" the heroes both encode the sense of shame, even of emasculation, that Doyle derived from his association with Newnes and his press.

In the narrative of those stories Holmes reveals the fictional causes of disorder; but in reality he was the medium of the real disorder, and he was interpreted by Doyle as its cause. A figure of such dialectic force was not easily disposed of, not even by death. In 1901 Doyle published a new Holmes story, *The Hound of the Baskervilles* — not a total surrender, as he carefully set it back in time, before Holmes had died. But this wasn't enough. In 1903 Newnes offered the stunning sum of £100 a thousand words, perhaps equivalent to as much as $20,000 a story now, and so Doyle resurrected Holmes in an adventure with the glum title "The Empty House." Doyle never did rid himself of the albatross he felt Holmes to be. In later life he was a busy public man — politics, patriotism, spiritualism, individual rights were all issues he spoke about a lot. But whenever he spoke, people always wanted to know about Sherlock Holmes. It irritated him: and so the figure was his private model of the selfish greed which his stories show as a manifest cause of disorder among respectable men.

It is only seen among men; that limitation, the exclusively masculine viewpoint of the stories, points towards another, more hidden, and perhaps ultimately more threatening source of disorder for Doyle and for his audience: the relations men have with women. The audience of the *Strand* was predominantly male; they bought the magazine, in shops, at bookstalls, especially on stations. They did take it home — there were sections for women and children, but they are just sections; they're kept in their place. Subordination has the structural reflex of insubordination: oppressors must fear the power of the oppressed. To keep women down and yet to need them as wives, mothers, housekeepers, lovers, means there is constant pressure, constant fear that the male dominance will crack. The stories show that pressure; it is certainly latent, and it often operates within the greed structure — it is the daughter's money that the aggressive father is after in several stories. Or is it? Perhaps the greed structure, being related to that acquisitiveness that is at least partly admirable, is itself a euphemism for the darker, less mentionable reasons why fathers desire daughters — which Freud worked out at just this period. Money may stand for the power women hold to attract, unbalance, even to destroy the controlled, organised Victorian male as he sees himself. This fear, like the fear of greed, is expressed most directly in a story written just after Doyle disposed of Holmes, when he had to cope alone with potential disorders.

The short novel *The Parasite* is little known and very hard to get hold of. Largely because Doyle suppressed it; it had only two early reprints, in quite small runs, and one U.S. edition. Doyle dropped it from the impressive list of publications that faces the title page of his books. Some have thought this was because its critique of mesmerism clashed with his later spiritual beliefs, but I suspect it may have been a bit too overt for comfort in the threats its hero discovers. He is a lecturer in medicine at Edinburgh . . . a plain enough projection of Doyle. He is happily engaged, respectable, settled — about to shape a family. He meets a Miss Penelosa, a mesmerist. She is fortyish, ugly, even crippled, from the West Indies; an exotic, foreign, grotesque figure, but she claims to have powers. He scoffs at mesmerism, offers himself as a subject. He becomes enslaved by her; he tries to fight it, locking himself in his bedroom so he can't get to her (or is it so she can't get to him?). But it's no good: he still gets out. Disgrace falls on him; he loses interest in his work; the university actually notices and he's suspended. Then he tries to rob a bank. Finally he goes off, under Miss Penelosa's control, to throw vitriol in his fiancée's face. But luck intervenes — or perhaps it's grace. The vicar calls while he's waiting to do the deed, the spell is broken, and the mesmerist herself dies, across the town, at that moment. There can be little doubt that mesmerism is really a displacement, a code, for sexual obsession. The disorderly and compulsive force of sexuality reeks and smokes through the writing: it's a brilliant piece of imaginative work, reaching into the dark underside of masculine confidence and domination. The woman who threatens masculine control is made foreign and ugly as a way of distancing and judging female power and sensuality together, a witch to remove guilt from her victim.

This fear of the seductive power by which women can bring men to the abyss is recurrent in Doyle's non-Holmes stories, outlasting and apparently deeper than the fear of greed. I'll give two very striking, even stunning examples. "The Terror of Blue John Gap," written in 1909,

enacts the fear of being engulfed by feminine sexuality. The hero pene-
trates a cave and then senses a fearful, powerful shuddering presence.
The phallic and vaginal imagery of the story is obvious. He finally es-
capes this debilitating experience and arranges for the mouth to be
blocked up for ever; that gap that the title tells us is blue, from a male
viewpoint obscene, is closed. If that seems a strained interpretation of
the name, what other explanation can be given for Doyle's frequent use
of versions of it, as in "The Gully of Bluemansdyke" and "The Parson
of Jackman's Gulch"? The story does rationalise "Blue John" as a type
of valuable stone — greed is brought in as a euphemism — but the
barely latent forces of the story are at work even in the title.

Another even more neurotic and savage way of immobilising the
sexual force of women is presented in a little known story "The Case of
Lady Sannox." It was written in 1894, that revealing year after Doyle
killed off Holmes and encoded his fears without the protecting hero to
minimise them. Lady Sannox is the wife of a London physician —
Doyle territory again. She is having an affair with a surgeon. Her lover
is called out to do an emergency operation on the wife of a wealthy
Turk. Lying drugged, shrouded by veils, in a darkened room, she appears to have an infected wound on her lower lip. The surgeon is reluc-
tant to operate, but the husband assures him it is crucial, and presses a
hundred sovereigns on him (greed for money is here too). So he acts.
With a quick double slash he cuts a thick "broad V-shaped piece" from
her bottom lip. Blood spurts. Pain cuts through the opium. As she jerks,
the veils fall away. Yes, that's right, it *is* Lady Sannox all the time. This
terrible story does not just present a sadistic disfigurement. It is a barely
coded version of the cruel operation called female circumcision — itself
a euphemism for the removal of the clitoris. It was recommended at
times in Victorian England for women who were "restless," a codeword
for improperly sensual. The husband makes this meaning of the story
quite clear as he turns to the stunned lover: "'It was really necessary for
Marion, this operation' said he, 'not physically but morally, you know,
morally.'"

Doyle wrote "The Case of Lady Sannox" while his wife was already
ill with the tuberculosis that would kill her in 1906. He remarked at the
time that their bedroom had become a sickroom. Sexual frustration and
the associated guilt sat on him heavily, but only some of the stories tell
the tale; he controlled himself otherwise. And before long he had more
specific pressures to control. In 1897 he fell in love with Jean Leckie.
They conducted a platonic and even courtly love affair till they married
in 1907, the year after his wife's death. Doyle coped with this situation

through a chivalrous moral structure more like that of his medieval historical novels than ordinary life, but the reflex of such containment strikes out in those stories which take fierce vengeance on the disturbing attractiveness of women. The circumstances of his wife's illness and the Leckie affair didn't create this hostile, fearful attitude to women; they only exacerbated it. The Holmes stories themselves, written before his wife was even ill, bear clearly the traces of the same fear that women tempt men to be disorderly, that they offer another path to the abyss. And just as that fear is realised, so there is a force to contain it — Sherlock Holmes himself. The importance of this structure to Doyle and to his audience is indicated by the fact that it's defined in the very first paragraph of the very first *Strand* story, "A Scandal in Bohemia." Watson states Holmes's position on women:

> He never spoke of the softer passions, save with a gibe and a
> sneer. They were admirable things for the observer — excellent
> for drawing the veil from men's motives and actions. But for the
> trained reasoner to admit such intrusions into his own delicate and
> finely adjusted temperament was to introduce a distracting factor
> which might throw a doubt upon all his mental results. (p. 32)

Masculine, delicate, scientific . . . the ideas go together to state the male self-concept, the delicate frailty it perceives in itself, and the protection it finds in a scientific hero. And even for Holmes, woman is a threat; vigilance must be eternal. Irene Adler is the heroine of this story. She's the discarded mistress of the King of Bohemia. She outwits not only the King, but Holmes as well, and he recognises her power. Watson actually opens the story by saying "To Sherlock Holmes she is always *the* woman." And so she is; she throws out the archetypal challenge to men. She's clever, determined, a royal mistress, a match even for Sherlock Holmes, a concise statement of the power of those seen as the enemy. In the early stories there are two distinct, but related, patterns of masculine fear. One is the fear of castration, directly losing potency. The other is the fear of being supplanted, losing control over a daughter or a wife — a less direct but equally severe threat to the potency of the possessing man. Greed is still the dominant force in the two stories where a past crime disturbs a present family, and in the two where a servant betrays a family's trust. The past and the male servants are forces beyond sexual anxiety. But the other eight stories are rich with masculine neurosis, underlying and often energising the greed motifs.

In "A Case of Identity," "The Copper Beeches" and "The Speckled

Band" a father refuses to let a daughter have her money and the independence to leave him. The most famous of the three stories, "The Speckled Band," indicates the primacy of the sexual force: Dr. Roylott attacks his step-daughter by driving a snake through a hole he has pierced in her bedroom wall. In "The Beryl Coronet" the father loses a daughter and at the same time the precious circlet is wrenched out of shape, a piece broken off: a clear token of the disturbing deflowering. The threat of Irene Adler in "A Scandal in Bohemia" has been discussed, and it's noteworthy that her most private place (it's a safe in the overt plot) is where she locks away the instrument of power by which she can politically emasculate the King. "The Noble Bachelor" loses his promised wife to a man with a prior claim, and different types of masculine debilitation are suffered in "The Man with the Twisted Lip" and "The Engineer's Thumb."

Against these disturbed states, the happy married life of Watson is an ideal: but it's so because you never hear about the wife; he spends all his time with Holmes. Mrs. Watson is a good housekeeper who makes no claim on her husband. To create this passive relationship seems the main reason why Doyle made Watson leave the rooms he shared with Holmes. I doubt if Doyle was ever bothered by the fear of a trace of homosexuality between the room-mates. Watson and Holmes have the sort of British male relationship which excludes all sexuality, including anything as positive as homosexual feelings. The French and the Americans tend to see and depict Holmes as a foppish dandy, with a distinct effeminacy, but they're misled by the languid manners that among the English are held to reveal effortless superiority.

It seems clear enough that the early Holmes stories realised fears the respectable audience had about their own weaknesses. Selfishness, greed, sexual tensions might disrupt the carefully poised bourgeois nuclear family. But these forces are not explored fully, not brought out into an analytic, unmasking light. Rather they are appeased by a figure from the very socioeconomic matrix that generated the disturbance in the first place, a helping hero who enacts a faith in rational individualism. So the ideological trick is turned, in a way so neat and so transitory that the fears remain and need to be assuaged again, and again — as each monthly issue appears.

The well-remembered icon of Holmes catches strikingly well the essence of the myth and its functioning force. Yet this powerful image is not Doyle's work: it's a notable example of the part the audience plays in the constitution of cultural ideology. The essence of the icon is itself a myth. In the early stories and illustrations, Holmes smokes a straight pipe, and like any other respectable gentleman of the period would only wear a deerstalker hat and Inverness cape in the country — not in town. But once an illustrator gave him a big curved meerschaum pipe, it seemed so right that it stuck, though it's in none of the early illustrations. You have to support a big curved pipe as you smoke, it's too heavy just for the teeth: a passive, thinking man's pipe. And though Holmes rarely uses a magnifying glass, that's what he has in the other hand in the familiar picture, to show how his thinking is applied, investigative. The original Holmes dressed smartly, striped trousers and bowler for business, a trilby for informal occasions, a silk hat on formal outings, and on one relaxed occasion even a straw boater. So the original illustrations tell us. But in our memory he must wear the country outfit, wherever he is, to stress that he's a hunter, stalking the fugitive weaknesses of his readers. And he never does say "Elementary my dear Watson." He says "Elementary" and he says "My dear Watson" often enough, but the completion process of a live myth has run them together, because together they perfectly catch the aloof and the friendly sides of his relation with Watson and, by extension, with the reader.

So even if you don't read the stories, Sherlock Holmes is memorable and functional; he lives. He won't live in a functional way for ever. He'll become a historical curiosity, like other heroes of the past. Nicholas Meyer's novel *The Seven-Per-Cent Solution,* and the film made of it, indicate a stage in this process: insisting that Sigmund Freud was a greater detective than Holmes — in Meyer's culture the subjective consolations of bourgeois psychiatry play the role that rational individualism fulfilled for Holmes's initial audience. That is an authentic and intimate development: the two medical men lived in similar metropolitan conditions but Freud made overt the forces that Doyle only covertly realised in fiction. Further developments will no doubt be more distant from Doyle's patterns: new societies, new cultures; new anxieties, new consolations.

For his period, Doyle caught in the Holmes stories an ensemble of attitudes, of fears and hopes. For anyone interested in seeing how dominant social groups use their literature to state and control fears, the Holmes stories are a fascinating source. They provide a means of recreating the structure of feeling in a complex period, one which has both continuities and contrasts with our own period. To illuminate the continuities and contrasts will illuminate our own patterns of disturbance, among them our own urgent and individualist quest for money and our still uneasy relations between the sexes — and just what are our hopes? What contemporary figures embody our values, act now as the great detective did for Doyle and his audience? Media figures? Industrialists? Paperback gurus? Politicians? Whoever they are, is their protective aura not in fact just as fictional, just as illusory — just as ideological — as that of Sherlock Holmes himself?

# CATHERINE BELSEY

# Deconstructing the Text: Sherlock Holmes

---

Belsey's essay on Holmes comes from her book *Critical Practice* (London and New York: Methuen, 1980), an introduction to contemporary, post-structuralist critical theory. What the various branches of contemporary theory have in common, she suggests, is a tendency to "question, not only some of the specific assumptions of common sense, . . . but the authority of the concept of common sense itself." They argue that "common sense itself is ideologically and discursively constructed, rooted in a specific historical situation": "the 'obvious' and the 'natural' are not *given* but *produced* in a specific society by the ways in which that society talks and thinks about itself and its experience" (Belsey 2–3).

As this emphasis on "society" and "authority" indicates, Belsey's own theoretical interest in the suppressed or ignored undertexts of literature is particularly an interest in "the limits of ideological representation." As she argues, following Pierre Macherey's Marxist precedent, "In its absences, and in the collisions between its divergent meanings, the text implicitly criticizes its own ideology; it contains within itself the critique of its own values," and so "[t]o deconstruct the text . . . is to open it, to release the possible positions of its intelligibility, including those which reveal the partiality (in both senses) of the ideology inscribed in its text" (Belsey 109). Like Knight, she finds the Holmes stories "elusive concerning both sexuality and politics" (p. 387). Attending particularly to the recurrent presence in the stories of "shadowy, mysterious and often silent women" (p. 385), she argues that these presences contradict and expose the stories' ideological assumptions.

---

In locating the transitions and uncertainties of the text it is important to remember, Macherey[1] insists, sustaining the parallel with psychoanalysis, that the problem of the work is not the same as its *consciousness* of a problem (Macherey 1978, p. 93). In "Charles Augustus Milverton," one of the short stories from *The Return of Sherlock Holmes,*

---

[1] ***Macherey:*** Pierre Macherey, *A Theory of Literary Production,* trans. Geoffrey Wall (London: Routledge and Kegan Paul, 1978). [Editor's note]

Conan Doyle presents the reader with an ethical problem. Milverton is a blackmailer; blackmail is a crime not easily brought to justice since the victims are inevitably unwilling to make the matter public; the text therefore proposes for the reader's consideration that in such a case illegal action may be ethical. Holmes plans to burgle Milverton's house to recover the letters which are at stake, and both Watson and the text appear to conclude, after due consideration, that the action is morally justifiable. The structure of the narrative is symmetrical: one victim initiates the plot, another concludes it. While Holmes and Watson hide in Milverton's study a woman shoots him, protesting that he has ruined her life. Inspector Lestrade asks Holmes to help catch the murderer. Holmes replies that certain crimes justify private revenge, that his sympathies are with the criminal and that he will not handle the case. The reader is left to ponder the ethical implications of his position.

Meanwhile, on the fringes of the text, another narrative is sketched. It too contains problems but these are not foregrounded. Holmes's client is the Lady Eva Blackwell, a beautiful debutante who is to be married to the Earl of Dovercourt. Milverton has secured letters she has written "to an impecunious young squire in the country." Lady Eva does not appear in the narrative in person. The content of the letters is not specified, but they are "imprudent, Watson, nothing worse" (p. 273). Milverton describes them as "sprightly." Holmes's sympathies, and ours, are with the Lady Eva. Nonetheless we, and Holmes, accept without question on the one hand that the marriage with the Earl of Dovercourt is a desirable one and on the other that were he to see the letters he would certainly break off the match. The text's elusiveness on the content of the letters, and the absence of the Lady Eva herself, deflects the reader's attention from the potentially contradictory ideology of marriage which the narrative takes for granted.

This second narrative is also symmetrical. The murderer too is a woman with a past. She is not identified. Milverton has sent her letters to her husband who in consequence "broke his gallant heart and died" (p. 283). Again the text is unable to be precise about the content of the letters since to do so would be to risk losing the sympathy of the reader for either the woman or her husband.

In the mean time Holmes has become engaged. By offering to marry Milverton's housemaid he has secured information about the lay-out of the house he is to burgle. Watson remonstrates about the subsequent fate of the girl, but Holmes replies:

> You can't help it, my dear Watson. You must play your cards as
> best you can when such a stake is on the table. However, I rejoice
> to say that I have a hated rival who will certainly cut me out the in-
> stant that my back is turned. What a splendid night it is! (p. 277)

The housemaid is not further discussed in the story.

The sexuality of these three shadowy women motivates the narrative
and yet is barely present in it. The disclosure which ends the story is thus
scarcely a disclosure at all. Symbolically Holmes has burnt the letters,
records of women's sexuality. Watson's opening paragraph constitutes
an apology for the "reticence" of the narrative: " . . . with *due suppression* the story may be told. . . . "; "The reader will excuse me if I conceal
the date *or any other fact. . . .* " (my italics).

The project of the Sherlock Holmes stories is to dispel magic and
mystery, to make everything explicit, accountable, subject to scientific
analysis. The phrase most familiar to all readers — "Elementary, my
dear Watson" — is in fact a misquotation, but its familiarity is no accident since it precisely captures the central concern of the stories.
Holmes and Watson are both men of science. Holmes, the "genius," is
a scientific conjuror who insists on disclosing how the trick is done. The
stories begin in enigma, mystery, the impossible, and conclude with an
explanation which makes it clear that logical deduction and scientific
method render all mysteries accountable to reason:

> I am afraid that my explanation may disillusionize you, but it has
> always been my habit to hide none of my methods, either from
> my friend Watson or from anyone who might take an intelligent
> interest in them. ("The Reigate Squires")

The stories are a plea for science not only in the spheres convention-
ally associated with detection (footprints, traces of hair or cloth, cigarette ends), where they have been deservedly influential on forensic
practice, but in all areas. They reflect the widespread optimism characteristic of their period concerning the comprehensive power of positivist
science. Holmes's ability to deduce Watson's train of thought, for instance, is repeatedly displayed, and it owes nothing to the supernatural.
Once explained, the reasoning process always appears "absurdly simple," open to the commonest of common sense.

The project of the stories themselves, enigma followed by disclosure, echoes precisely the structure of the classic realist text. The narrator himself draws attention to the parallel between them:

> "Excellent!" I cried.

"Elementary," said he. "It is one of those instances where the reasoner can produce an effect which seems remarkable to his neighbour because the latter has missed the one little point which is the basis of the deduction. The same may be said, my dear fellow, for the effect of some of these little sketches of yours, which is entirely meretricious, depending as it does upon your retaining in your own hands some factors in the problem which are never imparted to the reader. Now, at present I am in the position of these same readers, for I hold in this hand several threads of one of the strangest cases which ever perplexed a man's brain, and yet I lack the one or two which are needful to complete my theory. But I'll have them, Watson, I'll have them!" ("The Crooked Man")

(The passage is quoted by Macherey in his discussion of the characteristic structure of narrative, 1978, p. 35.)

The project also requires the maximum degree of "realism" — verisimilitude, plausibility. In the interest of science no hint of the fantastic or the implausible is permitted to remain once the disclosure is complete. This is why even their own existence as writing is so frequently discussed within the texts. The stories are alluded to as Watson's "little sketches," his "memoirs." They resemble fictions because of Watson's unscientific weakness for story-telling:

I must admit, Watson, that you have some power of selection which atones for much which I deplore in your narratives. Your fatal habit of looking at everything from the point of view of a story instead of as a scientific exercise has ruined what might have been an instructive and even classical series of demonstrations. ("The Abbey Grange")

In other words, the fiction itself accounts even for its own fictionality, and the text thus appears wholly transparent. The success with which the Sherlock Holmes stories achieve an illusion of reality is repeatedly demonstrated. In their foreword to *The Sherlock Holmes Companion* (1962) Michael and Mollie Hardwick comment on their own recurrent illusion "that we were dealing with a figure of real life rather than of fiction. How vital Holmes appears, compared with many people of one's own acquaintance."

De Waal's bibliography of Sherlock Holmes lists 25 "Sherlockian" periodicals apparently largely devoted to conjectures, based on the "evidence" of the stories, concerning matters only hinted at in the texts — Holmes's education, his income and his romantic and sexual adventures. According to the *Times* in December 1967, letters to Sherlock

Holmes were then still commonly addressed to 221B Baker Street, many of them asking for the detective's help.

Nonetheless these stories, whose overt project is total explicitness, total verisimilitude in the interests of a plea for scientificity, are haunted by shadowy, mysterious and often silent women. Their silence repeatedly conceals their sexuality, investing it with a dark and magical quality which is beyond the reach of scientific knowledge. In "The Greek Interpreter" Sophie Kratides has run away with a man. Though she is the pivot of the plot she appears only briefly: "I could not see her clearly enough to know more than that she was tall and graceful, with black hair, and clad in some sort of loose white gown." Connotatively the white gown marks her as still virginal and her flight as the result of romance rather than desire. At the same time the dim light surrounds her with shadow, the unknown. "The Crooked Man" concerns Mrs. Barclay, whose husband is found dead on the day of her meeting with her lover of many years before. Mrs. Barclay is now insensible, "temporarily insane" since the night of the murder and therefore unable to speak. In "The Dancing Men" Mrs. Elsie Cubitt, once engaged to a criminal, longs to speak but cannot bring herself to break her silence. By the time Holmes arrives she is unconscious, and she remains so for the rest of the story. Ironically the narrative concerns the breaking of the code which enables her former lover to communicate with her. Elsie's only contribution to the correspondence is the word, "Never." The precise nature of their relationship is left mysterious, constructed of contrary suggestions. Holmes says she feared and hated him; the lover claims, "She had been engaged to me, and she would have married me, I believe, if I had taken over another profession." When her husband moves to shoot the man whose coded messages are the source of a "terror" which is "wearing her away," Elsie restrains him with compulsive strength. On the question of her motives the text is characteristically elusive. Her husband recounts the story:

> I was angry with my wife that night for having held me back when I might have caught the skulking rascal. She said that she feared that I might come to harm. For an instant it had crossed my mind that perhaps what she really feared was that *he* might come to harm, for I could not doubt that she knew who this man was and what he meant by those strange signals. But there is a tone in my wife's voice, Mr. Holmes, and a look in her eyes which forbid doubt, and I am sure that it was indeed my own safety that was in her mind. (p. 256)

After her husband's death Elsie remains a widow, faithful to his memory and devoting her life to the care of the poor, apparently expiating something unspecified, perhaps an act or a state of feeling, remote or recent.

"The Dancing Men" is "about" Holmes's method of breaking the cipher. Its project is to dispel any magic from the deciphering process. Elsie's silence is in the interest of the story since she knows the code. But she also "knows" her feelings towards her former lover. Contained in the completed and fully disclosed story of the decipherment is another uncompleted and undisclosed narrative which is more than merely peripheral to the text as a whole. Elsie's past is central and causal. As a result, the text with its project of dispelling mystery is haunted by the mysterious state of mind of a woman who is unable to speak.

The classic realist text had not yet developed a way of signifying women's sexuality except in a metaphoric or symbolic mode whose presence disrupts the realist surface. Joyce and Lawrence were beginning to experiment at this time with modes of sexual signification but in order to do so they largely abandoned the codes of realism. So much is readily apparent. What is more significant, however, is that the presentation of so many women in the Sherlock Holmes stories as shadowy, mysterious and magical figures precisely contradicts the project of explicitness, transgresses the values of the texts, and in doing so throws into relief the poverty of the contemporary concept of science. These stories, pleas for a total explicitness about the world, are unable to explain an area which nonetheless they cannot ignore. The version of science which the texts present would constitute a clear challenge to ideology: the interpretation of all areas of life, physical, social and psychological, is to be subject to rational scrutiny and the requirements of coherent theorization. Confronted, however, by an area in which ideology itself is uncertain, the Sherlock Holmes stories display the limits of their own project and are compelled to manifest the inadequacy of a bourgeois scientificity which, working within the constraints of ideology, is thus unable to challenge it.

Perhaps the most interesting case, since it introduces an additional area of shadow, is "The Second Stain," which concerns two letters. Lady Hilda Trelawney Hope does speak. She has written before her marriage "an indiscreet letter . . . a foolish letter, a letter of an impulsive, loving girl" (p. 306). Had her husband read the letter his confidence in her would have been for ever destroyed. Her husband is nonetheless presented as entirely sympathetic, and here again we encounter the familiar contradiction between a husband's supposed reaction, accepted as just, and the reaction offered to the reader by the text. In return for her original letter Lady Hilda gives her blackmailer a letter from "a certain foreign potentate" stolen from the dispatch box of her husband, the European Secretary of State. This political letter is symbolically parallel to the first sexual one. Its contents are equally elusive but it too is "indiscreet," "hot-headed"; certain phrases in it are "provocative." Its publication would produce "a most dangerous state of feeling" in the nation (p. 291). Lady Hilda's innocent folly is the cause of the theft: she knows nothing of politics and was not in a position to understand the consequences of her action. Holmes ensures the restoration of the political letter and both secrets are preserved.

Here the text is symmetrically elusive concerning both sexuality and politics. Watson, as is so often the case where these areas are concerned, begins the story by apologizing for his own reticence and vagueness. In the political instance what becomes clear as a result of the uncertainty of the text is the contradictory nature of the requirements of verisimilitude in fiction. The potentate's identity and the nature of his indiscretion cannot be named without involving on the part of the reader either disbelief (the introduction of a patently fictional country would be dangerous to the project of verisimilitude) or belief (dangerous to the text's status as fiction, entertainment; also quite possibly politically dangerous). The scientific project of the texts require that they deal in "facts," but their nature as fiction forbids the introduction of facts.

The classic realist text installs itself in the space between fact and illusion through the presentation of a simulated reality which is plausible but *not real*. In this lies its power as myth. It is because fiction does not normally deal with "politics" directly, except in the form of history or satire, that it is ostensibly innocent and therefore ideologically effective. But in its evasion of the real also lies its weakness as "realism." Through their transgression of their own values of explicitness and verisimilitude, the Sherlock Holmes stories contain within themselves an implicit critique of their limited nature as characteristic examples of classic realism. They thus offer the reader through the process of deconstruction a form of knowledge, not about "life" or "the world," but about the nature of fiction itself.

Thus, in adopting the form of classic realism, the only appropriate literary mode, positivism is compelled to display its own limitations. Offered as science, it reveals itself to a deconstructive reading as ideology at the very moment that classic realism, offered as verisimilitude, reveals itself as fiction. In claiming to make explicit and *understandable* what appears mysterious, these texts offer evidence of the tendency of positivism to push to the margins of experience whatever it cannot explain or understand. In the Sherlock Holmes stories classic realism ironically tells a truth, though not the truth about the world which is the project of classic realism. The truth the stories tell is the truth about ideology, the truth which ideology represses, its own existence as ideology itself.

ROSEMARY HENNESSY AND
RAJESWARI MOHAN

# "The Speckled Band":
# The Construction of Woman
# in a Popular Text of Empire

This essay is drawn from a longer piece, "The Construction of
Woman in Three Popular Texts of Empire: Towards a Critique
of Materialist Feminism," first published in *Textual Practice* 3.3
(1989): 323–59. (The other two texts are an 1894 story by
Flora Annie Steel, "Mussumat Kirpo's Doll," and an 1895 political cartoon from *Punch*.) As its subtitle's reference to "materialist feminism" indicates, the essay develops from and participates in "feminist critiques within Marxism," critiques that
particularly consider "the social construction of gender" and
"women's positioning within patriarchal and capitalist systems"
(Hennessy and Mohan 324). Like Knight in this respect,
Hennessy and Mohan see Doyle's texts as "part of the general
work of crisis containment performed by ideology" in the late
nineteenth century (326); but they see this crisis as global and colonial no less than domestic, and political no less than social. Like
Belsey, they explore the "gaps and contradictions" in the text, and
find them "undermining both the coherence of [Holmes's] explanation and the obviousness of Holmes's authority" (p. 399).

The story's gaps and contradictions, Hennessy and Mohan
find, are particularly associated with Grimesby Roylott and
Helen Stoner and serve to signal their ideological relationship
both to English society and to Holmes. Roylott, with his links
to the Orient (his Indian animals, his friendship with gypsies, his
turkish slippers), is associated with "eastern irrationality" just as,
by virtue of his prodigality and his brutal and intemperate behavior, he is associated with "aristocratic dissipation" and
"lower-class un-respectability" (p. 392). Helen, poised ambiguously between the conditions (sexual no less than capitalistic)
of property and of property owner, cannot be granted her independence, of speech any more than of capitalistic or social
status. Holmes, ostensibly opposed to Roylott, is nevertheless
linked to him as the representative of that which Roylott has
failed to be — "western, rational," "the middle-class restrained

gentleman." As such, Holmes represents "a system of patriarchal gender relations that set both of them apart from woman as
other"; and his solution of the crime serves the purposes of that
system by managing and expediting Helen's swift transition
from daughter to wife. This, Hennessy and Mohan argue,
"comprises the ideological work of the story": "it eliminates the
threatening position of the independent, propertied female subject by means of the band of paternal protectors" (pp. 392–93).

---

"The Adventure of the Speckled Band" is one of several stories
Conan Doyle published in the *Strand* magazine in the 1890s which
negotiates these contradictions [present in late nineteenth century
capitalism's "articulation of racial, class, and gender difference"]
through a variety of narrative strategies: the construction of Holmes as
rational protector, the resolution of the narrative's enigma, and the positioning of the reader. The problem presented in the case involves a
father's control over his unmarried daughter's property. Thirty-year-old
Helen Stoner turns to Holmes for help in solving the riddle of her twin
sister Julia's death a fortnight before her marriage. Helen's anxiety is
based on vague suspicions sparked by the recurrence before her own
impending marriage of a series of events similar to those surrounding
Julia's death. The Stoner sisters live in a decaying ancestral manor with
their step-father, Dr. Grimesby Roylott, the last son of a pauperized
aristocratic family. In India where he practiced medicine, Roylott married
the Stoners' widowed mother who bequeathed a considerable sum of
money ("not less than a thousand a year") entirely to Roylott so long as the
twins lived with him, with a provision that a certain annual sum should
be allowed to each daughter in the event of her marriage (p. 155).
Holmes's detection discloses Roylott as his daughter's murderer, motivated by greed for the money he would lose when she married. In staging
the murder as symbolic rape (Roylott kills Julia by means of a poisonous
snake sent through a vent connecting his bedroom to hers) the narrative

dramatizes the sexual economy of patriarchy: the equation of woman
and property. At the same time, it presents Holmes as woman's protector, rescuing her from the villainous patriarch's domination and defending her right to control over her own property and person.

In the construction of Holmes as hero, the narrative draws upon the
codes of otherness such as irrationality, lack of control, and dissipation,
set by the discourses of alterity, and in so doing redefines subjectivities
in ways historically necessitated by the regional and global rearrange-

ments taking place in the late nineteenth century. Holmes's heroic status is constructed relationally in the narrative through a semic code[1] that links various subject positions. Examining these links makes visible a network of gaps and contradictions which are suppressed in the interests of the narrative's coherent resolution. These gaps, associated with both Roylott and Helen, are details which "exceed" the solution to the crime — details the solution does not and can not explain — specifically, Roylott's association with the gypsies, his possession of an excessive number of Indian animals, and Helen's silencing. As we will show, Holmes's status as hero depends on the down-played existence of these details.

Holmes's opposition to and complicity with the villainous patriarch, Roylott, indicates the articulation of a "new" masculine subject. Roylott is coded as a failed aristocrat whose decline is owing to a weakness of both moral fibre and blood, a hereditary mania that translates into lack of self-control and results ultimately in his criminal fall from respectability. His friendship with the gypsies upon his return from India is related to this fall, and is presented as simultaneously self-explanatory and suspicious. Helen's suggestion that the "band" of gypsies are linked to her sister's death draws on a commonly held suspicion of gypsies, but it does not explain the association between them and the lapsed aristocrat, Roylott. None the less, this unexplained contradictory class coding of Roylott helps valorize Holmes's status by positioning him in opposition to the negative upper- and lower-class alternatives associated with the villain. Holmes's amateur detective work (bearing the marks of an emergent professionalism: wage work as skilled yet artful dedication) takes on its value in opposition to Roylott's association with both aristocratic squandering and lower-class shiftlessness.[2]

---

[1] *semic code:* Roland Barthes's term for that aspect of narrative which contributes to the construction of characters. A *seme,* in this sense, is a minimal unit of semic code, a specific characteristic or trait. [Editor's note]

[2] Watson's introduction to Holmes in *A Study in Scarlet* makes clear Holmes's new professional class position (p. 25). Unlike the "armchair lounger who evolves all these neat little paradoxes in the seclusion of his own study," Holmes's theories are so practical that he depends upon them for his "bread and cheese" (p. 28). The kinds of knowledge he commands indicate a fairly "new" middle-class position. He has mastered the new natural sciences — chemistry and geology — is familiar with sensational literature (gained from sources like the *Daily Telegraph*), and also dabbles in genteel and manly leisure-time activities. As the skilled detective who applies practical scientific knowledge to protecting the social order, Holmes typifies a re-articulated masculine subject position which emerged with the transformation of the state accompanying Britain's transition to monopoly capitalism. The criminology Holmes both studies and advances exemplifies one feature of this transformation: the recruitment of science for increased state intervention in civil society, deployed through the free entrepreneurial subject who spontaneously serves the interests of the state by striving to maintain law and order.

In conjunction with his contradictory class location, Roylott's links to the Orient encode him with multiple semes for otherness in over-determined opposition to the western, rational, middle-class Holmes. Semically marked for aristocratic dissipation, lower-class un-respectabil-ity, and eastern irrationality, Roylott presents a profile of the criminal as all that Holmes, the middle-class restrained gentleman, is not. The semic association of Roylott with the wild Orient is also in excess of the requirements of the solution — Holmes's disclosure of the phallic mur-der weapon. Roylott has lived in Calcutta, has access to knowledge of poisons available only to "a clever and ruthless man who had had an Eastern training" (p. 172), keeps a baboon and a cheetah as well as the deadly swamp adder, and in his death scene is wearing turkish slippers. Like the gypsies, the Indian animals are decoys in the untangling of the enigma, possible suspects that establish a false lead but which ultimately are not required by the logic of the solution. However, Roylott's asso-ciation with the East blurs with his ties to the gypsies — long figures of alterity in the west — and qualifies *as explanation* for his violence. The hereditary mania blamed for his outbursts "had . . . been intensified by his long residence in the tropics" (p. 155), and it is his robbery by a native in Calcutta that incites Roylott to beat his butler to death, an act that lands him in prison. While Roylott's violence is associated causally with the East, its enactment in relation to three significant figures — the colonial servant, the white daughter, and the village blacksmith he as-saults — constructs him in opposition to a series of "others" arranged along race, gender, and class lines. However, Holmes's privileged posi-tion in the narrative as subject of knowledge with which the reader iden-tifies serves to dissociate him from these scenes of violence and to down-play any possible connections among imperial domination, patriarchal control, and class privilege.

Still, as opposed as Roylott and Holmes are made to appear, the narrative resolution that valorizes Holmes as hero depends on his links to Roylott in a system of patriarchal gender relations that set both of them apart from woman as other. It is the threatened disruption of this system that occasions the murder constituting the narrative's enigma. In his daughter's murder and symbolic rape Roylott enacts the ultimate patriarchal privilege: control over women *as* property that simulta-neously denies them access *to* property and to sexual consent. The nar-rative makes use of the twin sisters to negotiate woman's contradictory positioning as subject and object within capitalist patriarchal arrange-ments, simultaneously cancelling and affirming woman's claim to and status as property as she shifts positions from daughter to wife. It is the management of the "moment" of transition between these two highly controlled positions that comprises the ideological work of the story as it eliminates the threatening position of the independent, propertied female subject by means of the band of paternal protectors.

Questions about woman's status as subject in relation to property and sexual consent that are raised and quickly resolved in the narrative are symptomatic of the contest over woman's ambiguous social position, a struggle waged in the long campaign for reform of married women's property rights. The Married Women's Property Act (1882) overturned the common law of coverture according to which a wife forfeited all property upon marriage to her husband because husband and wife were one person and that person was the husband. While the formal arrangement of the family remained the same, legalized in the heterosexual monogamous Christian marriage, profound changes in property during industrialization — from land to money — created entirely new forms of wealth. By the late nineteenth century a transformation of entrepreneurial activity, brought about by the development of finance capital exemplified in the creation of the Stock Exchange and the legal recognition of limited liability companies, encouraged the investment of risk capital. These changes in economic practice meant that landed property inherited through a family line was no longer the sole source of wealth, a shift which paved the way for legal reforms relating to the family.[3] These legal reforms were also part of a process in the late nineteenth century by which the state, mediated by voluntary organizations, gradually intervened further in the private sphere in response to demands for civil equality from trade unions and women. These demands provided the state with opportunities to control and direct the emergence of an expanded and reconstructed middle-class workforce whose social position was grounded on education and business skills rather than inheritance. As a result, the division between public and private domains which undergirded the development of industrialization was re-articulated as the private family was gradually permeated by the disciplinary apparatuses of state intervention. In the process patriarchal gender relations were reshaped.

The Married Women's Property Act exemplifies the dynamics of this rearrangement. The contest over property rights simultaneously constituted and managed a crisis in woman's social position brought on by changes across the social formation which made visible woman's

---

[3] Abie Sachs and Joan Hoff Wilson, *Sexism and the Law: A Study of Male Beliefs and Legal Bias in Britain and the United States* (New York: Free Press, 1978).

contradictory social status, spanning positions as property and property owner. Legal reforms addressed this crisis by giving women control over their property; but by doing so in terms of male protection, the law kept in place woman's position as non-rational other.[4]

Because feminist histories of the Married Women's Property Act have been based on a liberal humanist understanding of social relations, they leave unquestioned the notions of equity, property, and the market-place western women struggled to gain access to. In opposition, our reading suggests a radical rethinking of these unquestioned categories in terms of the global exploitative relations they help to sustain. From this position, property reforms can be seen to readjust the patriarchal family alliance in Britain by perpetuating women's exclusion from full social participation. But this exclusion was only a regional aspect of the global social relations these reforms both depended on and affected. Reform of women's property rights also contributed to a shift in productive relations which would allow middle-class women in Britain to be recruited into a newly structured market-place. In turn, the emergence of the tertiary sector in Britain depended on the shift to the colonies of production and exploitable labour no longer viable in the metropole.

As the campaign for property reform made clear, the subject position most endangering the patriarchy — both sexually and economically — was the *femme sole,* a position made available by the shift in productive relations and threatening to elude the discourses of male protection that secured the feminine as other. Like all men, the single woman had legal control over her property. But because the skills thought to be needed for the administration of her property were locked in the male professions, the single woman's ability to exercise that control was curtailed.[5] Women's increasing demands in the late nineteenth century for access to the professions threatened the Victo-

---

[4]Feminist histories of this legislation have either applauded the reform as a landmark victory in feminist struggles for equality or in a more critical mode pointed to the ways equality under the new law was undermined by other legal and economic structures. For an example of the former see Lee Holcombe, *Victorian Ladies At Work: Middle Class Working Women in England and Wales, 1850–1914* (Hamden, Conn.: Archon, 1973); the latter position is exemplified in Dorothy M. Stetson, *A Woman's Issue: The Politics of Family Law Reform in England* (Westport, Conn.: Greenwood, 1982); Sachs and Wilson, op. cit., point out that although the act gave women the right to their separate earnings and property, it did not grant them legal status as persons.

[5]Women were not granted legal status as persons in British law until 1928 when an act of Parliament granted all adult women the vote: for an overview of the long struggle in the courts to grant women legal status as "persons" following the Second Reform Act (1867), see Sachs and Wilson, op. cit., pp. 22ff.

rian ideology of separate spheres by transgressing the paternalistic management of the division between the subject *of* property and the subject
*as* property that constituted the feminine as other. The unusual terms of
Mrs. Stoner's will in "The Speckled Band" — foreclosing the possibility
that either daughter will occupy the position of *femme sole* — functions
to suppress the availability of this dangerous feminine subject position,
one that by the 1890s — when large numbers of single middle-class
women were recruited into a newly formed clerical workforce — was
becoming increasingly available.[6]

The same discourse of protection used in the law to justify women's
limited liability and mystify the operation of patriarchal control underlies Holmes's defence of Helen's property right in "The Speckled
Band," and to a similar end. Holmes's opposition to Roylott's control
over his daughter's sexual and economic power might seem at first
glance to define a position that opposes traditional patriarchal domination. However, Holmes's inclusion in a circuit of exchange that enables
Helen's passage from father to husband makes his role as protector
problematic. As the go-between from the father who symbolically stran-
gles his daughter with his poisoned phallic band to the fiancé whose
power is encoded in his silencing of the daughter-wife's secret rape, the
position of Holmes is in collusion with a "band" of patriarchs implicated in suppressing that which poses an economic and sexual threat to
patriarchal gender relations. Holmes's position as opponent to the traditional patriarch defines him as a "new" man, but, as we will show, this
"newness" is more a re-articulation than a transformation of the sexual
economy of patriarchy.

The construction of Helen as "silent" provides the premiss for
Watson's narrative and allows Holmes the last word on it: Helen has
pledged Watson to secrecy and he can only tell her story now because
she is dead. Like Roylott's association with the gypsies and Oriental
beasts, this detail — that Helen's story must be suppressed until after
her death — is not explained. In this sense it lies outside the logic of the
solution to the case. Moreover, Helen's version of events is suppressed
as soon as Holmes takes over the case, and it never features in the official
report. In the absence of her narrative after Roylott's death, Holmes's

---

[6]For an overview of the conditions under which middle-class women were recruited
into the workforce see Holcombe, *Victorian Ladies At Work;* Jane Lewis, *Women in England, 1870–1950: Sexual Divisions and Social Change* (Sussex: Wheatsheaf, 1984), pp.
145–205; Joan W. Scott and Louise A. Tilly, "Women's work and the family in nineteenth
century Europe," in Alice Amsden (ed.), *The Economics of Women and Work* (New York:
St. Martin's Press, 1980), pp. 91–124.

"protection" of Helen elides easily with both the patriarch's phallic poisoning of his daughter until she "choked her words" (p. 158) and could not name her murderer, and the "protection" of her husband-to-be who censors Helen's narrative as "the fancies of a nervous woman" (p. 154). Silencing the rescued daughter effectively protects patriarchy's privileged "play": the inquest simply "came to the conclusion that the Doctor met his fate while indiscreetly playing with a dangerous pet" (p. 172). Firmly situated within a protective circle of male kin, Helen's position as consenting subject is so overwritten by paternal authority that it is virtually effaced. Thus, she serves the function of the feminine "other" in the economy of patriarchy: the conduit through which the phallus can be passed from father to son.[7]

The sexualization of the female body that serves as the symbolic ground for the narrative's enigma manages woman's contradictory position as property and property owner, a contradiction simultaneously being managed in the legal sphere by property reform and reform in the age of consent. Passed on the heels of the Married Women's Property Act, the Criminal Law Amendment Act (1885) legislated a complementary shift in patriarchal arrangements affecting the status of woman outside the home.[8] In raising the age of consent for girls from 13 to 16, the act and its supporters purported to defend and protect the interests of girls from sexual offenders. However, as with property reform, the discourse of protection, which threads its way through the reform campaign and the law, conceals the class and gender interests served by the amendment. The passage of the Criminal Law Amendment Act was punctuated by one of the first and most effectively waged campaigns of sensationalist journalism and inaugurated a broad-based social purity movement that would extend through the next few decades. The "Maiden Tribute of Modern Babylon," a series of stories written and published in *The Pall Mall Gazette* by its editor, W. T. Stead, provided the catalyst for passage of the Criminal Law Amendment Act by purportedly exposing extensive white slave trade between Britain and the continent as well as pervasive child prostitution in London. The exposé demonstrates the class lines along which the age of con-

---

[7]Several other examples of the containment of this figure in the Sherlock Holmes stories include "A Scandal in Bohemia" (1891) — the first of Conan Doyle's stories published in the *Strand* magazine and one of the few in which Holmes is outwitted, and by a woman no less; "A Case of Identity" (1891); and "The Adventure of the Solitary Cyclist" (1903).

[8]For an annotated version of the law see Earl of Halsbury, *The Laws of England,* vol. 10, 3rd ed. (London: Butterworth, 1955), pp. 750ff.

sent battle was fought and indicates the historical conditions of possibility for the overdetermined network of sexual and class codes in "The Speckled Band."[9] In targeting the foreign aristocrat as procurer and the "daughters of the poor" as his victims, the campaign for raising the age of consent used one of the most familiar themes of popular melodrama — the seduction of the poor girl by the wealthy lecher — to sexualize threats to capitalist production: foreign competition, collective unrest fueled by feminist and socialist reform movements, and the destabilization of gender arrangements by the recruitment of "redundant" single middle-class women into the workforce. The patriarchal gender ideology that commodified bourgeois woman as ornament of the home was thereby rearticulated in age of consent legislation and the social purity campaigns that this reform movement spawned. By constructing woman outside the home as sexual commodity in need of state protection, the law addressed the increasing numbers of single middle-class women working outside the home and helped contain the threat they posed. In the name of protecting girls against sexual abuse, the law went a long way in resecuring the destabilized patriarchal family: severely undermining the position of female "consenting" subject outside the private sphere by constituting it as a position in which woman was still encircled by patriarchal controls, *subject* to the "reasonable beliefs" of both her legal representative and her violator.[10]

Like the Married Women's Property Act, the age of consent law focused on issues central to patriarchal control — "protection" and "possession" — extending the protective arm of the state to girls and women outside the possessive claims of father or husband. But while the Married Women's Property Act emphasized woman as *subject* of property, age of consent legislation foregrounded woman *as* property. Both reforms managed complementary adjustments in the contradictory position of woman as the relationship between public and private spheres and middle-class women's place in both was gradually shifting. Most historical studies have treated one or the other of these reforms, but not

---

[9]Deborah Gorham, "The maiden tribute of modern Babylon re-examined: child prostitution and the idea of childhood in late Victorian England," *Victorian Studies,* 21 (1978): pp. 353–79.

[10]Two features of the consent law that bypass the state's "protective" role demonstrate how the law's "protection" of women actually safeguarded patriarchal privilege: the reasonable claim to possession — a husband could not be guilty of rape (upon marriage a woman forfeited her position as subject of consent to her husband's conjugal rights); and a "reasonable cause to believe" that the girl was over 16 in effect sanctioned child prostitution for first offenders under 23, granting them the chance to sow their youthful wild oats (Halsbury, op. cit., pp. 746, 751).

both in conjunction.[11] Seeing them in adjacency rather than in isolation makes visible the mutual determination of woman's position as married property owner and as sexualized subject outside the home. Taken together, they comprise two sides of the same coin of patriarchal control under capitalism.

The symbolic appearance of the incest motif in "The Speckled Band" is symptomatic of the contradictions which produced this de-securing of the patriarchal gender system from one set of social arrangements and its re-securing in another. As it is encoded in the story, the daughter's seduction demonstrates the class interests this sexualization of the family alliance served by dis-articulating the masculine subject from aristocratic aspirations and re-articulating it as the rational professional. Furthermore, the daughter's seduction enacts cultural anxiety about incest which helped reinforce the mutually supporting feminine subject of property — bound as non-person to patriarchal protection/possession within a father-daughter or a husband-wife relationship — and the non-subject of consent subjected to the state's (read Holmes's) protection in lieu of adequate protection from the father-husband. . . .

The sexualized subject of the late nineteenth century, inscribed by the disciplinary interventions of the state, did not supplant the subject of familial alliance. Rather, as Foucault has argued, the family provided an anchor of sorts whereby alliance and sexuality could be interchanged.[12] Universalizing the incest taboo made the law of the patriarch secure even in the new mechanics of power.[13] At the same time, the proliferation of incest motifs in the discourses of the social sciences — in particular, through the hystericization of the middle-class daughter — signalled a reformation of patriarchal gender arrangements that loos-

[11]See for example Lee Holcombe, *Wives and Property: Reform of the Married Women's Property Law in Nineteenth-Century England* (Toronto: University of Toronto Press, 1983); Mary Poovey, "Covered but not bound: Caroline Norton and the 1857 Matrimonial Causes Act," in *Uneven Developments: The Ideological Work of Gender in Mid-Victorian England* (Chicago: University of Chicago Press, 1988), pp. 5–88; Sachs and Wilson, op. cit., and Stetson, op. cit., on property. On reform of consent law see Edward J. Bristow, *Vice and Vigilance: Purity Movement in Britain Since 1700* (Dublin: Gill and Macmillan, 1977); and Gorham, op. cit.

[12]Michel Foucault, *The History of Sexuality. Vol. 1: An Introduction*, trans. Robert Hurley (New York: Vintage, 1980), p. 109.

[13]Incest was not penalized under civil law in Britain until 1908; prior to that time it was handled by the ecclesiastical courts. But it was a cultural preoccupation throughout the late nineteenth century, serving as a symbolic index of the vices of the lower-class residuum. See Sheila Jeffreys, *The Spinster and Her Enemies: Feminism and Sexuality, 1880–1930* (London: Pandora, 1985), p. 77.

ened the bonds of family alliance in order to construct an individual-
ized, sexualized feminine subject. The symbolic encoding of the
daughter's seduction in "The Speckled Band," including Holmes's
complicity with Roylott, is an instance of the ideological function of
incest motifs: managing the threat to family alliance posed by the indi-
vidualized, single, middle-class daughter by re-installing her within patriarchal control through a narrative of the family romance.

The narrative handling of the daughter's seduction in "The Speckled Band" demonstrates the alliance between the re-articulation of
woman as other and the discourses of scientific rationalism. The
daughter's seduction, along with the race, class, and gender hierarchies
it supports, is silenced by the narrative's coherent solution, a coherence
which depends on the reader taking up the position of the subject of
knowledge offered by Holmes. Holmes's ability to "explain it all" by
pointing to the perfectly obvious "elementary" details that have passed
before the reader's unwitting eyes (as well as the reader's stand-in,
Watson's) explains the enigma and gives Holmes his status as genius of
detection. Holmes's authority as rational, scientific investigator works
with the narrative movement toward resolution to seal over contradictions and gaps undermining both the coherence of the explanation and
the obviousness of Holmes's authority as subject of knowledge.

If read from the subject position the story invites the reader to take
up, these contradictory links and the fissures they open in Holmes's air-
tight explanation are invisible. This invisibility is in itself a clue to the
ideological force of both this position and the deductive logic it offers
as an obviously enlightened way of seeing. Reason is presented simultaneously as a universal human attribute and a gratuitous gift of birth
available only to a fortunate few. While the qualifications for those
"few" are not overtly explained — in this sense they are invisible — they
are none the less encoded in Holmes, the consummate rational subject.
The reader is invited to "identify" with this subject through Watson, the
classic participant-observer, in awe of Holmes's superior reasoning
power and yet similarly qualified in terms of class, race, and gender positions. Holmes's empiricist emphasis on the visible as self-explanatory
mystifies the ways the narrative's endorsement of deductive logic natu-
ralizes the visible marks of difference in order to sustain a social hierarchy. Thus, Roylott's associations with the Orient and with the gypsies
serve as obvious clues — visible signals to the reader — of his un-
reasonableness, just as mud splashes on a sleeve are visible evidence that
Helen has ridden in a dog cart.

The ratiocination that employs an empiricist mode of knowing as a

weapon for criminal justice explicitly sets the rational subject of knowledge apart not only from the criminal (who, as Roylott's over-
determined encoding indicates, is often a collective outlaw) but also
from the pedestrian masses: "Crime is common. Logic is rare,"
Holmes tells Watson. "What do the public, the great unobservant
public, who could hardly tell a weaver by his tooth or a compositor
by his left thumb, care about the finer shades of analysis and deduction?" ("The Copper Beeches") This subject position endowed with
heroic stature recruits the discourse of scientific rationalism increasingly taken up for state intervention into various domains of the social, to present as obvious and natural a hierarchy that protects the
interests of the middle-class, western, white male. By privileging this
subject position through Watson's narration, the narrative offers the
reader a way of making sense by which the contradictory links between the science of deduction and the interests of patriarchy and
imperialism are glossed over. . . .

The entangled encoding of the feminine and the Oriental as sexualized other in the Holmes story is an instance of the ways the sexualization of woman and Oriental male re-secured patriarchal and imperial
interests across a range of class positions. Both Helen and the Ori-
entalized Roylott are traversed by semes for un-reason, figured as a wild,
animal-like lack of self-possession. When Helen is first "unveiled" she
presents to Holmes a face "all drawn and grey, with restless, frightened
eyes, like those of some hunted animal" (p. 153), fitting complement to
Roylott, that "fierce old bird of prey" (p. 161). As with Roylott's unreasonable passions, Helen's feeble rational powers set her apart from
Holmes. The darkness that envelops Helen's mind makes her only able
to entertain "vague fears and suspicions" in contrast to Holmes's enlightened rapid deductions, "as swift as intuitions, and yet always
founded on a logical basis" (p. 153). This seme of animal irrationality
sexualizes both patriarch-predator and daughter-victim, entangling the
feminine and the Oriental as other in opposition to Holmes's rational,
reserved, western, middle-class norm.

The sexualization of western woman in the late nineteenth century
was the outcome of a complex of economic and political pressures ex-
erted on the sexual division of labour across the classes: working-class
women were gradually pushed back into the home as a result of the
decline in the predominantly female textile industry and the growth of
male-dominated heavy industry; unions won higher wages for men; and
a rigorous social purity campaign for working-class respectability

stressed woman's natural place in the home as health-conscious and efficient mother.[14] While the gradual movement of working-class women back into the home helped rigidify the sexual division of labour, the increasing recruitment of middle-class women into the developing tertiary sector in Britain bred a certain cultural anxiety over the residual flexibility of that division.[15] The construction of woman in the public space as object of desire in need of protection helped tame the threat independent women posed to the family (by implicitly calling into question the equation between domesticity and respectability) and to the male workers they at least potentially competed against in the market. At the same time, the sexualization of woman in the private sphere as reproductive body served to re-legitimate her invisible labour in the home not just as civilizing moral agent — the mid-Victorian angel in the house — but as mother of the race and domestic consumer; the concomitant re-articulation of her labour as a civic responsibility was aided by the increased permeability between the private and public spheres.[16] The overall effect was to mystify woman's role in both spheres as social producer.

[14]Anna Davin, "Imperialism and motherhood," *History Workshop Journal*, 5 (1978), pp. 9–65.

[15]Between 1881 and 1911 the number of middle-class jobs for women increased more than two times that of men during the same period (Holcombe, *Ladies At Work,* p. 216). This change in women's employment (an adjustment not so much in numbers as in the structure of occupations) was a response to the expanding service sector which created an increased demand for clerks, teachers, nurses, and civil servants — all areas opened up by capital expansion, the investment of capital in the colonies, and increased state intervention in civil society. The large numbers of educated "redundant women" provided a readily available and cheap workforce for this expanding market. For further discussion of the impact of shifting modes of production on British women's work see Margery Davies, "Women's place is at the typewriter: the feminization of the clerical labor force," in Zillah Eisenstein (ed.), *Capitalist Patriarchy and the Case for Socialist Feminism* (New York: Monthly Review Press, 1979), pp. 248–66.

[16]The sexualization of western woman as both reproductive mother and seductive, hysterical daughter is compatible with the emergence of a consumer society in which shopping is a feminine activity and woman both in the industrial workforce and in the home is the consummate consumer (Martin Pumphrey, "The flapper, the housewife and the making of modernity," *Cultural Studies,* 1 (1987), pp. 179–203). Moreover, the sexualization of woman in the Freudian family romance, as passive, narcissistic, and easily seduced fits readily with the construction of the willing feminine consumer (Rachel Bowlby, *Just Looking: Consumer Culture in Dreiser, Gissing and Zola* (New York: Methuen, 1985), pp. 30–2).

AUDREY JAFFE

# Detecting the Beggar:
## Arthur Conan Doyle, Henry Mayhew, and "The Man with the Twisted Lip"

---

Jaffe's essay is an example of what is loosely called new historicist criticism: she approaches the literary text by grounding it in its historical and social context, but she also attends particularly to those aspects of this context that the text would seem to obscure or deny. In "The Man with the Twisted Lip," she points out, the disguised and denied actual identity of the false beggar, Hugh Boone, is strangely intertwined with suggestions of another obscured or invisible identity in Doyle's society, that of the capitalist; and this intertwining implicates both in larger, unsettling questions about the arbitrariness of social roles and of professional and even personal identities. As soon as these questions are posed, other unexpected parallels appear and multiply: the anonymity of the opium den shadows the anonymity of the financial center; the pleasures of identity appear to lie in the possibility of movement between identities. Not only the capitalist and the beggar, ultimately, but even the detective and the writer (in this Jaffe echoes Knight) are caught in the story's exposure of the double life that serves, for their culture, "to preserve the fiction of an authentic self" (p. 426).

Henry Mayhew, a London journalist and self-made sociologist, massively surveyed and documented the lives and conditions of London's poor — the city's "street folk" — in a series of pioneering letters written for the *Morning Chronicle* in 1849–50 and then published in three volumes as *London Labour and the London Poor* in 1851 and again in a somewhat expanded four-volume edition in 1861. He not only reported on the poor, he interviewed them and let them speak for themselves; he even commissioned engravings of some of them.

Jaffe's essay originally appeared in *Representations* 31 (Summer 1990): 96–117.

---

TED KOPPEL: I wanted to get some statistics today, and so I asked our researchers to look into whether anyone had done a study or a master's thesis or a doctoral dissertation on the subject of begging, so that we know how many of these people — has anyone ever tried to find out how many of these people are legit, how many are, in fact, only collecting money so they can do some crack, how many of them are alcoholics? And you know what we found? Not one —

MR. SNYDER: Not one.

KOPPEL: — study. Not one study. Not a single study. Commissioner, how is that possible? How can you say what you're saying without there being any kind of underlying base of knowledge?

— *Nightline*[1]


# I

In Arthur Conan Doyle's "The Man with the Twisted Lip" (1891), Sherlock Holmes is uncharacteristically baffled by the disappearance of Mr. Neville St. Clair. St. Clair is a well-to-do gentleman who for years, while traveling to the City each day ostensibly to look after his interests, has in fact earned his living by disguising himself as a beggar named Hugh Boone, finding begging to be less arduous and more profitable than other professions available to him. Holmes, seemingly relying on his expectation that the case will yield the usual murder victim, advances the conclusion that St. Clair is dead — just as Mrs. St. Clair produces a letter she claims was recently written by her husband. Wedded to his interpretation — appearing, almost, to desire the death he has theorized — the detective attempts to explain away the clues that suggest St. Clair is still living: St. Clair's ring, included with the letter, "proves nothing," as "it may have been taken from him"; the letter itself may "have been written on Monday, and only posted to-day" (p. 125). The ease with which Holmes detaches the signs of St. Clair's identity from St. Clair, and the fact that it is his job to re-attach them, point toward the problematic of identity the story uncovers; Inspector Bradstreet's solemn insistence, at the end of the case, that there be "no more of Hugh Boone" reflects a determination to eliminate precisely the kind of instability Holmes implicitly acknowledges. For the possibility that

I would like to thank Catherine Gallagher, Mary Ann O'Farrell, and Peter Schwartz for their help.
[1] Quoted from "Panhandlers," program broadcast on ABC's *Nightline*, 1 September 1988, by permission.

identity can be dissociated from its signs undermines, even as it provokes the desire for, the stable categories of identity both detective fiction and Mayhew's studies of the urban poor seek to construct.

Holmes is called to investigate after Mrs. St. Clair, returning from an excursion into the City, looks up to see in the window of an opium den — where St. Clair puts on and off his disguise — what appears to her to be an assault on her husband but is actually his manifestation of surprise at seeing her. The story describes not a crime but a disturbance in the social field, a confusion of social identity, which it becomes Holmes's task to resolve. That such a disturbance should appear as a crime makes sense given the fantasy of knowledge and social control detective fiction represents; St. Clair's indeterminacy — the mobility that allows him to occupy two social places at once — disturbs the possibility of fixing identity on which that fantasy rests.[2] And that indeterminacy is expressed both in St. Clair's ability to transform himself and in the figures between which he oscillates — the gentleman and the beggar — who were, for the Victorians, ambiguous and often interchangeable entities.

The scenario wherein a beggar is revealed to be a gentleman or nobleman in disguise is a familiar one; behind "The Man with the Twisted Lip," according to Donald A. Redmond, lies Victor Hugo's novel *L'Homme qui rit*, which tells of a nobleman stolen as a child and disfigured, so he won't be recognized, with a scar across the mouth that makes him appear to be smiling or laughing.[3] In the late nineteenth century, the oppositions and similarities mobilized by a pairing of these figures are particularly charged: in the context of changing ideas about gentlemanliness, for instance, popular ideology had it that a beggar might very well be a gentleman; at the same time the increase in both financial speculation and unexpected, devastating crashes made it appear likely, at least from the gentleman's perspective, that a gentleman might someday have to beg. But rather than simply place a familiar tale in a new context, Conan Doyle's story demonstrates that the new context suggestively expands the problematic of identity implicit in that tale. For, even as it does away with Hugh Boone, restoring St. Clair to his proper identity, "The Man with the Twisted Lip" both constructs and disables detective fiction's fantasy of social control, performing its traditional task of establishing social identity only by disclosing the absence of the identities it seeks to expose.

---

[2] See D. A. Miller, *The Novel and the Police* (Berkeley, 1988).
[3] Donald A. Redmond, *Sherlock Holmes: A Study in Sources* (Montreal, 1982), 55.

*The man who does something in the City.* The figure of the finance capitalist confounds the attempt — central to both Henry Mayhew's project in *London Labour and the London Poor* and Holmes's in Conan Doyle's stories — to define identity in relation to work.[4] The person of the finance capitalist — both his body and "personal" identity — remains detached from the system of production in which he participates; where the laborer might suffer "in his existence." Elaine Scarry writes, the capitalist suffers only "in his money."[5] The legalizing of joint-stock companies in 1844 and the institution of limited liability soon after increasingly separated businesses from those who invested in them, enabling capital, effectively, to carry on by itself, with "not so much as a sign of the Capitalist to be seen."[6] And because of the detachment of "his own embodied psyche, will, and consciousness" from the manner in which he produces his income, as Scarry puts it, the capitalist might well be called an "exempted person": it is that absence of self, "that liberating relation, that attribute of nonparticipation," which "is summarized by the word 'capitalist'"(265).

Such an "exempted person" is Charles Dickens's Alfred Lammle, who, in place of the usual markers of identity and gentlemanliness, has "Shares":

> The mature young gentleman is a person of property. He invests his property. He goes, in a condescending amateurish way, into the City, attends meetings of Directors, and has to do with traffic in Shares. As is well known to the wise in their generation, traffic in Shares is the one thing to have to do with in this world. Have no antecedents, no established character, no cultivation, no ideas, no manners; have Shares. Have Shares enough to be on Boards of Direction in capital letters, oscillate on mysterious business between London and Paris, and be great. Where does he come from? Shares. Where is he going to? Shares. What are his tastes? Shares. Has he any principles? Shares. What squeezes him into Parliament? Shares. Perhaps he never of himself achieved success in

---

[4]Holmes characteristically identifies individuals by their professions: "By a man's finger-nails, by his coat-sleeve, by his boots, by his trouser-knees, by the callosities of his forefinger and thumb, by his expression, by his shirt-cuffs — by each of these things a man's calling is plainly revealed"; *A Study in Scarlet.* (p. 28)

[5]Elaine Scarry, *The Body in Pain* (New York, 1985), 263. Subsequent references are included in the text.

[6]Leland Jenks, *The Migration of British Capital to 1875* (New York, 1927), 234; quoted in Barbara Weiss, *The Hell of the English: Bankruptcy and the Victorian Novel* (London, 1986), 139.

anything, never originated anything, never produced anything? Sufficient answer to all; Shares.[7]

"Shares" substitute for cultivation, manners, principles, and production, replacing what had appeared to be substantive with what doesn't appear at all. In *Our Mutual Friend,* the sinister implications of such absence are manifest in Lammle's deceitfulness, as well as in the novel's essential image of the bodies Gaffer Hexam pulls from the river, devoid of any signs of identity but for their clothing and the money he retrieves from it. And it is in the atmosphere created by the novel's intertwining of finance and identity that Boffin engineers his "pious fraud"; in such a context, Dickens seems to say, not even well-intentioned characters need adhere to any notions readers might hold of consistency or legibility.

The identity of the "man who does something in the City," then, seemed as ungrounded as the City's prosperity itself did to many nine-teenth-century observers of it — a perception no doubt enhanced by the frequency with which, in the second half of the century, prominent businessmen were revealed to have built their empires on foundations of nonexistent capital.[8] (Of the seemingly unbounded proliferation and circulation of wealth in the City, one contemporary observer wrote, "We find many thousands here who live by supplying one another's wants; and the question arises, whence comes the original means by which such a state of things is rendered possible? What, in fact, is the primary fund of which these persons manage to secure a share?")[9] In his passivity and detachment, the disinterested relation he bears to his interests, the "man who does something in the City" exemplifies the kind of fungible identity that, his contemporaries feared, inhabited a realm of exchange divorced from production.[10]

*The "false beggar."* The middle classes in the nineteenth century re-garded the unproductive gentleman in a dubious light. Since neither he nor the beggar put in what they regarded as an honest day's labor, both

---

[7] Charles Dickens, *Our Mutual Friend* (Harmondsworth, Eng., 1977), 159–60.
[8] See Weiss, *Hell of the English,* chap. 7.
[9] Francis Sheppard, *London, 1808–1870: The Infernal Wen* (Berkeley, 1971), 81–82.
[10] On the connection between identity and exchange see Catherine Gallagher, "George Eliot and *Daniel Deronda:* The Prostitute and the Jewish Question," in Ruth Bernard Yeazell, ed., *Sex, Politics, and Science in the Nineteenth-Century Novel,* Selected Papers from the English Institute, 1983–84 (Baltimore, 1986), 39–62. Harold Perkin contrasts the "active owner-manager of the Industrial Revolution" with the "passive or remotely controlling financier of later corporate capitalism" in *The Origins of Modern English Society, 1780–1880* (London, 1969), 221.

were subject to general suspicion — the suspicion, in particular, of attempting to deceive those who did. A section of Mayhew's *London Labour and the London Poor,* included under the rubric "Those Who Will Not Work" and written by Andrew Halliday, discusses those "beggars and cheats" physically sound enough to perform "honest" labor, who choose instead to make their livings by deceiving the charitable. This "false beggar," as Halliday represents him, is a kind of actor, taking on specific costumes and mannerisms for the performance of his roles. Of one type of "street campaigner," for example, Halliday writes: "He is imitative, and in his time plays many parts. . . . His bearing is most military; he keeps his neck straight, his chin in. . . . He is as stiff as an embalmed preparation, for which, but for the motion of his eyes, you might mistake him."[11] And in order to see through this deceptive surface, the man on the street requires Holmesian powers of detection. In one instance Halliday, in the company of a friend who had once been a sailor, comes across what appears to him to be "a brother sailor in distress." "Of course you will give him something," he says to his friend. The friend replies negatively, with this explanation: "Did you see him spit? . . . A real sailor never spits to wind'ard. *Why, he couldn't*" (415). Unmasking the "false beggar" involves knowing the "true" version of the type he attempts to impersonate, and Mayhew's work attempts to codify these types, giving his readers the ability to distinguish "true" identity from "false."

Halliday is particularly offended by the figure whose pose conflates the beggar and the gentleman: the begging-letter writer, who "is the connecting link between mendicity and external respectability,"

> affects white cravats, soft hands, and filbert nails. He oils his hair, cleans his boots, and wears a portentous stick-up collar. The light of other days of gentility and comfort casts a halo of "deportment" over his well-brushed, white-seamed coat, his carefully darned black-cloth gloves, and pudgy gaiters. . . . Among the many varieties of mendacious beggars, there is none so detestable as this hypocritical scoundrel, who, with an ostentatiously submissive air, and false pretense of faded fortunes, tells his plausible tale of undeserved suffering, and extracts from the pockets of the superficially good-hearted their sympathy and coin. (403)

[11] Henry Mayhew, *London Labour and the London Poor,* 4 vols. (New York, 1967), 4:418. Subsequent references are included in the text.

For Halliday, the link between mendicity and mendacity is more than merely linguistic. But why should the begging-letter writer offend more than other beggars who, through various schemes, deprive the charitable of their "sympathy and coin"? Halliday's dislike of this character seems related to his pretense to respectability: the "intuitive knowledge" of the "nobility and landed gentry" that aids him in his deceptive practice. The begging-letter writer implies by his behavior that gentlemanliness is merely a matter of surfaces, disturbingly suggesting, in his capacity for imitation, the gentleman's own imitability.

Such a possibility had already been explored in Lord Chesterfield's 1774 *Letters to His Son*, which tells readers how to "act" the gentleman:

> When you go into good company . . . observe carefully their turn, their manners, their address, and conform your own to them. But this is not all, neither; go deeper still; observe their characters, and pry, as far as you can, into both their hearts and their heads. Seek for their particular merit, their predominant passion, or their prevailing weakness; and you will then know what to bait your hook with to catch them.[12]

As the general dislike with which Chesterfield's work was received by the eighteenth and nineteenth centuries demonstrates, the notion that the gentleman was imitable touched a particularly sensitive nerve. Robin Gilmour points out that the behavior Chesterfield recommends was in fact necessary for social advancement in eighteenth-century society. But by recommending particular forms of behavior rather than the cultivation of moral qualities, Chesterfield showed "how easily civilised behaviour could be reduced to the lowest common denominator" and "how weak the links between manners and morals" might be.[13] Chesterfield's advice about "catching" members of "good company" closely resembles Halliday's account of the begging-letter writer's scheme: both the gentleman, in Chesterfield's view, and the "false beggar," in Halliday's and Mayhew's, use knowledge of a group or class to imitate it, and advance themselves by means of that imitation. Both figures take dissimulation as their means of livelihood, cultivating exterior rather than interior; neither works in any sense Mayhew is willing to call work. Both, therefore, stand outside the wide realm of ordinary,

---

[12]Quoted in Robin Gilmour, *The Idea of the Gentleman in the Victorian Novel* (London, 1981), 15–17.

[13]Sheldon Rothblatt, *Tradition and Change in English Liberal Education* (London, 1976), 31; quoted in Gilmour, *Idea of the Gentleman*, 19.

middle-class life, which made work into a moral imperative and accused both the gentleman and the "false beggar" of "living off the toil of others."[14]

Potentially productive individuals not engaged in productive labor — regarded, as Mayhew's "will not work" implies, as refusing work — not only offended the age's emphasis on energy and productivity, but they also presented the Victorians with a constant threat of social unrest. Describing the Poor Law's inability to meet the needs of those in want, Halliday cites a letter to the *Times* that expresses this anxiety:

> It is an admitted and notorious fact, that after a fortnight's frost the police courts were besieged by thousands who professed to be starving. . . . It was the saturnalia if not of mendicancy, at least of destitution. The police stood aside while beggars possessed the thoroughfares. . . . We had thought that the race of sturdy vagrants and valiant beggars was extinct, or at least that they dared no longer show themselves. But here they were in open day like the wretches which are said to emerge out of darkness on the day of a revolution. (398)

The New Poor Law of 1834 had as one of its main objectives the separation of the able-bodied poor from those who could not raise themselves out of poverty, and Mayhew's system of identification, distinguishing those who "cannot work" from those who "will not work," fulfills the state's need to bring into the light of "open day" figures who represent a threat before they themselves choose to emerge. It is, at least in part, the goal of both Mayhew and Sherlock Holmes to put the gentleman and the able-bodied beggar equally to work.

But the anxiety about false beggary, like that about gentlemanliness, is also an anxiety about the theatricality of the social world, the susceptibility to manipulation of social identity. The "true beggar . . . who has no means of livelihood," Halliday writes, "has invariably commanded the respect and excited the compassion of his fellow men." But "the beggar whose poverty is not real, but assumed, is no longer a beggar in the true sense of the word, but a cheat and an impostor, and as such he is naturally regarded, not as an object for compassion, but as an enemy of the state" (393). What, however, is a beggar "in the true sense of the word"? What, for that matter, is a "false beggar"? For Halliday, the

---

[14]This is articulated for the beggar by Mayhew, as described below; John Ruskin wrote that "gentlemen have to learn that it is no part of their duty or privilege to live on other people's toil"; *Works*, ed. E. T. Cook and A. D. O. Wedderburn, 39 vols. (London, 1902–12), 7:344; quoted in Gilmour, *Idea of the Gentleman*, 7.

"false beggar" is not just a corrupter of images but a corrupter of language; the desire for a "true sense of the word," like that for a "true beggar," is a desire for an absolute correspondence between sign and referent. The "false beggar" is, for Mayhew and Halliday, a professional: one who knows the code of beggary and seeks to manipulate it, to sell what he considers to be a saleable identity. Both "true" and "false" beggars deal in images, exchanging identity for coin. The term *false* is important, however, because it maintains the possibility of locating "true" identity: identity not subject to the vicissitudes of representation.

As part of the apparatus of the Poor Law, the concern with "true" and "false" beggars reflects a desire to locate the truth of identity in the body by means of a separation of productive from nonproductive bodies. (The comment made by Halliday's friend — "Did you see him spit?" — defines identity in terms of the body's adaptation to labor.) Mayhew's work locates the truth of the beggar's identity in the presence or absence of the potential for production: the "true beggar" is one who cannot, for reasons of physical disability or illness, work. And if the unproductive body is "true," it follows for Mayhew that the productive body is at least potentially false; the capacity for productive labor without any signs of a product seems to suggest to Mayhew and his contemporaries that the impulse toward productivity is directed toward the body itself. On the one hand, a choice of profession may be regarded as a choice of identity. But on the other, the very idea of choice introduces the possibility of multiple identities — an instability that the idea of an identity divided between work and home, as I will discuss later, attempts to resolve. Productivity poses the threat of multiple identities; for Mayhew, the "false beggar" epitomizes this problem by making the production of identity a profession in itself.[15]

But the "false beggar" also disturbs because, in his capacity for producing representations, he endangers the identities of those who encounter him. As David Marshall has argued, sympathy — which Adam Smith[16] defines as the imagined reproduction of another's feeling within an observer's mind — is inherently bound up with representation and theatricality.[17] The beggar may be the focus of such intense concern about the possibility of separating "true" identity from "false," that is — for us as

[15]See Fredric Jameson, *The Political Unconscious* (Ithaca, N.Y., 1981), 249, on individualism and the choice of a profession.

[16]*Adam Smith:* Scottish political economist and moral philosopher; author of *The Theory of Moral Sentiments* (1759) and *The Wealth of Nations* (1776). [Editor's note]

[17]David Marshall, *The Surprising Effects of Sympathy: Marivaux, Diderot, Rousseau, and Mary Shelley* (Chicago, 1988), 21.

well as for the Victorians — because his confrontation with the potential charity giver presents an exemplary moment of theatricality in social life: a moment at which, in Marshall's words, individuals "face each other as actors and spectators" (136). And that confrontation involves an exchange not only of money but also of identity — identity already implicated in a system of representation and exchange.

When Halliday links sympathy and coin, he implicitly connects identity with exchange; the offer of money acts as a sign that the observer has involved his own identity — including his belief in his ability to tell "true" from "false" — in an exchange with the beggar's. Sympathy and coin, themselves within the realm of representation, are presented as guarantors of authenticity in the transaction between charity giver and beggar, offered as evidence of the charity giver's belief in the truth of the beggar's image, as well as in his ability to read that truth. (Hugh Boone is supported by the public, and tolerated by the police, because they know him to be a professional beggar; less important than the truth or falsity of the beggar's identity is the comfort they receive from being reassured of their ability to tell the difference.) What happens, then, when the observer fears that he has unwittingly identified with a representation? The category of the "false beggar" not only expresses the observer's anxiety about his ability to read identity, but it also reveals sympathy, coin, and identity to be mere currency: no single one of these, offered in exchange, can guarantee the authenticity of another. The "false beggar" makes visible the system of exchange wherein sympathy, coin, and identity can circulate endlessly, never drawing upon any fund of truth.

But the "false beggar" also takes advantage of the exchange between himself and the potential charity giver *as* exchange. Adam Smith argues that while sympathy involves the observer's projection of himself into the sufferer's situation, it also requires the sufferer who desires sympathy to imagine how he would appear to a spectator:

> As they are constantly considering what they themselves would feel, if they actually were the sufferers, so he is as constantly led to imagine in what manner he would be affected if he was only one of the spectators of his own situation.[18]

Both figures in "the scene of sympathy," as Marshall writes, "play the roles of spectator and spectacle" (173). The potential charity giver's

---

[18]Adam Smith, *The Theory of Moral Sentiments* (Oxford, 1976), 22; quoted by David Marshall in *The Figure of Theater: Shaftesbury, Defoe, Adam Smith, and George Eliot* (New York, 1986), 172. Subsequent references to Marshall are included in the text.

power inheres both in his ability to give money as well as in his imaginative projection: the former, in fact, depends upon the vividness and perceived truth of the latter. But that power is undermined by the charity giver's susceptibility to representation: his imaginative re-creation of the sufferer's situation is matched by the sufferer's need to imagine what will provoke his sympathy. And it is this reciprocity that underlies the anxiety about false beggary: the "false beggar" endangers the charity giver's identity by manipulating his sympathy, encouraging him to identify with a mere representation. The fiction of the "true beggar" is consolatory, therefore, in its construction of a figure who not only will not, but cannot, project — who is a vessel, pure and simple, for the charity giver's projection. The "false beggar" and the finance capitalist, then, prove to be not just exchangeable figures but figures *for* exchange — figures whose identities seem to inhere only in representation. And while Mayhew's project would protect the observer's identity by establishing the beggar's, his work finally undermines the safety of both. Similarly Conan Doyle, in a story not only destined for the popular market but to be sold in railway stations to businessmen commuting between home and City, simultaneously assures his readers that false identities can be done away with and implicates those readers, and himself, in the processes of exchange that bring such identities into being.

## II

Just as Mayhew's work pits the beggar and the journalist against one another in a battle of wits, so too does Conan Doyle's story associate Holmes and St. Clair through their use of disguise. In its opening section, Watson and his wife receive a visit from Kate Whitney, whose husband Isa has disappeared for two days, and who is known by his wife to be in an opium den in the City. Going to seek him out, Watson there encounters Holmes, disguised as a regular customer:

> He sat now as absorbed as ever, very thin, very wrinkled, bent with age, an opium pipe dangling down from between his knees. . . . It took all my self-control to prevent me from breaking out into a cry of astonishment. He had turned his back so that none could see him but I. His form had filled out, his wrinkles were gone, the dull eyes had regained their fire, and there, sitting by the fire, and grinning at my surprise, was none other than Sherlock Holmes. (p. 115)

Like St. Clair, who originally donned his beggar's disguise when he was a reporter writing a series of articles on begging, Holmes uses disguise to help him penetrate the opium den unnoticed. Both Holmes and St. Clair employ disguise in their professions; for both, disguise becomes a metaphor for profession. The transformation undergone in the opium den has its correlative, in Victorian life, in the imagined transformation of the husband and father who disappears mysteriously into the City each morning, returning at night to a family that has no firsthand knowledge of what he does there. And the idea of opium, like that of disguise, allows for a literalization of and play upon the idea of transformation: where Whitney enters the den a "noble" man and emerges "pale, haggard, and unkempt," St. Clair finds that he "could every morning emerge as a squalid beggar, and in the evenings transform [himself] into a well-dressed man about town" (p. 131). As Holmes describes him, even though St. Clair "had no occupation" his regular departure for and return from the City every day substitute for one, confirming his good character: he "was interested in several companies, and went into town as a rule in the morning, returning by the 5:14 from Cannon Street every night" (p. 118). And, indeed, St. Clair gets along very nicely without any evidence of a profession; as he describes his own situation, it was possible for him to continue this activity for years without anyone's actually knowing what he did during the day: "As I grew richer I grew more ambitious, took a house in the country, and eventually married, without anyone having a suspicion as to my real occupation. My dear wife knew that I had business in the City. She little knew what" (p. 131).

In moving back and forth between the City, the opium den, and the St. Clair home, the story plays St. Clair's various identities against one another: the figure who plies his trade as a beggar in the City every day, through the use of disguise — a painted face, a scar, a shock of red hair — and skillful acting — "the facility of repartee, which improved by practice and made me quite a recognized character in the City," versus the domestic St. Clair, whose concern about exposure manifests itself as concern for his appearance in his children's eyes: "God help me, I would not have them ashamed of their father" (p. 130). The alignment of disguise with travel into the City suggests the Victorian commonplace that the husband's and/or father's true self could be found only at home: that profession was a mask, a false self put on during the day but gladly relinquished "on the stroke of seven," when the husband and father became "himself" again ("When we come home, we lay aside our mask and drop our tools, and are no longer lawyers, sailors, soldiers, statesmen, clergymen, but only men").[19] But while the beggar's disguise reinforces this notion of profession as mask, the story also implies that St. Clair's true self may be located in his City life — a possibility enhanced by his desire to keep that life secret, by the use of his talents begging enables him to make, as well as by the fact that he confides his secret in the figure known only as the "lascar," who maintains the opium den, rather than in his wife.

But if St. Clair's true identity is located in the City, in what does that identity consist? The City appears here not as a place where the Victorian husband goes to take on a social role but as a place where he goes to lose one — where, in the anonymity of the financial center or the opium den, he can find privacy, freedom from the constraints of social and familial roles. Mrs. St. Clair's discovery of her husband results in what looks like an actual crime — the appearance that St. Clair is being assaulted — but it also appears as *her* violation of *his* privacy: she sees him while walking in the City, where he doesn't expect her to be. (Earlier, another wife acts as spy: Kate Whitney had "the surest information" that her husband had "made use of an opium den in the farthest east of the City." St. Clair later underscores the wife's role in policing her husband's identity: "It occurred to me that even a wife's eyes could not pierce so complete a disguise.")[20] The City and the opium den resemble one another as places where the usual constructions of identity can be abandoned, together mediating and dismantling the opposition between City and home: first, by suggesting that identity consists of freedom from identity — freedom found in exchange, in circulation — and, second, by implying that places serve not as loci of true or false identity but rather as switching points along a path of multiple identities. (Mrs. St. Clair in fact suggests this when she recognizes her husband's writing by its uncharacteristic nature: what she recognizes is "one of his hands. . . . His hand when he wrote hurriedly. It is very unlike his usual writing, and yet I know it well" [p. 125].) The den also resembles the City as a place where identity is replaced by habit — a habit, moreover, of consumption associated with the loss of identity. Holmes, lacking an occupation with which to identify St. Clair, identi-

[19]Mark Rutherford, *Mark Rutherford's Deliverance: Being the Second Part of His Autobiography* (London, 1885); quoted in Walter Houghton, *The Victorian Frame of Mind* (New Haven, 1957), 346; James Anthony Froude, *The Nemesis of Faith* (London, 1849); quoted in Houghton, *Victorian Frame of Mind*, 345.
[20]Wives safeguard their husbands' identities and are deceived by them, but it should be clear by now that the story's anxiety is focused on male identity.

fies him by his habits and his finances: St. Clair is "a man of temperate habits" whose "whole debts . . . amount to £88 10*s*., while he has £220 standing to his credit in the Capital and Counties Bank" (p. 118). It makes sense, then, that when the police search the opium den for St. Clair's body they find only a coat filled with coins — a coat more substantial, its pockets weighted with pennies, than the body which had inhabited it.

*The journalist.* A former actor, St. Clair uses his skill with makeup to devise the beggar's disguise; as Hugh Boone, he thus resembles one of Mayhew's "false beggars." But his journalistic background — which leads him to put on the beggar's disguise in the first place — connects him with Mayhew as well. Disguised as Hugh Boone, St. Clair expresses his culture's ambivalence about the activity of the "man who does something in the City." But his transformation also reveals what underlies the social scientist/journalist's project: the sympathy and identification responsible for Mayhew's success in collecting and transcribing the stories of those he interviews in London's slums also account for St. Clair's success as "false beggar," and both amount to a dealing in representation, a selling of the beggar's identity. Indeed, by making Hugh Boone the beggar and Neville St. Clair the (former) investigative reporter one and the same, Conan Doyle erases the distinction between identification and exploitation: to "know" the beggar is to trade in his identity, and to trade in his identity is to sell — as both Mayhew and St. Clair do — his words. (There is a difference, however: St. Clair finds reporting to be "arduous labor" but has no difficulty with the labor involved in creating Hugh Boone. In fact, he takes pleasure in his role. "Arduousness," here, would seem to stand for the visibility of labor, which can be perceived as difficult only after having been perceived in the first place. Since labor is only what a culture recognizes as labor, the refusal to see that begging involves labor keeps society from having to acknowledge its complicity in the creation of begging as an activity. The ease with which St. Clair takes on the character of Hugh Boone, and his pleasure in doing so, represents an effacement of labor that makes it all the more necessary to put the "false beggar" to work.)

And yet while unmasking the exploitative nature of Mayhew's project, Conan Doyle's story performs the same function as Mayhew's social science: in detecting the beggar, and making the "false beggar" confess the "truth" of his identity, it purports to distinguish "true" identity from "false." And, maintaining the opposition between "true" and

"false" in the figure of the beggar, both works appear to support the
possibility of doing away with the world of representation the "false
beggar" implies. It is this possibility, however, that they also finally undermine, since both Mayhew's structure and Holmes's reproduce the
system of representation they find so troublesome.

In his section on beggary, Halliday describes an encounter between
himself and a one-armed beggar claiming to be a soldier wounded in
battle. Quizzing the man, Halliday catches him in a factual error and,
after accusing him of lying, offers him a shilling — and his freedom —
in exchange for his true story (418).[21] In initiating and reproducing the
"false beggar's" business — the trading of identity, as narrative, for coin —
Halliday reveals the ideology underlying Mayhew's project: not the desire
to undo the system of exchange wherein identity is offered for money
but rather the desire to maintain it, reinstating the hierarchy the
beggar's imposture has upset by affirming the social scientist's position
as arbiter of social identity. The end of "The Man with the Twisted
Lip," similarly, has St. Clair telling his story to Holmes and the police in
exchange for a guarantee of confidentiality — a guarantee enabling
him, in spite of adjurations to the contrary, to keep Hugh Boone secret
from his wife.

The story's conclusion revolves around the question of whether or
not a crime has been committed. What St. Clair most fears — "exposure" — is exactly what the case requires, for Holmes discovers the solution to the crime in one of the most private of bourgeois spaces: "In
the bathroom." St. Clair's violation of bourgeois values is represented as
dirt; what is needed to restore him — to make him come clean — is a
sponge and water.

> The man's face peeled off under the sponge like the bark from a
> tree. Gone was the coarse brown tint! Gone, too, the horrid scar
> which had seamed it across, and the twisted lip which had given
> the repulsive sneer to the face! A twitch brought away the tangled
> red hair, and there, sitting up in his bed, was a pale, sad-faced,

---

[21]The passage is as follows:

> "You impudent impostor!" I said; "the Thirty — did not go out till the spring
> of '55. How dare you tell me you belonged to it?"
>
> The fellow blenched for a moment, but rallied and said, "I didn't like to
> contradict your honour for fear you should be angry and wouldn't give me
> nothing."
>
> "That's very polite of you," I said, "but still I have a great mind to give you
> into custody. Stay; tell me who and what you are, and I will give you a shilling
> and let you go."

refined-looking man, black-haired and smooth-skinned, rubbing his eyes, and staring about him with sleepy bewilderment. Then suddenly realizing the exposure, he broke into a scream, and threw himself down with his face to the pillow. (p. 129)

Holmes's washing reveals what might well be taken, for all its lack of specificity and interest, as a description of no one in particular; the passage's fascination lies with what it repeatedly invokes as "gone" rather than with what remains. As in the description of Holmes in the opium den, the narrative lingers over the moment of transformation, the moment at which identity is revealed to have been — and to be — mistaken. Indeed, these moments suggest that the pleasures of identity — and, for the story's reader, of identification — lie not in one position or the other but in the detachment from both and the possibility of movement between; when Boone's "face" (not mask) peels off, it reveals a man whose identity possesses little interest when he isn't being someone else. And in its repeated staging of recognition as assault — at least in the violence of the victim's reaction — the story exposes the violence of the attempt to stop that movement: in Holmes's symbolic "murder" of Hugh Boone (which, we might say, satisfies his desire for a victim) as in St. Clair's earlier start of surprise, revelations of identity are registered as murder not because they do away with identities — Boone or St. Clair — but rather because they produce them. Revealing one figure to "be" the other, these assaults annihilate the idea of a stable or unified identity altogether. (Suggesting in his own words that no one can be arrested because no one has disappeared, St. Clair articulates the social implications of his exposure by asserting that his identity is proof against his arrest: "If I am Mr. Neville St. Clair, then it is obvious that no crime has been committed, and that, therefore, I am illegally detained" [p. 130]. The story raises the possibility that the gentleman and the beggar are the same only to repudiate it, its ostensibly democratizing identification of the two figures, like that of Victorian popular ideology in general, in fact the expression of anxiety about such potential transformation.)

The suspected crime — murder — is found not to have taken place; what did occur was rather what Holmes calls an "error." And that error seems to have been in essence a crime against the family: "You would have done better to have trusted your wife," advises Holmes. But what does Holmes mean here — that, if St. Clair had confided in his wife, the beggar's disguise would have been acceptable? That his wife, apprised of St. Clair's plans, would have prevented the situation from occurring?

The actual crime of begging is regarded very lightly — "What was a fine to me?" — more serious, it seems, is St. Clair's violation of the rules of bourgeois family life: his failure to confide his true identity to his wife.

But the story only seems to resolve the problem of St. Clair's identity by entrusting it to his wife; in fact, while returning her husband to her, Holmes and the police keep the knowledge of his activity to themselves. ("If the police are to hush this thing up," says Inspector Bradstreet, "there must be no more of Hugh Boone.") "The Man with the Twisted Lip," like the Poor Law, seems to resolve the problem of the indeterminacy of social identity by locating identity in the body: a cut on the hand assures us that Boone and St. Clair are the same. But it goes a step further, requiring the subject to tell his story, to constitute his identity in (as) narrative. And, trading the confidentiality St. Clair desires for that story, the police and the detective protect the system they accuse St. Clair of having perpetuated, asserting their power to control an exchange that will remain, necessarily, in the realm of representation. For having divested himself of his multiple identities at the police station, St. Clair will have to invent another before he gets home, thus beginning life again on a foundation of representation. Rather than determining the truth or falsity of any particular identity, then, these texts demonstrate the perpetuation of a system wherein a subject is free to inhabit the identity designated as acceptable for him or her by the authorities. (Hence the unresolvable tension between fluidity and hierarchy in all these examples: Halliday's authority, for instance, lies not in his ability to determine the truth of the beggar's second story but in his ability to have the beggar tell it. Only the storyteller knows whether the narrative he tells is true, but that knowledge is not accompanied by power. The tale told by the beggar, like St. Clair's writing — and like the hand identifying Hugh Boone as St. Clair — may well be merely "one of his hands.") Truth matters less than the production and maintenance of the proper fiction, or rather truth lies not in the story but in the system of exchange that requires the storyteller to tell it: a system which unmasks that man, and then requires him to unmask himself, before the police, the detective, the social scientist, the journalist. What is understood as stable identity in these works is constituted within and produced by the very system of exchange Mayhew and Conan Doyle condemn.[22]

---

[22]What goes on here supports a definition of truth offered by Michel Foucault: " 'Truth' is to be understood as a system of ordered procedures for the production, regulation, circulation and operation of statements"; *Power/Knowledge,* ed. Colin Gordon (New York, 1980), 133.

And it is that system of exchange which links the "false beggar" to his detractors — Mayhew, Conan Doyle, Holmes, and St. Clair himself — as a version of the writer, not unlike the begging-letter writer whose profession it is to trade stories of poverty and decline for cash, providing the public with an opportunity to winnow "false" identities from "true" ones by means of narrative. Since Mayhew — or Halliday, who, appropriately enough, allowed his professional identity to be subsumed within Mayhew's — includes himself as a character in his own story, we can see that he is implicated in the exchange with his "false beggars": we see him constituting himself as social scientist at the same moment that he constructs the identities of his subjects. It is more characteristic of the writer, however, to hide that implication, and no writer is more famously effaced behind his creation than Conan Doyle, who, as a world of Sherlockiana attests, seems to have created an actual person rather than a fictional character. And Holmes, as fictional character, is also famous for self-effacement — for the skill with which he projects himself into "the criminal mind" while at the same time remaining aloof from it, as if his identity inheres, like the writer's, in the ability to project himself into the identities of others. Mayhew, Conan Doyle, St. Clair, and Holmes are all, literally or figuratively, writers, and the figure of the "false beggar" is a figure for the writer, involved in a sympathetic taking on of identity that is also an act of self-effacement, implicating its instigator in an ambivalent relationship not only with that other into whose identity he projects himself but with identity itself, so easily slipped in and out of.

Both Mayhew and Conan Doyle began to write out of financial need. Mayhew, in particular, may be said to have detached himself from his subjects precisely through the act of writing about them: the sympathy and identification which enable his work in fact keep away the possibility that he will actually occupy the beggar's place. And Conan Doyle discusses his decision to write in terms that parallel St. Clair's decision to beg: "It was in this year [1879] that I first learned that shillings might be earned in other ways than by filling phials."[23] (St. Clair says, "You can imagine how hard it was to settle down to arduous work at two pounds a week, when I knew that I could earn as much in a day by smearing my face with a little paint, laying my cap on the ground, and sitting still" [p. 131].) Upon discovering that he could make more money selling stories than as a medical assistant, Conan Doyle — like St. Clair — simply exchanged one profession for another, more lucrative one.

[23]Arthur Conan Doyle, *Memories and Adventures* (Boston, 1924), 24.

According to at least one critic, however, Conan Doyle felt degraded by the writing of mystery stories: Stephen Knight argues that "The Man with the Twisted Lip" expresses Conan Doyle's shameful feelings about writing "vulgar potboilers" rather than the historical novels by means of which he hoped to establish himself as a respectable author. Publishing in the *Strand* — a magazine sold, appropriately enough, in railway stations "to catch the commuting white-collar market" — Conan Doyle felt (according to Knight) that he was taking "profits made in the street from City workers."[24]

Knight's interpretation depends upon a number of elements — Hugh Boone as "degraded," mystery story writing as an "accidental discovery" which suddenly supplies Conan Doyle with large sums of money — that the story, and the biography, do not necessarily support. But the connection he emphasizes between writing and beggary may be drawn out in a number of ways: in terms, for example, of the need to appeal to an audience characteristic of both, or in terms of the movement from "filling phials" to "sitting still" that describes Conan Doyle's progression as well as St. Clair's — a movement, that is, from more to less visible labor. If Conan Doyle identified with his subject, as Mayhew appears to have identified with his, both suggestively turned that identification to account. An identification with illegitimate production is legitimated in a form of production — writing — that allows for vicariousness, for both imaginative participation and professional "disinterest."

On the one hand, stillness suggests the achievement of gentlemanly respectability; on the other, it evokes the degradation and loss of identity associated with the opium den. The identity Holmes and the police desire for St. Clair, in contrast, seems to depend upon incessant movement. And yet even as it seems to create such identity, this movement also dismantles it — and as he makes contemporary readers of "The Man with the Twisted Lip," commuting between home and City, into a *mise en abŷme*[25] for the story, Conan Doyle challenges the polarity between true and false identities he is attempting to establish. For what, we might well ask, is the identity of the man on the train, reading? Conan Doyle's story may indeed express an opposition between "true" and "false" selves he felt himself to be living: a structure in which the true, respectable self feels it necessary to trade on a false identity in order

---

[24]Stephen Knight, *Form and Ideology in Crime Fiction* (London, 1980), 70 and 98.
[25]*mise en abŷme:* A smaller version of a text embedded within that text; suggestively, then, an infinite regress. The term comes from heraldry, referring to a figure on an escutcheon that repeats the escutcheon in miniature. [Editor's note]

to survive. And yet if Holmes's creator maintained, along with many of his contemporaries, a notion of a "true" self that could be supported only at the expense of participation in the "false" identities of the marketplace, this passage between high and low culture has the same implications as St. Clair's changes of identity: in a characteristically Victorian movement between the poles of respectability and nonrespectability, the individual strives for the former because always kept from complete adherence to it by participation in the latter. The question is thus not what is identity but rather where, at any moment, is identity, since the story illustrates perhaps best of all the way the idea of respectability keeps identity in motion: the way the social self circulates endlessly in order to imagine itself drawing closer to the image of a desired, culturally valuable self that will finally (and paradoxically) sit still.

*The professional.* The irresistible continuity between "filling phials" and "sitting still" takes us back to the opium den, which evokes the same images of passivity and loss of identity that the figure of the City man does — and that also surround Holmes. The story displays anxiety about labor that appears not to be labor, often mentioning the fact that, when working, Holmes appears to be doing nothing. Both Holmes and Boone live by their wits; neither is perceived to be working when he is actually hardest at work. Thus Holmes, working on the case,

> took off his coat and waistcoat, put on a large blue dressing-gown, and then wandered about the room collecting pillows from his bed, and cushions from the sofa and arm-chairs. With these he constructed a sort of Eastern divan, upon which he perched himself cross-legged, with an ounce of shag tobacco and a box of matches laid out in front of him. In the dim light of the lamp I saw him sitting there, an old brier pipe between his lips, his eyes fixed vacantly upon the corner of the ceiling, the blue smoke curling up from him, silent, motionless, with the light shining upon his strong-set aquiline features. (pp. 126–27)

Indeed, Holmes at work resembles nothing so much as the habitué of an opium den. Producing the solution to the case in a scenario that highlights the absence of visible labor, Holmes resembles the "man who does something in the City" as well as the professional whose productivity the nineteenth century could not easily locate.

The beggar, the finance capitalist, and the detective are unproductive in the sense in which Adam Smith found many entertainers and professionals to be, since they produce no "vendible commodity . . . for which an equal quantity of labour could afterwards be procured."[26] The individual who professes rather than produces — whose speech, writing, or knowledge is his commodity — blurs the easily readable relationship between producer and product, laborer and commodity; the professional performs services whose merit, at least to some extent, the client has to take on faith. Having, as Harold Perkin writes, a "professional interest in disinterest," the professional also aroused suspicion during the period because of his "Protean" ability to "assume the guise of any other class at will."[27] It is therefore appropriate that it is in the figure of the professional as well as by means of professionals — the detective and the writer — that, in this story, the beggar and the gentleman meet and become indistinguishable from one another.

When Watson first meets Holmes, in *A Study in Scarlet*, he has difficulty figuring out his profession; given what Holmes seems to know, it's not clear what he's suited for. Watson actually draws up a chart, listing such items as "Knowledge of Literature. — Nil . . . Knowledge of Chemistry. — Profound," and, when finished, throws it into the fire in despair: "If I can only find what the fellow is driving at by reconciling all these accomplishments, and discovering a calling which needs them all. . . . I may as well give up the attempt at once" (p. 26). What is baffling about St. Clair, similarly, is his failure to fit into any obvious profession. Holmes's profession, of course, depends upon exactly the kind of indeterminacy he finds inappropriate for St. Clair.

Holmes, it has often been pointed out, is a model of the "gentlemanly amateur," "relaxed and disinterested."[28] His lack of specialization is his chief asset, this argument has it, since his work requires a collection of arcane bits of knowledge that would not appear necessary to a member of any other profession. Yet Holmes does not simply accumulate random information: indeed, by his own account his methods are supremely practical. His theory of the mind is based on an analogy with material labor:

> I consider that a man's brain originally is like a little empty attic, and you have to stock it with such furniture as you choose. A fool takes in all the lumber of every sort that he comes across, so that

[26]Adam Smith, *An Inquiry into the Nature and Causes of the Wealth of Nations,* ed. R. H. Campbell and A. S. Skinner, 2 vols. (Oxford, 1976), 1:330.

[27]Perkin, *Origins of Modern English Society,* 260 and 253. Perkin is referring here to a "new" professional class, differentiating themselves during this period both from older professionals — who might be represented here by Whitney and Watson — and from the capitalist middle class, more directly vulnerable to market fluctuations.

[28]Dennis Porter, *The Pursuit of Crime* (New Haven, 1981), 156.

> the knowledge which might be useful to him gets crowded out. . . .
> Now the skilful workman is very careful indeed as to what he takes
> into his brain-attic. He will have nothing but the tools which may
> help him in doing his work. (p. 25)

In fact, what Holmes knows signals his practicality. When Watson meets
him, he has invented a process for distinguishing blood stains; he also
reveals that he "dabble[s] with poisons a good deal" (p. 22). The one
element that signals "gentlemanly amateur" in its apparent lack of professional value is Holmes's violin playing, yet even that, as Watson describes it, may be geared not toward the ordinary production of music
as a means of relaxation but rather toward cogitation: "When left to
himself . . . he would seldom produce any music or attempt any recognized air. Leaning back in his armchair of an evening, he would close his
eyes and scrape carelessly at the fiddle which was thrown across his knee.
. . . [W]hether the music aided those thoughts, or whether the playing
was simply the result of a whim or fancy, was more than I could determine" (p. 26).

Despite his practicality, however, Holmes maintains an attitude of
gentlemanly disinterest; while asserting that "the theories . . . which appear to you to be so chimerical, are . . . so practical that I depend upon
them for my bread and cheese" (p. 28), he also claims that he may get
nothing out of a case but "a laugh" at the expense of the inspectors who
fail to solve it. Asserting his economic interest in his work almost at the
same time that he disavows it, Holmes maintains the professional's
characteristic tension between productivity and unproductivity. The
idea of Holmes as "amateur" is a mystification of professional labor: his
capital, Holmes's laugh suggests, is purely intellectual, his work a function of desire and source of pleasure rather than a matter of necessity. It
makes sense, then, that in "The Man with the Twisted Lip" Holmes
confesses to a fascination with that other professional who manifestly
enjoys his work: "I have watched this fellow more than once," he says
of Boone, "before ever I thought of making his professional acquaintance, and I have been surprised at the harvest which he has reaped in a
short time" (p. 120). Intrigued here by Boone's apparently effortless
production of income, Holmes boasts, at the end of the story, that he
solved the case merely "by sitting upon five pillows and consuming an
ounce of shag" (p. 132).

From the nonprofessional's perspective, such effortlessness is only a
step away from doing nothing, and professionals are found in the opium
den, in this story, because both professionalism and opium addiction
serve as focuses for Victorian anxieties about unproductivity. The

opium den was a fantasy about unproductivity: explicitly citing this threat, the anti-opium movement encouraged the idea that opium represented a particular danger for the working classes and raised anxiety about its spread to the middle classes; opium, wrote one physician in 1843, rendered "the individual who indulges himself in it a worse than useless member of society."[29] The lascar, similarly, was a figure of "surplus" population associated with unproductivity; considered, paradoxically, to be indolent himself — that is, likely to be a "false beggar" (for Mayhew, Asian beggars were figures of "extraordinary mendacity"),[30] this figure also aroused anxiety for his potential to take the place of English or Irish laborers, thereby producing unemployment — and "false beggars" — in the native population. In his fictional role as proprietor of the opium den, the lascar is an entrepreneur of passivity and unproductivity, his appellation signaling the kind of information — about race, profession, and social position — terms of identity are meant to supply.

As we saw earlier, the opium den undermines the possibility that St. Clair's "true" identity can be located either at home or at work; situated between the two, the den provides a place for transformation, for the constitution of identity in — and as — exchange. But, as we have also seen, the den suggestively associates opium addiction with professional identity. Like disguise, which functions throughout the story as a metaphor for profession, opium transforms appearance. Yet it does so more profoundly than disguise: opium makes Whitney into "a slave to the drug . . . with yellow, pasty face, drooping lids and pin-point pupils" (p. 112). Where disguise points to the existence of the authentic identity underlying it, evoking an easy movement between "true" and "false," Whitney's "slavishness" implies an inability to move back and forth — a fixedness and loss of identity. Indeed, we might say that while the story invites us to imagine disguise, profession, writing, and here, reading — Whitney begins his opium addiction, we are told, in deliberate imitation of De Quincey — as analogous movements in and out of identity, the idea of opium addiction deconstructs that movement, suggesting that the individual in motion may become stuck — not in one

[29] Anxiety about opium use in the late nineteenth century was associated with theories of the degeneracy of the middle class; the anti-opium movement helped spread the belief that "opium smoking was somehow threatening in its implications for the indigenous population." See Virginia Berridge and Griffith Edwards, *Opium and the People: Opiate Use in Nineteenth-Century England* (New Haven, 1987), 175, 198–99.

[30] See Mayhew, *London Labour*, 4:423–24; and Rozina Visram, *Ayahs, Lascars, and Princes: Indians in Britain, 1700–1947* (London, 1986).

identity or the other but in that very detachment from identity emblemized here both by the addict's stillness and the City man's incessant movement. As the professional, or the City man, that is, fancies himself to be moving freely between identities, his very movement registers his enslavement to the system which has him doing so. Whitney's "slavish" addiction — the presence of which disturbs the story's own regular movement between suburb and City — thus represents the other side of the coin on whose face St. Clair and, preeminently, Holmes enact the pleasures of disguise. And in fact when the police and Holmes require St. Clair to remain, visibly, in circulation, what they insist upon is exactly the kind of detachment from self that makes St. Clair into the entrepreneur of identities they accuse him of being. The professional, Whitney's addiction implies, is addicted not to one identity or another but to the detachment from self both opium, and profession, imply.

But the story establishes a difference between Whitney and St. Clair, on the one hand, and Holmes on the other. Holmes famously has no private life but only a bohemianism that dramatizes the absence of one; the uncovering of his "true" identity in the opium den requires no scrubbing but only, apparently, an act of will, a change of mood — or, on Watson's part, a slight change of perception. "His form had filled out, his wrinkles were gone, the dull eyes had regained their fire" (p. 115). Holmes "is" his professional identity: in him, enslavement to profession is disguised as the discovery of identity through it. (When, in the same scene, he remarks, "I suppose, Watson . . . that you imagine that I have added opium smoking to cocaine injections," Holmes emphasizes the bohemianism that seems to draw him away from his profession but in fact registers the absence, in his life, of anything else.) Dedicated to a profession he himself has invented, and of which he is the only member ("I suppose I am the only one in the world. I'm a consulting detective"; *A Study in Scarlet* [p. 29]), Holmes is a fantasy of professionalism as unalienated labor — of the highly specialized professional as a figure for whom slavishness cannot be an issue because his work so completely fulfills his nature, because his work is the complete expression of his nature. (Just as writing provides Conan Doyle with an alternative to medicine, so too is Holmes's professionalism contrasted here with the doctoring of Whitney and Watson.) His work, in fact, is no work at all but rather — as his night-long smoking session suggests — habit: "From long habit the train of thoughts ran so swiftly through my mind that I arrived at the conclusion without being conscious of intermediate steps" (*A Study in Scarlet* [p. 29]). In the figure of

Holmes, addiction is the same as fulfillment; for him, losing the self in one's work is the same as finding the self in it.

Yet this fantasy of professional identity exists alongside, and depends upon producing, everyone else's divided self; it is purchased at the expense of those who, imagining that they can wear one identity in public and preserve another, secretly, for themselves, provide their culture with the reassurance about identity it desires. Both Whitney and St. Clair become objects of official scrutiny, it is important to recall, not when they begin leading "double lives" but when they cease to do so; the police and Holmes require them not to abandon their double lives but simply to lead those lives in plain sight — and, above all, to keep moving. For Whitney's and St. Clair's cessations of movement reveal that the double life functions for them, and for Victorian culture, in the same way that disguise does for Holmes: to preserve the fiction of an authentic self. And this may be what Holmes and Boone are smiling about.

Having revealed this secret, however, the story must conceal it once again, if only to provide Holmes with something to do. For the detective's usual manner of proceeding is to find the strange in the commonplace: life, he claims, "is infinitely stranger than anything which the mind of man could invent" ("A Case of Identity" [p. 75]). In "The Man with the Twisted Lip" he is momentarily baffled by what has proven to be not so commonplace: St. Clair's choice of profession. The point of the case is therefore to return St. Clair the beggar — and St. Clair the gentleman — to the ordinary, middle-class world of work and family: the world that stands still while Holmes moves about, and that consists of identities into which Holmes will, temporarily, disappear. Thus assured that the ordinary world's lack of ordinariness will remain secret — until, that is, he discovers it once again — Holmes produces the commonplace world on which he depends for his labor, clearing the way for his own practice.

## III

*"There, sitting by the fire, and grinning at my surprise, was none other than Sherlock Holmes."*

The twisted lip is suggestively not quite a smile. As scar or deformity, it elicits sympathy even as it mocks those who are persuaded by it; both subservient smile and menacing grimace, it takes away with one half what it offers with the other.[31] As scar, the lip may be said to refer not only to the disability that would make physical labor impossible but to the body of the worker altered by such labor; Boone may thus be said to return to the arena of commerce the figure of the producer that has disappeared from it.[32] But what is returned is simulacra and spectacle: no longer seen in its productive capacity, no longer associated with objects produced, the worker's body, as Boone metaphorically represents it, appears only as something immediately transformed into money.

And yet as wound or deformity the twisted lip would not have prohibited the performance of physical labor. The lip is not a disability but rather the sign of one, alluding not so much to physical injury as to a knowledge of the codes that represent it. It is perhaps above all a knowing smile, providing another link between Holmes and Boone: Holmes, as we have seen, will take on a case requiring as payment only a "laugh" at those who fail to solve it. Glenn W. Most has interpreted the detective's smile as an acknowledgment of power: "This is the smile of wisdom, complacent in the superiority of its own power and tolerant of the weakness of mere humanity; the detective adopts it in the moment when he has understood something that no one else has."[33]

If the smiling detective understands something no one else does, what does the man with the twisted lip understand? Giving St. Clair the detective's freedom of disguise and fluidity of identity, Conan Doyle makes the beggar's smile detachable, preserving that realm of nonidentity for his detective by enabling Holmes to remove it from — by wiping it off — St. Clair's face.

---

[31]The connection between smiling and aggression is more fully developed in this character's latest manifestation, by way of the 1927 film *The Man Who Laughs*: the Joker in *Batman*. See Benedict Nightingale, "Batman Prowls a Gothic Drawn from the Absurd," *New York Times,* 16 June 1989, sec. 2, p. 16.

[32]Elaine Scarry describes the relation between worker and capitalist as a confrontation between an embodied figure and a disembodied one and suggests that, vampiristically, the capitalist's "absence" depends upon the worker's physicality; *Body in Pain,* 276.

[33]Glenn W. Most, "The Hippocratic Smile: John le Carré and the Traditions of the Detective Novel," in Most and William W. Stowe, eds., *The Poetics of Murder* (New York, 1983), 343.

# Appendices

# A Chronology of
# Arthur Conan Doyle

**1859**   Born in Edinburgh, May 22.

**1868**   Begins schooling at Hodder, the preparatory school for Stonyhurst.

**1870**   Enters Stonyhurst, a Jesuit college.

**1875**   Completes studies at Stonyhurst College; begins a year at a Jesuit school in Austria.

**1876**   Begins medical studies at Edinburgh University, where he meets Dr. Joseph Bell.

**1879**   First stories published.

**1880**   Voyage as ship's doctor on an Arctic whaler.

**1881**   Receives Bachelor of Medicine degree from Edinburgh University. Voyage as ship's doctor on a cargo steamer to West Africa.

**1882**   Medical practice as junior associate of another doctor in Plymouth; then sets up own practice in Southsea.

**1885**   Marries Louise Hawkins.

**1887**   *A Study in Scarlet.*

**1889**    Daughter Mary Louise born. *The Sign of Four.*

**1890**    *The White Company.*

**1891**    Studies ophthalmology in Vienna. Opens practice as an oculist in London, but soon gives up medicine for a career as a writer. First six Sherlock Holmes stories published in the *Strand.*

**1892**    Son Alleyne Kingsley born. *The Adventures of Sherlock Holmes.*

**1893**    Louise Doyle develops tuberculosis. "The Final Problem" tells of Sherlock Holmes's death.

**1894**    *The Memoirs of Sherlock Holmes.* Successful first American lecture tour.

**1897**    Meets and falls in love with Jean Leckie.

**1900**    Goes to South Africa in Boer War, serving as doctor in a hospital unit, February–July. *The Great Boer War.*

**1902**    *The War in South Africa: Its Causes and Conduct.* Knighted. *The Hound of the Baskervilles.*

**1903**    Sherlock Holmes returns in "The Empty House."

**1905**    *The Return of Sherlock Holmes.*

**1906**    Louise Doyle dies. *Sir Nigel.* Begins campaign to correct an egregious miscarriage of English justice in the case of George Edalji.

**1907**    Marries Jean Leckie. *Through the Magic Door.*

**1909**    *The Crime of the Congo*, an exposé of Belgian abuses in Africa. Son Denis born.

**1910**    Begins campaign on behalf of Oscar Slater, unjustly accused and convicted of murder. Son Malcolm Adrian born.

**1912**    *The Lost World.* Daughter Jean ("Dilly") born.

**1915**    *The Valley of Fear.*

**1916**    Announces his conversion to spiritualism.

**1917**    *His Last Bow.*

**1918**    *The New Revelation*, the first of Doyle's many books about spiritualism.

**1921**  Doyle's mother dies.

**1922**  *The Coming of the Fairies.*

**1924**  *Memories and Adventures.*

**1927**  *The Case-Book of Sherlock Holmes.*

**1930**  Dies July 7.

# Doyle's Favorite
# Sherlock Holmes Stories

In March of 1927 Sir Arthur Conan Doyle proposed a challenge to readers of the *Strand* magazine, where all his Sherlock Holmes stories originally appeared. Of the first forty-four Sherlock Holmes stories already then published in book form (in four books: *The Adventures of Sherlock Holmes, The Memoirs of Sherlock Holmes, The Return of Sherlock Holmes,* and *His Last Bow*), Doyle selected the twelve stories that he considered the best and invited readers to do likewise. A prize (£100 and an autographed copy of Doyle's *Memories and Adventures*) was offered to the reader whose list most nearly coincided with Doyle's own choices.

In June, at the close of the competition, Doyle wrote again in the *Strand* to explain "How I Made My List." He began by suggesting that all of his choices had come in for some international acclaim or recognition, then went on to list and justify several selections. He felt certain that "The Speckled Band" — that "grim snake story" — would appear on every list, and he placed it at the top of his own. He ranked "The Red-headed League" and "The Dancing Men" next on the strength of their "originality of plot." Rounding out Doyle's favorite half-dozen were "The Final Problem" (because it "deals with the only foe who ever really extended Holmes" and "deceived the public (and Watson) into the erroneous inference of his death"); "A Scandal in Bohemia" (as the first Holmes story, it "opened the path for the others" and "has more female interest than is usual"); and "The Empty House" (because it "essays the difficult task of explaining away the alleged death of Holmes" and "introduces such a villain as Col. Sebastian Moran"). Several of his second half-dozen choices, he readily admitted, were somewhat arbitrary, but he named his first six choices confidently.

Here is Doyle's complete list:

"The Speckled Band"
"The Red-headed League"
"The Dancing Men"
"The Final Problem"
"A Scandal in Bohemia"
"The Empty House"

"The Five Orange Pips"
"The Second Stain"
"The Devil's Foot"
"The Priory School"
"The Musgrave Ritual"
"The Reigate Puzzle"

# Sherlock Holmes on Film

The following is a list of those Sherlock Holmes films based more or less directly on the fourteen stories included in this volume. Some of these films, especially the earlier ones, are now available only in archives and research collections. Others, though, are screened or broadcast with some frequency; and a great many (including all those from the Jeremy Brett series, all the theatrically released films produced since 1945, all the Rathbone films, and some of the Wontner films) are now available on videotape.

Beginning with a brief (less than a minute) peep-show film of 1900, "Sherlock Holmes Baffled" (a burglar eludes and bests Holmes with the help of trick photography), Sherlock Holmes has been portrayed on film more often, and by more actors, than any other figure in literature; thus a complete list of Sherlock Holmes films and videos would be very lengthy indeed. On the other hand, a great many Holmes films have little or nothing to do with the Holmes stories themselves; instead, they cast the detective in new, apocryphal adventures — for example, *Sherlock Holmes in Washington* (1943, with Basil Rathbone and Nigel Bruce; Holmes versus Nazi agents), *Sherlock Holmes in New York* (1976, with Roger Moore and Patrick Macnee), *The Seven-Per-Cent Solution* (1976, with Nicol Williamson and Robert Duvall, and Alan Arkin as Sigmund Freud), and *Murder by Decree* (1979, with Christopher

Plummer and James Mason; Holmes and the Jack the Ripper murders). Many other Sherlock Holmes films, moreover, while ostensibly drawn from Doyle's stories, retain only the most tenuous of connections with the originals. Thus *Sherlock Holmes and the Secret Weapon* (1942, with Rathbone and Bruce; the secret weapon is a new bombsight) claims to be based on "The Dancing Men" but retains from it only the stick-figure code (and borrows from other Holmes tales both Moriarty and a few of Holmes's disguisings). Doyle's story about a marriage disturbed by a Chicago gangster connection from the American wife's past becomes instead a story about an eccentric scientist's militarily valuable invention and Holmes's efforts to preserve it from Moriarty (who is working for the Nazis). I have not included such films in this videography.

Still other Holmes films, finally, are based not on the stories but on Doyle's plays. *Sherlock Holmes* (1899) was co-authored and adapted for the stage by the American actor William Gillette, who became famous for his performances of the title role. The play, based very loosely on "A Scandal in Bohemia" and parts of "The Final Problem," gives Holmes both a formidable opponent, Moriarty, and a love interest, Alice Faulkner, who (like Irene Adler) possesses evidence of a potentially scandalous love affair (unlike Irene Adler, not her own affair) that Holmes is engaged to recover. It is this play, rather than any Holmes story, that lies most directly behind such films as *Moriarty* (1922, with John Barrymore; U.S. title *Sherlock Holmes*), *Sherlock Holmes* (1932, with Clive Brook and Reginald Owen), and *Sherlock Holmes* (1981, with Frank Langella and Richard Woods; a filmed stage production). Another play, *The Speckled Band* (1910), Doyle himself adapted for the stage from his own story; the play has been quite influential on some film treatments of this story.

Of the many actors who have portrayed Holmes, several have been particularly influential in defining the character for their time. First there was William Gillette, who created the role on stage in his dramatic adaptation in 1899 ("wonderfully acted," in Doyle's opinion), frequently revived it thereafter, and starred in it as late as 1932; he also recreated it in a full-length 1916 film, *Sherlock Holmes*, now lost. The most influential Holmes of the silent films was Eille Norwood, of whose performances Doyle also approved: "He has that rare quality which can only be described as glamour, which compels you to watch an actor eagerly even when he is doing nothing. He has the brooding eye which excites expectation, and he has also a quite unrivalled power of disguise" (*Memories and Adventures* 106). Norwood appeared in forty-five short and two feature-length Holmes films. Arthur Wontner accustomed audiences to an older, quieter Holmes in a series of five movies in the 1930s. Basil Rathbone in contrast presented a warm, vigorous Holmes in a series of fourteen increasingly apocryphal and modernized Holmes stories from 1939 to 1946. Now Jeremy Brett's contemporary (and still evolving) portrayal of Holmes in several series of television movies, emphasizing the character's eccentricity and egotism, seems to be influencing perceptions of Holmes as powerfully as Gillette's impersonation did almost a hundred years ago.

*Sir Arthur Conan Doyle.* 1927. 11½ mins. According to De Waal's *International Sherlock Holmes*, this is the only sound film ever made of Doyle. "He relates how, in 1886, he came to write the Sherlock Holmes stories, and for five minutes he gives a rich and humorous history of his scientific detective in a warm Scotch burr." In the last half of the film Doyle discusses his spiritualist faith.

"A Scandal in Bohemia"
   1921.  Eille Norwood, Hubert Willis. 35 min. Silent.
   1951.  Alan Wheatley, Raymond Francis. 35 min. TV.
   1984.  Jeremy Brett, David Burke. 60 min. TV.

"The Red-headed League"
   1921.  Eille Norwood, Hubert Willis. 36 min. Silent.
   1951.  Alan Wheatley, Raymond Francis. 35 min. TV.
   1954.  Ronald Howard, Howard Marion Crawford. 27 min. TV.
   1965.  Douglas Wilmer, Nigel Stock. 50 min. TV.
   1985.  Jeremy Brett, David Burke. 60 min. TV.

"A Case of Identity"
   1921.  Eille Norwood, Hubert Willis. 44 min. Silent.

"The Boscombe Valley Mystery"
   1912.  *A Mystery of Boscombe Vale.* Georges Treville, —— Moyse. 28 min. Silent.
   1922.  Eille Norwood, Hubert Willis. 40 min. Silent.
   1968.  Peter Cushing, Nigel Stock. 50 min. TV.
   1990.  Jeremy Brett, Edward Hardwicke. 60 min. TV.

"The Man with the Twisted Lip"
   1921.  Eille Norwood, Hubert Willis. 40 min. Silent.
   1951.  John Longden, Campbell Singer. 35 min. TV.
   1965.  Douglas Wilmer, Nigel Stock. 50 min. TV.
   1986.  Jeremy Brett, Edward Hardwicke. 60 min. TV.

"The Blue Carbuncle"
   1923.  Eille Norwood, Hubert Willis. 33 min. Silent.

1968.  Peter Cushing, Nigel Stock. 50 min. TV.
1984.  Jeremy Brett, David Burke. 60 min. TV.

"The Speckled Band"
1912.  Georges Treville (there possibly was no Watson). 28 min. Silent.
1923.  Eille Norwood, Hubert Willis. 30 min. Silent.
1931.  Raymond Massey, Athole Stewart. 90 min. Based on the play.
1949.  Alan Napier, Melville Cooper. TV.
1964.  Douglas Wilmer, Nigel Stock. 50 min. TV.
1982.  Geoffrey Whitehead, Donald Pickering. TV.
1984.  Jeremy Brett, David Burke. 60 min. TV.

"Silver Blaze"
1912.  Georges Treville, ——Moyse. 22 min. Silent.
1923.  Eille Norwood, Hubert Willis. 35 min. Silent.
1937.  (U.S. title: *Murder at the Baskervilles.*) Arthur Wontner, Ian Fleming. 70 min. Adds Moriarty.
1977.  Christopher Plummer, Thorley Waters. 30 min. TV.
1988.  Jeremy Brett, Edward Hardwicke. 60 min. TV.

"The Musgrave Ritual"
1912.  Georges Treville, ——Moyse. 22 min. Silent.
1922.  Eille Norwood, Hubert Willis. 29 min. Silent.
1943.  *Sherlock Holmes Faces Death.* Basil Rathbone, Nigel Bruce. 68 min. Loosely based on the story; the ritual now involves chess.
1968.  Peter Cushing, Nigel Stock. 50 min. TV.
1986.  Jeremy Brett, Edward Hardwicke. 60 min. TV.

"The Final Problem"
1923.  Eille Norwood, Hubert Willis. 28 min. Silent.
1931.  *The Sleeping Cardinal.* (U.S. title: *Sherlock Holmes' Fatal Hour.*) Arthur Wontner, Ian Fleming. 84 min. Based on "The Final Problem" and "The Empty House."
1985.  Jeremy Brett, David Burke. 60 min. TV.

"The Empty House"
1921.  Eille Norwood, Hubert Willis. 30 min. Silent.
1931.  [See under "The Final Problem."]
1951.  Alan Wheatley, Raymond Francis. 35 min. TV.
1986.  Jeremy Brett, Edward Hardwicke. 60 min. TV.

"The Dancing Men"
1923.  Eille Norwood, Hubert Willis. 44 min. Silent.
1968.  Peter Cushing, Nigel Stock. 50 min. TV.
1984.  Jeremy Brett, David Burke. 60 min. TV.

"Charles Augustus Milverton"
- 1922. Eille Norwood, Hubert Willis. 32 min. Silent.
- 1932. *The Missing Rembrandt.* Arthur Wontner, Ian Fleming. 84 min. Only loosely based on the story.
- 1965. Douglas Wilmer, Nigel Stock. 50 min. TV.
- 1991. *The Master Blackmailer.* Jeremy Brett, Edward Hardwicke. 60 min. TV.

"The Second Stain"
- 1922. Eille Norwood, Hubert Willis. 37 min. Silent.
- 1951. Alan Wheatley, Raymond Francis. 35 min. TV.
- 1968. Peter Cushing, Nigel Stock. 50 min. TV.
- 1986. Jeremy Brett, Edward Hardwicke. 60 min. TV.

# Select Bibliography

**TEXTS**

There is no one standard text of the Sherlock Holmes stories. The standard English edition is the two-volume set published by Murray in 1928–29, during Doyle's lifetime; the standard American edition is that published by Doubleday in 1930, the year of Doyle's death. Both editions contain a few errors. The Bantam edition (based on the Doubleday edition) has the particular value of being readily available in paperback. Baring-Gould's quirky edition, a monument of "Sherlockian" pseudo-scholarship (it arranges the stories and novels in "biographical" order and argues interminably about their actual dates, locales, historical occasions, and their intertextual consistencies or inconsistencies), is yet a mine of valuable annotative information about relevant details of late Victorian life.

Doyle, Arthur Conan. *The Annotated Sherlock Holmes.* Ed. William S. Baring-Gould. 2 vols. New York: Clarkson N. Potter, 1967.

———. *The Complete Sherlock Holmes.* Intro. Christopher Morley. Garden City, NY: Doubleday, 1930.

———. *Sherlock Holmes: The Complete Novels and Stories.* Intro. Loren Estleman. 2 vols. New York: Bantam, 1986.

———. *Sherlock Holmes: A Study in Scarlet; The Sign of Four; The Hound of the Baskervilles; The Valley of Fear: The Complete Long Stories.* London: Murray, 1929.

———. *Sherlock Holmes: His Adventures; Memoirs; Return; His Last*

*Bow and The Case-Book: The Complete Short Stories*. London: Murray, 1928.

## BIBLIOGRAPHY

De Waal's two massive bibliographies of writings (and plays, movies, radio shows, and more) about Holmes are a useful starting point for all research on the subject. The authoritative bibliography by Green and Gibson exhaustively catalogues Doyle's own writings, of which the Sherlock Holmes stories are but a small portion.

De Waal, Ronald Burt. *The World Bibliography of Sherlock Holmes and Dr. Watson*. New York: Bramball House, 1974.

———. *The International Sherlock Holmes*. Hamden, CT: Archon, 1980.

Green, Richard Lancelyn, and John Michael Gibson, eds. *A Bibliography of A. Conan Doyle*. Oxford: Clarendon, 1983.

## AUTOBIOGRAPHY AND BIOGRAPHY

Of the many biographies of Doyle, the three cited here seem the most useful. Carr was the first to have access to Doyle's unpublished biographical archives, and he uses and quotes them extensively. Nordon goes far beyond Carr in his attention to the stories themselves. Higham's biography also makes significant use of the Doyle archives and gives perhaps the most interesting and readable account of Doyle's career. Doyle's own *Memories and Adventures*, more memoirs than autobiography, is a series of reminiscences and commentaries written separately over a period of many years, then assembled and extensively filled out late in the author's life; three chapters deal particularly with Holmes. In *Through the Magic Door*, Doyle discusses the books that have most pleased and satisfied him as a reader.

Carr, John Dickson. *The Life of Sir Arthur Conan Doyle*. New York: Harper, 1949.

Doyle, Arthur Conan. *Memories and Adventures*. London: Hodder and Stoughton, 1924.

———. *Through the Magic Door*. London: Smith, Elder, 1907.

Higham, Charles. *The Adventures of Conan Doyle: The Life of the Creator of Sherlock Holmes*. New York: Norton, 1976.

Nordon, Pierre. *Conan Doyle: A Biography*. Trans. Frances Partridge.

New York: Holt, Rinehart and Winston, 1967. [Orig. French edition, 1964.]

## CRITICISM

The following articles, books, and collections will be of particular interest and value to students and critics of the Holmes stories.

Atkinson, Michael. "Staging the Disappearance of Sherlock Holmes: The Aesthetics of Absence in 'The Final Problem.'" *Gettysburg Review* 4 (1991): 206–14.

Barolsky, Paul. "The Case of the Domesticated Aesthete." *Virginia Quarterly Review* 60 (1984): 438–52.

Clausen, Christopher. "Sherlock Holmes, Order, and the Late-Victorian Mind." *Georgia Review* 38 (1984): 104–23.

Eco, Umberto, and Thomas A. Sebeok, eds. *The Sign of Three: Dupin, Holmes, Peirce.* Bloomington: Indiana UP, 1983. [A collection of essays sharing a semiotic approach.]

Jann, Rosemary. "Sherlock Holmes Codes the Social Body." *ELH* 57 (1990): 685–708.

Knight, Stephen. *Form and Ideology in Crime Fiction.* London: Macmillan, 1980.

Naugrette, Jean-Pierre. "Le rituel du récit: lecture d'une nouvelle de Conan Doyle." *Littérature* 53 (February 1984): 46–57. [On "The Musgrave Ritual."]

———. "Enigme de spectacle chez Conan Doyle." *Études Anglaises* 34 (1981): 448–53. [The importance of Watson as narrator.]

Ousby, Ian. *Bloodhounds of Heaven: The Detective in English Fiction from Godwin to Doyle.* Cambridge, MA: Harvard UP, 1976.

Priestman, Martin. *Detective Fiction and Literature: The Figure on the Carpet.* London: Macmillan, 1990.

Redmond, Donald A. *Sherlock Holmes, a Study in Sources.* Montreal: McGill-Queen's UP, 1982.

## FILM STUDIES

Of the several treatments of Holmes on film, the following are especially useful and informative. Both are heavily illustrated.

Pohle, Robert W., and Douglas C. Hart. *Sherlock Holmes on the Screen: The Motion Picture Adventures of the World's Most Popular*

*Detective.* South Brunswick, NJ: Barnes, 1977. [The fullest film-by-film review.]

Steinbrunner, Chris, and Norman Michaels. *The Films of Sherlock Holmes.* Secaucus, NJ: Citadel, 1978.

(*continued from page iv*)

Alastair Fowler, "Sherlock Holmes and the Dancing Men and Women." From *Addressing Frank Kermode: Essays in Criticism and Interpretation*. Edited by Margaret Tudeace-Clayton and Martin Warner. Copyright © 1991 by Alastair Fowler. Reprinted by permission of Macmillan Press Ltd. Reprinted in the United States and Canada with the permission of the University of Illinois Press.

Rosemary Hennessy and Rajeswari Mohan, " 'The Speckled Band': The Construction of Woman in a Popular Text of Empire." From *Textual Practice,* Vol. 3, No. 3 (Winter 1989). Copyright © 1989 by Routledge and Kegan Paul.

John A. Hodgson, "The Recoil of the Speckled Band: Detective Story and Detective Discourse." *Poetics Today,* 13 (Summer 1992). Copyright © 1992 by the Porter Institute for Poetics and Semiotics.

Audrey Jaffe, "Detecting the Beggar: Arthur Conan Doyle, Henry Mayhew, and 'The Man with the Twisted Lip.'" Copyright © 1990 by the Regents of the University of California. Reprinted from *Representations,* No. 31 (Summer 1990): 96–117.

Stephen Knight, "The Case of the Great Detective." From *Meanjin* 40.2 (July 1981): 175–85. Copyright © 1981 by the University of Melbourne.

Martin Priestman, "Sherlock Holmes: The Series." From *Detective Fiction and Literature: The Figure on the Carpet*. Copyright © 1990 Martin Priestman. Reprinted by permission of St. Martin's Press, Inc., and Macmillan Press Ltd.

# Index